Praise for *Conflicted Memory*

"Milton's careful attention to the intersection of human rights discourse and narratives of martial heroism makes the book an innovative contribution to scholarship on memory politics in Latin America and one that will likely resonate with researchers seeking to understand similar post-conflict dynamics in other parts of the world."
Memory Studies

"An original and engaging work which stands as one of the most important contributions to memory debates in Peru in recent years. It will be essential reading for any student of Peru's internal armed conflict for years to come."
Journal of Latin American Studies

"A laudable effort in the field of memory studies. . . . The response of the military and its defenders, as Milton skillfully shows in her nuanced account of the struggle over control of the narrative memory of events, became more sophisticated."
American Historical Review

"Brings to light how military 'entrepreneurs of memory' strategically place memory products in a memory marketplace. A major intervention in debates about Peru's internal armed conflict of the 1980s and '90s and its aftermath, which will interest scholars in many disciplines and regions."
Paulo Drinot, coeditor of *Comics and Memory in Latin America*

"Impressively documents the military's diverse interventions in Peru's culture— memoirs, 'truth' reports, films, novels, and memorials—and its numerous attempts to censor cultural productions that challenge its preferred narrative."
Jo-Marie Burt, George Mason University

Critical Human Rights

Series Editors
Steve J. Stern ❧ Scott Straus

Books in the series **Critical Human Rights** emphasize research that opens new ways to think about and understand human rights. The series values in particular empirically grounded and intellectually open research that eschews simplified accounts of human rights events and processes.

After the times of "dirty war," a predictable response of military officials is negation—denying the reality of massive state-sponsored violence against unarmed civilians and prisoners, or trivializing it by claiming that such atrocities amounted to an occasional "excess" in the heat of war. A complementary response is the imperative to forget—an assertion that in order to advance, a society must leave behind discussion of its troubled recent past. What happens, however, if soldiers conclude that such tactics will backfire and lead them to lose the culture war over memory, truth, and human rights? This profoundly original study of the Peruvian military, in the aftermath of the civil war with Shining Path in the 1980s and 1990s, confounds common analytical expectations. Military officials evolved beyond the predictable stance of negation and launched a cultural campaign to curate memory in ways that might resonate with an age of human rights values. The result is uncommon insight into the shifting terrain of human rights talk in the twenty-first century.

Conflicted Memory

*Military Cultural Interventions and
the Human Rights Era in Peru*

Cynthia E. Milton

The University of Wisconsin Press

The University of Wisconsin Press
728 State Street, Suite 443
Madison, Wisconsin 53706
uwpress.wisc.edu

Gray's Inn House, 127 Clerkenwell Road
London EC1R 5DB, United Kingdom
eurospanbookstore.com

Printed in the United States of America

This book may be available in a digital edition.

Library of Congress Cataloging-in-Publication Data

Names: Milton, Cynthia E., author.
Title: Conflicted memory: military cultural interventions and the human rights era
    in Peru / Cynthia E. Milton.
Other titles: Critical human rights.
Description: Madison, Wisconsin: The University of Wisconsin Press, [2018] |
Series: Critical human rights | Includes bibliographical references and index.
Identifiers: LCCN 2017015528 | ISBN 9780299315009 (cloth: alk. paper)
Subjects: LCSH: Peru—History—1980- | Peru—Politics and government—1980- | Human
    rights—Peru—Historiography—20th century. | Political violence—Peru—Historiography—
    20th century. | Memory—Political aspects—Peru. | Collective memory—Peru. | Peru—Armed
    Forces—Historiography.
Classification: LCC F3448.5 .M55 2018 | DDC 985.06/3—dc23
LC record available at https://lccn.loc.gov/2017015528

ISBN 9780299315047 (pbk.: alk. paper)

To Raúl Hernández Asensio

Contents

Illustrations

Acknowledgments

While my list of people to thank is long, despite appearances, I have attempted to keep it short. Since the topic of this book is military memories, and Peru remains a place where it is still difficult to talk about the recent past, my worry is that by publicly thanking individuals I might be placing them in a tough situation. Peru in the wake of the conflict of the 1980s and 1990s is a place where rumors circulate and may adopt a semblance of reality and where quotes taken out of context are reproduced in unanticipated, and sometimes harmful, ways. Better that I appear ungrateful than these generous individuals find themselves in a predicament because of me.

I have benefited from long conversations wherein individuals shared with me their insights on the conflict and on the role of the military in the past and the present. Some of these individuals come from the military establishment (some themselves active, others in retirement, some civilians employed by the military, and some members of military families), others come from human rights groups, and others are just citizens who have thought a lot about Peru's difficult history. Thoughts and memories percolate to the surface in various forms from academic studies, testimonies, memoirs, visual and performative arts, and fictional accounts of the past that express many different pasts from distinct angles. The generosity of time that these individuals spent with me, with a clear desire to grasp the past, is the wedge that opens up to a more understanding future.

So here are just some of the many individuals who have helped me along the way from Peru and elsewhere and to whom I wish to express my gratitude: Carlos Aguirre, Victor Armony, Rebecca Atencio, Manuel Balan, Claudio Barrientos, Karen Bernedo, Ksenija Bilbija, Jelke Boesten, Carlos Bracamonte, Jo-Marie Burt, Shelley Butler, Ricardo Caro, Jennifer Carter, Jesús Cossio, Ponciano del Pino, Geneviève Dorais, Laura Lee Downs, Paulo Drinot, Marc

Drouin, Philippe Dufort, Joseph Feldman, Kevin Gould, Regina Grafe, Olga González, Lourdes Hurtado, Nora Jaffary, Iris Jave, Elizabeth Jelin, Edilberto Jiménez, Denise Ledgard, Catherine Legrand, Erica Lehrer, Sofia Macher, Jean-François Mayer, Lourdes Medina, Françoise Montambeault, (the late) Luka Mutal, Nora Nagels, Leigh Payne, Stefan Rinke, Lucy Riall, Nicolás Rodríguez, Gustavo Salinas, Rocio Silva Santisteban, Margarita Saona, Daviken Studnicki-Gizbert, Javier Torres, Makena Ulfe, Rosa Vera, Alberto Vergara, Víctor Vich, Lucero de Vivanco, Markus Weissert, and Antonio Zapata.

Several institutions have generously provided me books, space, time, funding, and inspiration for this research: the Ibero-American Institute in Berlin, the Institute of Latin American Studies at the Freie Universität, the European University Institute, the Alexander von Humboldt Foundation, the Faculty of Arts and Sciences at the Université de Montréal, the Social Sciences and Humanities Research Council of Canada and the Canada Research Chairs program, the Fonds de Recherche du Québec-Société et Culture, and RÉLAM (the Latin American Research Network of Montréal).

The University of Wisconsin Press has been very patient and helpful in bringing this project to fruition, in particular Gwen Walker, Sarah Kapp, Sheila McMahon, and Terry Emmrich, as well as copyeditor Barbara Wojhoski. Thanks to Lori Ann Curley for yet another index. The Critical Human Rights series editor Steve Stern's scholarship opened up possibilities for generations of scholars from Latin America and abroad, but it is his generosity of spirit and mentorship across the decades that I feel most privileged to have received. I was fortunate for the lengthy insights from the two knowledgeable readers assigned my manuscript: Jo-Marie Burt and Paulo Drinot. Both have helped me at various points in the research and writing, and their own work is greatly inspiring and key to understanding the topic here addressed.

I also express my deep appreciation for my family: Peter, Lena, and Nora are so far from the stuff of this book, yet they are the bubble of love and "pas de chicane dans la cabane" that makes it possible for me to do this work. Vielen danke to the grandparents, Helga and Volkmar Dietsch, and, of course, a thank you to my mother, Elizabeth Milton (née Dutton), for countless reasons. I dedicate this book to a friend and scholar, Raúl Hernández Asensio: tu amistad atraviesa temas, continentes y siglos. Any faults in this book are *entirely* of my making. I could not have asked for a more supportive network of institutions, scholars, friends, and family.

Abbreviations

ADDCOT	Asociación Defensores de la Democracia contra el Terrorismo (Association Defenders of Democracy against Terrorism)
ADOGEN	Asociación de Oficiales Generales y Almirantes (Association of Generals and Admirals)
ANFASEP	Asociación Nacional de Familiares de Secuestrados, Detenidos y Desaparecidos del Perú (National Association of Relatives of Kidnapped, Detained and Disappeared in Peru)
APRA	Alianza Popular Revolucionaria Americana (American Popular Revolutionary Alliance)
APRODEH	Asociación Pro Derechos Humanos (Association Pro Human Rights)
CAEM	Centro de Altos Estudios Militares (Center for Advanced Military Studies)
CEP	Centro de Estudios y Publicaciones (Center for Studies and Publications)
CIDH	Corte Interamericana de Derechos Humanos (IACHR, Inter-American Court of Human Rights)
CLACSO	Consejo Latinoamericano de Ciencias Sociales (Latin American Social Sciences Council)
CMAN	Comisión Multisectorial de Alto Nivel (High-Level Multi-sectorial Commission)
CNDDHH	Coordinadora Nacional de Derechos Humanos (National Co-ordinator for Human Rights)
COMISEDH	Comisión de Derechos Humanos (Human Rights Commission)
CONCYTEC	Consejo Nacional de Ciencia, Tecnología e Innovación Tecnológica (National Council of Science, Technology, and Technological Innovation)

CONFIEP	Confederación Nacional de Instituciones Empresariales Privadas (National Confederation of Private Businesses)
CPHEP	Comisión Permanente de Historia del Ejército del Perú (Permanent Historical Commission of the Army)
CVR	Comisión de la Verdad y Reconciliación del Perú (Truth and Reconciliation Commission of Peru)
DED	Deutsche Entwicklungsdienst (German Development Service)
DESCO	Centro de Estudios y Promoción del Desarrollo (Center for the Study and Promotion of Development)
DINCOTE/ DIRCOTE	Dirección Nacional Contra el Terrorismo (National Counterterrorism Directorate)
DOPS	Departamento de Ordem Política e Social (Department of Political and Social Order)
ESMA	Escuela Superior de Mecánica de la Armada (Higher School of Mechanics of the Navy)
FIHRM	Federation of International Human Rights Museums
FOI	Freedom of Information
IACHR	Inter-American Commission on Human Rights; Inter-American Court of Human Rights
IDEHPUCP	Instituto de Democracia y Derechos Humanos, Pontificia Universidad Católica del Perú (Institute for Democracy and Human Rights of the Pontifical Catholic University of Peru)
IDL	Instituto de Defensa Legal (Legal Defense Institute)
IEP	Instituto de Estudios Peruanos (Institute of Peruvian Studies)
IFEA	Instituto Francés de Estudios Andinos (French Institute of Andean Studies)
INC	Instituto Nacional de Cultura del Perú (National Institute of Culture)
LUM	Lugar de la Memoria, la Tolerancia y la Inclusión Social (Place of Memory, Tolerance, and Social Inclusion)
MODIN	Movimiento por la Dignidad y la Independencia (Movement for Dignity and Independence)
MOVADEF	Movimiento por Amnistía y Derechos Fundamentales (Movement for Amnesty and Fundamental Rights)
MRTA	Movimiento Revolucionario Túpac Amaru (Túpac Amaru Revolutionary Movement)
NACLA	North American Congress on Latin America
NGO	nongovernmental organization
PNP	Policía Nacional del Perú (Peruvian National Police)

PUCP	Pontificia Universidad Católica del Perú (Pontifical Catholic University of Peru)
SIN	Servicio de Inteligencia Nacional (National Intelligence Service)
SSRC	Social Sciences and Research Council
UAP	Universidad Alas Peruanas (Peruvian Wings University)
VRAEM	Valle de los Ríos Apurímac, Ene y Mantaro (Valley of the Rivers Apurímac, Ene, and Mantaro)

Conflicted Memory

Introduction

The Countermemories of "los buenos militares"

n the field of memory studies in Latin America, *memory* implicitly connotes human rights, specifically the defense of human rights that had been transgressed, and the rights of victims to recount and seek social repair and justice.[1] Memory thus holds positive connotations, despite the negative memories themselves. It is through memory that we hope to attain the elusive "Never Again." That the pursuit of memory holds these positive connotations has been largely driven by survivor groups and nongovernmental organizations (NGOs) that argue that memory negates forgetting and oblivion, and academics have thus turned their attention to the myriad of ways that memory functions among individuals, groups, nations, and transnationally. Yet what about memories that do not necessarily promote a human rights narrative or may contort the meaning of "Never Again"? What about "memories" that script a present and future based on a distorted past? The potential exists to "abuse" memory.[2] These questions differ from concerns that memories become too generalized or that the speaking of them might open old wounds; rather, they ask about supposed memories that negate or alter the existence of such wounds.

In an attempt to consider such memories—not necessarily false or fabricated but contorted—I turn in this book to the memories of armed state agents of the Peruvian conflict from 1980 to 2000.[3] Peru makes for an intriguing case study for memory work since much of memory studies literature in Latin America tends to focus on clear instances of state violence against civilian populations, framed by the Cold War logic of repressive regimes stemming the encroachment of Communism within national boundaries, such as Guatemala, Argentina, and Chile. Though not completely outside this Cold War dynamic, Peru stands apart for its differences: the conflict took place during democratically elected governments, after a previous decade of left-leaning military rule, and was in response to a very serious subversive threat, that of the Communist Party of Peru-Shining Path (Partido Comunista del Perú-Sendero Luminoso), which committed most of the violence.

Peru's time of fear has a widely agreed upon starting point. The beginning is usually dated to the eve of the return to democracy after a reformist military regime (1968–80) when a contingent of the Maoist-inspired insurgent movement Shining Path burned the ballot boxes in a remote hamlet as a symbolic gesture of its refusal to recognize democratic means to societal transformation. Originally, Shining Path had the support of many campesino (peasant) communities that were attracted by its message of a more just society, by its intervention to resolve local conflicts, and by the failure of other political movements and parties to engage meaningfully with local communities.[4] Yet as its members turned bloodier and attacked the very people whom they purported to protect, Shining Path lost its rural strongholds by the mid-1980s.

Most accounts also agree that the state's response was inadequate and inappropriate to the threat posed by Shining Path. The president of the republic Fernando Belaúnde Terry (1980–85) did not initially grasp the gravity of the insurgency. Clouded by his own fraught relations with the military despite a kind of gentleman's pact that had facilitated his return as president, he sent the unprepared National Police into the emergency zones. Unable to contain the threat, by December 1982 the government transferred the task of routing out Shining Path to the reluctant Armed Forces so that they would "take over the initiative from the frightened police force."[5] The early years of police and Armed Forces involvement were marred by rumors and actual acts of violence, massacres, deaths, and disappearances. By the late 1980s, the Armed Forces became more selective in their use of violence and brought local participants in to help combat the insurgents, largely through the rural peasant patrols (*rondas campesinas*) and self-defense committees (*comités de autodefensa*), some of whom were given arms and training. This shift in military approach reaped success, aided in large part by intelligence gathering (importantly by the National Police) and by civil society's rejection of both Shining Path and state violence. In September 1992 Shining Path leader Abimael Guzmán was arrested, along with much of the Shining Path leadership thereafter. The active fighting diminished in the following years from 40 percent of the national territory being declared under a state of emergency in 1991 to 6 percent in 1999, though pockets continued to fight in the coca-producing regions of the Huallaga Valley under Guzmán's successor "Feliciano," who was captured in July 1999, and the Valley of the Apurímac, Ene, and Mantaro Rivers (VRAEM) under the Quispe Palomino faction.[6]

This narrative of events seems largely agreed upon in the accounts by the Armed Forces, academics, and civilians, though they may weigh differently the factors and participants that tipped the balance against Shining Path. Disagreement based on perceived memories emerges most starkly concerning who committed which acts of violence, who counts (or not) as a victim or a perpetrator, the percentage of responsibility attributed to different armed actors, and whether these acts of violence were legitimate and why they were committed. In short, how and what to recount became Peru's battle.

Like many other countries seeking to clearly delineate the periods "before," "during," and "after" the conflict, Peru held a truth commission. Formed in the wake of the collapse of Alberto Fujimori's quasi-authoritarian government in 2000, the Peruvian Comisión de la Verdad y Reconciliación (CVR, Truth and Reconciliation Commission) had the mandate to identify and determine responsibility for abuses and violations, to report on the experiences of victims, and to develop proposals for reparations and reforms from the beginning of Shining Path's "People's War" to the transition in 2000.[7] The CVR investigated assassinations, kidnappings, disappearances, torture, harm to collective rights of Andean and indigenous communities, and other grave violations of rights. They concluded that over sixty-nine thousand people were killed or disappeared, over twenty thousand women were widowed and forty thousand children left orphaned, and some six hundred thousand internal refugees migrated to cities in search of safety.[8] The CVR held the armed group Shining Path as the principal perpetrators, responsible for 54 percent of deaths and disappearances, and the much smaller armed group Movimiento Revolucionario Túpac Amaru (MRTA, Túpac Amaru Revolutionary Movement) for 1.5 percent. The truth commission also found that 36 percent of reported fatalities and disappearances were the product of actions by state agents; that is, the Armed Forces were responsible for almost 29 percent and the police forces for 7 percent.[9] This latter finding, which attributed over a third of the violence—described by the CVR as "systematic or widespread human rights abuses"—to state agents provoked outrage among the Armed Forces and some political elite.

The CVR was very clear in its condemnation of armed state actors:

> In the course of our investigations, and based on the norms of international law that regulate the civilized life of nations, we have concluded that during certain periods and at certain times the Armed Forces *were involved in systematic or widespread human rights abuses*, and that there are grounds for

the accusation of crimes against humanity, as well as violations of international humanitarian law.

As Peruvians, we are ashamed to have to state this, but it is the truth and we have the obligation to make it known. For years, the forces of order forgot that human beings are the supreme end of order. Instead, they adopted a strategy of massive violation of the rights of Peruvians, including the right to life. Extrajudicial executions, forced disappearances, torture, massacres, sexual violence against women, and, due to their recurring nature and widespread occurrence, other equally condemnable crimes *confirm a pattern of human rights abuses that the Peruvian state and its agents must recognize* in order to take a step toward rectifying their actions.[10]

In addition to naming the insurgents and armed state actors, the CVR also criticized political parties, elements within the Catholic Church, and the media for responding inadequately and inflaming hostilities. The CVR wrote, "The situation would not have been so grave were it not for the indifference, passivity, or simple ineptness of those who held the highest public offices during this time. . . . It is painful but true: those who sought the votes of their fellow Peruvian citizens for the honor of governing our state and our democracy, those who pledged to uphold the constitution, readily ceded to the Armed Forces the powers bestowed on them by the nation."[11] Morally, Peruvian society as a whole was held to account for having produced what historian Paulo Drinot has called "the grammar of violence,"[12] which made it possible for over sixty-nine thousand Peruvians to be killed or to disappear, three-quarters of whom were marginalized members of society and non–native Spanish speakers; their deaths and disappearances, which were previously estimated at some twenty-five thousand, went largely unnoticed by the urban middle and upper classes (or "integrated" members of society).

That the armed state actors and political elite should also be named as directly and indirectly responsible for this catastrophe provoked public debate about the truth commission's findings and the role of the Armed Forces during the conflict. As a consequence, over the decade following the truth commission's publication of its *Informe final* (hereafter referenced as *Final Report*), different claims about the past emerged in the public sphere as did different meanings and uses of terms at the heart of accountability and the transition to a democratic, inclusive society: *memory* and *human rights*.

My idea for writing about how various state actors' memories, in particular those of the "forces of order," enter the public sphere came about in response to comments by a historian to an article I wrote over a decade ago. This historian, in an earlier stage in his life, had been part of the Peruvian marines, stationed in the department of Ayacucho. He suggested to me that instead of

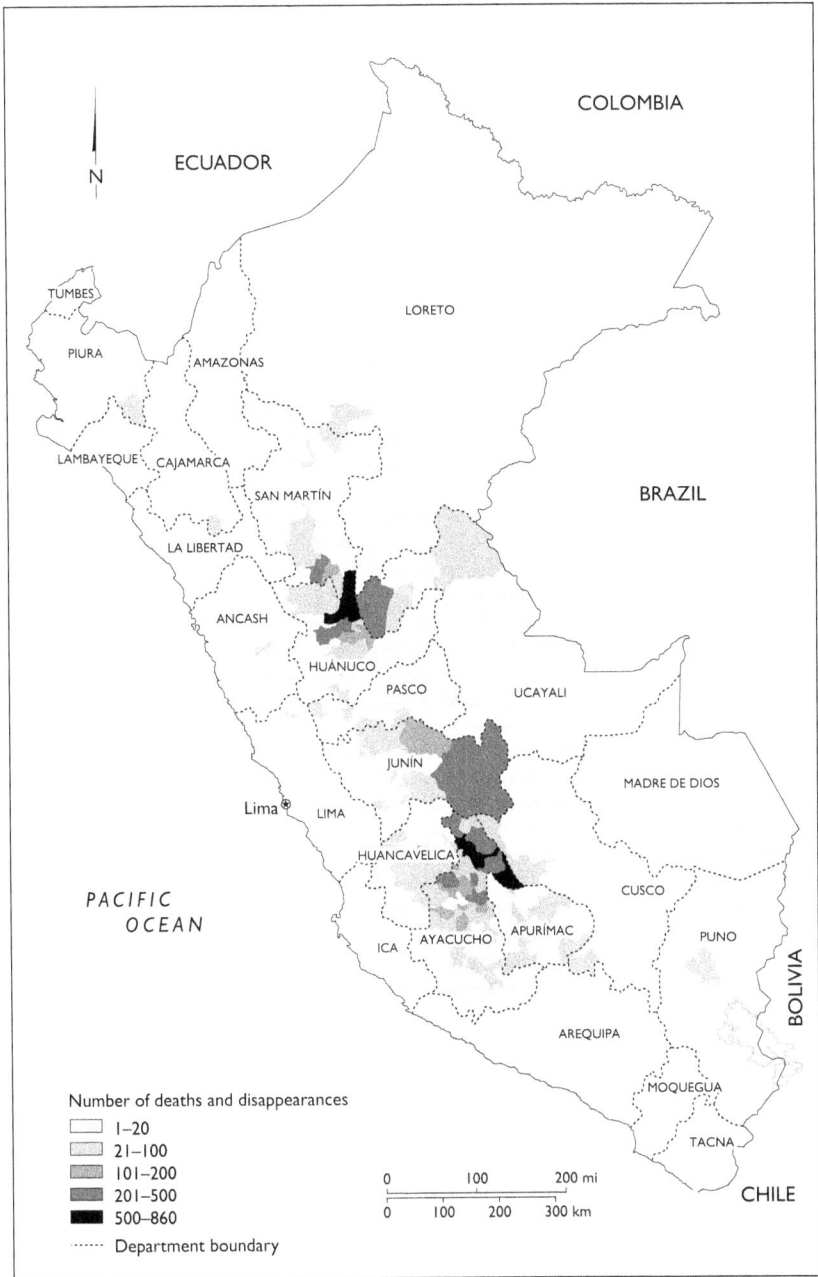

Map 1. Deaths and disappearances (1980–2000) according to the Comisión de la Verdad y Reconciliación, *Informe final* (Lima: Comisión de la Verdad y Reconciliación, 2003), vol. 1, 157. (Map by Bill Nelson)

qualifying the military's response to Shining Path as "brutal and indiscriminate," I should describe its response as "poorly discriminating" (the military that was sent to the region was Peruvian, not Swiss, he had remarked earlier).[13] A few years later, during a question-and-answer period following a talk in Lima, a military man pursuing a master's degree in the human rights program at the Pontificia Universidad Católica del Perú similarly asked me to reconsider my portrayal of the Armed Forces. He told me of the military's rescue efforts in the wake of a devastating earthquake in the 1970s: "Señorita Doctora," he said, "no olvide Usted que había buenos militares también" (Miss Doctor, do not forget that there were good military as well).[14] Rather than brush off such comments as remarks by military apologists or negationists, I realized that there is something to be taken seriously in their call for a more nuanced analysis of the military's role in recent history. Studies need to be done on how the military came to be an organization that instead of defending and helping its fellow citizens (such as the large campaigns in education, housing, health, and agriculture in the late 1960s and early 1970s) became a perpetrator, one that "poorly discriminated" when the use of violence was appropriate yet also studies that tell at times the stories of "los buenos militares."[15] Or perhaps rather than seeing "good" and "bad" military practices as oppositional, we need to see how development projects may operate in tandem with more repressive applications of raw force by the state.[16]

To further complicate matters, we must remember that the soldiers themselves were not always so distant in demographics from the victims. The Peruvian CVR determined that two-thirds of the victims were non–native Spanish speakers from rural regions, poor, and with weak literacy skills. They were Peruvians who were not "integrated" into the nation, many without basic markers of citizenship such as birth certificates or identity cards. As journalist Mirko Lauer notes, the discovery of tens of thousands of "new victims" beyond the twenty-five thousand already established by NGOs meant that "these Peruvians did not exist for the nation long before they ceased to exist in reality."[17] The tragic irony is that they only became citizens upon recognition of their death.[18] Yet this portrait of the victims of the conflict would also have described many of the soldiers who fought in the front lines of the conflict. According to military scholar Enrique Obando, much of the Armed Forces personnel, especially the Army, had a "modest social profile" coming mainly from "lower, middle class origins, often from the provinces outside of Lima."[19] Up until 1999, soldiers entered the military through a system of mandatory conscription, an obligatory service that the middle class and wealthy could more easily avoid, thus undermining the founding principle that the Armed Forces would be "a reduced image of the nation in which all social classes mix into a single ideal, sacrifice for the country."[20] Thus for much of the nineteenth century "the indigenous person was the principal face of the conscript," a demographic that may still hold today because becoming a soldier remains a means of socioeconomic mobility.[21] Some soldiers came from the regions where the conflict took place, such as Lurgio Gavilán, a young *senderista* from Ayacucho who once captured by the military converted into a soldier (discussed in chapter 3).[22] Furthermore, many young conscripts themselves may have suffered abuses within the military establishment.[23] That is, the profile of the victim as someone who does not form part of integrated society and who faces socioeconomic barriers and racial discrimination could resemble in some cases the profile of the perpetrator, either Shining Path or the armed state actor.[24]

There is a tendency in memory studies circles to slide the Peruvian experience into that of the Southern Cone, thus converting the Peruvian military into clear perpetrators against the civilian population, despite the more symmetrical acts of violence committed by the Maoist insurgent group and state forces.[25] This tendency does not help us to understand how the Armed Forces came to act the way they did, nor does it shed light on what it is they did do and the variations within this experience. We have to complicate this narrative.[26] My purpose in this book is in *no way* meant to suggest that we lessen our condemnation of armed state actors' abuses of human rights to criticism of mere excesses; the violations are clearly documented in the thousands of testimonies of victims and armed state and non-state actors gathered by the CVR and made evident through other sources.[27] A reanalysis of these testimonies suggests that the CVR may have reduced the number of abuses committed by state forces because of a decision to omit from its calculation individuals whose full names were unknown, and by separating those counted as dead and disappeared from victims of forms of nonlethal violence such as torture and sexual violations.[28]

Rather, this book seeks to shed light on military memories of the conflict and how state agents are curating this past in the public sphere since the transition in 2000. Categorizing the Peruvian military as like its counterparts in Argentina (1976–83) and Chile (1973–90) during their Cold War–induced conflicts limits our understanding not only of recent Peruvian history but also of how this past is wielded in the present. We need to analyze how armed state actors in Peru and those within their circle are writing, performing, displaying, reproducing, and projecting the conflict as a means not only to comprehend how such actors themselves see this past but also to grasp more fully the dynamic by which they promote their "memory" since the publication of the CVR's *Final Report* in order to undermine and rewrite the history presented in it. Military memory producers may be employing postconflict memory tactics similar to those of their Southern Cone counterparts, but their history is specific to them.

That said, while unique, Peru is not a case alone. Like many other Latin American militaries, the Peruvian Armed Forces have a long history of anti-democratic activity, obstructing democracy and assuming control of the governance of the country and then transitioning back to their role as a state institution ostensibly at the service of civilian and democratically elected governments.[29] In so doing, the military largely safeguarded the traditional order that worked in the interests of the oligarchic elite, such as the regimes of military men Augusto B. Leguía (1908–12, 1919–30), Luis Miguel Sánchez Cerro (1930–31), and Manuel Odría (1948–50, 1950–56).[30] Leguía served in the War of the Pacific and married into the oligarchy. His second mandate was preceded by a coup, and he was overturned by a coup in his eleventh consecutive year as president. The high-ranking military man who overthrew Leguía, Sánchez Cerro, himself only managed to stay in power for six months during his first round as president. Two years later, Sánchez Cerro was elected to office, a mandate cut short by assassination.[31] Odría was also twice president, the first time through the force of a military coup (1948–50); he resigned in July 1950 so that he could run for the office as a civilian and was elected president two months later. Though he had initially taken power to contain and later ban—much to the oligarchy's delight—the then-progressive Alianza Popular Revolucionaria Americana (APRA, American Popular Revolutionary Alliance), Odría's government also invested in social infrastructure such as schools, hospitals, and public buildings, and extended the vote to include women, all policies that are remembered fondly by the middle and poorer classes despite his authoritarian rule.[32] Odría did much to present the Army as a key institution within the nation and to fashion a manlier public image of the Army by naming General Francisco Bolognesi the Army's patron, with the slogan of fighting "until the last round."[33]

These examples are but a few of Peru's many military heads of state. According to Dirk Kruijt and María del Pilar Tello, Peru "has an established tradition of military involvement in national politics" with fifty-one of its seventy-two presidents coming from the ranks of military officers between independence in 1821 and 2000.[34] If we add Ollanta Humala, elected in 2011, the number becomes fifty-two. Yet the oligarchy's position was not always secure: by the late 1950s–early 1960s, some members of the Armed Forces linked social and economic concerns with national security, thus undermining the oligarchy–Armed Forces pact.[35] During the Revolutionary Government of the Armed Forces (1968–80), launched by General Juan Velasco Alvarado, a series of reforms were introduced in the fields of education, health, and housing as well as important efforts at agrarian reform and the nationalization of foreign-owned companies, among other measures typically consistent with demands of the Left.[36] In part, these reforms contributed to Velasco's support from lower- and middle-class Army soldiers.[37] Also, the thought at the time was to take the wind out of the sails of a revolutionary vanguard Left and thus replace a potential revolution from below with one controlled from above by joining the doctrine of national security with that of national development.[38]

It is important to note that the roots of the Peruvian Armed Forces' efforts to contain and combat insurgents does not lie in the Cold War alone, though the Cold War provided new techniques and language to interpret and describe internal challenges to the status quo.[39] Historian Eduardo Toche Medrano's important study on the history of the Peruvian military, which includes a close reading of the military magazine *Revista militar del Perú* (founded in 1897), locates two earlier threats to the nation, which readily morphed to suit the Cold War's lexicon: the indigenous person who stifled modernization, and APRA, which represented an "internal enemy." It was agreed that while the former could be "civilized" through assimilation, the latter had to be eliminated. The Armed Forces played a role in both. Through education, civics-building rituals (such as raising the flag), and obligatory military service, the "savage" could be turned into a soldier. In the case of APRA, their eradication meant confrontation, exile, and massacre.[40]

Much of the history of the Peruvian Armed Forces in the twentieth century is tied up with that of APRA. APRA emerged in the 1920s under the leadership of Víctor Raúl Haya de la Torre, who offered an anti-oligarchical discourse that appealed to the middle classes and workers. Fearful of Bolshevism and a "secret war" being coordinated by Russia, APRA members and Communists (and any potentially sympathetic institutions such as universities and unions) became suspect. Indeed, the term *subversive* and the concept of the "internal enemy" that came later to reference Shining Path and the MRTA were earlier applied to *apristas*. Toche gives a specific date when the Peruvian Armed Forces turned to defending the nation against internal enemies: July 9, 1932. On this day, the Armed Forces reclaimed the city of Trujillo from an *aprista* uprising. Three days later, the mutilated bodies of over thirty soldiers and civil guards-man, including officers, were discovered in police facilities. While the killers were never identified, *apristas* were held responsible. In a subsequent trial, forty-four prisoners were sentenced to death (and another fifty-eight in absentia), and another eighty-one individuals were sentenced to periods of incarceration. But it was not just through formal channels that the Armed Forces sought atonement for these deaths (as well for an earlier unsuccessful assassination attempt on Luis Miguel Sánchez Cerro). There were reports of the troops killing whomever they found walking in the streets of Trujillo. The massacre of over fifty *apristas* in the neighboring archaeological ruins of Chan Chan is remembered more than half a century later as the death of "hundreds of young *trujillanos*."[41]

According to Toche, these events provided the basis for the Armed Forces' contention that they fought an internal enemy, rooted in the popular classes, an enemy not as easily identifiable as rural indigenous people, and that the battle was not over national borders but a moral struggle. As the minister of war said in a speech shortly after the macabre discovery in the police quarters of Trujillo in 1932, these dead servicemen had not spilled "their young blood on the battlefield, [nor] before foreign enemies"; rather, they had died "defending order" and "to save the city of Trujillo from the advance of evil."[42]

❧

Despite the prominent role the Peruvian military played in the development of the nation, this field is understudied by professional historians. For many decades, there were few large-scale histories written about the Peruvian military, such as Brigadier General Carlos Dellepiane's classic *Historia militar del Perú* (1931) and Víctor Villanueva's *Cien años del ejército peruano: Frustraciones y cambios* (1972).[43] Academic studies in Peru have recently returned to military history while engaging themes beyond those of traditional institutional history to include questions of gender and the role of the Army in the formation of the nation state.[44] There is even a subfield in the curriculum of military studies dedicated to "the cultural cosmovision of war."[45] The expansion into new topics is noticeable in the journal published by the Permanent Historical Commission of the Army (Comisión Permanente de Historia del Ejército del Perú), such as film reviews.[46]

Among investigations into military history, there is an apparent preference to focus on the nineteenth century. The Permanent Historical Commission of the Army compiled a series of five volumes titled The General History of the Peruvian Army that spans the period from Tupác Amaru to 1899, when the Army was reorganized in imitation of the French model following the end of the War of the Pacific. The Permanent Historical Commission of the Army has yet to write the history of the twentieth century. Despite this preference for the distant past rather than the recent conflict of the 1980s, some historians have noted similarities between these two periods. For instance, historians Cecilia Méndez and Carla Granados have noted meaningful similarities between the wars of the nineteenth century and the recent conflict with regard to citizenship and state formation, based on the participation of Andean rural folk in the military campaigns.[47] In studies about the twentieth century, most scholarly attention—first by political scientists, then by anthropologists, and finally by historians—focused on the Revolutionary Government of the Armed Forces, which aimed to radically transform Peruvian society.[48]

In the field of Peruvian military history, Toche's *Guerra y democracia: Los militares peruanos y la construcción nacional* (2008) stands out as a significant history of the Armed Forces from their formation in the early republic to contemporary concerns of hemispheric security and conflicts in Peru's coca-producing regions. Toche's book does much to help clarify how the Peruvian Armed Forces came to see their role as extending beyond defense of the nation's borders and the constitution. In their own institutional aspirations to modernize and progress, the Armed Forces developed throughout the twentieth century a sense that they—rather than civil politicians—were the best trained and the best positioned to understand and address the needs of the nation; this *espíritu del cuerpo* (corporate spirit) was strongly critical of civilians' ability to govern, a position that Toche and others call "military antipolitics."[49]

It is interesting to note, however, that despite the mostly narrow focus and limited number of professional studies, military history has occupied a prominent place in public school curriculum. Military men dominate schoolchildren's pantheon of national heroes: though defeated, Grau, Bolognesi, and Cáceres, among others, are all held up as exemplary Peruvians. As historians Méndez and Granados note, it is impossible to study the history of Peru without knowing the role that the military played in it, an observation that points not simply to the military's intervention in Peruvian nation formation but also to how this history has been taught, a nationalistic narrative that highlights the struggle to defend the nation.[50]

Like many countries in the nineteenth to mid-twentieth centuries, the pedagogical aim of teaching national history was to make good citizens bound together by a common past. Yet in Peru, the military was also central to how Peruvians, especially indigenous and rural populations, were made into citizens.[51] It was a two-pronged approach: through military service and through the classroom. Military service was projected as a "civilizing mission": as one author explained in the *Revista militar del Perú* in 1898, "In learning the obligations as soldier he [the indigenous man] learns as well his responsibilities and rights as a citizen and as a man."[52] The other means of making citizens was educational curriculum. In 1939 president general Óscar Benavides introduced "the Law of Premilitary Education," which imposed military education on students all the way from elementary school to university so that young men could "fulfill their civic-military duties."[53] Premilitary education was later deemed unnecessary when General Velasco introduced obligatory military service, but in 1982 a general education law reintroduced it as part of civics and ethics education.[54] Premilitary education was suspended after the transition from Fujimori, but an *aprista* congresswoman in 2003 proposed bringing it back, arguing that "the deep sentiment of patriotism and of the heroes helps form a person who identifies with the country, and [premilitary education] favors the development of a military vocation in youth."[55] This military-civics-ethics principle comes to the fore each year in the parades of schoolchildren who march military style, with flags and in some cases pretend weapons, proudly demonstrating their patriotism. Such displays contradict the Ministry of Education's repeated resolutions since the transition in 2000 that school-children should display the country's cultural diversity, that is, "flags of peace" rather than "flags of war."[56] Carla Granados observed during her ethnographic fieldwork in the Central Sierra in 2013 and 2015 that the ministry's efforts have had little local effect, in part because the teachers themselves, especially in rural zones, argue that "these policies threatened a practice that traditionally served to inculcate civic patriotic values in schoolchildren."[57]

But it is not historians and schoolchildren alone who are reflecting on the history of the Armed Forces. In the wake of the collapse of Fujimori's regime, the return to open elections, and the publication of the findings of the CVR's *Final Report*, the military has undergone an internal self-examination, especially, it seems, within the Army. Toche identifies two factors driving reform: The first impetus is the successive events in which the military was embroiled (the subversive threat against the state, the battle against narcotrafficking and production, the frontier dispute with Ecuador known as the Cenepa War, its political support for Fujimori, and its implication in his web of corruption). The second impetus is the need to evaluate how best to reinsert the military into the new democracy being developed after the Fujimori government, along with other related issues such as international pressure to reform and a mobilized civil society that is quick to respond to perceive injustices.[58] To Toche's list, we should also add the prosecution of Peruvian security forces, especially since Fujimori's extradition to stand trial in 2007, as factors promoting self-reflection within the ranks of the Armed Forces.

Indeed, the transition in 2000 from the government of Alberto Fujimori to Valentín Paniagua—that is, from authoritarian governance to open democracy—had a profound impact on the Peruvian Armed Forces, weakening and discrediting them. When Fujimori fell, so too did the military establishment, which had aligned itself closely with his regime. Particularly damning for the military were a series of videos, known as the *vladivideos*, leaked in September 2000, that showed the head of the Servicio de Inteligencia Nacional

(SIN, National Intelligence Service), Vladimiro Montesinos, bribing high-ranking military men among others, and another subsequently released video showed top military and police commanders and hundreds of officers signing a document supporting Fujimori's 1992 self-coup. In addition, the Armed Forces were found to be involved in corrupt arms deals, narcotrafficking, and stealing from state coffers, including their own pension system.[59] Though drawing what appeared to be less condemnation in the media, the military was also accused of human rights violations.

Despite apologies from the Armed Forces' leaders for their having been co-opted by Fujimori and their promise to remain loyal to the interim government and the constitution, major purges within the military took place immediately after the transition. Some personnel offered their resignations to President Paniagua, others were removed, and some were convicted in courts. Paniagua replaced all the high command of all branches of the Armed Forces. Generals who had been forced into early retirement or exiled by Fujimori were reinstated in prominent positions during the transition.[60] Those who had risen to the top through Fujimori's system of rewarding the most loyal, but not the most talented, tumbled.[61] Both the head of the Armed Forces from 1991 to 1998, General Nicolás Hermoza Ríos, and his replacement, José Villanueva Ruesta, were arrested, charged, and sentenced to prison.[62] Hundreds of officers were eventually charged with corruption. In 2001 alone, over 486 military men were retired, and during Paniagua's eight-month administration "not a single day passed without at least one major Peruvian newspaper carrying a story detailing corruption within the military."[63]

Notwithstanding these early efforts at lustration and accountability, which focused more on corruption than human rights violations, attempts at reforming the Armed Forces in the spirit of a transition to democracy were weakly applied. The military has maintained important political positions and is often in the public eye. Major cuts to the military's budget were initially announced, yet campaigns against narcotrafficking have kept the budget robust.[64] Civilians and members of the Armed Forces have headed the Ministry of Defense since the transition (up until 2015, four out of fourteen were military men, and all except one was retired). During the presidency of Ollanta Humala (2011–16), himself a former colonel who fought in the emergency zones, the very public General Daniel Urresti was minister of the interior, an office that has authority over the Peruvian National Police.[65] While minister, Urresti often made public appearances, hosted a radio show, and subsequently attempted unsuccessfully to run as the presidential candidate of the Partido Nacionalista in the 2016 elections (Humala's then-governing party). During his campaign, Urresti was embroiled in court proceedings over the 1988 death of a journalist and faced a possible sentence of twenty-five years in prison, making him "Peru's possible prison president."[66]

Peru's Memory Knots and Memory Camps

Historian Steve Stern's notion of "memory knots," introduced in his study on memory struggles in post-Pinochet Chile, is useful in considering the public conflicts in Peru over its recent past.[67] The metaphor of knots invokes the pain inflicted on bodies by traumatic events (and more quotidian knots in the stomach or the throat) and the potential hindrance this pain poses to language in the wake of trauma. A knot also points to processes: social actors with competing memories tie knots (politicians, victims' groups, and the military, for instance), and thus the labor of memory that seeks to construct broad democratic narratives entails working out (or untying) knots in the social body. In this metaphor, the tying of a knot might foment social discord, yet the untying of knots necessitates agreement on an inclusive narrative to which various social actors contribute their competing memories.[68]

Peru's memory knot is pulled tight by a myriad of actors. It is too simple to say that there is an official versus a nonofficial version of the conflict. A plethora of camps exists, each with its own experiences and memories. Moreover, "memory" as an intellectual or political project is not likely on the minds of most Peruvians in their daily lives but simmers, percolates, and, at times, erupts into the public sphere, for instance when a case comes to trial, the memorial to victims El Ojo que Llora gets defaced, or prominent figures are accused of human rights violations. The two most notable memory tropes may be characterized as "human rights" memory versus a "salvation/heroic" memory, each of which takes distinct positions regarding the CVR's *Final Report*. When these "eruptions" occur, pubic response often adheres to one of these two memory frameworks.[69] These narratives of the past circulate, compete, and structure the present. It should be noted that *senderista* memories remain on the fringe, despite efforts by the political wing of Shining Path, Movimiento por Amnistía y Derechos Fundamentales (MOVADEF, Movement for Amnesty and Fundamental Rights), to intervene in public spaces to advance its vision.[70]

The first memory camp, which might be considered that of "human rights," is for the most part closely aligned with the conclusions of the CVR, though at times members of this camp may contest specific findings or inadequacies without necessarily wishing to dismantle the CVR's narrative as a whole. This camp is largely composed of various human rights and victim-based NGOs and other educational and developmental NGOs, without a political movement or party that consolidates it.[71] The massive protests that precipitated the ousting of Fujimori—los Cuatro Suyos (the Four Regions)— largely represent the same social sectors. This camp situates the violence as the outcome of entrenched social, economic, and political inequalities, of which Shining Path was a symptom and on which Shining Path could build its movement. Rather than seeing the end of the conflict as the victory over terrorism, this memory camp emphasizes the ongoing inequalities that were both the cause and a continuation of the conflict, and that Fujimori and subsequent governments have yet to root out (in part because of their failure to implement fully the CVR's recommendations): endemic poverty, racism, and unequal access to resources and the full benefits of citizenship. While most in this camp would agree that Shining Path was the main instigator and perpetrator of the violence that engulfed the country as of 1980, the camp highlights the state's disrespect for the rule of law and points to the Armed Forces' illegal use of force that caused great harm, especially to highland communities. In its structuring of the recent past, the "human rights" version pits Shining Path and the Armed Forces against each other (and thereby somewhat erroneously positions Peruvians as caught between these "two fires") while celebrating the laudable role of civil society, the self-defense patrols (*rondas*), and individual acts of heroism in bringing the conflict to its end.

In the decade following the CVR's *Final Report*, efforts of the human rights camp focused on implementing the CVR's recommendations, including those for symbolic and financial reparations. Because it is impossible to compel Shining Path—largely disbanded, with its members decimated, imprisoned, or morphed into narcotraffickers—to make financial reparations, this demand is solely intended for the state. Also, captured Shining Path members were tried in courts prior to the CVR, so further efforts at accountability have concentrated on the remaining state agents. Thus this quest for reparations and accountability has shifted the focus of public debate to state actors' abuses rather than to those of Shining Path. A sense of skewed justice is further exacerbated by the release of prisoners previously charged with terrorism who have completed their sentences, individuals such as MRTA's Peter Cardenas Schulte and Lori Berenson, whose release gained much public attention. Thus "terrorists" are freed, while the "defenders of the nation" are placed in prison.

The second trope, the "salvation" or "heroic" memory, is espoused by conservative and neoliberal sectors, composed mainly of supporters of Fujimori's political movement, known as *fujimoristas*, APRA, the Armed Forces, the National Police, more conservative elements within the Catholic Church such as Opus Dei, and affiliated media outlets, all of which had been named by the CVR as contributing to the escalation of the conflict. The salvation story line arose during the time of the Fujimori government: it portrays Fujimori and Montesinos as the central protagonists, the Armed Forces and the National Police as secondary, and institutions and citizens as marginal to the successful outcome.[72] In this version of the past, human rights violations were committed by a few bad apples within the security apparatus; Fujimori's heavy hand and disregard for human rights were deemed necessary (and his decisiveness commendable) in the eradication of the terrorist threat; and Shining Path, as instigator, was held as wholly responsible for the violence. Furthermore, a large swath of the educated and "integrated" society was absolved of wrongdoing, for the "we" in Lima were unaware at the time of the human toll of the conflict.

Since Fujimori's fall from grace and his incarceration, the "salvation" memory, whose protagonist was Fujimori, has shifted toward a "heroic" memory of the Armed Forces in their battle against terrorism. This latter "heroic narrative," which came to supplant the "savior narrative," portrays state security actors as heroes of the nation and the defenders of democracy; like the earlier salvation memory, it describes *ronderos* and *arrepentidos* (former insurgents who had surrendered) as merely "useful," thus largely downplaying their importance to the final victory. Little if no mention is made of the role of civil society in Shining Path's demise, despite its activism and ongoing defense of human rights.[73] Whether "salvation" or "heroic," the memories advanced by this camp are not the same as "forgetting," though elements of the latter are at times evoked, that is, the need to move on, to turn the page, and not to reopen old wounds.

At the time of the CVR's report in August 2003, these conservative actors came together in a united attack on the CVR's work: a public campaign was launched to discredit the CVR's findings, which led to accusations of conflicts of interest among commissioners, claims of malfeasance, and the labeling of the truth-telling exercise as a "lie commission."[74] That the statistical findings concerning the number of dead and disappeared were nearly three times higher than previously reported became the Achilles' heel of the CVR, and much doubt was cast on the methods used to calculate the number of victims and attribute responsibility.[75] Critics also took issue with what the CVR considered the root causes: a historical account of entrenched inequalities and racism; rather, they pointed to the violence as having been started by Shining Path. Terminology was also a sticking point: Was the episode an internal "conflict" or a "war"? Was it "violence" or "terrorism"? Who should be called a "victim" and who a "perpetrator"? These were just some of the linguistic choices that served as clues to one's alignment with or against the CVR. To return to Stern's metaphor of the memory knot, these were the words that would get caught in the throat of some who did not necessarily want to be categorized one way or the other.

The Many Members of the Salvation/Heroic Camp

The salvation/heroic memory camp itself is not homogenous. Despite the factions' readiness to unite in its disdain at the time of the CVR's *Final Report*, the interests of the political and economic elite and those of the Armed Forces do not always align. Peru's conservative sectors remain rather fragmented, despite their common cause. Indeed, the political right is not one group but rather is fractured into what appears to be two dominant factions, one that adheres to the economic policies of Fujimori and yet believes in human rights and democracy, and one pejoratively referred to as "La Derecha Bruta y Achorada" (The Stupid and Arrogant Right), whose quest for liberty allows the trampling of others' rights, and which fosters a belief that the means to the ends may require a *mano dura* (strong hand).[76] Even within these groups there are tensions and shifting opinions about the work of the CVR. Two-times presidential candidate and daughter of the incarcerated former president, Keiko Fujimori caused great controversy among political circles including her own political movement, Fuerza Popular (Popular Force), when, following a pre-pared talk at Harvard University in September 2015, she stated that the CVR was "an advance for [the] country" and that she recognized its "diagnostic work." However, she also stated that the CVR had not sufficiently considered "the opinion" of the military and the National Police.[77] In the months pre-ceding the 2016 elections, she incorporated aspects of the CVR's recommen-dations into her presidential plan, in what she referred to as the promotion of "effective protection" of human rights. If elected, her administration would have contributed funds for finding and returning the remains of the "forced disappeared" to their families and would have complemented the recommen-dations of the CVR by providing civil reparations to the families of fallen military personnel.[78] The latter proposition was criticized as opportunistic by the then-president's wife, Nadine Heredia, who saw it as an attempt by Keiko Fujimori "to curry favor with the military, which her daddy had abandoned."[79] Indeed, most had already received financial reparations.

Apart from the conservative sectors, even the armed state actors' accounts of the past differ noticeably regardless of their shared aim to discredit or at the very least place in question the CVR's *Final Report*. Peruvian security forces consist of many units: the National Police (composed of the Civil Guard, the

Republican Guard, and the Investigative Police of Peru), the Armed Forces (Army, Navy, and Air Force), special forces within them, and state-supported civil defense units. Each has its own version of the past, which may share a similar core but emphasize divergent points as *its* memories.[80] These differences may reflect schools of thought about the role of the Armed Forces in society—for instance, that of "reformers" versus "hardliners" within security forces—or military rank (officers versus troops) and the experiences of generational cohorts of graduating classes and promotions.[81] These differences undermine the Armed Forces' attempts to present a united public front since they point to inner dissent and discord.[82]

Since the transition in 2000, the Armed Forces have gone from a mild acceptance to a strong rejection of the CVR. Initially the Armed Forces (along with the *fujimoristas* and the political elite) were weakened by the scandals surrounding Fujimori and his security advisor, Vladimiro Montesinos, and their original response to the project of a national truth commission was shaped by the sudden "collapse of the authoritarian regime" and their own embedded position within Fujimori's web of corruption and interests.[83] In response to the public disclosure of damning videos, the Armed Forces issued an apology, the top brass resigned, and the Armed Forces publicly supported the launch of a truth commission as they attempted to distance themselves from the Fujimori regime.[84] Yet this initial support came from a position of weakness. This weakness dissipated over the subsequent decade as the military repositioned itself in the Peruvian political scene, most notably in the election of Ollanta Humala in 2011, and as it contended with an active judiciary. The process of holding perpetrators to account succeeded in the sentencing of Alberto Fujimori in 2009 as well as convicting some military men and tarnishing the reputation of many more.[85] According to retired general José Williams Zapata (considered by many a national hero for his role in the successful release in 1997 of the hostages held by the MRTA), 537 military personnel faced judicial proceedings as of May 2016.[86] In their individual and collective defense, military men turn to discrediting the CVR.

Though united in their derision of the CVR, the Armed Forces appear uncomfortable about where to place the former president within their recounting of the past, in part because of their own role in his regime and any potentially lingering sympathies, but also because Alberto Fujimori continues to wield political power despite residing in prison; his daughter, Keiko, lost the 2016 election by a fraction of a point. Instead, different armed state actors and conservative sectors tend to place the blame almost entirely on Montesinos, Fujimori's close advisor and the head of the SIN, the parent to all the Armed Forces' intelligence divisions.[87]

The complexity of the Peruvian conservative sector's and the armed state actors' narratives is expressed in a review of the Peruvian Army's 2010 publication *En honor a la verdad* (In honor of the truth). One reviewer wrote in the conservative daily *Expreso*, avoiding mention of Fujimori: "We have repeated in this column, speaking about the large penance that members of the Armed Forces and the National Police seem obligated to pay, thanks to campaigns led by their internal enemies. Enemies who pass the bill to the institution to pay because of the excesses of a few in the fight against terrorism, and the corruption of the highest leaders during the imperial reign of Montesinos."[88] This quote also illustrates what other sources indicate: state actors do not have a single, homogenous narrative, and state actors and conservative elites are not simply blaming human rights groups or zealous and politically motivated judges for the prosecution of members of Peru's security forces. They point to the guilt of a few bad apples and corrupt heads in order to preserve the purity of the many. This was a similar sentiment to how the CVR was perceived as treating the Armed Forces in 2003, as not wanting to tarnish the image of the institution as a whole, only "bad elements who had committed crimes" (figure I.1).

In a chapter by the scholars Kruijt and Tello on the relationship between civilian political figures and the military, the authors provide a *postdata* written just after Fujimori's resignation in which they describe the scrambling by military personnel with close connections to Montesinos, whom they "blamed as the Rasputin of the regime, [and who] had to be sacrificed, notwithstanding his support in army circles."[89] Military hierarchy and order fell apart: in an act of protest to the corruption of the Fujimori regime and the co-optation of the Armed Forces, a group of mid-ranking Army officers (including the brothers Humala) led an unsuccessful uprising against Fujimori in October 2000 (the Peruvian congress later pardoned them).[90] Young military personnel periodically leaked news to the press, perhaps to express their frustration with corruption.[91]

Yet younger military personnel were not just concerned about corruption. Some were also deeply affected by human rights violations committed by the military during the conflict that they had witnessed directly or had participated in. Mining the CVR archives as part of his undergraduate thesis, Javier Pizarro Romero read around thirty testimonies by former lower-ranking Police, and Army and Marine servicemen. Some expressed fear of reprisals and death threats if they recounted to the CVR what they had witnessed. Some requested protection for themselves and their families. These testimonies not only challenge the official heroic and honorable discourse of the National Police and the Armed Forces but also illustrate "invisible fractures" that belie a homogenous group's

Figure I.1. Caricature of the president of the CVR, Salomón Lerner, throwing a bin full of garbage at the Armed Forces, saying that he is not against the institution as such but only against some "bad elements" who committed crimes. Drawing by Miguel Ángel. (*Diario Expreso*, August 31, 2003, A2)

espíritu del cuerpo. They tell us about daily life, the relationships between officers, troops, training, and hazing. They also provide details of corruption and the torture and massacre of local people (whom some described as innocent), memories that they chose to recount to the CVR despite the risks involved.[92]

The gap between high-ranking and subordinate members of the state security forces points to a generational difference, one that was also apparent in the presidency of Ollanta Humala, who prematurely promoted members of his and his brother's graduating cohort. But there is also a generational difference between those generals and military men from the Velasco era and those who came to power during Fujimori. Importantly, based on interviews from the 1990s, Kruijt and Tello perceived a tension between how those interviewed felt about the military before the Fujimori era and at the end of the twentieth century. In their conversations, retired officers spoke with visible pride of the years of the Revolutionary Government of the Armed Forces, when they had held important posts in public service; in particular they expressed respect for Velasco and his team, who came to represent "patriotism, honesty, discipline

Introduction

and respect for the common people."[93] By contrast these same officers saw the Fujimori regime as having led astray their honorable institution, especially by men such as Montesinos and the powerful National Intelligence Service, which implemented the practice of "subtle promotion of corruption-prone, spineless officers to the commanding ranks."[94]

Any fissures were quickly patched over, however, when the CVR came to a close. Despite the Armed Forces' official but tentative initial support for a truth commission, in the days leading up to the publication of the CVR's *Final Report*, individual members of the state security forces began their critique of the not yet public findings. The only military member on the truth commission, a retired Air Force general, Lieutenant General Luis Arias Graziani, reluctantly signed the final report. He noted several objections to the CVR's conclusions, in particular the pejorative interpretation of the Armed Forces' role in the conflict, in a letter submitted to the president of the CVR, Salomón Lerner, which was included in the CVR's eighth volume.[95] The content of this letter circulated widely in public and on social media. New associations also sprang up in defense of the Armed Forces with their own speaker series, websites, blogs, Facebook pages, publications, and news magazines with investigative journalism. For instance, Arias Graziani's letter to the CVR president denouncing the CVR's findings was published along with other critiques by the Confederación Nacional de Instituciones Empresariales Privadas (CONFIEP, National Confederation of Private Businesses), the Asociación de Oficiales Generales y Almirantes (ADOGEN, Association of Generals and Admirals), among others, in a book titled *Omisiones a la verdad ¿Y la reconciliación?* (Omissions of truth: And reconciliation . . . ?) by the newly formed association of retired generals, the self-described Asociación Defensores de la Democracia contra el Terrorismo (ADDCOT, Association Defenders of Democracy against Terrorism). ADDCOT was short lived, but it actively railed against the CVR through various publications and its website in the years following the CVR's *Final Report*.

This distancing by the Armed Forces from the CVR became more overt and hostile with the mounting efforts by human rights groups to hold armed state actors accountable for violations. These groups worked to bring to trial the initial forty-seven cases that the CVR had turned over to the prosecutor general.[96] The ruling by the Inter-American Court of Human Rights on the 1991 killing by a clandestine military death squad of fifteen people gathered for a party in the Barrios Altos neighborhood of Lima included the annulment of the 1995 amnesty laws. Early verdicts in Peruvian courts focused on well-known cases and established important precedents, such as classifying the forced disappearance of student Ernesto Castillo Páez as a crime against humanity.

Success in retributive justice culminated in the 2009 conviction of Fujimori for crimes against humanity (among other charges), a decision in which the CVR's *Final Report* played a determining role. Political scientist Jo-Marie Burt, who has closely monitored the cases before the Peruvian judiciary, noticed that since Fujimori's sentencing the number of prosecutions with sentences had dropped significantly by 2010, a shift that began during Alan García's term. Burt attributes this decline to these earlier judicial gains. The efficiency of the judiciary in the early years of the transition pushed conservative sectors of society to regroup and actively seek to subvert efforts of accountability, to come to the legal defense of accused military personnel (such as the work of the Asociación Civil Patria [Association Civil Homeland], formed by members of the Armed Forces), and to boisterously denounce in the public sphere such efforts to hold their members accountable for past crimes.[97]

The Human Rights Trials in Peru project, headed by Burt in collaboration with the umbrella organization National Coordinator for Human Rights (Coordinadora Nacional de Derechos Humanos), amassed information on investigations and prosecutions in Peru.[98] They organized their findings according to sentences, number of convictions and acquittals, and information about cases in trial or close to reaching that stage. They also collected data from the Public Ministry on the 2,880 denunciations of human rights violations received between 2001 and 2012. According to their findings, from 2006 to 2012, 187 state agents had been prosecuted. Some of the verdicts included high-profile cases, such as those of Alberto Fujimori, Vladimiro Montesinos, the former head of the Armed Forces retired Army general Nicolás Hermoza Ríos, retired general Julio Salazar Monroe, the operative head of the Colina Group, Army major Santiago Martin Rivas, and retired Army chief of staff Carlos Pichilingue. Yet of these 187 state agents, only 66 were convicted (12 of which were civilians: Fujimori, Montesinos, and 10 *ronderos*), while 121 were acquitted. Whereas Argentina had had a 90 percent conviction rate at that point, Peru had only 35 percent.[99] Less than 1 percent of the cases came to trial due to lack of evidence or turpitude.[100] This contrast led Burt and others to ask why the same court that produced important sentences from 2006 to 2009 appeared in the following years to produce a high rate of acquittals, a partial answer to which involved changing "political winds [that] have narrowed the space for accountability efforts . . . and raises important questions about the independence of the judiciary vis-à-vis other powerful actors, primarily the Executive and the armed forces."[101] Burt referred to these powerful actors as forming an "impunity bloc," a coalescence that began with the election of Alan García and solidified with Ollanta Humala, both of whose governments included top officials who made public statements in various forums that absolved the Armed Forces of wrongdoing or lessened their culpability.

Dressing Up Past Actors in New Clothes

Peru is not alone in the resurgence of military memories in the face of an active judiciary: Valentina Salvi similarly notes the power of trials in Argentina to bring diverse members of the political Right together in a cohesive organization. In the midst of trials against state perpetrators, various family associations of fallen soldiers, civil organizations that support the military, and sympathetic media outlets consolidated into an umbrella group known as Complete Memory that adopted some of the methods of human rights movements to establish and disseminate its own version of Argentina's "Dirty War." The implication in its name is that human rights memories are partial.[102]

As political scientists Felipe Agüero and Eric Hershberg note of Southern Cone militaries, all have tried to reposition and reaffirm their institutions in the new order.[103] The ability of former participants and beneficiaries of authoritarian regimes to repackage themselves successfully within democracies is perhaps extreme in the case of one former torturer in Argentina studied by Leigh Payne, whom she gave the pseudonym of Major Martinez. Martinez had served as an intelligence officer in La Perla, one of Argentina's most infamous detention centers during state terrorism. Twenty different survivors identified Martinez. Fearful of being held accountable during the initial trials and after a failed coup attempt against the Alfonsín government, Martinez lost his position in the Armed Forces. Swapping his uniform for an Italian-style suit, he reinvented himself as a successful consultant for an environmental group and as a political scientist. In his interview with Payne, Martinez displayed no discomfort with his past, even offering to travel at his own expense to speak at her university about the "Dirty War."[104] Leslie Gill, who interviewed former students of the School of the Americas, might consider Martinez "a Teflon assassin" much as she does other military men who despite accusations of assassinations, massacres, and torture manage to ascend in their careers and live well off and in relative freedom, in some cases even enjoying visas to the United States.[105] Winifred Tate in her study of human rights activism in Colombia similarly describes a process of dressing up the past whereby the military has come to embrace the term *human rights*. The Colombian military sees the importance of human rights discourse in its efforts to "win the hearts and minds" of citizens and international actors. Such a lexical turn, however, is in tandem with its postulation that human rights denunciations against state agents are fabricated by local NGOs or are the product of an international conspiracy.[106]

For the most part, the arguments of Peruvian conservative and armed state actors leveled against the CVR are more nuanced criticism than outright negation. These critics are not saying that the conflict did not happen, as seems to be largely the case for Guatemalan state agents and elites (even with the initially successful sentencing of General Rios-Montt for committing the act of genocide and the later Sepur Zarco ruling against soldiers guilty of sexual slavery). Rather, they are ever so subtly altering the argument and thus shifting the debate. Take, for instance, the term *caviar* in the Peruvian context: by designating human rights as a concern of *los caviares* ("those who eat caviar"; the English equivalent slur would be "champagne socialists"), conservative actors insert a distance between the mostly humble origins of the victims and survivors and the individuals and groups that aim to help them in seeking justice and social repair. Thus, the terrain is altered from one of universally shared human rights to that of class divisions.

Furthermore, one of the successful legacies of the neoliberal and quasi-authoritarian Fujimori presidency (or "electoral authoritarianism") has been the indelible stain on the Peruvian Left, coloring anything considered politically left with the same genealogical origins as Shining Path, a stain that may mark not only Peruvians but also foreigners.[107] Thus, in a swift brush of a pen, the vice president of Peru during the second government of Alan García (2006–11), retired admiral Luis Giampietri, discredits the statements by Hidetaka Ogura, the former secretary of political affairs for the Japanese embassy and one of his fellow hostages during the nearly four-month MRTA siege of the ambassador's residence in 1996–97. In a sworn statement, Hidetaka stated that he had seen three MRTA hostage takers surrender themselves, yet none of them survived the military evacuation of the residence; his testimony thus raised the possibility of extrajudicial execution. Giampietri reminds readers of his memoir about this shared harrowing experience, titled *Rehén por siempre* (Forever prisoner), and that Hidetaka had come to Peru to study "the doctrine of José Carlos Mariátegui . . . from whose ideas emerged the bloodiest Peruvian terrorist group, who had the name of 'Shining Path.'"[108] Giampietri does not directly contradict Hidetaka's statement about the three dead MRTA; he just casts doubt on Hidetaka's motivations for producing this sworn statement.

Questioning why specific individuals or groups remember and what it is that they choose to recall creates a wedge that enables conservative and state agents to cast doubt on the fidelity of others' memories and permit them to offer their own versions of the past. For instance, in the long process of building a national memory museum in Lima (2009–15), called the Lugar de la Memoria, la Tolerancia y la Inclusión Social (LUM, Place of Memory, Tolerance, and Social Inclusion), conservative sectors originally opposed the erection of such a place. In a controversial gesture, President García turned down the German government's donation for its construction but later changed his mind. Subsequently, the military also expressed interest in building its own memory museum. Yet such a military museum would be a space in which to house the military's memories of the conflict years and of its injured and fallen soldiers.[109] Thus the foundational story shifts: not only do the memories contained in a potential museum become those of state agents (which the CVR found to be perpetrators of systematic abuse) rather than those of the victims of state agents and Shining Path, but in an odd twist the military museum would have housed the memories of the Armed Forces' victimization. Reinforcing this image of the war as one-sided, the 2012 proposed Law of Negation (Ley de Negacionismo), if adopted, would have allowed the criminal sentencing and imprisonment for up to eight years of anyone who placed in question, down-played, or attempted to justify the violence committed by Shining Path.[110] As historian Nelson Manrique has commented, without taking into considera-tion the human rights abuses committed by other actors, this law "negates part of the story."[111] It is noteworthy that President Ollanta Humala chose to submit the proposed law on August 28, the ninth anniversary of the presentation of the CVR's *Final Report*.[112]

These examples are but a few of many that show an emerging and sustained pattern by prominent public figures and members of the Armed Forces (through widespread media, publications, interviews, commemorations, parades, blogs, and websites) to disseminate armed state actors' narratives of the past: the de-fense of human rights are frivolous endeavors by leftist human rights groups that share the same genealogy as Shining Path; that memory should be of the heroic efforts of state security agents, who themselves were victims of Shining Path violence and who died saving the nation and democracy at the behest of the government; that Shining Path alone was responsible for the violence, and that not only its violent means but its aims and those of its supporters were illegitimate.[113]

In the decade following the CVR, armed state actors have appropriated the language, imagery, and mechanisms of human rights memory "entrepre-neurs" to advance their own narratives of Peru's conflict.[114] That is, the tools and lexicon of the human rights memory camp equally serve the Armed Forces in advancing their version. This is not to say that the Armed Forces have not previously used "soft power" in the public sphere to align the public to their point of view.[115] Promoting military memory is nothing new, despite aca-demia's only recent interest in memory studies. The streets of most Peruvian towns—named after generals and heroes from different conflicts (especially that of the War of Pacific)—mark urban topography with the nation's military past as do the many triumphant memorials and monuments to Peru's various battles from the colonial and republican periods. Each year, these military memories are embodied and performed by schoolchildren around the country as they march military style to the drum and tuba of *fiestas patrias* (patriotic celebrations) of the nation's birth on July 28, 1821, in imitation of the Armed Forces' Great Military Parade held each July 29 in Lima.

That the military occupies civic memorial spaces is not new, but some of yesterday's modes seem out of date and too crude in the era of human rights. In the post–Shining Path and post-Fujimori period, in which human rights discourse has come to the fore, the military struggles to find new methods to advance its perspective of the past. Thus the Armed Forces engage in a "culture battle" as they protest the diminishment of their previous hegemony: they use cultural means to shift public memorial culture. Previously obvious attempts at persuasion appear in bad taste and perhaps not even possible when attempted in the post-CVR political context. For instance, Alan García had proposed during his second mandate to rename numbered streets after military heroes from the recent past (including the Chavín de Huántar Operation), but nothing came of it.[116] The even heavier-handed and overt tactics of the conflict years (of blatant censorship and silencing of dissent through human rights abuses, kidnapping, and foreclosing pathways of information dissemination) appeared, after the transition, too obscene for the political elite and the Armed Forces, according to their public statements that condemned such acts.

Perhaps such abuses seem obscene in the new era, but they are not beyond imagination. Democracy remains very fragile, and, worrisomely, remnants of Peru's violent past echo into the after years, especially in the ongoing conflict in coca-producing regions and in the state response to local protests to extractive industries, for instance, Bagua, Conga, and Tía María.[117] While a far cry from the "war through other means" taking place in post-genocide Guatemala, the prevalence of previous logics and their iterations into the present day are also true for Peru.[118] Hence, it is more accurate to place a hyphen in *post-conflict* to demarcate the questionable *post* and to point to ongoing connection between the still-violent present and the lingering past.[119] Furthermore, as the defense of civil rights and the rule of law remain weak in Peru, the Armed Forces' projections into public space take on a cautionary valence: while the military is fundamental to the stability of democracy, it remains an institution whose own history is undemocratic, as we were reminded of by rumors of the Armed Forces' negotiations with candidates and political parties during the 2016 presidential election.[120]

Yet democracy is not necessarily counter to the interests of authoritarian segments in society. In her book *Uncivil Movements*, political scientist Leigh Payne studies the emergence of an armed Right in three transitional countries: coup attempts by a group of military leaders in Argentina after the return to democracy, waves of violence committed by landlords in Brazil as they attempted to maintain their wealth and cultural identity in the face of government efforts at agrarian reform, and the rise of paramilitary squads in Nicaragua. The novelty of Payne's argument is that while destabilizing for democracy, these groups—what she calls "uncivil movements"—are not necessarily geared toward overturning or replacing democracy; rather, they use violence and their powers of persuasion as a means to shape democracies while also using "democratic institutions, discourse, and practices."[121] She writes, "[Uncivil movements] show that the same institutional processes designed to channel demands from civil society also give political expression and power to uncivil groups. Uncivil movements also employ the same mobilization strategies used by social movements within civil society: like social movements, they claim to identify and empower a new political constituency, conscious of its identity while struggling to overcome its marginal status in the political system."[122]

By contrast, the Peruvian military has perhaps been more successful in regrouping in democratic times than the cases studied by Payne, for in the election of Ollanta Humala to the presidency in 2011 (himself dogged by rumors of human rights violations about his time as a captain responsible for a military base in the Upper Huallaga Valley), the Armed Forces reentered the democratic system, thus overcoming any marginalization they might have suffered since the transition from Fujimori.[123] In the 2016 elections, at least another half-dozen former security personnel were elected to office. This trend, of course, does not necessarily indicate the democratization of the military or the militarization of democracy.[124] Furthermore, the military's return to grace does not mean that its members are exempt from prosecution by the independent judiciary or that the state security forces are beyond criticism by the media.

Peru's military does not fit neatly into Payne's definition of uncivil movements.[125] However, its efforts to use the channels designed for civil society and the mechanisms favored by civil society to express its version of the past are similar to those of the groups studied by Payne, and these similarities demonstrate the importance of considering how perpetrators seek legitimacy within democracies and in the era of human rights.[126] That is, armed state actors' versions of past violence are presented in the public domain as part of a strategy to improve the public perception of their involvement in this past; like Payne's cases, "they used similar myths to overcome negative images and develop support among constituents."[127] To do so, state security members draw on a series of cultural mechanisms and practices often associated with the promotion of human rights and actively employ memory discourse in order to shift public perception of the validity of trials and to counter nonheroic images of the Armed Forces' participation in the conflict. They hotly contest several of the findings of the CVR: the number of victims, the ratio accorded to the Armed Forces and National Police, and the CVR's assessment that the Armed Forces "systematically" committed human rights abuses. The CVR's findings do not coincide with *their* memories and experience of what took place.

Countermemories:
Curating the Military's Past

Because of the limited political weight of the CVR to establish its report as *the national* account of Peru's internal conflict, culture became a key site of Peru's memory struggles. In the years following the CVR, we saw the opening of public spaces for recounting the past through creative modes from the originally victim-focused memories to include those of agents of violent acts. The Peruvian Armed Forces actively participated in these debates by "curating" their version of Peru's recent past and in so doing countering victims' memories of human rights violations and the CVR's narrative.

Curating refers to the active process of choosing objects and shaping and ordering them. This creation of a mise-en-scène means making the past meaningful and interpretable so that we might bear witness to the past. But what happens when this past is contested or when the knowledge imparted is "difficult," that is, knowledge of uncomfortable truths about a nation's past rather than comfortable knowledge that allows nations to build happy, unifying national myths? Such efforts at curating may attempt to direct political transformation, such as reconciliation, but they may also silence experiences, contort the past, and contribute to further injustices. *Curating* in its most basic linguistic root also means "to care for," as in "attend to." Important ethical questions are raised when the past displayed is contested, the aftermaths of which perdure, and whose historical actors are still present. Curations can both settle and unsettle established meanings of the past.[128]

Curating the past in public spaces necessitates cultural engagement. Several studies point to the link between cultural memory production and institutional truth-seeking and accountability mechanisms. For instance, in my own research and that of Margarita Saona and Victor Vich, among others, the emergence of the Peruvian truth commission gave space and legitimacy to cultural expressions of previously suppressed and underacknowledged subaltern "truths" of human rights violations.[129] Rebecca Atencio similarly notes "cycles of cultural memory" in Brazil, showing how cultural interventions beget more cultural works and how official mechanisms of truth telling and accountability can speak to previous cultural initiatives as well as stimulate new public engagements.[130]

This book, *Conflicted Memory*, addresses this interplay of "memory's turns" of culture to culture, of institutional mechanisms to culture, and vice versa, but it takes as its focus armed state actors' memories and their cultural efforts. Since Peru's transition in 2000, the Armed Forces have responded both to cultural interventions—in particular the various artistic and creative works disdainful of the military—and to official mechanisms of truth telling and accountability, that is, the CVR and prosecutions. They have done so in several ways: by speaking out vociferously against those who seek to tarnish the military's image and against a judiciary that holds them accountable; by employing cultural means to combat this negative image; and by refashioning themselves and carving out for themselves a legitimate place in democratic Peru in the era of human rights.

Yet it may surprise some that the military came to use many of the terms and mechanisms of truth telling and recognition often considered part of the domain of human rights groups. While scholarship has mostly considered memory producers coming out of human rights and victim associations, Elizabeth Jelin, in her foundational work on memory, also notes the importance of not losing sight of memory advocates whose work undermines victim-based memories by placing their own memory products on what Ksenija Bilbija and Leigh Payne refer to as a "market."[131] Simply put, memory and human rights are double sided: they may be employed to *counter* "victim-oriented" memories and to promote *countermemories* that go against common understanding of whose memories are to be publicly remembered. Here the focus is on memory producers who are not the victims or the survivors of state violence but rather emerge from within the state apparatus. State agents' memories may run counter to a human rights discourse that emphasizes the rights of victims and survivors or they may adopt a similar logic and lexicon that is counterintuitive. The latter risks diluting the saliency of the terms *victim* and *human rights* or displacing those to whom these terms are applied.

By different means and great effort, state security forces have sought to counter human rights memories with their own curation, thus shifting public imagination since the CVR. Employing a range of cultural interventions—including memory books and novels by military personnel, a "truth report," films, museums, and memorial sites—the Peruvian Armed Forces and those closely related to them have sought to write and present their version of the past. Their efforts have also sought to edit this past, that is, to control what is said and how, suppressing inconvenient "truths" and portrayals of Peru's conflict in the public domain. Culture matters in post-transitional societies and in the era of human rights, and debates over the past may take subtle forms. Despite the perception of truth commissions as often ineffectual in the implementation of their recommendations, they do have the means to guide the course of public debate, so much so that those with access to institutional power feel obligated to enter into a cultural struggle, a conflict over competing memories. Yet terms such as *memory, truth,* and *human rights* cut many ways, and when used by agents of violence they may take on different and changing meanings, moving us beyond the conventional arguments of forgetting, denial, and salvation.

Military Memory Books

Picking up Pens to Recount Their Truths

n *Memory's Turn*, Rebecca Atencio studies the interplay between transitional justice mechanisms, such as trials and
truth commissions, and cultural forms of recounting in post-dictatorship Brazil.
While other scholars have argued that truth commissions provide an opening
for cultural works, Atencio points not to causality but to timing and imaginary
connections between transitional justice mechanisms and cultural artifacts.
These connections may lead to yet more interventions and perhaps even to
what she identifies as "a cycle of cultural memory."[1] We also see such patterns
(or "turns" in the cycle) in Peru—though over a much more condensed period
of time than in Brazil—whereby the truth commission shed light on extant
cultural texts and gave rise to a myriad of new artistic engagements, and such
creative works may have helped to promote further reckoning and reparations
as well as inspire other cultural endeavors.

During the work of the Peruvian truth commission and in the period
following the publication of its *Final Report*, a series of books flooded the
Peruvian literary scene and continue to do so. While literature on the conflict
had been written in the 1980s and 1990s (by authors such as Mario Vargas
Llosa, Julio Ortega, Carlos Thorne), the theme of the conflict burgeoned in
the CVR's wake. In 2006, for instance, Alonso Cueto's *La hora azul* (The blue
hour) and Santiago Roncagliolo's *Abril rojo* (Red April) both won the prestigious Spanish-language awards Anagrama and Alfaguara.[2] In that same year,
Peruvian American author Daniel Alarcón published the award-winning
novel *War by Candlelight*, followed by the much-acclaimed *Lost City Radio*.

Other authors soon joined them on the theme (for example, Iván Thays, *Un lugar llamado Oreja de Perro*; Raúl Tola, *Toque de queda*; and Claudia Salazar Jiménez, *La sangre de la aurora*), while others revisited the conflict years (Carlos Thorne's *En las fauces de las fieras*, to name one), or others saw their books reprinted after many years out of print, as in the case of Félix Huáman Cabrera's *Candela quema luceros*.[3]

The above-mentioned books—all fictionalized accounts of the past, many of which have their roots in the awareness prompted by the Peruvian Truth and Reconciliation Commission—broach the conflict years from the perspective of characters who were victims of the violence, are undertaking a personal quest to understand the past, or are haunted by this past. These works have had an impact on Peruvian memory debates by making imaginable what happened. Thus fiction plays an important role in how culture attends to this difficult past.

Fewer are the books, however, that take the perspective of those who perpetrated acts of violence, whether Shining Path or a state actor, whether fictional or not.[4] This makes sense, for in the spirit of reconciliation after transition, the narrative of reconciliation emphasizes returning victims to the fold of the nation, with full rights of citizenship, and restoring their dignity. More potentially unsettling for reconciliation are narratives of those who committed the harm, who had suspended their humanity and that of their victims.[5] In the literature boom following the CVR, the "perpetrator" perspective is fairly recent. They include such nonfictional works as Alberto Gálvez Olaechea's *Con la palabra desarmada: Ensayos sobre el (pos)conflicto* (With the unarmed word: Essays on the [post]conflict), a series of reflections about the conflict by a formerly imprisoned member of the MRTA; Lurgio Gavilán's experience as a child soldier for Shining Path and later in the service of the Peruvian Army (*Memorias de un soldado desconocido: Autobiografía y antropología de la violencia*, translated as *When Rains Became Floods*); and José Carlos Agüero's hybrid memoir-treatise, *Los rendidos: Sobre el don de perdonar*, which reflects on what it means to be an orphan of *senderistas* killed by state security forces.[6]

Despite their smaller number in the memory book niche, books written by regime insiders and from the perspective of armed state actors shed light on how cultural memory is constructed and employed. What about military memories that emerge through these writings? And for what ends are these books written? In the black-and-white binaries of postconflict Peru that structure much of public debate, in particular the oppositional categories of "victim" and "perpetrator," these writings present the other side of the *letrado* (lettered) coin.

In Atencio's study of culture and transitional justice, she tracks four stages in the "cycle of cultural memory": the first stage is the apparent *simultaneous emergence* of cultural works and processes of truth telling or accountability; the second phase consists of the *imaginary linkages* perceived between the two; the third phase involves attempts to *leverage* this association, whereby social actors who are aware of the connection choose to use it to promote their own vision; and the fourth phase is *propagation*, whereby new cultural works emerge out of those preceding them, thus potentially prompting yet another turn of the cycle of cultural memory. The latter three phases that Atencio identifies in Brazil seem particularly pertinent to contextualizing the emergence of military writings about the past in Peru. We see in Peru that cultural works have emerged in response to transitional justice mechanisms, that social actors leverage this linkage, and that they propagate new cultural works in an effort to advance their memories into the public sphere. For the most part scholars, myself included, have tended to consider memories advanced by human rights groups and victims. Yet as we see in Peru, state agents also produce cultural artifacts of memory. While forgetting would seemingly best serve the interests of regime insiders, they have sought to remember instead through cultural mechanisms.

For the members of the Armed Forces—considered by the CVR as "perpetrators" of 36 percent of the deaths and disappearances during the conflict—one mode of remembering and placing their memories in the public sphere is to pick up a pen, perhaps heeding the adage that the pen is more powerful than the sword, and indeed in times of peace and transitional justice it is one of the few weapons available to them. Such writings can take several forms, such as memoirs, testimonials, documentary publications, blogs, and imaginary public letters.[7]

While they have written some novels, for the most part these memory books by regime insiders and armed state actors are works of nonfiction.[8] These nonfiction memory books differ from the many novels produced in the wake of the CVR, for they lay a claim to truth that works of fiction do not (though the authors of fiction may do so, they are not obliged). Most of these books take the form of a testimonial or an autobiographical memoir of the conflict years. These memory books either directly challenge the truth commission as a whole or challenge in part its findings, based on what their authors consider to be their "truths."[9] Indeed, along with more-professional publications, a cottage industry of works by key protagonists in the political arena and the armed conflict, especially from the 1990s, emerged after the CVR. These writers include former president Fujimori (who is rumored to be presently writing "Memorias de mi encierro," at least as a blog); his former security advisor and head of the National Security Service (SIN), Vladimiro Montesinos; former admiral and vice president Luis Giampietri, the former archbishop of Ayacucho Cardinal

Juan Luis Cipriani; some imprisoned servicemen (for instance, Jesús Sosa, a secret service agent and member of the Colina Group); several retired military men (such as generals Eduardo Fournier Coronado, José Cabrejos Samamé, César Ramal Pesantes, and Edwin Donayre Gotzch), and military clubs like ADDCOT, an NGO formed by retired generals of the Peruvian Armed Forces.[10]

In this chapter, I analyze books in which the authors claim firsthand knowledge of the events therein described. My overview of these military memory books is based mainly on works that I found while researching at the Ibero-American Institute in Berlin, through the Internet, at the Ricardo Palma Book Fair in Lima 2014, or were recommended to me by colleagues and military personnel. These books were not collected in a systematic way. Some were very easy to find, such as Luis Giampietri's *Rehén por siempre* (Forever hostage), which is available in many bookshops in Lima, while others were more difficult to obtain, such as Donayre's tribute to the military men who had fought against Shining Path and the MRTA, *El silencio de los héroes* (The silence of the heroes).

The appearance on the literary scene of these memory books written from the perspective of state agents occurred not just as a reaction to the Peruvian Truth and Reconciliation Commission and the general upsurge in books and films about the conflict years, but perhaps more importantly they emerged as a response to escalating prosecutions of members of the Armed Forces, in particular of the National Police and the Army (figure 1.1). That is, there is an imaginary or real (most likely the latter) link between mechanisms of accountability and cultural interventions in the guise of memory books and other forms, to borrow from Atencio's phases in a memory cycle.

Efforts to bring perpetrators to account after the transition from Fujimori to Paniagua enjoyed early success.[11] The Inter-American Court of Human Rights (IACHR) ruled in March 2001 that the Peruvian state was responsible for the Barrios Altos massacre and repealed the amnesty law that Fujimori had put in place in 1995. The case was returned to the Peruvian judiciary, where in 2010 the courts issued a guilty verdict, sentencing nineteen members of the Colina Group (including the former Army chief General Nicolás Hermoza Ríos and Vladimiro Montesinos) to sentences of fifteen to twenty-five years in prison. This sentencing was preceded by the other important rulings. In 2006 the National Criminal Court sentenced four police officers for their part in the forced disappearance of Catholic University student Ernesto Castillo Páez. In 2007 three separate cases of accountability resulted in the conviction of six Army officers for their role in the forced disappearance of municipal authorities, the murder and disappearance of Efraín Aponte Ortiz, and the

Figure 1.1. The reproduction of a "wanted" for human rights violations poster by the Association Pro Human Rights (APRODEH) on its website in November 2015. Of the nine individuals shown, all members of the Peruvian Armed Forces, three have been detained and six are fugitives as of this writing. (APRODEH)

murder of journalist Hugo Bustíos. In 2008 former head of the SIN and Army general Julio Salazar Monroe and eleven other Army officers were convicted in the disappearance and murder of nine students and one professor from La Cantuta University. The pinnacle of accountability was reached in April 2009 with a guilty verdict issued against Alberto Fujimori for human rights violations. This was the context in which state agents' memory books entered the literary scene.

In the transitional justice era of truth telling and subsequent prosecutions, books are one medium by which state agents attempt to set the record straight about their participation in the internal conflict. They do so by mixing research and documentation with personal lived experience and passionate opinions. Many of these books are fairly polished productions that include color images, tables, maps, and the like and were funded by prominent institutions such as the private university that grants decrees to upwardly mobile military personnel, the Universidad Alas Peruanas (UAP, Peruvian Wings University). Others are self-published and of fairly low production quality. All the authors claim to be telling the "truth" (the words *verdadera verdad* or *verdadera historia* are often featured in the titles or the introductory pages). When the authors mention the toll that the conflict took (usually referred to as the "internal war," "*guerra interna*"), they cite the earlier figure in circulation of twenty-five thousand victims rather than the nearly seventy thousand estimated by the CVR.[12] To substantiate their claims, the authors insert conversations in the texts; use journalistic, private, and Armed Forces' photographs; and supply tables, footnotes, and appendices of documents. Most authors begin with a dedication to those who defended the nation (to the Armed Forces, the National Police, and the *ronderos*) and end with an epilogue that bemoans the present-day situation in Peru and the way Peru's servicemen are treated. Almost all are written by individuals who feel somehow betrayed, mostly by the post-2000 Peruvian state.

Despite being at odds with the CVR, these memory books share a lexicon similar to that of the human rights memory camp from which the CVR emerged. Often in these works, the authors cite the refrain "*un pueblo que olvida su historia está condenado a repetirla*" (a people who forget their history are doomed to repeat it) or some version of this warning, which also lay at the heart of the CVR's work. Several key terms appear repeatedly in their writings: *para no olvidar* (in order to not forget), *human rights, justice*, and *truth*. Occupying a prominent place in this lexicon is the concept of "memory." State actors do not wish to forget; what they want is that the past be remembered correctly, thus countering the memories advanced by groups who act against the interests of the Armed Forces. These terms are the centralizing nodes or the building blocks by which state agents organize their cultural arguments about the past as the military's collective memory.

The Right to Forget and to Remember

Let us consider, for instance, the right to forget and the obligation to remember in Luis Giampietri's accounts of his experience as a hostage in the Japanese ambassador's residence for nearly four months from 1996 to 1997. Giampietri is a retired admiral and a former vice president during the second García government. He wrote two books (the first in English with the help of an American journalist and former Navy Seal in 2007, the second in Spanish in 2011) about his experience as one of the seventy-two hostages held by the MRTA in the Japanese ambassador's home and the Chavín de Huántar operation that led to their successful release.[13] While all the hostages managed to escape alive, all the hostage takers died, a ratio that raised the possibility that they were executed. (This operation is discussed further in chapter 4.) According to Giampietri's Spanish account, for years he did not wish to speak about his participation in the affair because he did not want to draw attention to himself when others were openly using the experience for their own political gain (he cites Kenji Fujimori, Alberto Fujimori's son, as one example), and also because he did not wish to place his family at risk of retaliation.[14] Despite this call for privacy, at different junctures Giampietri has participated in interviews and written and republished his account of what took place.

The timing of both books on his experience as a hostage seems linked to prosecutions. The first publication, *41 Seconds to Freedom*, published in 2007 (second edition in 2008), appeared after Alberto Fujimori was arrested in Chile and during efforts to extradite him to Peru to stand trial. The 2007 English account situates the contested memory of Chavín de Huántar as a political attack aimed at discrediting Fujimori; according to Giampietri, "In their zeal to discredit him, Fujimori's enemies turned their attention to what had been the president's crowning achievement in the War on Terror: the hostage rescue."[15] For the Spanish account, *Rehén por siempre* (Forever hostage) (2011, second edition 2012), Giampietri shifted his concern from Fujimori (by then in jail) to what he viewed as the political persecution of the commandos and the high command in this operation. Giampietri's book hit the market at a time of increasing criminal proceedings against state agents for their participation in the Chavín de Huántar operation. As stated in *Rehén por siempre*, Giampietri would have liked to have forgotten this event, but he chose to write of his experience once trials began: "I could not allow myself the luxury of forgetting something, [though doing so is] *inherently a human right*, because one contradiction of forgetting in our judicial system [is that it] may mean the difference between being a witness and [being] an accused."[16] Thus, he explains, he chose to write a Spanish account of his experience only after he had been subpoenaed as a witness to the events in a court case against General Nicolás Hermoza Ríos, Vladimiro Montesinos, and others involved in the rescue operation. In the appendix, Giampietri includes an image of this subpoena dated January 12, 2011. Thus, in his Spanish-language account, *Rehén por siempre*, the "hostage forever" alludes not to his time held captive by the MRTA in the Japanese ambassador's residence but rather to his ongoing subjugation to a political climate that continuously seeks to victimize the Armed Forces.

In his earlier English account, *41 Seconds to Freedom*, Giampietri describes his decision to write about his experience as part of his campaign as García's vice presidential candidate. He used the opportunity of this book to explain to the reader why he, as a former member of the Armed Forces, would chose to align with APRA, a political party with which the Armed Forces had historically tense relations.[17] Yet other histories have entwined APRA and Giampietri. Giampietri does not mention the fact that he had led the naval forces to regain control in the 1986 Fronton prison mutiny, which resulted in the extrajudicial execution of more than one hundred inmates. In 2007 the IACHR requested that Peruvian courts reopen the case against García, Giampietri, and the then-minister of the interior Agustín Mantilla as intellectual authors of the massacre. None of these facts are mentioned in Giampietri's account.

Giampietri's selective recounting of the past reflects in part his contradictory stance on remembering. In the epilogue to his Spanish account, Giampietri lays claim to "the human right" to forget, a right denied him and the other hostages by "human rights defenders, the Public Ministry, and the judiciary."[18] Yet at the end of the English account, Giampietri cites the names of three colleagues who died because of terrorist acts, and he concludes with the reminder "lest we forget," a reference to the victims of the havoc that the terrorists had wreaked.

Not forgetting the past (and the risks that such forgetting might entail) is also the theme of several publications by Vladimiro Montesinos, a pivotal member in the successful Chavín de Huántar rescue operation and Fujimori's main advisor and chief of the SIN. According to the inside jacket of one of his books, he has produced seven works, and all of them raise alarms that he believes should jolt Peruvians out of their complacency.[19] The two-volume book *Sin Sendero: Alerta temprana* (Without Shining Path: Early warning) forewarns of Shining Path's strategies in the twenty-first century. The back cover attempts to arouse the Peruvian public's fear that Shining Path might emerge as a serious challenge to the peace and security of the country. He informs the reader that somewhere in Lima, sometime in 2011 or 2012, Shining Path held a "second party congress" in which Shining Path decided to expand its operations beyond the regions where it remained active, with new techniques and tactics that would, as a whole, present a second strategic surprise "like it did in 1980," the year it launched its People's War to topple the government.

Nowhere in the book does Montesinos indicate that he is issuing these warnings from prison. Indeed, his dedication at the beginning of the book (to the Armed Forces, the National Police, the SIN, and the self-defense committees) is simply signed by Vladimiro Montesinos Torres, Lima, July 4, 2011. It would have been more accurate for him to indicate the part of Lima where he was residing: on that date he would have been in a penitentiary on the Naval Base of Callao, where other inmates such as Víctor Polay Campos (MRTA), Óscar Ramírez Durand (Sendero Luminoso), Miguel Rincón Rincón (MRTA), Peter Cárdenas Schulte (MRTA), and, most famously, Abimael Guzmán (Sendero Luminoso) were held.[20] Rather than mentioning his present infamy, the book jacket describes Montesinos's impressive career, from which he was at the time in a "military situation of retirement."

Montesinos does not refer to a "pueblo forgetting" as many other authors do in their memoirs but rather states that the readers have been warned, "*estamos advertidos.*" That is, readers who choose to look to the past are warned by Montesinos of weak and inept governments in the face of the Shining Path threat. Indeed, Montesinos's book is not so much a memoir as an attempt to give security advice to the Peruvian government and the broader population by making them aware of the various risks in the present day. He warns readers that Shining Path's members can wait out their twenty years in prison and change their strategy from one of arms to that of a nonarmed movement, a reference to MOVADEF, an organization that seeks amnesty for those engaged in the conflict and legitimation as a political party.[21] According to Montesinos, Shining Path simply adjusted its tactics from that of war to that of peace, a "fight without arms."[22]

Montesinos's account of the past and his concerns for the future cannot be taken as indicative of any position other than his own, at least not openly. The figure of Montesinos is the focal point for many in the military (and Peruvians as a whole) of everything that went wrong with Peru. Different armed state actors and conservative sectors tend to place the blame almost entirely on Fujimori's former security advisor and the formation of the SIN, which came to hold special powers over traditional military branches, rather than on Fujimori himself or the military establishment that swore its allegiance to him. As the journalist and columnist Eddie Álvarez Sotomayor has written, the past to be remembered (and thus avoided in the future) is not the conflict but rather the need to not forget Montesinos: "Let us not forget, for as Jorge Santayana said: 'People who forget their history are doomed to repeat it.' If we have not learned the lesson, we are doomed — *let us never forget it* — to continue suffering from the injustices, the ill treatment, the teasing and the scorn of sinister minds such as that of Vladimiro Montesinos Torres, snitch and father of all lies."[23]

In many of the post-CVR books, the authors highlight the web of corruption built by Montesinos and their attempt to distance themselves from it.[24] We see this, for instance, in the writings by Giampietri, Cipriani (who wrote his account as mediator in the MRTA hostage taking), and former president Alan García (who assumes an "I-told-you-so" tone in his hybrid short stories and memoir, *El mundo de Maquiavelo*, written in 1994 while in self-exile in Colombia and published ten years later, after the fall of Fujimori).[25] Indeed, writing memoirs seems a way for the authors not only to keep their past success in the public spotlight (their battles against Shining Path, the hostage-release operation Chavín de Huántar, and, for many former servicemen, their rural developmental efforts) but also to settle accounts with other actors from the period and to point a blaming finger at other governments: Giampietri and Cipriani cast aspersions on Montesinos; García derides Montesinos and Fujimori; Montesinos criticizes present and past governments (except for that of Fujimori) for being weak on national security, and the general Peruvian public who chose them; and retired general Fournier Coronado blames the transitional government of Paniagua for placing him in premature retirement "for the simple fact of having worked for the disbanded SIN, despite his unquestionable honesty that kept him at the margins of the embarrassing events that were discovered years later."[26]

Human Rights, Justice, and the New Rules of Peacetime

This latter theme, that of maligned military men who have been victimized by political maneuverings and a faulty justice system, is the narrative that structures several works and is a theme that melds into that of the "human rights" of the military. That is, who are the victims of human rights violations? Though this may be counterintuitive to the usual understanding of human rights victims, in their writings military men situate themselves and other members of the military as both victims of the conflict (injured and killed by Shining Path) *and* of the transitional justice era ("persecuted" by the judiciary).

During the CVR's investigation and at the conclusion of its mandate, the CVR handed forty-seven cases to the prosecutor general to investigate, of which all but one implicated members of the National Police and Armed Forces. Some of these initial cases led to successful prosecution, a process that culminated in the much-publicized proceedings against and the sentencing of Alberto Fujimori in 2009. It is likely that the military memory works produced during this period of accountability are a direct response to these prosecutions. The authors state that such judicial proceedings against military men are unfair for they had been following the orders of democratically elected governments, and that the transitional Paniagua administration (and subsequent governments) had changed the rules on them and were putty in the hands of the "caviar" Left. The Armed Forces and the National Police had been following the "rules of war" and subsequently were being held to account according to the "rules of peace." The authors thus place military men not as perpetrators of human rights violations but as individuals who have had their own rights trampled in peacetime.

In the style of a coffee-table book, measuring 9.5 × 11 cm and printed on heavy, high-gloss paper, *El silencio de los héroes* (The silence of the heroes) by General Edwin Donayre visually assaults the reader/viewer with this question: what about the rights of the men who defended the nation against terrorism? Similar to other books in this large format, the pages consist mainly of pictures, accompanied by short segments of text; yet the pictures are not of the sort one would expect to find on an actual living room table. We see detailed, high-resolution photographs of amputated limbs, scarred torsos, and pitiful military men now behind jail bars.

This book is a visual (and to less extent textual) account of 107 dead and 367 handicapped army personnel (officers, petty officers, technicians, and troops) who had been deployed in confrontations during the armed conflict and of former military men now serving sentences in prison related to their time in service.[27] The book is divided into two unequal parts called "chapters," one that focuses on victims and the other on military relations with communities in the emergency zones that led to their "pacification," the term used by Fujimori and many others to refer to the military defeat of Shining Path and to the campaign to win over communities that might have previously supported the insurgents.

The first part, "Chapter 1" (constituting nearly two-thirds of the book, or 256 pages), pairs photographs that graphically show wounds with brief texts about the difficult lives these men have led since suffering the injuries. Three subchapters consist of short *testimonios* grouped into "the testimonies of the handicapped heroes," "the testimonies of the families of fallen heroes," and "the testimonies of survivors," followed by an interview, a text on changing legal codes, testimonies and photographs of those on trial or in jail (and of Donayre visiting soldiers who had been sentenced and were "unjustly suffering"),[28] and a text on the psychological effects of the conflict on military personnel.

The second "chapter" focuses on "the decisive factors in the tenacious battle for national pacification."[29] It includes accounts of specific operations, the role of self-defense committees and *rondas campesinas*, and the fight since the 1990s in the coca-producing regions. Donayre also offers a few pages (including a short testimony) about the program to involve repentant Shining Path members or supporters (*arrepentidos*) as collaborators with the Armed Forces. This chapter's structure and content advance the argument that the conflict was finally won because of military intelligence (gained through collaboration with informants and other means) and because of an important shift in military tactics in the 1990s to win the hearts and minds of the people in the affected regions. Thus the last section of Donayre's book recounts the civic actions of the Army, especially work with orphaned children and youth. The theme of the Army's engagement in civic action for the defenseless and innocent is reinforced by the book's cover image: a photograph of a young soldier, not much older than a teenager, surrounded by four children under the age of five.[30]

Retired Peruvian Army general Edwin Donayre probably had many reasons to produce this book. He may have been inspired by the visit of a commanding general of the Colombian Army who gave Donayre a similar book about the heroes of the Colombian military's battles.[31] Another reason might be his political aspirations, for this publication would have helped establish his credentials as a heroic, caring, and decisive leader.[32]

One reason in particular stands out as motivating Donayre to write his book: his very strong identification as an Army man, a soldier just like the rank and file. Donayre is known for his comic and colorful public persona. He makes fun of himself as a Quechua speaker from the highlands in public interviews, yet he is obviously very proud of his roots and his success in the Army: the opening photograph in this book is of Donayre wearing his uniform with an Andean poncho over it (figure 1.2). This combination of being a local (indeed from the region where the conflict emerged) of humble origins as well as someone who has risen to the top of the military establishment make him both able to understand how the soldiers feel and obliged to speak on their behalf in ways that are reminiscent of Velasco's earlier patriotic discourse of the Revolutionary Government of the Armed Forces.[33] As Donayre wrote in his first paragraph, "[My account is] from the perspective of a soldier who has participated in the defense of life, having been born in the land where the terrorist violence germinated and developed, having suffered the painful confrontation with my own brothers. I gather in this present publication the brave actions and successful operations carried out by our Army in the long battle for pacification, facts that we should not and cannot relegate to oblivion; rather they must occupy a space in the history of our patria."[34]

While critical of the CVR, the book levels its harshest criticism at Peruvian society in general for turning its back on the heroes of pacification, many of whom are unable to work or are incarcerated. Take, for instance, the interview with a "major" titled "Message to My Nation: 'I did not commit excesses.'" It is unclear from this text if this is an imaginary interview by Donayre with his younger self (as implied by the photographs of him as an Army major in Ayacucho that accompany the interview) or if it is an actual interview that Donayre conducted with a major, "an official who contributed to the pacification," who was either facing charges or in prison for unnamed crimes and with whom Donayre felt enough commonality to append photographs of himself at the same stage in his career.

In this interview, the major (whoever he might be) takes issue with the use of the word *excess* as a means to categorize and explain the violent acts committed by military personnel. When the CVR came to the conclusion that "during certain periods and at certain times the Armed Forces were involved in systematic or widespread human rights abuses,"[35] the Armed Forces vehemently rejected the idea that human rights abuses were "systematic." Rather, Armed Forces officials stated that specific acts of violence were "excesses" produced by individuals and were not part of institutional procedures or of the military's culture. Yet Donayre's major challenges the heads of the Armed Forces by not accepting either the CVR's description of "systematic" or the official military

Figure 1.2. A photograph of General Donayre at the beginning of his book, *El silencio de los héroes*. (Universidad Alas Peruanas)

explanation of "excess." The major states that the term *excess* individualizes the acts and does not explain the context. Rather, Donayre's major prefers the word *error* to describe the "emotional state" in which soldiers found themselves because of the war. This emotional state, the major explains, was the consequence of excessively long tours of duty in conflict zones. He likens the resulting emotional stress to that of a pregnant woman who after giving birth "experiences an emotional state such that she could kill her newborn child." Had the soldiers served shorter tours and received more psychological support (as did American soldiers in Vietnam, he argues), these "errors" could have been avoided, for the perpetrators would not have reached the emotional state that led to fratricide. For the major, to kill one's child or brother is an error, not excess.[36]

By not accepting the term *excess*, Donayre's book thus distances him not only from the findings of the CVR but also from the official position of the Armed Forces. Furthermore, his book expresses a complaint by many members of the Armed Forces, and especially within the Army, at the time: that the few served as scapegoats to protect the many. Donayre imparts a feeling of being sacrificed and abandoned, not just by the Peruvian state but also by the high command of which he was once a member. His opinion is supported by the political scientist Jo-Marie Burt, who notes that changes in judiciary sentencing patterns meant that actual perpetrators of the crimes (the lower-ranked soldiers) rather than those who gave the orders were being sentenced despite "a now robust international jurisprudence emphasizing the need to hold accountable those who impart orders."[37]

Donayre's career trajectory may in part explain his opposition to both "systematic" and "excess" categorization of the violence committed by members of the Armed Forces and his preference to consider such violence as "errors" made in the context of war. After serving as head of the Army in its highest position, that of commanding general, he was summarily forced into early retirement in December 2008 for provocative comments about Chileans that he had made in a private context (something about placing them in coffins, perhaps a not uncommon sentiment among members of the Peruvian Armed Forces).[38] His sense of betrayal by the Peruvian Army, to which he had dedicated his working, if not personal, life, is clear both in this book and in other public interventions. In a video taken by someone in the audience during Donayre's book launch at the Universidad Alas Peruanas in Puno, General Donayre states to a lively audience (who laugh regularly in sympathy with his comments) that he does not hide anything under the table but says things as they are ("in black and white"), raising the specter of political corruption and irresponsible journalism in "this country where there is no justice."[39]

A common complaint made by the incarcerated Army men included in Donayre's book is the absence of justice in post-CVR Peru, a sense that the rules of war changed in peacetime, and for this reason the soldiers were serving sentences, despite their having successfully defeated Shining Path. "This sentence is unjust," stated Private Pedro Miguel Lozada Rázuri in prison for his part in the torture, death, disappearances, and other violations of the residents of Cayara in 1988. All these imprisoned military men seem to be unjustly incarcerated since the link between the events and their incarceration was tenuous, in their opinion. The major interviewed earlier argued that the cases against them were fabricated by the families of Shining Path members, who "weave false stories."[40] Some military personnel claimed that they were not present at the place of the crime or that they have witnesses who could testify to their good conduct. For instance, reenlisted sergeant Óscar Alberto Carrera Gonzales (serving a twelve-year sentence) claimed that seventeen soldiers testified that he had nothing to do with extortion; "Never did I act in an inappropriate way," he adamantly asserted. Many of the imprisoned military men mentioned the impact of their incarceration on their families: "The sentence is not only against me but against my family," bemoaned Carrera Gonzales; yet he asserted that he would still fight terrorism on behalf of his country, if asked again.[41]

As the unnamed major interviewed by Donayre asked rhetorically, "Why has the successful strategy and tactic waged by the Army in the battle for pacification now become an act against human rights?"[42] Here the major expressed a concern held by other military personnel that international laws had taken precedence over the Peruvian Constitution and laws, at the behest of zealous human rights lawyers and NGOs, and that these legal theories and laws were prejudicial to them since they had emerged from Europe (the major cites the post-Holocaust judgment of Nazis) and Argentina, "which are completely different contexts." In his contribution to *En el silencio de los héroes*, Brigadier General Wilfredo Mori Orzo complained that the incarcerated military personnel do not have lawyers who specialize in international law, whereas "*senderistas* have lawyers with experience."[43] At the time when Donayre's book was published, Mori stood accused of being the intellectual author of the 1985 Accomarca massacre, for which he was later sentenced *in absentia* to twenty-five years prison in September 2016.

The contributors to *El silencio de los héroes* primarily criticized the internationally lauded CVR for false assumptions and bias. In a three-page chapter prepared by Colonel Pablo Morán Reyna, the author states that it is unfair to judge the Armed Forces based on post-CVR rules, principally because the CVR was wrong. According to Morán, the CVR did not seek information from the Armed Forces. Furthermore, the CVR was biased because of its focus on rural victims and because the CVR favored those who "had complaints about the forces of order." Possible reparations for victims further compounded this bias since only those who were harmed by state agents would receive monetary compensation; thus "the witnesses changed their versions," and this was how military men "became responsible for disappearances and other crimes" (thereby implying that they did not commit these acts). Though the CVR recognized that the Armed Forces succeeded in defeating Shining Path, "the [CVR] disseminate[d] with greater intensity [the military's] errors."[44]

Yet if it is military men who suffer from injustices and who have had their rights trampled on, then who are the victims of human rights violations? In the era of transitional justice, when renewed democracies advocate for the rights of victims, offer reparations, and attempt to restore citizenship, it rings odd that regime insiders would make such complaints. While Donayre's book positions soldiers as the victims of injustices that he conflates with the abuse of human rights, other books do not make quite as grand an assertion but rather seek to downplay (as "excesses") or explain away actual violations (as a consequence of war), or they deny them outright (as fabrication). In all these attempts to correct or qualify the perception of the Armed Forces as a perpetrator of human rights violations, honor plays an important role.

Honor and Masculinity in Times of War

In all the military memory books considered here, honor structures relations within and between the sexes, across ages and socioeconomic and ethnic status. Honor works to define both personal quality and virtue of individual members within the Armed Forces ("an honorable man") as well as social precedence (of rank or class) that places the Armed Forces as a superior institution within Peruvian society. The flipside to honor is shame. In this honor/shame complex, the authors refute the Armed Forces as reproachable; it is individuals who have been dishonorable.[45]

An example of concern with honor can be found in retired Army general Eduardo Fournier Coronado's descriptions of his successful capture of the Shining Path leader "Feliciano" (Óscar Ramírez Durand), in which he points to the good comportment of military personnel despite their deep dislike of the enemy (figure 1.3). Fournier's closing introductory remarks, titled "Advertencia," warn readers that they "will be surprised by the behavior" of the SIN members of the Armed Forces who treated the "recently captured terrorists" in a "friendly" way, "in particular the women." This was difficult for them to do, according to Fournier, for as military men they had to "shed their natural rejection" of the subversives, especially knowing that the insurgents had killed many soldiers. "Conversing," however, was "one of the many forms used by [the] Intelligence [division] to know the enemy."[46] In the epilogue, Fournier reminds readers that because his Special Intelligence Team could "not forget that *senderistas* are also human beings with ideals, even if mistaken ones," they managed to capture the Shining Path leader Feliciano "without bloodshed," all the while "respecting human rights."[47]

Fournier's account includes lengthy conversations between Fournier and Feliciano (Ramírez), who assumed command of Shining Path after Guzmán's arrest until he too was captured in 1999. Fournier presents these conversations as dialogues that took place often at mealtimes and while sharing cigarettes. Although Ramírez did eventually collaborate with authorities in return for a reduced prison sentence and also apologized to the CVR for the crimes committed by Shining Path, these conversations seem remarkable not only for the good rapport between the captured and the captor but also for Fournier's ability to remember the dialogue (though the conversations may have been recorded).[48] For instance, when Fournier first came to Feliciano's cell (which is described in the book as being more like a room in a three-star hotel than a holding cell), Feliciano did not at first recognize Fournier as his captor. Once he realized who Fournier was, both men commented on how their appearances had changed.

Figure 1.3. Publications by or about members of the Armed Forces on display at the LUM. Eduardo Fournier Coronado's *"Feliciano"* is second from the left on the top row. (Photograph by author)

> —*Oh! You are the general with whom I spoke on the plane?*
> —*Yes, I am General Fournier.*
> —*What a pleasure, but you* [formal "you," *Usted*] *do not seem . . . then you had longer hair, more of a beard, thinner . . . if I had seen you in a different place, I wouldn't have recognized you.*
> —*And you* [informal "you," *tú*] *have also completely changed,* [you are now] *well dressed, rested from the bad life, and you are still well accompanied . . .* —I [Fournier] was referring to the neighboring cells where the women who had been with him the day he was captured were [being held].

In the same conversation, they congratulated each other for having outwitted each other for so long:

> —*I congratulate you, General . . .* said "Feliciano," looking at me with curiosity.
> —*And I congratulate you for having made fun of the forces of order for eighteen years, because you are an expert at evasion and escape.*[49]

In another conversation, Feliciano gave advice to Fournier about how to get other members of Shining Path to "reintegrate into democratic Peru." Fournier thanked him for his suggestions, to which Feliciano responded, "General, they have told me that you write and have various publications. . . . If I could get one of your books, I would like to read it." Fournier promised to bring him a copy the next day.[50]

Their exchange is reminiscent of a cinematic and literary trope of two adversaries who regard each other with mutual admiration, a dialogue that effaces the violence yet highlights their masculinity. Fournier and Feliciano sit smoking cigarettes and commenting on each other's skill in war, while female prisoners are held in the next cell. They are worthy, masculine opponents.

This dialogue illustrates the gendered dynamics apparent in other military memory books as well, both in the authors' wartime memories and in their perception of their persecution in peacetime. Key is the gendered notion of honor and the military's insistence on the integrity of the Armed Forces' members. While few of the memory books examined here speak directly of sexual violence, gendered power (male-male and male-female) is clearly woven throughout the texts.[51] Rather than highlighting the violence committed against subalterns, the authors of these books stress their masculinity and correlated honor while defending the nation, doing developmental work, and taking care of orphans like good *paterfamilias* (their legal and cultural status as patriarchs).

These memory books give a sense of what Jean Franco has described as "hypermasculinity," the presence of a heightened masculinity that not only signaled the authors' heroism but also served to justify or to reduce the significance of their violent actions.[52] Gender disparity in Peru's color-class hierarchy was further aggravated by the conflict that dehumanized members and suspected members of Shining Path in the eyes of state agents, thus producing an extreme gendered political culture that made socially and politically legitimate the exercise of violent power over subalterns. The books employ a discourse of dishonorable women and virile soldiers, whereby the latter's virility and aggressive masculinity was praised in military culture.[53] This sense of honor is deeply entwined with the same gender codes that allowed military personnel to commit extreme violence against rural Andean women and girls, acts that might make General Fournier's claim that the captured women in the cell adjacent to Feliciano's were "treated well" something more than a mere lie. The Armed Forces' mistreatment of subaltern women was part of a larger wartime pattern.[54] As Jelke Boesten notes, military masculinity that condoned wartime sexual violence remains deeply embedded in gendered power configurations: during the conflict, superiors would "give simple punishments" for what were considered "minor errors," and in peacetime, ongoing official silence and impunity reinforce the perception of sexual violence as permissible in war.[55]

In these books, members of the Armed Forces are virile, strong, courageous, and responsible for their dependents. Honor provides the context for the "excesses" committed by individuals: a momentary lapse in control of one's actions is what led to excess, or errors, and thus tarnishes the honor of the individual. When military men did commit "errors," according to Donayre, it was because the war had transformed them: the soldiers who committed abuses became female, like a crazed woman after childbirth. The members of Shining Path, though often portrayed as demented in military memoires, are also framed as worthy opponents. Shining Path is not feminized but rather the caviars, the CVR, and the justice system are gendered "female"—such as weak governments that are too "tolerant."[56] The caviar Left is vengeful in the judiciary, like a woman scorned. It is this caviar Left that is dangerous since because of their misinformation and political intrigues, future generations risk being "condemned to repeat [history] with graver consequences."[57]

"Truth" That Comes from Knowing

The authors of these books attribute the lack of justice, or more specifically the injustices committed against the Armed Forces, to an avid judiciary that is the product of political machinations and susceptible to the misinformation of the CVR's *Final Report*. All the books considered here contest the CVR's findings and offer other facts that the authors argue were either not known, un(der)acknowledged, or distorted by the CVR. These books challenge the CVR's version of truth by claiming that the CVR could not possibly have accessed these truths, first, because of the political bias of those who advocated for a truth commission and who were the commissioners; second, because the CVR did not seek testimonies from the military (an accusation that was not the case but has subsequently been repeated often enough to be considered so by the Armed Forces, conservative sectors, and some of the media);[58] third, because the commissioners had not been present in the emergency zones; and, fourth, because only military personnel can understand the military.

Several of these books are offered as correctives to the CVR and are packaged as a mixture of research-based texts with memoir-*testimonio*, in which the authors combine accounts of their personal experience with what they consider to be facts unknown to or disregarded by the CVR. Since none of the commissioners participated in the war, at least not as members of the "forces of order" that actually fought against Shining Path (at times, authors even describe CVR members as "pro-terrorist"), the memoirists write from what they *know* as individuals who were there, on the front lines, a kind of knowledge that the CVR members could not have possessed. Indeed, the inclusion of one member of the Armed Forces on the CVR commission reinforced this view of CVR members as not having relevant personal experience: Lieutenant General Arias Graziani came from the Air Force, which played a minor role in the conflict.[59]

It is this knowledge, or "truth," that comes from experience that most of the authors claim in their accounts. Having had these experiences, the authors cannot remain silent: as retired general Fournier writes in his epilogue, "The history that you have read is the outpouring from [my] conscience that does not allow [me] to hide or silence the truth, before the circumstances in which we are still living in this country, with the latent danger of [another] outbreak of terrorist subversion; I don't intend to alarm, just warn." Fournier had tried during the transition to tell this story, he explains, to the commanding general of the Army, the minister of defense (at the time a civilian), and the president of the republic (then Paniagua), but was not received by any of them. The only recourse left to Fournier, "*como última opción*," was to write this book, "because it constitutes a transcendental episode in the fight against the violent maelstrom that subversion unleashed in the last two decades of the twentieth century."[60]

Donayre's *El silencio de los héroes* takes this impossibility of knowing by outsiders a step further by suggesting not only that the CVR commissioners could not know what the war was like but also that as a Quechua-speaking Ayacuchan he has knowledge that would not be shared by many in the high command. Donayre asserts that his position as an Ayacuchan Quechua speaker makes him more similar to the rank and file of the Army, whose principal recruits would also have come from such a demographic. By including a photograph of himself draped in an Andean poncho at the beginning of his book, Donayre is letting soldiers know that he is one of them, not just an Army man but an Army man like them.

Even though these authors consider their personal experiences to be well-founded "truth," they probably realize that subjective truth is open to doubt and erosion over time. Thus, several of the memoir-style books also present their arguments as research based and adopt an academic-like approach. The former commanding general of the Armed Forces Pedro Villanueva Valdivia, who contributed the prologue to César Ramal Pesantes's book *La paz después de la violencia en el Perú: Seguridad y defensa nacional para una política de estado* (Peace after the violence in Peru: Security and national defense for a state policy), also published by the Universidad Alas Peruanas, similarly claims that the book is "based on real facts lived by the author" and "statistical information." The author himself describes the book as emerging from his own experience, as someone who "participated for four years in this delicate and important task of achieving peace."[61] The diagrams, tables, statistics, color photographs, and bibliography reinforce the visual impression of the book as based on research and not his experience alone. "Appendix 4," for instance, "intends to inform [the reader] of the professional means by which the soldiers were educated, and exercised their professionalism while respecting human rights." To such an end, Ramal offers to the reader a simplistic diagram meant to explain the "strengthening of the forces of order's moral"; it indicates the different factors that produced a good image of the Armed Forces among the people and thus encouraged their support. Circles, squares, and arrows link concepts such as "psychological operations" and "well-being" to the Armed Forces; an arrow titled "good image" then leads from the Armed Forces to the encircled "population," from which another red arrow, titled "adhesion," points back to the Armed Forces.[62] Statistics strengthen Ramal's argument about the significant gains made by the Armed Forces; yet for the most part, the sources for these statistics are not provided. Similarly, "Appendix 13" offers a projection of the "social costs" of the conflict with or without "pacification." The units of measurement are the number of lives lost: with "pacification" "approximately 25,000" people died versus "the million" who would have died if it had not been for the "pacification policy."[63] The author does not provide the source for this projection.[64] Fournier also adds statistics and tables in his account, though he does cite his sources at least in one case: the author's own database.[65]

One of the earliest books to emerge after the CVR's *Final Report*, three years later, at the beginning of prosecutions of security forces members for crimes against humanity and human rights abuses, is retired colonel Pablo Morán Reyna's *Complot contra los militares: Falsedades de la C.V.R.* (Plot against the military: Untruths of the CVR); he later also contributed a chapter in Donayre's *El silencio de los héroes*. As the title implies, Morán sees a coordinated conspiracy against the military, of which the formation of the truth commission was but one element. While not the first work that attempted to dismantle the findings presented in the CVR's *Final Report*—the first was probably a publication by retired army generals, ADDCOT's *Omisiones a la verdad ¿Y la reconciliación . . .?* (Truth omissions: And reconciliation?), just three months after the *Final Report* appeared—*Complot contra los militares* was the first work by a single author to combine the claim of knowledge through experience with what the author argued was an attempt to be "didactic with the reader."[66] According to the book's editor, César Reátegui Alvarado (a journalist for the daily *Expreso* who prior to the transition had written favorably of Montesinos and Fujimori), Morán was in the emergency zones, and in recognition of his service he received the honor "Cintillo de la Pacificación" (Pacification Sash). Thus Morán personally witnessed the deaths of comrades and campesinos and also experienced firsthand, "like the majority of Peruvians," the surprise of seeing the "defenders of human rights converted into the legal arm of terrorists," which, he explains, prompted his decision to "write this book" and thereby "offer to the reader analytical pages about the work of the CVR," after his own "intense investigation and collection of data."[67]

The latter assertion promises a quality of scholarship that seems questionable given the few sources cited in the book. The page-and-a-half bibliography lists seven newspapers and journals and sixteen books, many of which are only tenuously connected to the topic of the Peruvian truth commission or the recent conflict.[68] Furthermore, the chapters do not include footnotes; at most, sources are only partially indicated in the text itself.

Most of the book's 239 pages are filled with blustering reflections. Morán begins his book with a discussion of the evolution of the human species and society that led to the emergence of philosophers who became politicians and then leaders who needed armies to protect their interests. The introduction ends with a call to remember the soldiers now betrayed by Peru who had died or were injured while defending the nation. Morán repeats throughout the book that international and foreign actors colluded with Peruvian NGOs against the Armed Forces ("Like them, [representatives of] the Red Cross and the NGOs always get together, have lunch, and coordinate with politicians, above all with those in government, and thus they always go against the militaries").[69] In these pages, the author has chosen to place in bold font particular points that he wishes to draw to the attention of the reader, for example: "'**In war God is invoked and the soldier solicited; in peace, God is forgotten and the soldier slighted.**' In the last year, with the knighting of the caviar Left, strengthened by the Paniagua and Toledo governments, to this adage one can add, '**And after the terrorists are defeated, God is abandoned and the soldier sacrificed.**'"[70]

Morán's rage is tangible. He seems genuinely upset by what he believes is a changing of the rules (an argument that he repeats later in his contribution to Donayre's *El silencio de los héroes*): the state had mandated that the Armed Forces protect the nation, yet the state was punishing them for having fulfilled their duty, which they did successfully since Shining Path was no longer a threat. But his argument reduces the prosecution of military men and the CVR's report to a narrative wherein the government has been taken over by caviar leftists (he names Paniagua and Toledo) and supported by predatory NGOs. He sees abuses committed by the Armed Forces as legitimate acts of war, rather than the military acting outside the law. His contempt for the CVR is tangible on nearly every page as he lumps the CVR and NGOs together with communists and socialists and at times with narcoterrorists (the term he seems to prefer when describing Shining Path and the MRTA). The problem, as he describes it, is not simply within Peru, for the NGOs are part of a global network (according to Morán, sponsored by George Soros) that works against militaries worldwide, and truth commissions are tools designed to undermine these militaries (which he considers to be the case in El Salvador and Argentina).[71] Internally, he perceives conspiracy within all institutions of the state except the security forces. Governments also seek to tarnish the image of those still living who defended the nation, and the state has abandoned the 953 handicapped men who served the nation and the 1,186 who died, who, he proclaims in bold, are "¡Presente!" Listing each man, these 54 pages of names of injured and dead military personnel make up over a fifth of the book. Citing General Carlos Tafur Ganoza (who later fell from grace when it was discovered that he too was one of the generals shown in the *vladivideo* who signed the document swearing his allegiance to Fujimori), Morán concludes his book by saying that "the poor conduct of some of its members should never damage the essence of the organization in exclusive service of the patria."[72]

One might take Morán's rants as the opinions of an individual raging against what he perceives as a conspiracy, yet his book echoes other opinions at the time of its publication, and many of his complaints and concerns can be found in more recent military memory books and cultural interventions. Though *Complot contra los militares* is difficult to locate in Peruvian bookstores or at book fairs (I found it in the Ibero-American Institute in Berlin), it has influenced subsequent publications and generations of military thought about the conflict's aftermath: it is cited in the bibliography of several other books (such as ADDCOT's publications and the Peruvian Army's *En honor a la verdad*) and was donated by the Universidad Alas Peruanas to the Chorrillos Military School for the cadets to read.[73] Morán's views also resonate with conservative sectors outside the military. The Freemasons of Peru extended an invitation to Morán to give a keynote lecture in May 2015 on "the untruths of the CVR."[74]

Nonconfessional Scripts

Although the books discussed in this chapter often feature first-person accounts of the authors' experiences, these books should not be confused with "confessions," at least not in the common understanding of the word, since they do not acknowledge wrongdoing or admit behavior that the authors now consider shameful or embarrassing. Indeed, in Peru "confessions" about the internal conflict in general by perpetrators are rare, and they tend to come from repentant Shining Path and MRTA members.[75]

In this regard, the Peruvian journalist Ricardo Uceda's book, *Muerte en el Pentagonito* (Death in the little Pentagon), is both unique and representative. It is unique in that through investigative journalism involving lengthy interviews with different state agents, Uceda could describe in great detail the violence employed by state security forces against citizens and to depict this violence as endemic to the chain of command and a culture of "common sense among the military for fifteen years."[76] Yet the book is also representative in that none of his informants express remorse for what took place or their role in it. An institutional logic and a shared "common sense" allowed torturers and executioners to dispassionately perform their task, all the while maintaining a sense that they were protecting democracy and the nation. As Uceda states, the notion that democracy could be legitimately defended through violence was reinforced by the views of the highest level of government: even the president of the republic commended his countrymen for acts of vigilante justice.[77]

Uceda's *Muerte en el Pentagonito* revolves mainly around one key protagonist, Jesús Sosa. Uceda describes how Sosa was transformed from a scared twenty-one-year old-recruit, who was sent to Ayacucho as an undercover operative posing as a lingerie vendor when the military took over the region, to a seasoned torturer and executioner and a member of the secret squad Grupo Colina. Sosa's regret stems not from his actions but from his disappointment with his superiors, who had abandoned him and others for months on end, if not longer, in the emergency zones. Indeed, another member of the same group interviewed by Uceda also shows no regret over killing *"terroristas"*; rather, he is sorry that he did not give the victims a proper burial and expresses concern for their families, who do not know where the bodies are located.[78]

This lack of remorse for acts of cruelty also emerges in a televised interview with Jesús Sosa by another journalist in which Sosa discusses his involvement as a member of the Colina Group in both the Barrios Altos and the La Cantuta massacres.[79] In this interview, titled "No Regrets," Sosa describes himself as a soldier, not an assassin: "I don't feel like an assassin. I feel that I fought hard against terrorism." Nor does he shy away from his involvement: "I accept my responsibility; I have been a soldier. I am aware. If they wish to judge me for having fought against terrorism, for having made a sacrifice [*sacado la cara*] for Peru, well, what am I to do?" And when confronted with the fact that one of the Grupo Colina's victims was an eight-year-old boy, he responded, "It was unfortunate [*desgracia*] what happened." In such a "moment," according to Sosa, "you don't think, you just act, that's all; you leave, and then you forget, otherwise you drive yourself crazy." When the journalist questioned him about the victims of La Cantuta, if they deserved to be assassinated, buried, dug up, and buried again, Sosa responded flatly with a question: "And the victims of Tarata?" a reference to the middle-class victims of a Shining Path car-bomb attack.

Following his extradition to Peru, former lieutenant Telmo Hurtado (referred to in the media as the "Butcher of the Andes") similarly expressed no regret during court proceedings in April 2012 over his participation in the 1985 massacre of sixty-nine residents of Accomarca (August 14, 1985), for he had thought his thirty-one victims to be "captured terrorists." Rather, Hurtado was angered that he had been forced to "make a fool of himself" before a congressional hearing about the case shortly after the event, because his superiors ordered him to conceal the involvement of the military high command.[80] His outbursts in the courtroom were reserved for maligning those who had given the orders; he showed little emotion when clarifying for the court the number of deaths for which he was responsible.[81] He pointed to the culpability of his superiors, including the Army general turned author José Cabrejos Samané, who had published in 2006 his own account of the massacre, *La verdad sobre Accomarca* (The truth about Accomarca).

Jesús Sosa's seemingly similar indifference to the consequences of his actions contrasts with his animated description of the terrorist threat posed by Shining Path and the Armed Forces' job to eradicate the threat as justified under such exceptional circumstances. His nonchalance led scholars Jean Franco and Rocío Silva Santisteban to invoke Hannah Arendt's notion of the "banality of evil," though Franco reminds readers that torture "can never be banal for the tortured."[82] It seems important to Sosa that viewers understand that while he may have killed—a job that he performed because he was ordered to do so in the defense of democracy—he was neither corrupt ("*no soy corrupto*") nor a thief: "We did not kill to steal or because we were delinquents. We killed because unfortunately the commander [Hermoza Ríos] told us 'you have to kill the terrorists because this way we defend the democratic system.' And we defended the democratic system, *pues*, in their way. Because they are the ones who lead, who give orders, and us, we just comply with orders."[83] These statements shed much light on how individual perpetrators of violence justify their acts: they were following orders, and such acts were deemed necessary by their superiors for defending democracy. How they envision democracy appears reduced to references of working within the framework of the 1993 Peruvian constitution (which Fujimori designed).[84] But their statements also illuminate what they think would be bad, immoral behavior: to kill in order to steal, to be delinquents, or to be corrupt. Indeed, in the transition away from Fujimori's government, the worst criticism that one could level at others seems to have been not that they were assassins, torturers, or murderers but that they were corrupt and had used their position of power and authority to steal from state coffers. The transitional government of Paniagua charged many higher-level military personnel for corruption, and such acts of corruption provoked discontent within the military rank and file. The accusation of human rights abuses did not appear to arouse the same sense of disgust or moral outrage.

An exception to this pattern of indifference to human rights abuses that sheds light on the rule is a small act by former Army major Collins Collantes. Stepping out of the prosecutions' truck in April 2013 after a day of court hearings concerning the forced disappearance of three adults and one minor from the district of Chuschi in 1991, Collantes approached the family members of the disappeared. He asked their forgiveness for his part in the loss of their loved ones. There was no media present, only the family and some lawyers. One person took a photograph. This single photograph made its way into the news, but it was a story that only a few newspapers picked up: a former member of the military asked for forgiveness.[85]

Collantes's request for forgiveness by those affected stands out not just because it may be one of the few times that a former military man in Peru had done so but also because it looked unstaged, unscripted, and not part of a larger project of exculpation.[86] His request for forgiveness was quiet, rather private, and seemingly spontaneous. His feelings of remorse were not apparent in his testimonial contribution to the *El silencio de los héroes*, though this may be the result of the way the book was edited and organized. However, his feelings were apparent in a documentary, *Caminantes de la memoria* (Walkers of memory, 2014, directed by Heder Soto Quispe), in which Collantes presents himself as someone who regrets his actions and was suffering, at least financially and personally, for what he had done. Recently released from prison, he could not find employment and had lost the affection of his family. His regret as thus expressed in the film was more about the personal consequences of his actions than what they meant for others.

Writing Books for a Niche Readership

In Leigh Payne's study of perpetrator confessions in four different countries (Argentina, Chile, Brazil, and South Africa), the cases she examines started as controlled confessions, in prearranged settings, and within a larger political project of attempting to restore the reputation of security forces within democracies. Though these confessions might follow a narrative that demonstrated remorse, such displays were done publicly with a particular objective in mind: explaining and justifying the past in the new political context.

In their attempts to account for the past, Peru's military memory books are similar in their narratives to the "confessional scripts" adopted by the perpetrators, or regime insiders, in Payne's study. Yet in Peru the memories and versions presented in the memory books did not elicit much reaction from other members of the heroic memory camp or from human rights, victims, and survivor groups; nor did they gain traction according to Atencio's phases in the cycle of cultural memory, in the sense of inciting other significant cultural interventions or transitional justice mechanisms. One wonders then to what ends and for whom such books were written? And how was reading them supposed to affect the reader?

For the most part, reading the above-mentioned books written from the perspective of former members of the Armed Forces—mainly Army men—is a frustrating exercise. With the exception of the books that are written primarily as memoirs (such as Giampietri's), where specific memories are recounted about specific events as they evolved, these memory books are loosely strung-together statements of opinion presented as facts. The narrative thread running through them is poorly defined, and indeed the arguments that link one paragraph or even a sentence to another are often unclear, leaving the reader uncertain of the message the author wishes to impart. As a result, I feel that I acquired little substantial information from reading these works.

Yet I am not the intended reader, so perhaps the apparent absence of a narrative thread or clear argumentation would not pose a problem for the intended public. But then who is this intended public? Their readership must be a niche market, though the actual number of copies in print is good sized (most seem to have a print run of around five hundred copies, Donayre's book had one thousand, and Giampietri's second edition had two thousand).[87] There may also be a pirated market for them. When the books are announced in the media, the publication launches are hosted in venues such as military establishments and addressed to small circles, such as the Masonic society's Lima chapter, which invited Pablo Morán to speak about his book.[88] It is difficult to measure the impact of these books as there is little mention of them in the media, except on the occasion when an accused military man might publicly display a military publication to bolster his claim of innocence, or in the case of Donayre's *El silencio de los héroes*, when Donayre was running as a candidate for congress in the 2016 elections, a story of plagiarism emerged.[89] That there is little public discussion of these books is in itself interesting though difficult to interpret (for instance, is it due to poor distribution, little public interest, or simply lack of media attention?).

Given a likely limited readership, the question, then, is why write these books at all? First and foremost, the authors, as many state straightforwardly, are writing against the CVR's *Final Report*, which they simply frame as a "version" of the past. In exchange, they offer their account, their heroic narrative. By publishing books, the authors are putting in print what they had already expressed within their inner circles and in public, thereby reinforcing their narrative of the past. The louder they are, the more their versions appear in print, the more likely their narrative and arguments will gain traction and shift the public debate and perception. The authors also wish to dislodge the scholarship and intellectual authority of the CVR's report. The decision to publish printed books, rather than web books, probably has much to do with the cachet attached to printed works, "the lettered city" of official and scientific discourse, and the weightiness to counter the CVR's nine volumes. Books published in part or in whole on websites have a greater potential to reach a wider audience, but they do not have the same cultural heft as old-fashioned printed books. One can point to books on the shelf as evidence of a counternarrative, or a soldier accused of crimes can hold up a copy as proof of innocence. This was how retired general Clemente Noel posed for a photograph in response to a warrant for his arrest (he died peacefully at home at the age of seventy-five in 2005): declaring his innocence, in his hands he clasped ADDCOT's *Omisiones a la verdad ¿Y la reconciliación?*[90]

A second reason that some military men write their accounts is to reach not necessarily a general public but rather individuals and groups that like themselves already hold heroic views of their past actions in the battle against Shining Path. We might consider such writings as public engagements and performances by agents who in the post-transitional process of truth telling and judicial proceedings need to bolster their command of this past and reinforce internal cohesion when threatened by the disclosures of human rights violations and corruption. Indeed, the spurt of military memory books came not only at a time of a human rights–centered literary boom and judicialization but also when the chain of command and the pact of silence were falling apart. Telmo Hurtado's and Jesús Sosa's very public denunciations of their commanders must have sent shock waves through the military establishment, as did the publication of Uceda's investigation based on interviews with unnamed military personnel, and perhaps as well Collantes's intimate request for forgiveness.[91] They broke what one member of the Colina Group described as "*nuestra ley,*" or their law by which they "don't speak about or incriminate others."[92] Payne has described potential audiences for perpetrators' heroic confessions as "not only victims but also colleagues and supporters who may need to be reminded of the official line."[93] Thus these memories may be directed internally for the political elite and armed state actors themselves, reinforcing their own imagined heroism in the present context of ongoing judicial proceedings against their members as perpetrators of violence. Rejecting the category of "perpetrators," they pick up pens to tell their version of this contested past, thus entering into a cycle of cultural memory.

A third reason for the Armed Forces to write about this contested past is not necessarily to critique the CVR (though they do so) but rather because they perceive themselves as agents in a historical drama. That is, the authors have a historical consciousness: they see themselves as actors in and witnesses to important historical times. They all seem to hold the strong conviction that history is on their side and that time will eventually absolve them from present accusations of wrongdoing. Furthermore, the influence of the literary genre of memoir writing and perhaps even more so of the *testimonio*, and the role of the *testimoniante* in constructing knowledge of this past, is not lost on them.

This use of *testimonio* by regime insiders might seem surprising, given the roots of the genre. Testimonial literature grew out of an urgent need to seek redress and prompt action against social injustices and in the absence of sanctions. Perhaps the most famous *testimonio* is that of Rigoberta Menchú, who, assisted by an anthropologist, recounted in the early 1980s the violence committed against indigenous peoples of Guatemala at a time when there was little international awareness of the humanitarian tragedy unfolding. Menchú's book did much to bring outside attention to the state-led violence in Guatemala and may indeed have helped to bring about foreign policy changes. She was awarded the Nobel Peace Prize in 1992 in recognition of her *testimonio* and activism. Because of the roots of *testimonio* in subaltern experience, the genre tends to be understood as giving voice to victims and ordinary people typically excluded from the technologies of reading, writing, and publishing who speak truth to power and against silence. Yet in the more than fifty years of this genre, the form of *testimonios* and who writes them have changed. No longer is an interlocutor, an anthropologist or a historian, necessary to transcribe and organize the other's experiences. Neither is it only subalterns who wish to speak against injustices who turn to this literary form to denounce. Nor do these books need to be pitched to an international audience.

The binary of speech against silence has also morphed into one of memory versus forgetting. Both, however, slide over the fact that what is at play is not a choice between the two but rather what Elizabeth Jelin describes as "memory negotiations" that involve various social groups, some of which have louder voices than others.[94] Steve Stern has conceptualized such competing memories as taking place within an open-air tent in which dissonant memories vie for the position of emblematic or dominant memories.[95] Yet as Nancy Gates-Madsen notes, even silence does not simply mean "not talking" or "not remembering." As she demonstrates at various junctures in cultural production in Argentina, memories may take the form of silences, whether literary or societal; that is, they are full of meaning.[96] Nor are silences restricted to those who would rather "forget," "turn the page," or "move on," positions that ultimately benefit perpetrators and are helpful for maintaining the status quo. Victims may choose to be silent. Perpetrators and state agents may wish to speak, and they may choose the testimonial genre as a means to do so. That their books are often poorly written and structured without outside assistance may reinforce the perception of their authenticity in breaking the silence.

State agents who take up the *testimonio* are playing with at least two aspects of the genre: first, because the genre is associated predominantly with victims, state agents-turned-authors place themselves as the victim-*testimoniante*; and second, the authors want to access a reader who, by virtue of the genre, is situated as someone prepared to be moved by the injustices described. Yet as Kimberly Nance notes, rarely does this genre lead to action. Rather, it positions readers as armchair judges and jury who are moved to morally condemn the injustices described but not necessarily to take to the street or to write their local representatives to complain.[97]

It seems that authors of military memory books primarily want readers to agree with their moral outrage. Atencio's work on the narratives by former guerilla in post–amnesty law Brazil (which granted amnesty to both state and insurgent groups) is helpful here: she sees former guerillas turned *testimoniantes* as "invit[ing] readers to substitute the act of reading for meaningful social action, such as demanding trials and truth commissions," because the guerilla authors benefited from the amnesty.[98] Similarly, because the truth commission and subsequent trials go against their interests, some Peruvian military men turn to *testimonio* because they want to transform the reader into a judge, one who they hope will give them a more sympathetic hearing as well as condemn trials and truth commissions as the work of *los caviares*. The authors do not necessarily want to promote social action; rather, they seek to encourage moral condemnation of what they perceive as the ungratefulness of the Peruvian state and their persecution by prosecution.

The desire to convince readers of the wrong done to those who had sacrificed their youth (and sometimes their lives) in the service of their nation seems to be a key factor motivating the production of a book that reached me by a circuitous route at the end of my research and writing on military memories.[99] Having heard that a North American historian was looking for books by military men, Jesús Sosa sent a copy of his 2014 memoir, *Sueños de justicia: La verdad del llamado Grupo Colina* (Dreams of justice: The truth about the so-called Colina Group) from his maximum-security prison, Piedras Gordas (Ancón, Lima), to a mutual acquaintance who then delivered it to me. I know very little about this publication, how he came to publish it, how many

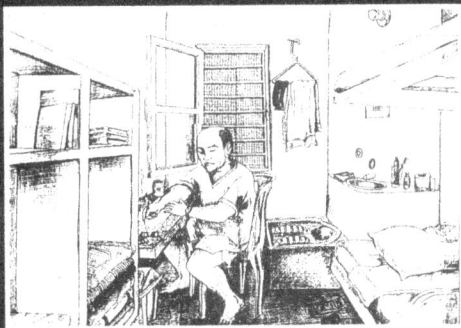

Figure 1.4. The cover of *Sueños de justicia: La verdad del llamado Grupo Colina* by Jesús Antonio Sosa Saavedra. (Scan by author)

copies were made, its circulation, and who has read it. Yet Sosa's reasons for writing the book are clearly stated, and they illustrate many of the points made in the earlier military memory books examined here. Feeling misunderstood and maligned by Ricardo Uceda in *Muerte en el Pentagonito* (he refers to Uceda as participating in the "plot fabricated by the caviars") and falsely imprisoned for simply having followed orders because of retroactively applied laws (he maintains that the Armed Forces won on the military field, but "today [they] lose on the political field"), Sosa is informing the Peruvian people, to whom he dedicates the epilogue, sharing with them his "truth." Perhaps Sosa had hoped that by getting his book to me, I might assist in the process of letting others know and perhaps even help him to write about his experiences in English. Regardless of his reasons, there Sosa sits in his cell, as depicted in the book's cover image, a black-and-white drawing of him at fifty-four years old and five and a half years into a twenty-year sentence for crimes against humanity, pen in hand, writing in the hope of being read (figure 1.4).

2

The Army's
Memory Entrepreneurs
and Their Truth Report

n the many works written from the perspective of armed state actors since the Peruvian CVR, one book stands out for the gravity and grand scale of its endeavor: the nearly 350-page *En honor a la verdad: Versión del Ejército sobre su participación en la defensa del sistema democrático contra las organizaciones terroristas* (In honor of the truth: The Army's version of its participation in the defense of the democratic system against terrorist organizations).[1] Published originally in 2010 and again in 2012, *En honor a la verdad* is the Army's official account of the conflict in response to the findings of the CVR and was published at the same time as the Army's recounting of the Chavín de Huantár operation, which successfully freed hostages held by the MRTA.[2] Compared to the works of the retired generals of the Armed Forces association ADDCOT and retired colonel Pablo Morán Reyna's *Complot contra los militares*, which appeared shortly after the CVR completed its mandate, *En honor a la verdad* does not display the rage of these earlier books and seems less a direct attack on the CVR than an institutional grappling with what took place and with the CVR's findings. It is a more fine-tuned and measured response to the CVR than the other books produced by military men up to that point, examined in the previous chapter.

Rather than stating that the CVR's *Final Report* was "false" or "lies," *En honor a la verdad* attempts in a less vitriolic way to insert the memories of the military into a national discourse, something that the authors believe the CVR neglected: "This book seeks to not omit an important voice in the history of the Republic . . . a voice [the Army's] that does not present excuses, but explains the facts, as they happened."[3] Though some might consider the book an attempt to "clean the institution's honor," the authors insist that their intention, rather, was to "recompose the history [*recomponer la historia*] . . . about which many have spoken but few have studied academically or exhaustively."[4] That is, *En honor a la verdad* is their effort to "write a part of this history that until now [was] invisible [that of the experience of the Army]."[5] "True reconciliation," they argue, necessitates recuperating the Army's history so that "these tragic deaths of our countrymen do not happen again."[6] Perhaps because of the seriousness with which the conflict is studied from the perspective of one branch within the Armed Forces and because it was produced by an investigative team of professional civilian and military historians with the support of the Armed Forces' high command, *En honor a la verdad* came to be known informally as the Army's "truth report," the counter report to the CVR's *Final Report*.

The Permanent Historical Commission of the Peruvian Army

The important task of writing an official Army version of the conflict in the period after the transition fell to the Comisión Permanente de Historia del Ejército del Perú (CPHEP, Permanent Historical Commission of the Peruvian Army), a few historians housed on the imposing grounds of the Army's headquarters, "El Pentagonito" (the Little Pentagon), in what appears to have originally been built as a temporary one-story structure. For the CPHEP, a small, rather neglected unit within this massive compound, writing *En honor a la verdad* gave it a renewed raison d'être within the military since its illustrious beginning in the early 1970s.

The CPHEP's own foundation and trajectory follow that of what might be considered the *letrados*, or intellectuals, within the military establishment.[7] Established in 1973 first as an "executive" commission, which later became a "permanent" commission, the CPHEP was charged with studying, writing, and disseminating the history of the Army, a task that won its publications official recognition as of "cultural interest to the nation" by supreme decree in 1984.[8] General Mercado Jarrin, the founder of the CPHEP as well as a similar institute for the Navy, was part of a cohort promoted around the same time as a group of broadly educated and talented men with progressive sensibilities beyond that of military strategy.[9] In the 1950s and 1960s, these men received professional training in law, economics, history, agrarian studies, and other fields, and they were the men who came to surround the reformist-minded military president Juan Velasco Alvarado (1968–75), though Velasco was probably the least educated among them, for he had not studied in the Centro de Altos Estudios Militares (CAEM, Center for Advanced Military Studies). These *letrados*, referred to by the scholars Kruijt and Tello as the "institutionalists," combined a strong nationalist sentiment with cotemporary theories of underdevelopment.[10]

The Velasco era was a period of grand publications that coincided roughly with the 150-year-anniversary of independence (1821) and the 100-year anniversary of the War of the Pacific (1879–83) and was a "revolutionary time, of agrarian reform, of foreign policy, and Third World nationalism."[11] The roots of the CPHEP most likely lie in the collaboration between Velasco and a group of civilian historians to celebrate the sesquicentennial of Peru's independence. With the 150th anniversary approaching in 1971, the Velasco government created a national commission headed by a general and composed of seventeen other members, including distinguished civilian historians. This commission produced an eighty-six-volume compilation of documents related to Peruvian independence (for instance, on Túpac Amaru, travelers' reports, and military affairs in the *Colección documental de la independencia del Perú*); organized parades and contests; erected monuments; and created paintings, bronze friezes, two short documentaries, and short promotional clips, the latter shown in theaters and on television. According to historian Carlos Aguirre, this precursor to the CPHEP was a key element in the Revolutionary Government of the Armed Forces' efforts at self-fashioning.[12]

At times when military men of that generation (such as General Felipe de La Barra, who wrote on independence-era history) or prominent Peruvian civilian academics (such as renowned anthropologist and archaeologist Luis Lumbreras, who has worked extensively on pre-Colombian societies) headed the CPHEP, the commission was prolific in its writings about Peru's military past. As its emblem states, "History [is the] soul of the Army" (figure 2.1). Yet by the mid-1980s, the CPHEP and intellectuals within the Army fell out of favor as military culture became less intertwined with that of the *letrados*, and technocrats and hardliners rose to the top. With the rise of hardliners within the military establishment, the CPHEP was headed by military personnel who were less engaged in the commission's work. When Fujimori fled, however, the Army's high command turned to the CPHEP to write a counternarrative to that of the CVR, which had placed significant responsibility for the violence on the Armed Forces. To do so, the Army reanimated the CPHEP, thus leading to a new florescent period for the commission and marked the first time that the CPHEP plied their trade to study the twentieth century.[13]

Figure 2.1. The CPHEP emblem, which states, "History [is the] soul of the Army." (CPHEP Facebook page)

Important educational reforms to military training also contributed to changes in the composition of the CPHEP team. In 1997 the military academy in Chorrillos began accepting female cadets. In order to train these women, the Army brought in female professionals at the level of officers in the fields of engineering, law, accounting, and other professional degrees.[14] Later, disgraced by the fall of Fujimori and Montesinos—and with them the highest level of the Armed Forces command—the Army sought to further build a "professional corps," perhaps not so much in the image of the *militar letrado* of the Velasco years but rather as an organization that trained its members not only in strategy, armament, and the like but also in a whole range of professional and civilian fields. These steps to professionalize the military were also deemed necessary as a means to attract new recruits since mandatory service had ended in 1999.[15] Around 2010, this professionalization expanded to include training in the humanities and social sciences in degree-granting institutions outside military schools for both servicemen and women.[16] Soon afterward, the Peruvian Army put out a call for young professional historians to join the Army, thus combining their careers in academia with the military rank of lieutenant.[17] As a result of these changes, in 2015 the CPHEP team consisted of three civilian historians who had been part of the CPHEP for several decades, a few military men (two with undergraduate history degrees), and a half-dozen young military personnel, including women, studying in the humanities and social sciences.[18]

As its Facebook page in 2015 indicates, the CPHEP actively engaged the public through different media.[19] At the republic's Congressional Book Fair in March 2015, the CPHEP advertised over forty-five publications. Prominently displayed on its exhibition table were *En honor a la verdad* and *Operación militar de rescate de rehenes Chavín de Huántar*. The CPHEP members also issued a quarterly journal, *Documenta de historia militar* (Military history document), and contributed to the handsome volumes on General Francisco Bolognesi (a hero from the War of the Pacific, who despite his military defeat was undergoing a revival in literature and on the screen for his 200th birthday in 2016) and General Andrés Cáceres (another ultimately defeated hero of the War of the Pacific, who served as president three times).[20] In addition to producing publications presented at various book and cultural fairs, the CPHEP members regularly hosted a radio program ("Peru through its history"), conducted research for history-based television series and film scripts, were invited as guest speakers on other media programs, gave talks to schoolchildren, and taught military history as instructors in many military institutions. In the realm of cultural activities, CPHEP members participated in occasional historical reenactments (of battles in the War of the Pacific), helped to mount cultural exhibitions such as one commemorating the Battle of Callao (May 2, 1866), and attended several consultative workshops with the newly opened national place of memory, the Lugar de la Memoria, la Tolerancia y la Inclusión Social (LUM), to discuss their museological script. To the one-thousandth person who "liked" its Facebook page in April 2015, the CPHEP gifted a copy of the most recent edition of its quarterly journal and of *En honor a la verdad*.

It is in this context of creating a more professional corps with links to society outside military compounds that specific military "memory entrepreneurs" or promoters should be understood, individuals such as Brigadier General Marco Merino, a historian with a degree from the Pontificia Universidad Católica del Perú (Pontifical Catholic University of Peru, PUCP) who helped lead the *En honor a la verdad* project and who in 2016 was the head of the National Geographic Institute;[21] Major Carlos Freyre, a published writer and active soldier, tasked with writing *En honor a la verdad* based on the research of the CPHEP; and Lieutenant Carla Granados, a master's student in history and anthropology who was active in the dissemination of the Army's version of events in various cultural venues. While these memory promoters might not be representative of the average military personnel, they do signal a turn to professionalization within the institution and indicate the public face of this professional corps that the military wishes to present (this face is sometimes that of a young woman). As part of the CPHEP, they participate (with civilian members of the CPHEP) in public events on issues of human rights and the Armed Forces; attend the sessions at the LUM; speak in panels at the progressive think tank, the Instituto de Estudios Peruanos (IEP, Institute of Peruvian Studies); present at book fairs; and contribute to publications that many in their institution would consider *de los caviares*.[22] The CPHEP serves as a bridge between the military and the larger public on questions about the past, including the conflict years. And while it is often the same members of the Armed Forces who attend these events, one must remember that within the world of NGOs and human rights groups, it is often the same fifty or so individuals as well. In both cases, it is a small circle whose members are self-selecting to a certain extent because of a shared interest in common themes.

The CPHEP's turn to recent history came at the behest of the commanding general of the Army during the García government, Otto Guibovich (who holds a master's degree in philosophy).[23] It is likely that members of ADDCOT and similarly minded individuals from within the military, some of whom had already written accounts (such as Giampietri, Cabrejos Samamé, and Morán), felt that the Armed Forces had to take an official position in print, and they lobbied Guibovich to do so. By 2007, when conversations about producing such a book were taking place, the CVR's *Final Report* was being used in the prosecution of former armed state agents, and negative images of the Armed Forces were circulating widely, not just of the corruption of the Fujimori years but also of the military's human rights abuses. There was a growing sense within the military that its voice was absent in public debates and not sufficiently known or understood.[24] Also, those being tried in the courts could use an official Army report in their legal defense (which they subsequently did with *En honor a la verdad*).[25] Thus, in response to these demands for an official account and the perception that the Army in particular needed its version to be firmly established within public and academic realms, Guibovich charged the CPHEP with the task of compiling and writing such a report; then–vice president Luis Giampietri advocated for the report; the minister of defense, Rafael Rey, financed the project; and the Universidad Alas Peruanas published the work, as it did with some of the individual memoirs written by military men discussed in the previous chapter.

There are few equivalents to Peru's *En honor a la verdad*. The closest Southern Cone text was produced by the Brazilian Centro de Informações do Exército (CIE, Center of Army Information), after the Archdiocese of São Paulo's report *Nunca mais* appeared in 1985. Commissioned by the minister of the Army, over thirty officers worked for three years under the code name "Orvil," using classified documents to produce in 1988 two volumes titled

Tentativas de tomada do poder (Attempts to seize power), which disseminated the Brazilian Army's version of the years 1964–85. The book was publicly given to the president but was later archived and classified as "reserved." In 2000 a group of civilians and military called Terrorism Never Again (Ternuma) posted forty pages on the Internet. Today, the entire 953-page document is available, with the link bearing the title "suffocated truth."[26]

An important Peruvian precedent to *En honor a la verdad* comes from the tradition of writing *libros blancos* (white papers) on defense policies and other ministerial reports, such as the *libro blanco* produced after the coup d'état in 1962, a document that justified the military seizure of power to prevent APRA's Víctor Raúl Haya de la Torre from wining the elections.[27] Indeed, the cover of the 2010 version of the *En honor a la verdad* is a simple white cover. White papers are intended mainly for internal government use, though they may also be made available to the public; they summarize the institution's work and identify strategies for the future. In 2005 the Ministry of Defense produced a *libro blanco* that summarized the different organizations under its supervision (Joint Chiefs of Command, the Air Force, the Navy, and the Army), the Peruvian Armed Forces' domestic and international role, and possible reforms. *En honor a la verdad* shares a similar official stature to the *libros blancos* commissioned and approved by the commanding general of the Army and with the support of the Ministry of Defense. A review in the daily *Expreso* at the time of the original publication of *En honor a la verdad* and *Operación militar de rescate de rehenes Chavín de Huántar* points to this precedent:

> It is an "official" version of our Army about its participation in the defense of democracy and against terrorist organizations since 1980 to date as well as of the successful actions of the commando who rescued seventy-one of seventy-two hostages from the Japanese ambassador's residence in 1997. It is not a "white paper" or clandestine, but rather a true, intense, and rigorous account of [the Army's] perspective on the aforementioned events. . . . Many crimes—literal and metaphorical—have been committed in the name of truth over the last six years. It was time already that the truth of our Army also begins to open up spaces of reflection.[28]

Yet while similar to a white paper in that it provided assessment of an institution, *En honor a la verdad* is different in the scope of what is studied and its aims. Its authors attempt to explain the origins of the conflict and the role of the Army in it as well as to draw lessons from this specific conflict as a way to come to terms with this past for both Peruvians and for themselves.

The original edition of *En honor a la verdad* was published in 2010 with a print run of five hundred copies, which were mainly given away, mostly within the military and to libraries, though some individuals from NGOs also received copies.[29] According to historian Antonio Zapata, when the 2010 version appeared, the Army realized that it had an unanticipated problem. Because the Armed Forces had previously told the CVR that it did not have certain documents (because they did not exist, had burned, or had been lost), human rights groups and lawyers such as Gloria Cano of the Asociación Pro Derechos Humanos (APRODEH, Association Pro Human Rights) immediately requested access to the documents cited in *En honor a la verdad*, such as those pertaining to the August 1985 Accomarca massacre of sixty-nine community members by state security forces.[30] At this point, the Armed Forces stepped back and did not draw much attention to its report ("no hicieron tanta bulla," according to Zapata), thus dampening the potential initial impact that this document might have had on public debates.[31] Indeed, except for a short mention of the book in some newspapers in 2010, *En honor a la verdad* received little media attention, and few copies were in active circulation.[32]

In 2012 the Army reissued a slightly revised version of the report with some minor changes made in the text, the addition of color photographs, and the front cover changed from that typical of *libros blancos* to feature a photograph of soldiers in the VRAEM region preparing to go on patrol (the smiling soldier in the center died during that patrol) (figure 2.2).[33] One of the reasons given for producing a second edition was that the initial five hundred copies had run out; the second version had a print run of five thousand copies.[34] But the decision to reissue *En honor a la verdad* might also have been a response to a perceived change in the climate for public debates. In 2012 the country had reached a different juncture, one possibly offering a more propitious opening for dialogue: Ollanta Humala, a military man, was president; many in the media feared that the political wing of Shining Path, MOVADEF, was on the rise and that the younger generation needed to be taught about the past (and implicitly those who supported the *En honor a la verdad* project felt that the CVR did not do this adequately); and various government organizations in conjunction with congress had launched the "Todos contra el Terrorismo" (All against Terrorism) educational campaign the previous year. There was also a sense that the attitude of some of the CVR commissioners had changed, a sentiment reflected in the statements of several members of the Armed Forces in conversations with me. They were referring to a 2012 interview of former CVR commissioner Sofía Macher in which she expressed her regret that the CVR had not conducted an *audiencia pública* (public hearing) with the military.[35] Taken out of their original context, her remarks were subsequently reconfigured by these military men to mean that some members of the CVR have acknowledged that they had not sought the military point of view for the *Final Report*. This

Figure 2.2. The cover of *En honor a la verdad*, 2012 edition. (CPHEP)

was not so, however; the chapters in the CVR's *Final Report* on the Armed Forces and Police Forces draw on military and police testimonies, which are today archived by the Defensoría del Pueblo (Ombudsman's Office) and available to whoever wishes to review them.[36]

The Army's Alternative Truth

En honor a la verdad is a valuable text for understanding the Army's account of the conflict, the narrative that it wishes to register in the public sphere as the subtitle of the book indicates: "The Army's *version* of its participation in the defense of the democratic system against terrorist organizations" (emphasis mine). By using the term *version* in the subtitle, the authors imply that other "versions" are in circulation. Rather than considering the CVR's nine-volume *Final Report* as the result of a government-mandated truth commission tasked with producing a coherent report about what took place for the nation's collective memory, the Army implies that it is simply another "version," or interpretation, of the past. One objective, then, of *En honor a la verdad*, perhaps the primary one, is to diminish the stature of the CVR's *Final Report*, presenting it not as the findings of a rigorous investigation conducted by an interdisciplinary team and multisectoral commission but as a mere "version," and in doing so to displace the CVR's report with its own.

The end product of the Army's efforts is close to 350 pages long, including three appendices, a glossary, and a short bibliography. After the introductory front matter (dedication, presentation, and introduction), the main body of the text consists of five chronological sections: the background to the conflict and the various actors involved prior to 1983; the entry of the Army into the conflict to replace the Police Forces, 1983–85; the expansion of the war, 1985–89; the successes in the war, 1989–95; and the defeat of the two adversaries and the price of peace, 1995–2000. The sixth and final section offers in two and a half pages the "conclusiones y lecciones aprendidas por el Ejército del Perú" (conclusions and lessons learned by the Peruvian Army).

The heart of the conflict as experienced by the Army is structured according to presidential periods—Belaúnde (from the Army's entry into the conflict in 1982–85), García (1985–89), and Fujimori (1990–95, 1995–2000). These periods are further divided into thematic "chapters" with descriptive titles such as "Una nueva organización terrorista irrumpe en el scenario: El Movimiento Revolucionario Túpac Amaru" (A new terrorist organization breaks into the scene: The Revolutionary Movement of Túpac Amaru), "Lima, la caja de resonancia" (Lima, the sounding board), "Los frentes inclinan la balanza" (The tipping of the scales on the front), and "Las ciudades: El regreso a la vida cotidiana" (The cities: The return to daily life). Each chapter is further broken down into subsections, usually consisting of one or two paragraphs, related to specific events such as the "creation of the Huallaga front" and the "liberation of the Dog's Ear [Chungui]."[37] The structuring of the book into these short subsections makes the reader feel as if she is perusing an annotated list.

The Army's overarching story line is one of learning how to engage the enemy. *En honor a la verdad* starts with the Army arriving in the emergency zones, where they confronted a poorly understood adversary and with little guidance or coherent plan on the part of civilian governments. The Army was ill-equipped with out-of-date counterinsurgency manuals from the 1960s (based on those of the United States Army and translated into Spanish).[38] The war shifted in favor of the state once new manuals were issued, when greater emphasis was placed on intelligence gathering, with the incorporation of communities in the fight, and when new legislation was enacted that combined "pragmatism and cold calculation" in response to the public outcry for "a strong-handed" government.[39] The book ends with some notes of self-critique over the Army's role in the conflict, recognition of the sacrifice made by the men in uniform and others, and the emphatic denial of an "extermination policy dictated by military hierarchy."[40]

En honor a la verdad is the product of three years of labor by the CPHEP's investigative team, composed of three civilian historians, two military historians (then colonels, Merino and Torrico both became brigadier generals), one Army major and fiction writer (Carlos Freyre), and two journalists, as well as at various points psychologists and lawyers.[41] The documentation amassed comes from a wide variety of sources, including the Army's own archives; published works found in public and military libraries such as Clemente Noel's memoir *Ayacucho, testimonio de un soldado* and Edwin Donayre's *El silencio de los héroes*; and academic studies, including some by scholars who participated in or were close to the CVR.[42] Indeed, there is some irony in the CPHEP's references to the works of CVR commissioner and anthropologist Carlos Iván Degregori and historian Nelson Manrique, both of whom were members of insurgent leftist movements in the 1970s and 1980s.

In order to compete with the CVR's *Final Report* as an official account of the past, *En honor a la verdad* claims to have followed scholarly practices in the composition of its team, in its methodology, in the use of primary and secondary sources, and in the literature reviewed. The appearance of serious scholarship is further bolstered by footnotes, graphs, appendices, and the like. The authors attempt to gain scholarly legitimacy by referring to established historians and social scientists throughout the text.[43] Yet despite these efforts, the scholarship in this book is mixed. The reader does not learn much about the actual battles that took place, and it is difficult to reach any larger conclusions about the conflict and the Army's military engagement because of the episodic structuring of the book.[44] The footnotes vary in style (and have significant typos) and do not always lead the reader to the source of the information indicated. For instance, single-page numbered documents on gray-shaded pages with short titles, such as "Una larga noche" (A long night) and "El problema de viajar" (The problem of travel), are scattered throughout the text. The authors of these short texts are not identified, and their origin is not indicated, though they most likely came from the CPHEP's interviews with military personnel in 2009.

The authors and investigators of *En honor a la verdad* draw from published studies and accounts to present their version of the past. Unlike many of the previous military memory books examined in chapter 1, *En honor a la verdad* uses the work of the CVR (it is cited twenty-four times). Whereas ADDCOT and Morán cited the CVR only to discredit it, *En honor a la verdad* borrows from the CVR's findings to provide global context and background to the conflict and when the CVR conclusions resemble its own. For instance, the CPHEP description of the Uchuraccay massacre, which resulted in the deaths of eight journalists and their guide, comes almost entirely from the CVR's chapter in the *Final Report* and cites the CVR's conclusion that neither the Marines nor the *sinchis* (of the former Civil Guard) were direct perpetrators in these deaths.[45] Other than one footnote to Clemente Noel's memoir noting the impact of Uchuraccay on Shining Path's tactics, not a single military or police document is cited in this section of *En honor a la verdad*, although there must have been at least some internal correspondence about the death of these journalists in the region under their command.

The authors of *En honor a la verdad* also draw on the media as a primary source of information about events as well as a barometer of public perception of the Army, even though the authors of *En honor a la verdad* are rather critical of the role of the media in the conflict.[46] Similar to some authors of books examined in the previous chapter, the authors of *En honor a la verdad* use media-based opinion polls as a means to measure public support for their conduct. For instance, in July 1982, 60 percent of respondents to a poll by *Caretas* magazine thought that the Armed Forces should intervene, which the authors of *En honor a la verdad* interpret as an implicit mandate from the people, though the actual number interviewed was fewer than two thousand urban citizens.[47]

The style and tone of argumentation undermine the quality of scholarship. The authors of *En honor a la verdad* tend to declare opinions as facts, which are backed up by self-referencing sources. For instance, the CPHEP asserts that some human rights organizations were fronts for Shining Path, including the umbrella organization the National Coordinator for Human Rights; while members of some conservative sectors and of the Armed Forces held this opinion, the only evidence offered to readers of *En honor a la verdad* is a vaguely titled "Official Document of the Army."[48] This self-referencing (or the use of a circular argument that "this is so, because we say so elsewhere") is also noted by historian Antonio Zapata, whose principal criticism of the work is that it is one-sided, and "its point of departure and arrival is the same Peruvian Army, and other actors only appear in this capacity. For this reason, their opinion is often biased, and various passages consist of a closed defense of the actions of its members."[49]

Zapata gives as an example of this "closed defense" the CPHEP's coverage of the massacre in Accomarca, a section of the book that demonstrates the authors' tendency to reference internal sources as evidence. This case received much attention both in the CVR's *Final Report*, one of the forty-seven cases it passed to judicial authorities to pursue, and in the Peruvian judiciary, where the trial began in November 2010 and a verdict was reached nearly six years later. The Army's version of this massacre was written after the publication of the CVR's findings and before the trial began. The 2012 version was published during the trial. Though *En honor a la verdad* does not provide this information, this military operation resulted in the deaths of sixty-nine peasants (twelve men, twenty-seven women, and thirty children); rather, the CPHEP vaguely titles the subsection "Los lamentables hechos de Accomarca" (The unfortunate events of Accomarca).[50]

The authors of *En honor a la verdad* present two main protagonists in "the unfortunate events," the then-political-military chief of the zone, General Wilfredo Mori, who staged an operation to capture or kill Shining Path members said to be gathering in the Province of Cangallo, and the head of one of the patrols that he dispatched to complete this mission, Second Lieutenant Telmo Hurtado. According to *En honor a la verdad*, the returning patrols' reports made no mention of a massacre, and it was not until later that "a series of denunciations" prompted a congressional commission to investigate. When evidence emerged of a massacre of peasants by state agents, Hurtado told the investigating congressional commission, "Ultimately I made the decision that I considered correct, to eliminate them." Hurtado's commanding officer, Mori, recounted to the CPHEP in his April 2009 interview that he had not been informed of events (and thus had no knowledge of the massacre of civilians): "According to what Hurtado said in his reports, he arrived in the zone, accompanied by a guide, who was a terrorist, and [the guide] told them [the soldiers] that they [the community members] were all terrorists, so he [Hurtado] captured them and shot them. But he [Hurtado] did not tell [us, his superiors] about this. Hurtado's written and oral accounts were uneventful. . . . I didn't hear of the matter [until] later [when] the photos of the bodies came out in the newspapers. Then the investigations started." According to *En honor a la verdad*, once Mori realized that he had let Hurtado run rogue, Mori requested his own demotion, and his troops were sad to see him go: "The troops had come to hold him [Mori] in high regard, and they did not stop cheering him." Though the subsection had been vague about the deaths of the campesinos, the last sentences stand in sharp contrast with details and dates of continued Shining Path attacks in the month that followed "the un-fortunate events of Accomarca."[51]

When the original *En honor a la verdad* was published in 2010, this version of events in Accomarca might still have found a sympathetic hearing or may have been given the benefit of the doubt by some; yet when Telmo Hurtado, who had fled to the United States after the transition fearing that his earlier amnesty might be repealed, was extradited back to Peru in 2012 to face trial, his newer version of events differed significantly, and this public account made the front page of the main newspapers. In his trial, Hurtado described having been ordered to "act [as though he were] crazy" in order to save the careers of his superiors. Hurtado claimed responsibility for thirty-one of the dead but not for all sixty-nine victims, and he named his superiors as responsible for having ordered the massacre, including General José Williams Zapata, who had later led the successful Chavín de Huántar operation, and General Wilfredo Mori, on whose 2009 testimony much of *En honor a la verdad*'s account rests.[52] This section in the 2012 version of *En honor a la verdad* was probably printed too early in the Accomarca trial to take into account Hurtado's testimony, yet his extradition from the United States the previous year would have accorded time for the authors to make some changes from the 2010 publication besides that of slightly different spacing between two paragraphs.[53] Despite new infor-mation and evidence coming to light in the trial, Mori's 2009 testimony to the CPHEP and Cabrejos Samamé's 2006 book "The Truth about Accomarca," both generals whom Hurtado implicated in the crime remained the key sources of information about the massacre for *En honor a la verdad*.

While history as a discipline has been dislodged from its pedestal of objec-tivity, there remains a foundational principal that information can be repre-sented as historical fact only if others given access to the same sources could reach similar conclusions. While others might indeed reach comparable con-clusions as those of the authors of *En honor a la verdad*, it is nearly impossible to do so using the same materials, because they are poorly identified, because they are not identified at all, or they are deemed too sensitive and thus are "off-limits" to nonmilitary personnel. Yet perhaps this criticism of the scholar-ship is beside the point and a bit petty, since as the book's title indicates, this is the military's "version." Though weak in truth value because of the tendency to rely heavily on internal documents and testimonies as evidence, *En honor a la verdad* has great value for the insight it provides into how the military perceives its past, one that, as Zapata notes, places the Army as the "point of departure and arrival" for any understanding of this past.[54]

Zapata's observation about the closed or circular argumentation holds since the most sources cited in *En honor a la verdad* come from internal military material: documents referred to as "official documents of the Army" are cited 166 times (for instance, what might be intelligence reports, personnel files, and counterinsurgency operations); the *Memoria anual del Ejército* (yearly report) and documents from the Joint Command of the Armed Forces are cited 41 times (mainly strategic manuals and assorted texts such as a daily reports, supreme resolutions, and recommendations). These are the kinds of documents petitioned by human rights lawyers, prosecutors, and judges but whose existence was denied by the Armed Forces (they were lost, burned by accident, or never existed, so the Armed Forces claimed).[55] These sources might not have been available for the purpose of accountability, but they were for the purpose of the CPHEP's investigation and thus provide insight into the military's collective memory. An important addition to these sources is the more than seventy testimonies gathered by the CPHEP for this book and *Operación militar de rescate de rehenes Chavín de Huántar*. The testimonies, however, do not simply provide raw material for the Army's narrative; they also give it heft: direct citations project the appearance of truth value, and the single-paged gray-shaded documents interspersed throughout the book give the impression of documentary evidence.

CPHEP and the Gathering of Testimonies

In studying the conflict years, the CPHEP historians turned to recent history and adopted methodologies beyond the analysis of archival documents: they interviewed actors from the time. Just prior to this investigation, some members of the CPHEP had assisted General Donayre in gathering testimonies for his *El silencio de los héroes*.[56] As well, the CPHEP had conducted interviews in the early 1980s for a centennial project on the Breña Campaign (a Peruvian resistance movement against Chilean occupiers); members of the CPHEP followed the route of the War of the Pacific (1879–83) and interviewed descendants about the epic war (all while the National Police were fighting against Shining Path in Ayacucho) (figure 2.3). The War of the Pacific is not a conflict subject to much public controversy among Peruvians; despite Peru's defeat, it is a point of patriotism and pride for many, and it is from this war that both the Army and the Navy draw their patron heroes (Bolognesi and Grau). Yet the task at hand for the CPHEP in studying the recent past differed greatly from the Breña Campaign project; while the Breña project work involved interviewing Peruvians a century after the event, documenting the battle against Shining Path and the MRTA required interviewing direct actors

Figure 2.3. Members of the investigative team of the CPHEP in the Central Sierra of Peru on the one hundredth anniversary of the Breña Campaign, 1981–83, as displayed in their promotional pamphlet. (CPHEP)

over a contested past that was still fresh in their lived memories. According to a CPHEP member, the three civilian historians were somewhat reluctant to engage in the study of the recent past, especially since they themselves had experienced and remembered these years.[57]

None of the historians involved in this aspect of the project had formal training in conducting interviews. Nevertheless, they organized a system to do so: they wrote questionnaires tailored to different ranks of military personnel (troops, technicians, commissioned and noncommissioned officers, and commanders) that were meant to start a conversation, and then the interviewers would let the interviewees speak, sometimes interrupting for clarification, asking questions. The interviews were conducted and recorded by at least one civilian member, sometimes in the company of military personnel. Brigadier General Marco Merino described the testimonies as providing "anecdotes and conversation."[58] According to civilian CPHEP historian Lourdes Medina, some of the interviewees would talk for "hours and hours," as was the case of a general who spoke six hours in one session. Medina saw this opportunity to speak as "cathartic" for the participants, especially for the hostages who gave their testimonies for the CPHEP book on Chavín de Huántar.[59] One commander who had fought in the emergency zones and later became an evangelical asked all those present in the room to bend on their knees and pray prior to his testimony. Those interviewed were "people very affected" by the conflict, noted Medina.[60]

Military personnel provided their testimonies voluntarily, overcoming fear that they might be identified by still-unrepentant Shining Path members or fear of prosecution.[61] The CPHEP made announcements on loudspeakers on the Army headquarters in San Borja, Lima (El Pentagonito), and then the project passed by word of mouth. The CPHEP also sought testimonies through the veteran's association and the association of those who had fought in the border dispute with Ecuador (the Cenepa War, 1995) and from members of the association of those who had been wounded. Most of the interviews came from the latter. The CPHEP investigative team also spoke with the still-living commanders of the emergency zones. The CPHEP did not, however, seek the testimonies of Fujimori or Montesinos, supposedly because of concern that their inclusion would politicize the publication's reception. Though Fujimori indicated that he wanted to be interviewed for the project, Major Carlos Freyre was not granted permission to visit Fujimori in prison, and the civilian members of the CPHEP were too uncomfortable to do so.[62]

The CPHEP conducted a total of seventy-one interviews, and these testimonies form the core of *En honor a la verdad*.[63] Of these seventy-one, fifteen interviewees are identified in the footnotes by name, including retired colonel César Martínez Uribe Restrepo, a controversial figure who was later accused of giving the orders to kill residents of Accomarca but died prior to sentencing, and Mori, who later had a warrant for his arrest issued as part of his sentence of twenty-five years in jail for the same massacre. Of the fifteen named men who were interviewed, all but two are retired, and eleven of them are generals (plus two colonels, one captain, and one technician). The remaining fifty-six testimonies were coded to maintain the participants' anonymity. Most of the anonymous interviewees are cited only once, and their quotes range from a few sentences to a paragraph. Six or seven interviewees are cited more than once. Another eleven untitled, stand-alone "documents," which may come from these testimonies, appear throughout the text. Unfortunately, because the interviews are scattered throughout the book, it is difficult to piece together the larger story from which they were extracted, thus diminishing some of the potential value of these testimonies as sources of individual memories.

Winning Hearts and Minds:
The Bread Strategy

The three and a half pages dedicated to the period of Commanding General Adrián Huamán Centeno is indicative of the kind of content that constitutes the Peruvian Army's version of the past and of how the Army builds its narrative through several sources, including testimonies. Huamán was the second general put in charge of the emergency zone of Ayacucho as the political-military commander of the Second Division of the Infantry in December 1983, a position he held for eight months (until the end of August 1984).

According to the authors of *En honor a la verdad*, Huamán was chosen for his intelligence and decisiveness, his past experience in fighting the guerrillas in 1965, his successful studies in the School of the Americas, and his physical fitness. Like his predecessor, Clemente Noel, he received little instruction or strategic planning from the Belaúnde government and arrived in the region to discover that the local population was hostile to the Armed Forces, a sentiment that the authors attribute to the previous actions of the police group known as the *sinchis*.[64] To improve relations with the local population and to counteract Shining Path's ideological gains in the region, Huamán sought to implement "the bread strategy," that is, to employ a traditional Andean practice of sharing bread.[65] This strategy was part of a larger effort to win the hearts and minds of the local populations that Huamán had proposed to Belaúnde prior to taking up his new post and also drew on the sentiments held by the descendants of Velasco in the military that to tackle insurrection necessitated not only security but socioeconomic development. Yet according to *En honor a la verdad*, despite Huamán's positive reception locally and in the national media, the government did not make the necessary funds available, and those funds that could have been made available were poorly used by the civilian-led government, which Huamán came to openly criticize on national TV and newsprint. The authors state that Huamán's criticism of the government led to his dismissal.[66]

According to *En honor a la verdad*, the general nonetheless did what he could with limited direction from above and too few resources; in addition to sending out patrols, he "took protective measures" and introduced civic projects related to "health, fixing roads, various infrastructural works, controlling the operation of schools, and principally to counter *senderista* propaganda though the practice [of instilling] national values." As part of the latter, he further introduced literacy programs and obligated local villagers to attend the flag-raising ceremonies. According to the authors, Huamán "tried to fill the empty space created by the state," which Shining Path had used to its advantage. The text does not mention that just four years earlier the state would have been a military one.[67]

Despite Huamán's efforts to reach a political solution and his "willingness to dialogue," many fights and violent acts "presented themselves," including declarations of human rights abuses and the existence of mass graves near Huanta. These denunciations led to "countless judicial investigations." As a means to "ease these inconveniences," Huamán introduced a system of registering troops returning from patrols. According to one CPHEP testimony, these controls were humiliating "but necessary": "We had hardly left the helicopters, when a group of superior officers registered us, and even at times stripped us naked and took away whatever might have been stolen."[68]

In an attempt to assure better comportment of his troops in order to improve relations with the local population, General Huamán introduced other measures as well: he banned alcohol and ordered the police to look into "supposed" cases of disappearances. An official communication was issued, stating, "All those individuals who believe that in one way or another they have been made vulnerable or have had their rights denied are to make their complaints known to the political-military chief and the senior prosecutor in order that corrective measures may be taken."[69] That is, local community members were to make known to Huamán or to the senior prosecutor in Ayacucho their complaints of abuse at the hands of military personnel.[70]

The only concrete example of misconduct given in the section corresponding to the period of Huamán's mandate is the story of a thieving captain. As recounted in one testimony, a captain stole three motorboat engines from a village that he knew to be involved in narcotrafficking and brought them back to the Army base. When the villagers returned, they complained about the missing engines. According to the interviewee, the captain was therefore severely sanctioned ("*con rigor*"), "his career ruined, and he also had to pay I don't know how much, and [he] was removed from the base."[71]

The testimony about the stolen engines is immediately followed by a paragraph stating that during the eight months when Huamán was commander of the region, there was an average of five confrontations with Shining Path per week, not including the Marines and the National Police. The authors state that despite Huamán's "strong social and economic push," he did not manage to establish more efficient intelligence channels. This lack of a system for gathering intelligence meant not only that the Army could not adequately evaluate its opponent but also that there was a "lack of control over certain subordinate elements" (i.e., military personnel). "The decentralization of the military command required constant and extreme control measures that were not helped by the shortage of air facilities [i.e., helicopters], the only way by which the control elements could supervise performance within the law without affecting other tasks according to rank. This has been wrongly translated [by the CVR] as actions of 'systematic violence,' which is absolutely alien to the armed institutions and the laws of the republic."[72] The section ends with a description of Huamán's last order before leaving the region, another humanitarian effort whereby he sent soldiers, teaching tools, building materials, and food to the community of Santa Rosa, which prompted one campesino to declare loudly for a radio program in 1985: "The Army respects us as human beings and brings us progress. For this reason, we will not forget General Huamán. We send him our greetings and our appreciation. He recovered this forgotten village not by force but by labor."[73]

This section on the period of General Huamán is rather typical of how much of *En honor a la verdad* is structured: testimonies by key protagonists and subordinate personnel describe events decades earlier, complemented by print sources of the time. In this section, the former commanding general of the zone, Huamán, now retired, provides his 2009 account of the situation in 1984; several short testimonial fragments by soldiers also gathered in 2009 offer anecdotes or description. Two extracts from newspapers provide second-hand information from the period: a 1984 article in *Caretas* that commented favorably on Huáman's development work and aid, and another article in *La República* that described secondhand the taking of a patriotic oath and the flag-raising ceremony in Vinchos. The only actual source offered in this section that might be directly related to events of the time is an "Official Document of the Army. Part Number004/HGF/ 2a DI, 9 April 1984." This citation is appended to a description of the death of Lieutenant José Reátegui Schutt, who was shot in the head in an ambush on the outskirts of Ayacuchos's airport in 1984. It is odd that the authors did not access original sources from the time to describe the brutality of Shining Path, such as accounts of local populations being forced to hide in the mountains, where they lived in misery. Rather, the authors of *En honor a la verdad* chose a 2009 mediated description of the terrorists' violence: a book review in the weekend supplement of *La República* of Ayacuchan anthropologist and artist Edilberto Jiménez's collection of testimonies and his related drawings.[74]

This section reads like an exculpatory text that not only explains away human rights abuses while not directly mentioning them but also limits the culpability of the Armed Forces and contradicts the CVR's findings. While the content of *En honor a la verdad* is not necessarily incorrect, how the authors choose to structure this content indicates the kind of message that they wish to transmit. For instance, each time the authors state that "inconvenient" acts might have been committed (acts such as abductions, human rights abuses, and the killing of citizens buried in mass graves), the actual examples given of misconduct and the measures implemented to correct such misconduct address thievery: upon leaving the helicopters, the soldiers were searched for stolen goods and a captain's career was ruined for having stolen three motorboat engines. When responding specifically to the CVR's finding of "systematic violence" (the actual terms used by the CVR were stronger, "systematic human rights violations"),[75] the authors state that this was not the case because such comportment is "absolutely alien to the armed [state] institutions and the laws of the republic," and that the CVR got this false impression due to the lack of a centralized military command, made all the more difficult by the too few helicopters to adequately oversee personnel.

Furthermore, this section allocates more space to the good deeds and intentions of General Huamán than to foul play, and these good intentions begin and end the section dedicated to his mandate as commanding political-military chief. Thus one leaves the section with the impression that Huamán, a *quechuahablante*, was a strict but good-hearted general who did his best in the worst of times. This picture stands in stark contrast to that of the CVR's findings, which were based not on opinion but on evidence, such as survivor testimonies and documents from the era produced by human rights groups and military sources. The CVR concluded that the worst peak of the violence was precisely during Huamán's command: according to the CVR, his mandate was "the year in which the largest number of victims was registered during the twenty-year period studied by the CVR."[76] This infamous record is not noted in *En honor a la verdad*. Indeed, it is his contact with and affinity for the people—those most affected by the violence—that the CPHEP chose to highlight. A segment from a 2009 interview with General Huamán begins the introduction to *En honor a la verdad*: "I am from the land of the indigenous, and being from such a place, I was always in contact with my countrymen [*paisanos*]." Similarly, in one of the documents scattered across *En honor a la verdad* ("Document 5"), the archbishop of Ayacucho from 1979 to 1991, Federico Richter Prada, compares General Huamán to the Inca Manco Cápac: "[Huamán was] a stout young man who spoke in Quechua to our indigenous [people], and they took him seriously. Pleased with this, he [Huamán] brought them many things, to the extent possible: seeds for new plants, food for livestock, [materials] to help improve schools, and [new measures] to watch over authorities; in sum, he was a man who worked hard and collaborated greatly with the community."[77] The text is silent about the spike in violence committed by both Shining Path and the Armed Forces during his command, or his subsequent legal imbroglios following the CVR's *Final Report*.

Internal Divisions

The attention paid to describing Adrián Huamán Centeno—his character, his career, his bond with Quechua speakers—is comparatively greater than that devoted to his predecessor General Noel and his successor, General Mori, despite Huamán's having served a shorter time as chief of the emergency zone in Ayacucho.[78] This lengthy description of Huamán, especially his relationship with local populations, may hint that *En honor a la verdad* is not just about setting the record straight in response to the CVR's version but also about establishing a narrative of the conflict for internal use, one in which the Army reasserts its position as of the people (*del pueblo*) and that it has their interests at heart. In particular, one notices in reading *En honor a la verdad* that certain periods and commanders are remembered more positively than others, and that those who are presented more favorably tend to be adherents of the "developmentalist" approach to conflict resolution from the Velasco era rather than the "hardliners" who drew from the later counterinsurgency logic. General Adrián Huamán Centeno had replaced an earlier "hardliner," General Clemente Noel, the first military commander of the Political-Military Command in Ayacucho, who pursued what Burt describes as "a typical 'dirty war' strategy based on national security doctrine."[79] Huamán's replacement as the political-military commander in Ayacucho, Colonel Wilfredo Mori Orzo, returned to Noel's approach of national security detached from development work.[80]

According to Obando, sectors within the Army—especially in the early years of the conflict—did not support "dirty war" tactics:

> Although human rights violations did not cause friction between the military and the civilian government, such abuses did cause internal problems within the Armed Forces. The Peruvian Armed Forces (especially the army) were made up largely of officers from lower middle class origins, often from the provinces outside of Lima. This modest social profile was one of the reasons that, when military officers took over the government in 1968, they sought not to defend the oligarchy but rather to destroy it and modernize the country. The experiment ultimately failed but in 1983 some military sectors still favored social change and did not want to resort to a purely repressive counterinsurgency policy. Some officers thought that the best solution would be to win the support of the population through economic and social assistance from the government.[81]

Human rights violations may have generated tensions within the military, but they did not provoke government sanctions. Although President Belaúnde had opposed Noel's repressive approach, he did not ultimately support Huamán's call for social and economic assistance either, which was deemed too costly. Nor was the government willing to arm local defense groups; according to Huamán's 2009 interview with the CPHEP, though he had requested five thousand weapons to arm local campesinos, the government gave him only five hundred.[82] And despite President García's early claims to favor a more comprehensive approach to the conflict and one that was supposed to be more respectful of human rights, he too switched to a repressive counterinsurgency policy.[83] Thus, according to Obando, "the civilian government had rejected proposals for a military policy oriented toward social assistance, yet still lacked an alternative to the strategy of the military hardliners, whom the civilians ended up defending."[84]

This possible wish of the CPHEP authors to distance the Army of today from the years of the hardliners is most evident in their treatment of the civil-military alliance between Fujimori and the Armed Forces. While, on the one hand, the authors of *En honor a la verdad* point to this period as decisive in the victory against Shining Path, precisely because of important policy and strategic changes, little direct mention is made of this alliance. They tread carefully when discussing this period of civil-military alliance. One of the criticisms made of the CVR's *Final Report* was its heavy focus on the Fujimori presidency. This criticism cannot be made of *En honor a la verdad*. For while two of the seven sections cover the years of Fujimori's two mandates, Fujimori himself is mentioned only seven times in the text, two of which are references to these years but not directly to his person. The absence of Fujimori is noticeable, especially considering that the period of his presidency is credited in *En honor a la verdad* as the turning point in the war. His government is described as having used the *mano dura* (firm hand) that the population wanted and employing a combination of "pragmatism and cold calculation."[85] The Fujimori government introduced the "ley de arrepentimiento" (the repentance law), which pardoned those who laid down their arms in the wake of Abimael Guzmán's letters of surrender while also introducing stronger antiterrorism legislation.[86] Also, the Fujimori government is credited for having given the Armed Forces clear directives (as opposed to the earlier governments) through the newly formed Comando Único de Pacificación (Single Pacification Command), headed by the president of the republic. Montesinos is not mentioned a single time by name in *En honor a la verdad*.

Nor do the authors explain how this civilian-military collusion came about. A series of decree laws issued around the time of Fujimori's self-coup in April 1992 facilitated a partnership that benefited the military's hardliners, thus pushing the *velasquista* remnants and their beliefs to the margins.

Through these decree laws, Fujimori ceded civilian governance in the emergency zones to the military, meaning that large swaths of the national territory and half of the country's population was under military control.[87] In another law, the president appropriated the power to promote and retire military officers. This law was followed by purges within the National Police and the Armed Forces, and officers deemed sympathetic to the executive assumed prominent positions. It was at this time that General Hermoza Ríos was named head of the Army and the Armed Forces, a position he held for nearly seven years in contrast to the typical assignment of one year. This rise to the top and the dismissal of others led both to the politicization of the Armed Forces and to grumblings of dissent within the Armed Forces, especially among mid-ranking officers who saw Montesinos and the SIN as having too strong a control over the Armed Forces.[88]

This close alliance that subsumed all the high command of the Armed Forces into the Fujimori regime—buying their compliance in exchange for advantageous posts, protection, or hard cash—is not evident in *En honor a la verdad*. For instance, there is no mention of the video showing the top brass of the National Police and the Armed Forces signing their fidelity to Fujimori in support of the 1992 *autogolpe* and impunity from human rights investigations or the slew of other videos showing Montesinos bribing military commanders and public officials. Rather, the problem of corruption among some members of the Armed Forces is only alluded to in a subsection titled "Aprovechamiento político de los éxitos obtenidos en la guerra" (The taking political advantage of the successful gains in the war), in which the authors write that "the Peruvian Army has determined that the political interference in the institutional development of the Armed Forces was real and widespread to levels unexpected [at the time], and that [this political interference] not only caused a rupture within [the Armed Forces] but also ended up undermining the efforts made by thousands of officials and soldiers who in one way or another were assigned the responsibility of confronting the war." The following paragraph credits Fujimori for having taken the political decision to follow a "more holistic strategy" already designed by the Armed Forces (which included improving relations with local populations as advocated earlier by General Huamán), and it was this decision that brought about the end of the war. Yet the corruption in the Armed Forces meant that the successful victory over Shining Path was tarnished. In a note of regret, the authors write, "If these events [the components of the more holistic strategy] on their own had concluded the peace process and returned the country to tranquility, there would be no doubt about applauding the merits of those who were able to point the way to success." Rather, the text continues, "personal appetites" ended up corrupting officers and creating a "kind of interior mechanism [the SIN] that served only to attempt to increase revenues and to obtain illegal benefits for a few."[89]

Honor and Human Rights

A few sections in *En honor a la verdad* offer the reader what Zapata calls a "mild self-critical tone," such as the note of self-reproach over the corruption of a few by Fujimori that tarnished the honor of the Armed Forces as a whole.[90] According to the CPHEP, had it not been for some individuals who sought personal gain, one could have easily commended the work of the Armed Forces. Not only were some individual acts not honorable, but they also placed in question the honor of the institution.

Featured in the title of this publication are the words *honor* and *truth*; this publication pays honor to the truth (*honor a la verdad*). *En honor a la verdad* does not dwell on the past or provide detailed explanations (though lists are provided sporadically) but rather foregrounds the military value of honor. Even though the authors believe that "those who do not know the Army from within [could] not [possibly] understand the high values that run through the veins of its members,"[91] they nevertheless try to bring outsiders to a kind of understanding of the Army's moral rectitude. Here, honor becomes both a key description of the military (military men are honorable; the institution is honorable) and an explanatory factor (to explain the comportment of the military). The military did what it did in honor of the nation and democracy; its honor *is* the truth.[92] If readers do not understand this, so goes their argument, it is because as outsiders they cannot fully appreciate the extent and depth of the Army's honor.

The flipside of honor is shame. The Army members who committed illegal acts jeapardized not only how outsiders see the institution but also how they see themselves, no matter how deep or intrinsic honor may be to them. How can the Army explain these crimes that went against "the high values that run through the veins of its members"? *En honor a la verdad* responds in several ways to this question: the authors blur the kinds of crimes committed; certain crimes, such as rape, are left vague, and when mentioned other members within the Armed Forces may be imputed to be the perpetrators; the crimes were committed by bad individuals and thus were not systematic or inherent to the institution; the crimes were a consequence of the kind of war being waged (which the Army did not choose or initiate) and were the result of the political inadequacies of democratic Peru. Furthermore, the geographical realities made much of the country difficult to access, and thus it was impossible for superiors to fully supervise the comportment of their subordinates.

A principal point of tension or discomfort in *En honor a la verdad* is how to explain or contextualize the shame of having committed human rights violations. According to the CPHEP, there were thirty-seven cases against members of the military in 2010 (a number that is significantly less than the number of denunciations at the time), and the charges of human rights violations by state agents were a matter of public discussion.[93] The authors seem torn between acknowledging individual members who should be tried and punished and defending others whom they consider innocent, ensnared in political machinations.[94] Within this dichotomy of the guilty and the innocent, the authors categorize the former as individuals who committed crimes for "reasons strictly personal" and the latter as individuals who are the victims of political intrigue, whereby "those who defended the rule of law" are unjustly placed "in the same bag" as terrorist organizations.[95] In the former—the cases involve theft, malfeasance, abuse of authority for personal aggrandizement—the authors of *En honor a la verdad* strongly condemn the individuals (though they mostly remain nameless). The latter—the charges of human rights abuses and crimes against humanity both directly and indirectly (as *autoría mediata*, or intellectual authors)—are described by the CPHEP as the product of rivals' political vengefulness during the transition from Fujimori and afterward.

The authors of *En honor a la verdad* carefully tread a fine line: on the one side they acknowledge that illegal acts, such as theft and corruption for personal benefit, took place, yet on the other side they do not accept human rights abuses as emerging from military culture, as systematic, or as the result of orders from above. As a consequence, when the authors mention acts that would be considered human rights abuses (e.g., torture and forced disappearance), the description of the violations remains vague or the actual examples given are most often that of theft or corruption. Though this may not have been the authors' intention, by continually returning to examples of theft and opportunism when the charges laid against military personnel are human rights abuses, the authors end up conflating the two.

While not making mention of specific human rights violations, the authors of *En honor a la verdad* raise at several points in the text the Army's respect for the rule of law, the Peruvian constitution, and human rights. For instance, in his January 1985 tour to inspect the troops and the newly formed *rondas campesinas* in Ayacucho and Apurímac, the commanding general of the Army at the time, Germán Ruiz Figueroa, gave speeches to officers and soldiers about the need to "act with the constitution in hand . . . respecting human rights . . . and acting in accordance with the Geneva Convention." One of his speeches resulted in a "curious" incident. According to one story recounted in *En honor a la verdad*, the general told his subordinates that they should make the local population feel their friendship and camaraderie, which led to a scene of campesinos fleeing the embrace of overly eager soldiers: "But soldiers have the tendency to obey orders . . . running; and in their attempt to comply with what the general had asked [to embrace and make their feelings of friendship known to the locals], they scared the peasants, who started to run away. A Quechua-speaking soldier had to intercede to explain [to the campesinos] what was happening." That is, the Quechua-speaking soldier explained to the scared locals that the soldiers were not attacking but rather wanted to befriend them.[96]

In their attempt to explain both to locals and to readers of *En honor a la verdad* their respect for human rights, the CPHEP might at times go overboard, so much so that what might have been genuine sentiments of respect may be read as though the authors are trying to convince skeptical audiences. In this text, the term *derechos humanos* appears sixty-two times, and several important passages address this term and the Army's incorporation of human rights principals into its institution, including a five-page section titled "El Ejército con relación a los derechos humanos" (The Army in relation to human rights) and two pages dedicated to "Juzgamiento de miembros del Ejército por delitos de derechos humanos" (The prosecution of Army members for human rights crimes).[97] In addition to the glossary entry for *human rights*, the authors of *En honor a la verdad* provide a definition of the term within the text, one that rings of the preamble to the UN Universal Declaration of Human Rights:

> Human rights are those that man possesses for the simple reason of being. They are inherent in the person, universal at all times and places, and are proclaimed sacred, inalienable, permanent, and beyond the reach of any political power. Human rights are guaranteed by the Peruvian constitutional framework, whose first article states that "the defense of the human person and the respect for his dignity are the supreme goal of society and the state."[98]

The paragraph, however, goes on to insert caveats and qualifiers to these universal human rights that end up being subverted because of the state's shortcomings and their manipulation by rapacious NGOs: "But as in many other instances, [because of] the gaps created by the failures of the state that, due to underdevelopment, lacked the capacity to meet all the country's needs, [human rights] were addressed by institutions not linked to the state sector [NGOs] that inserted themselves in society for secondary motives for the purpose of addressing these shortcomings."[99] Thus this convoluted sentence undermines the very principal of human rights as inalienable; the authors write that they are in practice violable because of the Peruvian context. Furthermore, human rights were also, according to *En honor a la verdad*, susceptible to manipulation, picked up by some NGOs ("facade organizations") that used human rights ("needs") for their own ends.[100] So despite the Army's high regard for human rights, in practice human rights and their defense, and who is defending them and for what ends, depend on context.

The authors present readers with a different, though not unrelated, series of core tenets to human rights that guided the Army personnel's conduct, published in 1983 at the peak of violations in the twenty years studied by the CVR. These *criterios básicos* (basic criteria) governed the actions of the commanders and their troops: "Basic Criteria. They guide our actions, individually and collectively; because of them we must govern our actions with *honesty*, *loyalty*, and with the full conviction of fulfilling *duty*, in addition to consolidating and maintaining the image of the Army as the *guardian* institution of the patria, by way of *impeccable* individual and collective comportment of its members, the *respect* for society, and the *support* for national development."[101] These basic criteria make clear what the authors of *En honor a la verdad* mean by the term *honorable soldier*: an honest, loyal patriarch who protects the country, through respect and the full acceptance of his duty.[102] Thus, honor is presented as proof that these military men did not commit systematic human rights abuses. The violation of human rights is antithetical to the very core of what it means to be part of the Army; it goes against their sense of honor.

These "basic criteria" were added to and it seems transformed over time into the military's human rights discourse. Through the years, the Army "slowly" came to understand the "necessity to clearly define its own policies on human rights," to which end it offered more courses and instruction.[103] By 1989, teaching human rights was considered "obligatory" in military schools, and from 1992 to 1993 the Army developed a plan to improve the teaching of human rights.[104] The original "basic criteria," from which the Army's human rights discourse emerged, took effect in the emergency zone in 1985, and they are credited in a footnote in *En honor a la verdad* for having prevented behavior by Army personnel similar to that of the *sinchis* (a special division within the Police Forces known for its brutality), whose conduct was "unfortunately, not the most correct."[105] Once introduced into the emergency zones, according to "an Official Army Document" dated March 27, 1985, if the "basic criteria" were not respected, the perpetrators "should be punished with much rigor so as to serve as an example."[106] (It should be noted that these "basic criteria" had come into effect some months prior to the Accomarca massacre.)

In an attempt to control distant military units, General Mori (like later generals) conducted a series of approximately one hundred inspections, which "in their majority ended in drastic results for officers, petty officials, soldiers and police" who had not followed these "basic criteria." The CPHEP provides a rare detailed list of the infractions committed, presumably based on the findings of Mori's inspections: twenty-one accidents caused by firearms or grenades; sixteen cases of abuse of authority; twelve cases of administrative irregularities; eleven automotive accidents; eight cases of theft of weapons, explosives, or ammunition; five brawls between National Police and Army personnel; five terrorist ambushes; four human rights denunciations; and three cases of rape. According to the authors, a few other cases involved suicide, police irregularities, negligence, disobedience, drug trafficking, and desertion, which were not "made public" for fear of the negative impact this revelation would have had on the troops and not for reasons of "collusion."[107]

The authors of En honor a la verdad do not deny that these "basic criteria" were not always followed, hence the above-mentioned list of "accidents," "incidents," "irregularities," and "denunciations." However, they place such occurrences, and especially human rights violations, in the context of an unconventional war and attribute them to individual actions rather than a collective failure of their institution. Several explanations are given for why individual members would commit such acts: stress, revenge against Shining Path, racism that they themselves experienced, ignorance of local language and culture, and insufficient or ineffective means of control of subordinates by their superiors. One testimony provides insight into the tensions between its members over such comportment, vaguely referred to as "abuse of authority," and the difficulty commanding officers had in controlling those in their charge:

> Reaching the top of the hill, I could see the townspeople gathered [below] and the other officer committing an abuse of authority . . . so I went down to where he was and I scolded him. We argued and finally we fought hand to hand. I said, "You're crazy! You think you can do whatever you want with people! I'm the one in charge here!" . . . Then the patrol soldiers separated us. For these things outside my control [cosas ajenas], I have asked Peru for forgiveness many times.[108]

The authors of En honor a la verdad state clearly in several places in their book that any violations that took place did not result from the orders of superiors: "Human rights violations unfortunately took place during the war but it was not a systematic practice, not ordered or orchestrated by the higher-ups [*los entes rectores*] of the Army."[109] By ignoring military doctrine as enshrined in the manuals used to teach soldiers (and studied by the CVR), the authors can dismiss the possibility that foot soldiers and others were trained to respond violently. Furthermore, the accusation that the upper echelons of the military establishment would give orders that ran against their principals of conduct, their honor, not only seems morally impossible in *En honor a la verdad* but furthermore logistically improbable because of the kind of warfare that took place, guerrilla war. According to the authors, the higher levels of command did not give orders to their subordinates since each patrol and each base was under its own counsel: "The planning was centralized, but the execution decentralized."[110] This argument not only seems to absolve the high command from accountability—from the legal accusation of *autoría mediata*, which some generals already faced and others feared—but also maintains the integrity of the institution.[111]

Lessons Learned and Atonement for the Past

In addition to the authors' efforts to contextualize the Army's actions and to highlight their respect for human rights, they also express regret over offenses and errors committed.[112] There are three places in *En honor a la verdad* where contrition is conveyed: one section in which the Army recognizes some "errors" were committed during its efforts to vanquish terrorist organizations, one instance when the Army explicitly apologizes, and the third, in the book's concluding section, where the Army acknowledges a shared responsibility for the mishandling of the conflict.

The first self-critical reflections are toward the end of *En honor a la verdad* in a section titled "Los errores en la conducción de la guerra" (The errors in the handling of the war). In this section, the authors state that the Army "made the decision" to "lay out the errors that were committed during the more than seventeen years of counterterrorism war" in its publication *En honor a la verdad* because of its "respect for the institution, for order and the law, and for the clear concept of individual and collective justice." While the authors note that displaying these errors "does not diminish the pain and suffering of those who suffered or experienced directly [*en carne propia*] these errors and excesses, it leaves for future Peruvian generations a fountain of lived experience from which they should drink."[113]

These victims, the authors argue, were the social cost of the war, a cost that disproportionately affected the "poorest," which they consider to be the case with most conflicts.[114] But these victims were also the product of Shining Path's violence, which pushed Armed Forces personnel to commit excesses, thus altering the "comportment of many people who entered into combat." Fear "created the sensation—not justifiable—that 'the best terrorist is a dead terrorist' [el mejor terrorista es el terrorista muerto]."[115] The authors give a rare testimony, one in which a once young second lieutenant describes how the war changed his "own morals, even though he came from a solid family":

> I walked for several hours during the night in order to arrive at the house in which the (intelligence) agents had said that a terrorist lived, so as to capture him. When I arrived, he was not there, only the wife and a son who was around four years old. I asked her about the man, and she did not want to say anything, so I pulled out my gun and pointed it at the boy. The woman immediately confessed where the terrorist was. Now that years have passed, I have started to think about what I did. I didn't do anything to the boy; I would not have been able to. But I have thought about this boy, and I think about my kids, and I can't imagine how I would feel if someone were to point a gun at them [my children]. . . . I think that it was related to the moment, in 1988 or 1989; there were a lot of dead, almost every day, and I was so young; I was twenty-one years old. I have felt badly about this.[116]

Ill-prepared troops may have felt fear when sent into the countryside, such as this second lieutenant. Yet it was not fear alone that pushed soldiers to violent crimes. Though the authors of En honor a la verdad do not state this, manuals taught to soldiers the military doctrine "el mejor terrorista es el terrorista muerto." The authors situate this "sensation" of "better a dead terrorist" as an individual experience rather than a collective dogma. Ultimately, the unconventionality of the war, not superior orders or an institutional culture, explains for the authors many of the "errors" that individual Army personnel committed.[117]

Despite regarding these "errors" as individual acts, the authors of En honor a la verdad feel compelled to offer a group apology. The apology is buried between some paragraphs about the secret organization Grupo Colina, a clandestine military unit responsible for over fifty death-squad-like killings between 1991 and 1992 (such as the killing of fifteen people at a private party in the Barrios Altos neighborhood of Lima and the death and disappearance of one professor and nine students from La Cantuta University). The authors, assuming the voice of the institution as a whole, express sorrow and ask for forgiveness.

The Peruvian Army *laments* that officers and petty officers who emerged from its ranks have participated in acts outside the law, which have overshadowed the brilliant work of many of its members, who renounced life, their youth, the warmth of their homes in order to end the terrorist scourge. In the same way, [the Peruvian Army] thanks the citizens of our country for their display of confidence and affection for their soldiers and offers our *most sincere apology* for all the harm that *some individuals* may have caused any citizen and society in general. For this reason, [the Peruvian Army] commits itself to greater possible control over any system in which active Army personnel are officially involved, no matter how small.[118]

By placing this "most sincere apology" in the section on the Colina Group (which is vaguely described as having committed "*actos no legales*"), the Army's expression of regret concerns individuals whom the authors state might have had an affiliation with the Army at one time (i.e., training and the like) — individuals such as Jesús Sosa who became well known for their participation in the Grupo Colina — yet who, according to the authors of *En honor a la verdad*, acted without the knowledge of the Army (even though they were still on active duty when the killings occurred), since the Colina Group was in the SIN's realm and "did not involve the Army." This factual misrepresentation places the Colina Group outside the military structure, although such an assertion should have been recognized as complete revisionism not only to the authors of *En honor a la verdad* but also to the Peruvian public who had followed the trials against members of the Colina Group, as well as the head of the Army, Nicolás Hermoza Ríos, and Alberto Fujimori (the latter two were convicted for several Colina Group crimes), which concluded prior to the first publication of *En honor a la verdad*.

This is not an open-ended or blanket apology; it covers only the Colina Group and some other unidentified individuals who had acted "outside the law." Yet while apologizing for the Army's oversight, the authors do not pass an opportunity to commend other servicemen and Peruvians. The Army mixes the contrite tone with a reaffirming, positive one by stating that its apology is addressed to the citizens of the country whom they commend for having supported their Armed Forces throughout the conflict, and the authors restate the heroism and sacrifice of most of its members. This apology does much more than simply say, "Sorry"; it isolates the violence and its perpetrators while reinforcing the Army's own heroism and reminds readers of a supposed mandate that Peruvians had bestowed on them.

The only instance in *En honor a la verdad* where the Army broaches the need for a broader forgiveness occurs at the very end of the book, in the section

"Lecciones aprendidas" (Lessons learned), a single page that again raises the participation of citizens. This segment begins with the advice that for the nation to overcome the "trauma" of the past, it must shed the bad memories ("*mal recuerdo*") of what took place and at the same time not forget them so that the nation can identify any future signs of danger. The authors state that it is from such "an objective vision" (one not burdened by bad memories) that reconciliation may emerge, and that the country must "follow the path of reconciliation and respect the memory of those fallen in war." But they insist that for this "true reconciliation" to take place and before "our own forgiveness," "[we] must recognize our mistakes as a nation before attributing them to others." Thus it is not the Army alone that must look into and atone for the past.

> There exists a shared responsibility of the state, the Army itself and other units of the Armed Forces, of the public institutions that make up the state apparatus, and many other actors that were involved to a greater or lesser degree in the conflict. But in the same way, there also exists the responsibility of those who did absolutely nothing, indeed aggravated the situation, because it did not interest them or was very far from shattering their individual stability. This critical reflection applies to all the estates of our country, authorities and common citizens. The most important lesson for the future is that war is a completely avoidable phenomenon, [one that will] inevitably arise; it is an effort that fully involves all the citizens that make up the country.[119]

This request for "forgiveness" stops short of asking for pardon. The Army states a shared responsibility should be acknowledged by the state, by all the units of the Armed Forces, by public institutions, and by all those citizens who chose to ignore the conflict. In the absence of such an acceptance of a shared responsibility, the Army—the authors seem to suggest here—does not seek its specific forgiveness. As well, what is being asked forgiveness for is a hazy statement of "our nation's errors."

Despite the convoluted formulations and vagueness of the acts for which the Army expresses contrition, these sections of *En honor a la verdad* are considered "apologies" by some Army personnel with whom I spoke, but also by some individuals whom the Army might consider "caviars." These sections that touch on their errors and their regrets are perhaps the closest the Armed Forces will come to saying they are sorry. They do not, however, by any means accept a collective responsibility or acknowledge a culture of violence and disregard for citizens that fostered systematic human rights abuses. Indeed, in the very last sentence of *En honor a la verdad*, the authors transform human rights violations into a juridically more difficult crime to prosecute, that of genocide, a "policy of extermination," something of which the CVR did not accuse the Armed Forces:[120] "The Peruvian Army condemns acts against the law committed by certain members of the Armed and Police Forces who acted individually and not as part of a policy of extermination [*política de exterminio*] dictated by some military hierarchy."[121]

Dialogues for Peace and Memory beyond the Barracks

En honor a la verdad is a text written for both an external and an internal audience. Published after the CVR and in the midst of prosecutions against the Armed Forces, it was the Army's official response to the public charges laid against it. Among individuals with whom I have spoken in the realm of human rights NGOs, there seems to be a consensus that this is an important document, and they treat it with high regard, some even commending the Army for having apologized (though the actual text seems to do so only weakly). Yet I got the impression that few within the human rights community had read *En honor a la verdad* in its entirety but rather read only the introduction and the concluding "Lessons Learned" section. This is understandable: the book is difficult, slow reading. Indeed, the book may have been written with the intention that most would simply read its bookends. While providing us snippets of testimony and technical details about weaponry, patrols, and advancements in the conflict zones, the book's middle sections offer little beyond the emblematic cases identified by the CVR, cases such as Uchuraccay, Accomarca, and Cayara. *En honor a la verdad* does not provide much information about lesser-known confrontations. That is, the authors do not shed light on events that were not already in the public domain, and the events that are mentioned are presented case by case without an overarching analysis or synthesis.[122] Indeed, the authors of *En honor a la verdad* remained completely or nearly silent about some cases that were being publicly discussed: for instance, the military headquarters in Ayacucho Los Cabitos N°51 (notorious for torture and forced disappearance), Chumbivilcas (the 1990 massacre of 16 peasants), Lucmahuayco (the 1984 massacre of 34 peasants), Chilliutira (the 1991 extrajudicial execution of 4 detainees being moved to a military base in Puno).[123] The single footnote that refers to Putis implies the Army's innocence in the 1984 deaths of 123 peasants who sought safe refuge on a military base.[124] By contrast, the authors expend much effort enumerating the core values of the Army in a way that suggests that members within this institution were struggling at the time with a moral crisis internally and externally. Reading *En honor a la verdad*, one senses the Army's sorrow and prickly sensitivity over its lost honor. The few mildly self-critical sections in *En honor a la verdad* are useful for gaining insight into the military establishment in the decade following the transition. It is an institution shamed by and ashamed of aspects of what happened, but whose members strongly believe in what they did and why they did it. They wish not only to convince those outside the institution of their honor but to assure the newer generation within it that they belong to an honorable institution. Thus, the book is given to new cadets as part of their training and to the CPHEP's Facebook friends, to *ronderos* whom they wish to thank for their role in the pacification, as well as to those facing prosecution.

En honor a la verdad is also an olive branch to the human rights community and others outside the military who speak out against the actions of the Army but who, according to the CPHEP authors, do not sufficiently understand the experience or position of the Army. A singular event gave the Army and the human rights community the opportunity to enter into dialogue over this past. On January 24, 2013, to mark the publication of an autobiography by Lurgio Gavilán, a former *senderista* and soldier (discussed in the next chapter), the Army also presented its publication, *En honor a la verdad*. It was an event made possible by the close collaboration between historians Cecilía Méndez and Lieutenant Carla Granados, who had wanted to have a discussion of *En honor a la verdad* when it was originally published and revisited the idea upon the publication of Gavilán's book.

The dialogue was also accompanied by an exhibition of artwork by Ayacuchan artist Edilberto Jiménez Quispe, *Universos de Memoria*, some of whose pieces very graphically show the violence committed by Shining Path and the forces of order. For instance, the wooden relief triptych (*retablo*) *Huamanguino* (1988) depicts the military attacking villagers one night, stripping them of their clothes, tying them up, beating and torturing them, and eventually throwing them into a pit where birds feast on the cadavers. Among those who came to attend the launch of *En honor a la verdad* were young soldiers who also took the time to view Jiménez's work prior to the evening's main event.

Held at the Instituto de Estudios Peruanos, a location that many within the Armed Forces would consider the den of *los caviares*, many active and former military personnel came to hear the two panels dedicated to Gavilán's book and the CPHEP's *En honor a la verdad*. Six presenters spoke on *En honor a la verdad* to an overflowing room: General Marco Merino, Major Carlos Freyre, Lieutenant Carla Granados, a civilian historian and member of the CPHEP, as well as two historians who came from military families. The event was described as tense,[125] but gave many the sense of an opening for dialogue between the Army and the civil society of human rights intellectuals and activists, a meeting that "until recently would have seemed like a dream."[126] As one journalist wrote, "It was an unusual show, not in enemy territory, but yes, in the unknown."[127] Though an event of this size and nature happened only once and was the product of a small group of memory entrepreneurs within the Army and civil society, it was remarkable, for it brought together groups previously seen as antagonists. While not as meaningful as an apology would have been, at least this gathering was a recognition of the need for dialogue.[128]

3

Guerra fratricida

The Parallel Lives and Writings of Carlos Freyre and Lurgio Gavilán

They [the members of Shining Path] created a *fratricidal confrontation* in order to satiate the appetite of their convictions, and they bathed in the country's blood by bloody means when what was needed more than ever was unity and development.

CPHEP, *En honor a la verdad*, 21

The previous week, [members of] Shining Path approached the Army: using intimidation, they tried to convince the military base Los Cabitos 51 that they should not take action against them, "since *senderistas* and *soldiers* are both *children of the people* [*hijos del pueblo*]."

CPHEP, *En honor a la verdad*, 48

One of these nights, we exchanged shots. An eerie silence gripped the world, and from the darkness of the forest a terrorist started to shout: "Soldier, you are of the people [*pueblo*]. *You are like us*. Give us your officers, those dogs, those wretches [*desgraciados*]. Don't suffer, soldier. Look at how badly they treat you. They insult you; they take your things.

"Soldier! We are your friends. You won't regret it.

"Go to hell!" [the patrol members] shouted back, almost in unison.

Freyre, *Desde el Valle de las Esmeraldas*, 60

And so, as suddenly as this, I was running with the soldiers, beginning *over again*, providing information. The party [Shining Path] had probably denounced me, or maybe they thought I had died shouting chants to Chairman Gonzalo. . . . And so, my socialist utopia dipped like the sun beneath the horizon, only to rise on a new and very different day.

Lurgio Gavilán, *When Rains Became Floods*, 42

espite the tendency in public discourse in post-CVR Peru to lapse into the use of binary categories to describe and identify different actors in the conflict—of perpetrator/victim, of terrorists/heroes, of them/us—one of the central tensions in the CPHEP's *En honor a la verdad* is that the members of Shining Path, though influenced by the foreign ideology of Maoism, were Peruvians. They were not foreign enemies but fellow countrymen and women. How then should one explain the direction that Shining Path members took that nearly brought the nation to its knees? While the conflict is most often referred to in the public sphere as an "internal war" (*guerra interna*) or a "political internal conflict" (*conflito político interno*), *En honor a la verdad* introduces fleetingly another term that complicates these binaries: *guerra fratricida*, a fratricidal war, a war between brothers.

This theme of a war between brothers and the ease with which one could slide into one camp or the other are central to Carlos Enrique Freyre Zamudio and Lurgio Gavilán Sánchez in their respective works: Freyre's novel *Desde el Valle de las Esmeraldas* and Gavilán's memoir, *Memorias de un soldado descono-cido: Autobiografía y antropología de la violencia*. Contemporaries, and only a few years apart in age,[1] Freyre and Gavilán were both protagonists in the con-flict, sometimes in the same regions though not at the same time. Their works similarly suggest the fluidity of identity that challenges the binaries that frame much of the public dialogue over the past such as the writings discussed in the previous chapters. They do so as military insiders, each having served in the Army.

Carlos Freyre, an active-duty career soldier and fiction writer, joined the military of his own volition, enrolling in the military academy in Chorrillos in the mid-1990s (Peru's equivalent to the United States' West Point). Upon graduation in 2000, he entered active duty, mostly in the VRAEM area, known at the time simply as part of the "emergency zone."[2] While stationed near the frontier with Ecuador, just after the completion of the CVR, he wrote an essay called "Verdad sesgada" (Biased truth), which won a military history contest in 2005. Around this time, Freyre began working on his novel *Desde el Valle de las Esmeraldas* (From the Emerald Valley). Later in 2007 the then–commanding general of the Army, Edwin Donayre, invited Freyre to write the script for the film *Vidas paralelas* (Parallel lives, 2008, directed by Rocío Lladó) produced and funded by the Armed Forces through the Universidad Alas Peruanas. In 2009 Freyre joined the CPHEP as a researcher and as the main writer of *En honor a la verdad* (discussed in the previous chapter). Later, Freyre continued fighting in the VRAEM against narcotraffickers and the few remaining Shining Path clusters. At the time of our interviews in 2016, he was stationed as a lieu-tenant coronel in Arequipa, where he continues to write in his free time fiction and a biweekly column about military experiences in the conflict zones, "Diarios de guarnición" (Daily garrison), for the IDL, a legal rights organization.[3]

Lurgio Gavilán's personal story, *Memorias de un soldado desconocido: Autobiografía y antropología de la violencia* (Memories of an unknown soldier: Autobiography and anthropology of the violence), proved to be an instant sensation: published twice in Spanish in 2012 and not long afterward in English as *When Rains Became Floods: A Child Soldier's Story* (2015), the book also has a film adaptation pending with the collaboration of Mario Vargas Llosa. In this book, Gavilán recounts his experiences as a former child soldier for Shining Path, then as a soldier for the Peruvian Armed Forces, then as a Franciscan novice, and finally as a social anthropologist pursuing postgraduate studies. His memoirs and the public response to them highlight the difficulty of defining "victim" and "perpetrator." Though largely read for its insight into the experience of a child *senderista*, the book might as well be equally, if not more so, considered the memoir of a state soldier, though it was largely not received as such in Peru. Gavilán's book could be described as a *testimonio* from a *rendido* (repentant), a term applied by the military to individuals who left Shining Path.[4] After his capture, Gavilán was placed under the informal guardianship of a lieutenant and lived in the barracks. He went to school, learning Spanish and how to read and write. After having completed obligatory military service, Gavilán reenlisted and remained in the Army, almost reaching the rank of petty officer. In total, he fought with Shining Path for roughly two years and served in the military for nearly a decade.

Despite their contrasting personal trajectories and their different choice of literary genres, this chapter juxtaposes the works of Freyre and Gavilán. I avail myself of the concept of "brothers in war" to encompass these contemporary authors and their parallel works. Both men write from the perspective of someone within the military, an institution that had been discredited in the media and disavowed by others in private since the unraveling of Fujimori's network. Both authors offer the perspective of witnesses and of historical agents. While it is perhaps unfair to compare a work of fiction with a testimonial account, I do so here because both authors are military insiders and the public has interpreted their work as providing insight into the authors' experiences and that of their cohort.[5] Members of the military and Peruvian academic circles also made this comparison when they jointly organized and participated in a conference to discuss these authors' works together (in this case *Memorias de un soldado desconocido* and *En honor a la verdad*, not *Desde el Valle de las Esmeraldas*) as part of a conference titled "Diálogos por la paz y la memoria: Fuentes y testimonios para la reconstrucción de la guerra reciente: *Memorias de un soldado desconocido* y *En honor a la verdad*" (Dialogues for peace and

Figure 3.1. Authors Major Carlos Freyre and Lurgio Gavilán at the colloquium "Diálogos por la paz y la memoria," held at the Instituto de Estudios Peruanos, January 24, 2013. (Photograph by IEP)

memory: Sources and testimonies for the reconstruction of the recent war: *Memorias de un soldado desconocido* and *En honor a la verdad*), held on a late afternoon in January 2013, nearly a decade after the publication of the CVR's *Final Report*, at the IEP, and discussed briefly at the end of the previous chapter.

Placing the works of Freyre and Gavilán beside each other permits an understanding of how the military may wish its conduct during the war years be remembered as opposed to how the actual experiences are remembered. Though *Desde el Valle de las Esmeraldas* has been described as a *testimonio* by some, it is a fictional account, though one written by an active member of the Peruvian military, Carlos Freyre.[6] It is a novel that depicts the heroic story of a fictional character (supposedly based on a real individual), his decisiveness, his camaraderie, his fidelity, and his comportment, which was appropriate to an honorable soldier, "*un soldado hecho y derecho.*"[7] This portrayal of heroism and self-sacrifice, however, is challenged by an actual testimony written by another military man, Lurgio Gavilán. Despite parallels in their affiliation with the Army, their age, and the regions where they fought and have written about, Freyre and Gavilán have produced very different accounts of the Army in the conflict. Yet both authors ultimately, perhaps unintentionally, erode a clear portrait of "heroism" by blurring the necessary dichotomies at the heart of the heroic memory camp and the other military works examined here so far, in particular, *En honor a la verdad*.

Brothers on the Battlefield:
The Works of Carlos Freyre

When I first encountered in the official Army's account, *En honor a la verdad*, the phrase "a war between brothers," I was surprised. *Guerra fratricida*, at least to my mind, places Shining Path and the Army on the same footing, something that the Armed Forces had lambasted the CVR for having done. Such a phrase draws a parallel between the two armed camps, making soldiers and *senderistas* of the same origin.[8] Although the Army may have sympathized with the adversary and perhaps even understood the insurgents' demands during the confrontations of the 1960s, this discourse of fighting fellow citizens was far from the official stance of the Armed Forces in the early twenty-first century, when they tended to depict Shining Path in terms that served to "other" or dehumanize its members and in so doing made it unnecessary to consider the roots of the movement or its sociopolitical demands.[9] Yet when we take into consideration that Carlos Freyre, at the time a captain and member of the CPHEP team, was placed in charge of writing up the Army's official version, the use of the designation *guerra fratricida* is less surprising. It is a narrative framework that Freyre has used in at least two of his other cultural works: the script that he wrote for the film *Vidas paralelas* (2008) and the novel *Desde el Valle de las Esmeraldas* (2009). *En honor a la verdad* (2010) is the Army's voice, officially sanctioned by the institution, but perhaps the few instances when the idea of *guerra fratricida* is evoked are moments when Freyre's own voice and understanding of the past conflict slip into the Army's "truth report."

Freyre first introduced to the general Peruvian public his use of the trope of two brothers in the Universidad Alas Peruanas' feature-length film *Vidas paralelas*, for which he wrote the screenplay. According to the promotional posters, the film is "based on a true story," that of two childhood friends, Sixto and Felipe, "united by friendship, separated by violence, and confronted by destiny."[10] Each boy chooses a different path once history intervenes in his life: Sixto, portrayed as an intellectual, is forcibly recruited into Shining Path but then willingly continues in the footsteps of his father, who had left earlier to fight alongside the insurgents; Felipe, the son of the local mayor, eventually joins the military following the officer who had adopted him after his own father had been killed by Shining Path. In Freyre's later novel *Desde el Valle de las Esmeraldas*, the connection between the two main characters is even tighter; they are actual brothers (though estranged) some ten years apart in age. The older one, Germán Goicochea, an intellectual, receives a grant to study abroad and unbeknownst to his family returns to Peru and joins Shining Path, known as "*camarada* Tuchía," fighting in the Amazonian watershed. The younger brother, Leoncio, surprises his family but also pleases them when he chooses the path of his uncle and joins the Army. After graduation, Leoncio is sent to rebuild an Army base in La Constitución (whose name evokes the Peruvian constitution) in the humid region that he refers to as "the Emerald Valley," where Leoncio has adopted the pseudonym "Elías," after his much-admired grandfather (22).[11] As in the film, the two brothers meet again years later on the battlefield. Germán's last words while he lies dying in Leoncio's arms returns to their familial bond: "Leoncio. My little brother. Don't let me die. It's me, your brother Germán. Do you remember me?" (179).

While a creative contrivance that allows the author to both surprise the reader and bring the narrative full circle—spanning from their shared childhood memories to their battlefield reunion—this literary trick also projects a possible military view of the conflict. The theme of two childhood friends or brothers estranged but reunited on the battlefield suggests the folly of war, of an ideology (referred to in *En honor a la verdad* as "a fratricidal confrontation that was launched in order to satiate the appetite of their [Shining Path's] convictions"[12]) that pitted men of the same origin against each other who, at least in the novel, not only look alike but even "have the same voice" (155). The scrolling text at the end of the film *Vidas paralelas* similarly points to the common origins of this "history lived among brothers of race, blood, and culture."[13] The differences between the adversaries that led them down divergent paths is one not of birth but of negative influences.

I am not a literary scholar or a novelist, so I am not the best suited to comment at length on the literary merits and weaknesses of Freyre's novel. Overall, I found *Desde el Valle de las Esmeraldas* an engaging read, fast-paced, and at some points elegantly written. The story is fairly smooth even though the narrator jumps between memories of the conflict and memories of his childhood, interrupted at times with a reminder of the present moment from which the protagonist reflects back. I found abrupt, however, the introduction halfway through the book of a second main character, a high-ranking member of Shining Path whose thoughts also go back and forth from the period of conflict to the years leading up to his decision to join Shining Path. When it becomes clear later in the book that these two key protagonists are brothers—Leoncio, who has joined the Army and become Elías, and Germán, the older brother who has joined Shining Path and become *camarada* Tuchía—the arrival of this other inner voice (that of Germán/Tuchía) makes sense, for his voice is the counterweight to (and nemesis of) that of the main protagonist, Leoncio/Elías.

Eventually a third main character takes shape, though she had been present since the middle of the book under various names: la Mestiza, Angelita, and Chola Bonita. She serves as a link between the adult brothers, one whom she had recruited into Shining Path and the other whom she attempts unsuccessfully to seduce (most likely with the intention of killing him). While as a plotline, this triangle of Tuchía, Elías, and Chola Bonita asks the reader to suspend disbelief, it is an important triangle for understanding how the author frames the conflict: as one between brothers, a contemporary version of Cain and Abel, but ultimately, a conflict caused and inflamed by the actions of a woman, Chola Bonita.[14]

Chola Bonita (meaning in pejorative slang "a pretty girl of mixed origins") is presented as a stock femme fatale figure: her unnerving beauty ("especially her eyes: they were two brown spheres that provoked disquiet" [145]), seductive ("under the dictatorship of her hips that cause waves in the imagination of live beings" [181]), mysterious ("It's that I am a witch" [151]), and educated (she sang with such a voice as to suggest that she had been trained [144], and she wrote with fine penmanship, "a rare thing in a place where women were so poor that only a few finished elementary school" [146]). Though it was Germán's time in Europe that gave him the penchant for radical ideology, it was Chola Bonita who drew him to Shining Path: "Yes, now my president will be Gonzalo [Shining Path's leader], Angelita. Climb into my bed, show me those breasts, Mestiza. Be yourself, show me your blood; mine, I will give to the revolution. I have opened my eyes, thanks to you" (117). Later in the novel, and over a decade since she had last seen her comrade and lover (with whom she conceived her first son), Chola Bonita realizes that the second lieutenant heading a patrol in La Constitución is Germán's younger brother, Leoncio/Elías.[15]

Chola Bonita represents danger, but at least she is constant in her ways. According to her cousin, "she has always been involved in trouble" (143). Elías is able to resist her charms by remembering something a fellow soldier had told him before dying in an ambush: "You don't know how many men have died because of a pair of panties" (151–52). Perhaps more ruinous—according to the moral compass of the author—than Chola Bonita is Isolina Cossío, Leoncio's love interest back home in Lima. Isolina appears throughout the story through Leoncio's memories of his life before entering active duty and on the few occasions when he was granted leave to return to Lima. Isolina is worse than Chola Bonita in that she is not constant but changes in her ways. What begins as an idyllic story of love at first sight for this girl from a prominent family turns into a story of betrayal. Isolina in his imagination is perfect: beautiful, pious, faithful, and playful. As the war wears on, however, her love becomes inconstant; perhaps she has set her heart elsewhere, as Leoncio suspects. Despite his loyal affection, Isolina, who has dyed her hair red (perhaps not coincidently the color of Shining Path), abandons Leoncio when he needs her most as a place to rest his heart and mind when he is in the thick of the war's chaos. Leoncio, however, remains steadfast in his sentiments: "It never occurred to me to change you for another" (165).

Years later, during the postconflict period of transition, Leoncio and Isolina encounter each other at an event in Lima: she has put on the weight of a woman in her forties ("*su gordura cuarentona*"), aged (indeed, prematurely since she was first introduced at her fifteenth birthday party while Leoncio attended military academy), divorced, and full of regret. She has become a prominent lawyer, "worthy of a page in a magazine and of the best qualifications of a social class that was accustomed to bashing or praising justice and their stars." Perhaps she has become a human rights lawyer. "I am not happy," she says to Leoncio. Most disconcerting for Leoncio is that she has lost the shine and excitement in her eyes: "those eyes had died without any epitaph to mark them" (174). Isolina represents a certain sector of Lima society that has lost interest in the war, if they ever had it.

Isolina, with her mercurial heart, ends up betraying Leoncio/Elías. She is not the only character in the book, however, who is a traitor. Indeed, many characters are disloyal. Muca, a small dog "of uncertain race or the product of a disorganized cross breading, a black torso, stripes without direction, and an elongated snout," has been a useful companion in the patrols of Elías and his fellow soldiers, yet he too changes sides. Muca saves them from falling into a trap and alerts them to two attacks before eventually leaving them to join another military patrol, and after that patrol, the dog joins a Shining Path contingent (83–84).[16]

More unsettling to Elías and his men and more tragic than a dog of "uncertain race" changing sides is the betrayal of one of their own men, a sergeant in a parallel battalion named Cholo Negro (Black Cholo, a name that also connotes a racial slur), a soldier of such trust and diligence that he has "counted for two." Cholo Negro surprises everyone by assisting in an ambush that kills fourteen of his fellow soldiers and his commanding officer. Cholo Negro's act of treachery is beyond Elías's comprehension; he wonders, "How many years in the planning for this evil, this lethal step? Two years in active military service. Then he [Cholo Negro] reenlisted and was in his first year. We patrolled together. We fought. He was one of the best in the battalion. He never shirked his obligations. That sergeant, he was an example to others: one of those men worthy of being called 'trustworthy.' And so?" (149).

Freyre dislodges the binary on which heroism rests primarily with the frequent switching of sides that occurs in the book: in addition to several "repentant" *senderistas* who act as guides and informants to the military, Elías captures a *senderista* only to later discover that he had once been an Army private in another battalion, "an *infiltrado*," and that the battalion "had been sleeping with the enemy" (107–8). In another example, a youth who was not allowed to reenlist in the Army after his obligatory military service because he had not finished secondary school decides to join Shining Path "to try it out." He later becomes an *arrepentido* who is of much use to Elías (168). Another soldier leaves the Army because he has entered into a relationship with a local girl, and upon discovering that her father is a drug lord, he has no choice but to abandon his military post and live at the largess of his future father-in-law (112).

It is noteworthy that Germán, Leoncio's brother, for all his heinous acts, is not portrayed as a traitor to his country or as having betrayed his class or his family (though Germán sees his own family as bourgeois lackeys). Rather, Germán is portrayed in the novel as someone for whom fate has chosen a certain path: "It's just that destiny dealt us a bad hand," Leoncio says to his father in an attempt to alleviate the older man's sense of guilt over his eldest son's actions (188).[17] Germán had become radicalized because of his time in Europe, because of the disquieted spirit of youth, and because of a woman. While some of Germán's inner thoughts suggest that he may have later come to question his reasons for having joined the revolution, he remains steadfast in his path. He does not waver even when he discovers the identity of his principal adversary, Leoncio/Elías.

The plotline of two brothers on opposite sides of a battle suggests one way that some military men may conceive of the main actors in the conflict. This plotline may also hint at how members of the military envision the possibility of reconciliation: while a mutual understanding would not be possible between extremes, a rapprochement might be possible between brothers. Leoncio Goicochea, a faithful brother to the end, who, though aware of the barbaric acts his sibling has committed, nevertheless calls an Army medic to attend to his dying brother, whose blended identity (that of a middle-class Peruvian and a Shining Path militant) is noted in his name at the time of his death: Germán Tuchía Goicochea Guzmán Reynoso de la Flor (179). Even Leoncio's supervising commander raises the possibility of reconciliation or forgiveness when he writes to the distraught Leoncio that he knew Germán was in heaven because he was Leoncio's brother (181).

The possibility of rapprochement between the two brothers, however, is ultimately placed in question by Germán/Tuchía's unwavering commitment to the revolutionary movement. Through Chola Bonita, we discover that reconciliation would not have been possible, even if Tuchía were to have survived, for he would not have renounced his convictions. Toward the very end of the novel, after the brothers' fatal encounter, readers are made privy to Chola Bonita's thoughts. Now in prison, she reflects back on the twists of fate that have connected her to both men. Upon discovering the familial bond, Angelita/Chola Bonita had sought out comrade Tuchía in a nearby hamlet. He has become a hardened man since she had seen him ten years earlier: "Germán had changed. His was not the development of an adult, but a messianic narrowing that changed his individual perspective and converted him into a monstrous being whose religion was a party and for whom death became a way of life. To see his face was enough to know his penchant for bad deeds. The [former] young man whose radical thoughts were expressed loudly in the classroom was a European product, a slave to a metamorphosis that had blurred him forever." So she is not surprised by Comrade Tuchía's unwavering response to the revelation that the head of the patrol whom he has tried to kill is his brother: "I don't know who this *cachaco* [slang for soldier] is. He may have come from the same womb as me, but he is a pariah of the system" (183). That Freyre presents reconciliation as both possible and impossible suggests an unresolved tension within the narrative and perhaps within the military.

At the core of *Desde el Valle de las Esmeraldas* is memory: the narrator recounts his story in the postconflict period Peru (around 2005), over a decade after the main events of the book had taken place, that is, the years that Leoncio Goicochea was stationed in the Peruvian jungle. The state had won the war against Shining Path, but the Army now confronted different challenges: judicial prosecutions of its members in a hostile democracy and an apathetic population "with an incredible capacity for *desmemoria* [to undo memory]" (186). By contrast, Leoncio is filled with memories, even if he would rather not have had them: the emergency zone "would follow [him] forever" (186). The book is structured so that memories are inserted inside his bouts of remembrance, that is, the memories he had of his memories. Major Leoncio Goicochea recounts his memories back to his time in the emergency zone (when he was Elías), where he spent many hours seeking refuge in his memories of his life prior to the war (when he was Leoncio), of his family, of his childhood growing up in middle-class Lima, of his pure love for Isolina.

Temporal leaps between the present and remembering the past and past perfect push the narrative along. These temporal and spatial jumps between the different pasts and Lima and the Valle de las Esmeraldas break up the long stretches of rain, hunger, strenuous physical demands, lack of sleep, and the constant threat of Shining Path suffered by the main protagonist and his men. The monotony of their time on duty is otherwise only interrupted by a visit to a village, a helicopter bringing provisions, unintended skirmishes with other patrols, and occasional ambushes by Shining Path and the resultant tragedies. It would be a slow, grueling read if not for Elías's turns of memory to his past before the war and his leaps forward to the present day.

Because of the first-person vantage point, the book reads somewhere between a story and a memoir. Though the author makes no claim for his book other than a fictional "novella," Freyre included in his novel an epilogue in which the narrator states that he had interviewed over six long days Major Leoncio Goicochea de la Flor, a pseudonym for a real soldier, and that the novel was based on these interviews. This epilogue describing the interviews between the major and the narrator (Freyre?) may simply be the author's literary trick to lend veracity to his novel.[18] In this way, the author lays claim to truth while also falling back on the fluidity and imagination of fiction. Thus, the author employs both meanings of *historia* in his account: story and history.

Yet the novel is not entirely fictitious or based on someone else's accounts. Author Hugo Martínez Garay, who wrote his undergraduate thesis on Freyre's novel, categorizes it as an "ethnographic fiction of the violence" because of Freyre's combination of the imaginary with his own knowledge as a military man. Martínez notes that Freyre offers readers "a version of the facts and a truth, from the place of enunciation that has been disavowed and discredited."[19] Freyre began writing the manuscript that would become *Desde el Valle de las Esmeraldas* while he was a lieutenant stationed in the northern Peruvian jungle. He had patrolled and fought in the regions he described: Pangoa, Alto Chichireni, Somabeni, and Valle Esmeralda, and other places "that are not part of any map."[20] He, too, would have known what it was like to go to a military school and later what it was like to be stationed in the VRAEM, though Freyre was there over a decade after it was a main theater of conflict. (By then, the conflict mainly involved a small holdout group of Quispe Palomino, and the battle was over drug production and trafficking, void of ideology.) Thus, when Freyre writes of the humidity, the heat, the heavy weight of the backpacks, the camaraderie of the soldiers, the respect and affection for their superiors, and the sorrow over the loss of fellow soldiers in confrontations, he too knows of this experience.[21] He has the kind of insider's knowledge that makes him able to write with an experienced eye and to interview the supposed "Leoncio," like others he would have actually interviewed while a member of the CPHEP research team.

This sense that average Peruvians, or at least urban Peruvians, have too easily forgotten the war may have been what pushed Carlos Freyre to write this novel. In one scene, years after the conflict, Leoncio drives with his father along the highway that hugs the coast in Lima on the morning of Leoncio's wedding day. His father points to the people enjoying the hot summer day: "Look, it is for all those people that you fought. Look at him who is kissing his girlfriend, and the other who is running after a ball, and those who are throwing themselves in the waves. They don't know it, but you fought for them." In

Leoncio's eyes, his father, a civilian who represents the political class, was the one "most mixed up in the events of this story/history" (186).

That most Peruvians "did not know" who had "fought for them" is restated in the book's epilogue (which could be read either as an explanation by the author of the book or as a fictional extension of it): "The most pathetic aspect of this war is the terrible tendency we have to forget it. . . . The protagonists have become the victims of *olvido*." This book thus combats forgetting: "If every one of those who fought in one way or another undertook the labor of telling his individual story, many such volumes would emerge" (190). Yet most soldiers, it seems, would have preferred not to remember but were forced to because of Peru's entry into the transitional justice era. The narrator (Freyre?), according to this epilogue, does not want to write about his "real profession, that of being a soldier in [his] country"; however, "the compelling reason arose because the voice [that of the novel] is the same cry that escapes simultaneously from many throats, and instead of being written, spreads through the streets, squares, markets, offices and that if you are not careful [this cry] is distorted in such a way that its resemblance to reality is purely coincidental" (190). When Freyre began this novel in 2005 (the same year he won a military prize for his essay "Biased Truth"), these "were hard times for the military" because its members were being prosecuted for human rights abuses.[22]

The fact that Freyre's "real profession" is that of a soldier is central to the origin of this novel and some of his other works, as well as to his literary success. Because Freyre was a writer who worked within the military, General Donayre commissioned him to write the script to *Vidas paralelas*. Freyre was chosen to write up the final version of *En honor a la verdad* even though he was not a historian because most of the CPHEP was composed of civilians, and it was thought at the time that unless a member of the military wrote the report, it would not have been taken seriously by the Armed Forces.[23] Freyre's is a military discourse.[24]

Yet his military discourse came from a relatively untainted point of departure. Freyre entered into active duty a decade *after* the conflict described, and this distance might make his views on the conflict differ from those of the military men of the previous generation. Freyre had gone to military school once the conflict had switched to the Ene-Huallaga Valley and after the introduction of new manuals. He did not fight in the highlands during the height of the dirty war tactics of the early and mid-1980s. Indeed, by situating his novel in the "Emerald Valley," he could avoid some of the messiness that came to haunt the Army because of its earlier actions in the highlands and for which it faced prosecution.[25] Freyre, thus, already represented a different generational cohort within the Army, and as such his views and experiences may diverge from the established Army account.

This generational divide is also present in Freyre's portrayal of Shining Path. While he describes horrific violence inflicted by Shining Path, there are also several moments in the novel when this villain characterization is undermined or at least complicated by other passages in the book, as also noted by Hugo Martínez. Indeed, the very brutality of the war brought soldier and *senderista* together. For instance, after arriving too late to help a fellow battalion in one particularly bloody confrontation, Elías takes stock of the scene around him: "The bodies were strewn all over. Maybe the most suggestive image was that of a soldier and a terrorist who had fought until they killed each other, and they seemed to have *become brothers* in the pain of the shooting" (137, emphasis mine).[26]

This generational difference might also be apparent in the portrayal of civilian-military relations and military conduct during the war. Freyre is of the generation that attended the military academy as the Fujimori-Montesinos-Hermoza Ríos triumvirate was unraveling and entered active duty in the period of transition. To join the Army and then to serve at a time when the institution was under attack and repudiated from both within and without must have made it difficult to easily adopt a heroic view of the military. At the very least, it would have been difficult to accept Fujimori as an untarnished savior. Freyre avoids this problem by only obliquely alluding to any of the crimes of which the Army's members were accused and by not mentioning any collusion or the close alliance between the Army and Fujimori. Indeed, Fujimori is briefly mentioned in relation to the Repentance Law and as "a strange candidate of Asian descent (could he be a samurai or a kamikaze?)" who surprisingly won the elections (71). Freyre does not justify abuses by stating that this was a time of war or that the armed state actors were defending the nation (and thus implying that their actions were just); rather he simply does not disclose any human rights violations. For instance, though the CVR identified the unrealistically low number of 538 reports of sexual violence, mostly against women, and 83 percent by members of security forces, Freyre does not mention rape by military personnel in this novel.[27] The main protagonist does worry at some point, however, that he might have spent so much time in the emergency zone that he now considers local women "too beautiful." For instance, he has heard stories of officers and petty officers who "under the effect of isolation had ended up flirting with natives. [He] didn't think this could be possible, but who knows?" (67). That rape produced children noted in actual local birth registries as fathered by "Pedro Militar" or "Señor Capitan" ("Military Peter" and "Mr. Captain")[28] is explained away indirectly by Freyre as the result of an entirely different kind of encounter, the practice of naming military men as godfathers. While on patrol, Elías stumbles across a woman in labor being attended by a midwife. He is present during the birth of the baby; Elías is made the godfather ("*teniente padrino*"), and the child is named after him: Elías (147).

Personal aggrandizement and links with narcotrafficking are also explained away as something other than what they seem: they are attempts by narcotraffickers to entrap military personnel, men of impeccable and irreproachable character, such as Elías's much-admired commanding officer Sánchez Ortiz: "He was a good man, married with three kids. He had to abandon the woman he loved in order to enter this all-out war." But because of the machinations of some narcotraffickers, Sánchez Ortiz must suffer "the humiliation of legal investigation, tiring subliminal interrogations, and the distrust of investigators who could not believe his honor" (162).

When the main protagonist does mention specific infractions, they seem rather insignificant and cause internal confusion rather than harm to others. These improper acts are strictly sanctioned. For instance, a few of Elías's men steal the consecrated wine from a local chapel. Drunk, a private fires his gun in the air, causing all the other soldiers to wake up, thinking they are under attack. Furious, Elías tells the private "that when [they get] back to the base in Suinabeni, he [is] going to pay" (74).

To the accusation that the military committed human rights abuses through its chain of command, this novel posits a different interpretation. As in *En honor a la verdad, Desde el Valle de las Esmeraldas* suggests that geography made communication difficult so that individual heads of patrol units had to make their own decisions. Indeed, communication was so poor at times that the patrols accidentally fired on each other. In the moments just prior to the pinnacle confrontation between the two brothers, Elías radios the command post to make sure that what they heard in the distance was not just another military patrol in the area. When the answer comes back "negative," Elías's scouts inform him that it is an approaching Shining Path column of some fifty armed men, along with women and children. An exchange of words over the radio ends with the base commander ceding authority (and responsibility) to Elías:

> —Elías, I cannot authorize you to open fire in the presence of women and children. Out.
> —Engineer [the commander], it is the life of my men or their lives. Enemy at 700 meters. Out.

—Look for an alternative. Out.

—Engineer, there are no more alternatives. Enemy at 600 meters. Under my responsibility [*bajo mi responsabilidad*].

Therefore, he did what he what he had to do: he [the commanding officer] gave me all the weight of responsibility. "Proceed, under your authority" (177).

This is the culminating passage in the novel, for all the preceding narrative has been leading up to this moment of battle but also to this moment when Elías becomes "*un soldado hecho y derecho.*" While in earlier parts of the novel Elías has struggled with his angst over proving himself a worthy and upright soldier, when he is given full responsibility to confront the oncoming Shining Path contingent, he has finally matured into that soldier, "ready to fight," "solid, strong." The transformation has made him one with his natural surroundings, but he is still human: "[I could be] an upright officer and good soldier, and . . . that under any random condition I would never renounce the humanity with which we leave a mother's womb." Now a complete soldier, he can bear the weight of his decisions, even if in his judgment he must fire on a Shining Path column that includes women and children.

That it is Elías, and not his commanding officer, who gives the orders and makes the decision that leads to the killing of women and children was important in the period after the conflict had ended and peace had returned. This novel portrays the heads of patrols, men such as Telmo Hurtado (mentioned in chapters 1 and 2), as ultimately responsible for events, thus countering post-CVR accusations of a chain of command that made high-ranking military men the intellectual authors of the crimes committed.

Even though Freyre wrote this novel during a cascade of accusations against Armed Forces personnel and the prosecution of some for violations and crimes against humanity, the judicial proceedings are seldom brought up in the book. The trials are mentioned once when Leoncio encounters Isolina in an event in Lima, and she states that she has become a lawyer. He tells her, "Even some of my *compañeros* are facing trials; even now I don't know why. It's complicated" (174).[29] That the military was being judged in this transitional era is mentioned obliquely in the last paragraph of the book, when Freyre in the voice of the narrator states, "We have left this long fight so hurt that we mix up the heroes and the villains, the victims and the victimizers, the ideologues and the orphans, and the moment came when police, military, *rondero*, *senderista*, or *emerretista*, all became synonymous and are weighed in the same scale [of justice]" (190).

It is against these accusations and the possibility of being judged unfairly that Elías's logbook, his *bitácora*, takes on a special importance. Throughout the novel, from the beginning to the end, Elías continuously makes notes in his logbook. Originally the *bitácora* was meant to serve as a means to record information for when he later has to send in reports, but it turns into his personal diary and a metaphor for his time in the emergency zone. He is not the only one to have a journal.[30] At the Army base, Elías meets officers who have shared experiences: "Not only did they have in common the years of war, but as well the constant fear for their families. Many fought subversion from its early days, when it was thought that it was a blind evil, and they unjustly thought it was a strange revolution whose actors mixed with the campesinos." These officers each had their own *bitácora*, "an entire life to recount, a particular internal struggle" (168–69). Theirs are the notebooks from which "many such volumes [as the story of Leoncio's] [c]ould emerge" (190). After labeling the *bitácora*, placing the location and the date, Emerald Valley, March 11, 1990, he writes his opening sentence: "Our country is bleeding itself" ("*Nuestro país se desangra*"). Two years later, after his last confrontation, he closes his *bitácora* in a similar fashion: "Our country bleeds. And so do I" ("*Nuestro país se desangra. Yo también*") (179).

The *bitácora* is a metaphor for how Leoncio/Elías and others are changed by the war, but it also serves as evidence, proof of what took place just in case memory is not sufficient. While waiting for the rain to stop, while riding in a helicopter, or at night by the light of a candle, Elías diligently writes in his notebook, "day after day": "I got used to writing scrupulous texts, following a well-established sequence where I detailed events in exact order and in such a way that the facts could be used in the future for a good cause" (70). And this cause does come later. Because of a series of postwar accusations, Major Goicochea must dust off his notebook that he had earlier stored in the attic of his house at the war's end, "trying to distance" himself from his memories (23).

While *Desde el Valle de las Esmeraldas* makes very few direct references to the trials against military personnel for their conduct in the war, such as Major Goicochea retrieving his *bitácora* for legal defense, the film *Vidas paralelas* is very explicit. The film follows much of the plotline of *Desde el Valle de las Esmeraldas* with a notable exception: a lengthy scene at the end of the film that is absent in the book. This cinematic scene portrays the hero, Major Felipe Cano (similar to Leoncio Goicochea), who is unjustly accused, tried, and sentenced for a crime he did not commit—indeed, for a crime that did not even happen—the forced disappearance of a *senderista* teacher. Justice is denied by the failure to respect the principal of a person's innocence until proven otherwise and by an obstinate failure on the part of the female prosecutor to listen to the defense's arguments.[31] This final scene of *Vidas paralelas*, in which Major Cano is being sentenced (despite the judge's claim that "it was a very difficult verdict to reach"), draws on the same sentiment about the injustices of the post-CVR era raised in the nonfictional accounts discussed in chapter 1 and in the reflections of Freyre's narrator in *Desde el Valle de las Esmeraldas*, who attributes the pain caused by the war as resulting in confusion over who were the victims and who were the perpetrators, who were the heroes and who were the villains.

By writing this novel, Freyre may have wanted to separate the heroes from the villains, and despite some moments of confusion, of blurring, of "*fratricida*," he clearly sees the soldiers as "*los buenos*," and it is to future soldiers that his book ultimately speaks. For Freyre, the most meaningful readership of *Desde el Valle de las Esmeraldas* is not Lima's literary circles or media, who tend to frame the novel as remarkable because its author is a military man who can write.[32] Rather, what gives Freyre satisfaction is the book's reception by cadets and soldiers, who "know the book better than [Freyre]"; having read it many times over, they can recite entire passages from memory.[33]

For the men pursuing military careers after Freyre, *Desde el Valle de las Esmeraldas* has taken on a veracity and become a kind of guide that the author had not intended or imagined. Many cadets have carried Freyre's work in their backpack as well as perhaps *En honor a la verdad*. According to one journalist, *Desde el Valle de las Esmeraldas* "is read religiously in the barracks, and it tells about the soldiers sent into combat against terrorist columns in Quispe Palomino [VRAEM]. The novel is read even during the breaks in military school. It is not uncommon for an instructor to call on his cadets, shouting at them 'Sit down, dogs,' before reading with great feeling a chapter from the novel. They have made it their own."[34] So much so that the soldiers in the region where the book takes place sometimes blur lines between fiction and reality and mistake episodes from the novel as having actually taken place where they are stationed. Carlos Freyre gives the example of Cholo Negro, the moment in the story when a soldier's betrayal led to the death of over a dozen men. The "real" "Cholo Negro" was inspired by an incident that Freyre had heard about that took place in the highlands, which he transplanted to the Emerald Valley. Yet the soldiers later stationed in the VRAEM claim it as their own story.[35]

The soldiers who read Freyre's novel are most likely drawn to the heroic narrative of the battle fought by men who defended the country and in particular "La Constitución" (the constitution), the name of the town where Elías and his troop were sent to rebuild an Army base. And as the novel was written by one of their own, a soldier, this heroic narrative takes on a truth value or authenticity that lends it credibility as a *testimonio*. This is how fellow author Hugo Coya categorized the novel in the prologue to *Desde el Valle de las Esmeraldas*, a testimony that shows the honor, the camaraderie, the bravery of the men in adverse conditions. Yet it is a novel. Through fictional means, Freyre is able to offer a more searing, impactful, and coherent account of the conflict than the nonfictional *En honor a la verdad*, which is burdened by a cumbersome episodic structuring of a chronological account interspersed with tables, graphs, and scattered testimonial cameos. Both works, as well as the film *Vidas paralelas*, advance in their own way the same heroic narrative and vision of the military's past in the conflict, one that resonates and appeals to the postconflict generation of soldiers: they were the heroes.

While Freyre's story may ring true to some—even so far as to be considered a *testimonio* of a soldier who places himself in harm's way to protect his fellow soldiers and citizens—there is little mention in the novel of potential "excess" and even less of human rights abuses. This heroic narrative, however, is placed in question, if not entirely undone, by *Memorias de un soldado desconocido*, an actual testimony by another military man, Lurgio Gavilán. In the space of the twenty-five pages of his memoir that he dedicates to his time as a soldier in the Peruvian Army, Gavilán recounts bribery, theft, rape, the systematic abuse of lower-level personnel by their superiors, forced disappearances, extrajudicial killings, confrontations staged to hide the bodies of Shining Path prisoners, the burning of corpses in ovens, and the disposal of remains in ravines, rivers, and gullies.

The Many Lives of Lurgio Gavilán

While in his writings on the conflict, Carlos Freyre employs the motif of separated brothers whose lives follow different trajectories, in Lurgio Gavilán Sánchez's memoir these parallel lives are sequential rather than coterminous, and they are lived in a single life, his own.[36] *When Rains Became Floods* is an autobiographical account of the life of a boy from Ayacucho between 1983 and 1997 who joined Shining Path, then when caught in combat entered the Army, later as a young man shed his uniform for a Franciscan habit, and in 2007 returned to his earlier stomping grounds as an aspiring social anthropologist. Originally published in Spanish in 2012 while Gavilán was pursuing his master's degree in Mexico City, and subsequently at the IEP as *Memorias de un soldado desconocido: Autobiografía y antropología de la violencia*, Gavilán's memoir quickly became a great success, selling out the initial thousand copies and leading to further print runs, and it was swiftly picked up by

Duke University Press, translated, and published in English in 2015. Shortly after the Spanish edition appeared, Mario Vargas Llosa wrote a highly appreciative review of the book in the Spanish daily *El País*, stating that "it should be read by all those youth who believe that true justice is at the end of a barrel."[37] The Nobel laureate subsequently worked on the screenplay for the film based on this story.[38]

Gavilán's memoir took most by surprise, for it was an unprecedented work. Though some interviews, artworks, and fictionalized accounts reflected personal experiences, there were few memoirs outside a handful that came from well-known political and military elites, and these books had the air of being written with exculpatory or political intentions (such as the memoirs by Noel, Cipriani, and Giampietri).[39] That someone of humble origin, an "unknown soldier," would produce a memoir was not in the realm of the imaginable at the time, not simply because of linguistic or educational challenges and access to publishers but also because of the inhospitable context of Peru's ongoing memory debates.[40] A journalist asked Gavilán the question if "we [Peruvians] are ready for this story."[41] As Vargas Llosa wrote, "It is a miracle that Lurgio Gavilán survived this atrocious adventure. But it is even more remarkable, that after having experienced the horror for so many years, he left without the shadow of bitterness, with a clean heart, and has produced a testimony so persuasive and so lucid of a period that still incites great passions in Peru."[42]

Since the publication of *Memorias de un soldado desconocido*, there has been a surge of memoirs by other little-known historical actors who have chosen to write of their experiences, but none has come near the impact and uniqueness of Lurgio Gavilán's account.[43] The reverberations of his book can be measured by the sheer number of reviews, blogs, interviews, and budding dissertations on this work. Now in English, *When Rains Became Floods* will join others in the canon of testimonial literature, such as the accounts of Rigoberta Menchú and Domitila Barrios, and depending on how it is read, other perpetrator accounts such as those of the Chilean Luz Arce and of child soldiers, such as the Sierra Leonean Ishmael Beah.[44]

What contributes to making Gavilán's book so extraordinary is the extraordinary life he led, despite his own description of his life as "ordinary." He writes early in his memoir,

> This is not a history of violence, but rather a series of stories about an ordinary life, devoid of theatrics and party politics.
> In no way do I try to justify the atrocities committed by Shining Path or the Peruvian Army; I simply tell the events as they occurred. For this writer, these are ordinary memories, as if I lived them only yesterday. An

unknown soldier's life takes many twists and turns. They are not all here, perhaps because some of the memories are distant now, or some are less important.[45]

Perhaps Gavilán sees his life as "ordinary" because many other Andean youth were caught up in the violence of the 1980s: they voluntarily joined Shining Path or were recruited against their will, and when captured switched to the Army; young men were conscripted because of their age into obligatory military service or joined because few options were available to Quechua-speaking rural adolescents; even some, like Gavilán, subsequently entered monasteries.[46] For Gavilán, someone born in a small village in the Central Andes and growing up in the 1980s, his story would have been shared by many, at least in part. Gavilán considered his life "normal" given the time and place.[47] As he stated in an interview with sociologist Javier Torres, "It is so cruel looking back [on this time] from here [years later]; it was so atrocious this violence, what we went through, but it was so normal, for me, to live through this violence."[48]

But for Peruvians living in Lima during the internal conflict, Gavilán's reality was far from "ordinary" and "normal"; that his memoir has been received by the capital city (*la ciudad letrada*) as "exceptional," "extraordinary," and "amazing" reveals the socioeconomic, ethnic, and geographical gulf between those engaged in the conflict and those who were far away, and the tendency of *limeños* especially to see these years in "black and white."[49] The experiences and atrocities would not have been "believable," according to Mario Vargas Llosa, if not for the "austerity and humility" with which Gavilán wrote.[50] Gavilán's bare prose makes visible, and perhaps understandable, a reality that for others such as urban Peruvians seems strange and beyond imagination. As Carlos Iván Degregori writes in the prologue:

> Hundreds of child soldiers and thousands of adolescents or very young adults were drawn to the organization [Shining Path] by its discourse and some of its actions. They weren't aliens from another planet. Sufficient time has passed for us [urban, middle- and upper-class Peruvians] to try to understand in greater detail who these people were, why they did what they did, how a totalitarian ideology took them in—at least for a time— and how the terrorist project came to describe a veritable parable.[51]

The parable to which Degregori refers is that of the would-be revolutionary zeal that led to this Peruvian tragedy. But the larger tale lies in the fluidity of identities and the care with which one should treat engulfing ideologies and institutions. The three "total institutions" (described as such by Degregori) to which Lurgio Gavilán belonged during the conflict years were Shining Path (1983–85), the Army (1985–95), and the Catholic Church (1995–99).[52]

The Changing Flags of an Unknown Soldier

The book begins with the first of Lurgio Gavilán's three identities during the conflict years when as a twelve-year old boy he had gone in search of his older brother who had earlier joined Shining Path. In emulation of his brother and also caught up in the fervor of the moment, young Lurgio voluntarily joined the armed insurrection: "At that time, Shining Path was expanding; everywhere you went they were talking about social justice" (6). It was early 1983, just after the Army had replaced the National Police in the emergency zone and the violence was escalating.

Gavilán's narration of the two years he spent in Shining Path elicits revulsion and compassion: his squad participated in the burning of villages and the savage murder of its inhabitants, yet this child was also fearful of *rondas*, of the military, and of his own comrades, who would easily kill one of their own for the slightest of reasons, such as falling asleep while on watch duty. These traumatic events that Gavilán lived as a child caught up in the floods of history serve to "humanize" Shining Path and move nonrural and non-Andean readers "past the simplistic idea that they were a kind of incarnation of evil," all the while not "accepting the organization's project, which continues to be radically unacceptable," explains Degregori.[53]

One feels sympathy for this child. His youth is central both to how the book is narrated (a simple voice that grows more reflective and mature with the years, as noted by writer Margaret Randall, who translated from the Spanish version) and to how it was received by Lima's literary and academic circles, a child soldier's experience. His youth makes him a victim despite the crimes he committed and allows Peruvians of this distant, urban, and educated social class to engage with Gavilán's past without the risk of being deemed pro-*senderista*. Had he been fifteen years old, and not twelve, when he entered Shining Path, one wonders if this book would have elicited as much sympathy and if it would have been possible to publicly discuss Gavilán's experiences.

Gavilán's youth is felt in his constant hunger, a growing boy with little to eat. Except for the first year, in 1983, when he and his fellow *senderistas* had their "three square meals," he was constantly hungry, a sign that the communities that had once supported Shining Path had turned against them: "We had become common thieves. . . . After burning the houses and killing the traitors the first thing we looked for was food, then clothes. We took everything we found; it was our war booty" (17, 32). By 1985 his hunger was severe, his dreams of social justice reduced to "a lot" to eat.

> Some comrades said: "The Incas never lacked for food; the Spanish are the ones who brought hunger." I dreamed of great quantities of food. . . . But when I woke up, all I could hear was my stomach growling. And we looked at one another like squalid dogs, but the party was there, always watching. . . . The person in charge ordered: "Today we are only going to eat one mouthful." That's the way it was back then: one mouthful of soup. I don't think it even reached our stomachs.
>
> We could walk barefoot, with lice in our hair, but without eating we could not walk. And so we thought and we dreamed: when we win, when communism arrives, we will eat a lot. (31)

Reading the first chapter of Lurgio Gavilán's memoir, one gets the sense that Shining Path had been reduced to tiny, filthy, marauding bands of poorly armed youth, always on the run, hiding in mountain caves. At least, this is what Gavilán's contingent had become when the soldiers attacked their small camp one morning in March 1985. The *senderistas* fell easily, no match for the "many rounds of bullets, grenade launchers, and mortars [whose] sound shook the rocks." There was no escape for Lurgio; his end was near: "What to do? Pretending that a bullet had ended my life, I rolled over a rock and remained face down at the end of it. I stayed motionless like that for almost half an hour. The firefight continued. I thought of my Peruvian Communist Party, of my [dead] brother Rubén, of Rosaura who I knew was splayed on the ground in her own blood. I believed death would come at any moment" (38). Yet death did not come; "chance changed the story" of his life (38). Gavilán was taken prisoner by the lieutenant heading the patrol and was used as a guide to lead them back to the Army base. Though the *ronderos* prodded the soldiers to "kill that terrorist," arguing, "Even those as small as him have burned our houses," the soldiers "neither understood nor paid attention" (39). And just like that, the first chapter in Lurgio Gavilán's memoir ends. The next chapter—his life at a military base—begins with him running through the streets in uniform chanting songs about capturing and eating terrorists, his former comrades.

Gavilán's transition—from a squalid revolutionary to wearing a soldier's uniform and running through the streets belting out military chants—is swift. The passage from one identity to another is marked in the book by a paragraph consisting of a single sentence: "And so, my socialist utopia dipped like the sun beneath the horizon, only to rise on a new and very different day" (42).

The reader is left with the feeling that this metamorphosis from one side of the battle to the other must have required some time, rather than simply that the lieutenant who had saved him had burned his "ragged clothes and made [Gavilán] into a solider," and the transition was made "from one day to the next" (42).[54] Gavilán's explanation of this transformation and how it occurred is sparse, perhaps for reasons too painful to describe (though hinted at when he mentions the Army's treatment of other Shining Path prisoners) or simply because, as Gavilán describes, the two organizations were not so different from each other, though on opposite sides of the battlefield.

Gavilán's trajectory was not unique. He was not alone in his experience of switching sides from Shining Path to the Army, or as an adolescent who was taken in by military men and provided shelter by the Army, and in some cases, an education. *En honor a la verdad* recounts a similar story in a testimonial excerpt titled "a *senderista* seeks protection." In this excerpt, a former member of Shining Path who was increasingly alarmed by the senderistas' violent actions sought to desert. He joined the Army because it offered him protection from his former comrades. With time, this *senderista*-turned-soldier "learned to love the Army." One of the photographs included in *En honor a la verdad* shows a boy wearing Army "greens," including a cap, with the arm of an officer gently resting on his shoulder. The caption reads, "The Army rescued several children who were orphaned or abducted by the terrorist organization Shining Path. In many cases, the officers adopted them due to the extermination of their [children's] families. Others lived in barracks, under the care of the same soldiers."[55]

Gavilán's life changed dramatically once he set foot on the base in San Miguel, despite the similar hierarchical order, obedience due, and poverty ("though there was a bit more to eat" in the Army).[56] The lieutenant who had saved him, who, as we can piece together later in the memoir, had the alias "Shogun," became a father figure to the adolescent Lurgio. Shogun asked Lurgio if he wanted to go to school, a proposition he enthusiastically accepted. Lurgio entered a primary school for boys. Later, he moved to the military base in Huanta, where he spent most of his adolescent years (where the photograph that graces the cover of the English version was taken in 1986, when Gavilán was around the age of fifteen) (figure 3.2).[57] This same lieutenant continued to guide him, and Lurgio stayed in school. In Huanta a teacher helped Lurgio acquire a birth certificate (44). Because of rotation, his military "father" eventually left, and Lurgio never saw him again, but Shogun sent him a package with sweets the following Christmas, and Lurgio carried throughout his Army years a small blue-striped suitcase that the lieutenant had given him.

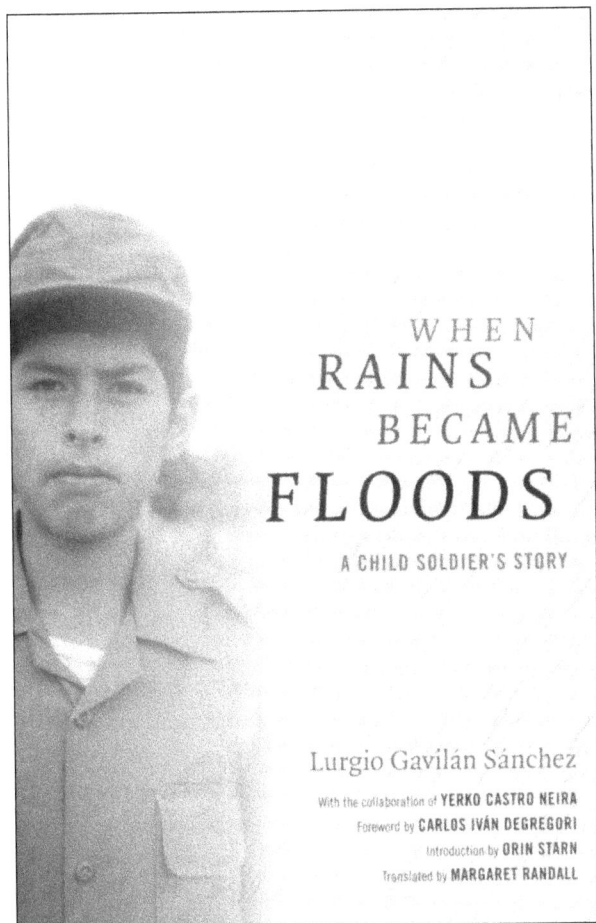

Figure 3.2. The cover of *When Rains Became Floods* by Lurgio Gavilán. (Duke University Press)

Like many young people of his socioeconomic and ethnic background, when Gavilán reached majority age, he fulfilled his obligatory military service. He later reenlisted in the Army as an instructor. At this point, Gavilán was no longer a prisoner, an errand boy, or a *"perro"* ("dog," the term used to designate conscripts), and he began to earn a salary as a professional member of the military corps. He had chosen the institution despite what he had witnessed up to that point and perhaps because of the few other avenues available to someone of his background. As an instructor for the incoming cohort, he too participated in the brutal hazing and possibly even the hypermasculine culture he describes of others. But in what seems a change in trajectory as swift as his previous transformation, an encounter with a nun planted in him the seed of an idea that he might become a priest. After taking a short vacation, upon his return to the Army base he declared to his superiors his new vocation; he shed his uniform in search of a habit.

The chapter on the nearly ten years of his life spent with the Army ends with Gavilán changing not only his clothes but yet again flags; this time instead of the "red-and-white flag it would be the white one that would accompany [him] for a while" (65). By joining the Franciscan order, he could return to an earlier vision he had of himself, of helping the poor, a vision that distanced him from the violence and atrocities he had experienced since making the decision at twelve years old to become an armed actor:

> The [religious] mother's words caused me to dream that I was wearing a sackcloth, curing bullet wounds, giving water to the thirsty, *and mediating between members of Shining Path and the soldiers.*
>
> But, more than a dream, this seemed like the opportunity I had been waiting for since childhood. To be able to do something for those who had nothing, for my countrymen *we had so brutally mistreated, stealing from them and raping their women.* (64, emphasis mine)

He saw the possibility to act as a mediator between his two previous organizations as well as "to do something" for those whom these organizations to which he had belonged had "brutally mistreated."

During his time as a novice of the Franciscan order, Gavilán wrote an earlier version of these two chapters of his life as a *senderista* and a soldier. Encouraged by a philosophy professor from Lima's School of Pontifical and Civil Theology, he began "to write in a notebook," and it was in the silence of his cell that he "was able to engage with long-relegated memory" (76). It was later, as a student of social anthropology, that he came to realize the importance of his memories as both a genre and a societal memory tool. According to Ramón Pajuelo, "in a large part due to his membership in this discipline [that of anthropology], he was compelled to remember and tell the facts of his own experience, clearly aware that it is a humanly tragic life story as well as a pedagogical story for today's Peru."[58]

Perhaps it was his experience in a monastic order and exposure to parables, or perhaps the orchestrated sessions in Shining Path where its cadres were expected to publicly display self-loathing and reflection, or perhaps his years as a student of anthropology that attuned him to the importance of testimony; regardless, what emerges in *When Rains Became Floods* is a life put into a narrative and compartmentalized into distinct chapters of experience. What are sharp turns for the reader, who upon ending one chapter is launched immediately into a new reality in the next, for Lurgio Gavilán were seemingly smooth transitions as he crossed over from the Shining Path to the Armed Forces to the Catholic Church. Gavilán changed his threadbare clothes for Army greens for brown habit and put down one flag in exchange for another: the yellow hammer and sickle on red, for the red and white bands, for a white flag. His songs also changed from *huaynos* and Maoist anthems to soldiers' barked-out choruses to Franciscan prayers and hymns.

Yet from one "total institution" to the next, aspects of his life remained disconcertingly constant in these affiliations, in particular the dogmatic, authoritarian structure of the institutions in which he resided: his life was governed by others and by their visions; in all three he was a soldier—first for Gonzalo/Guzmán, then for the state, then for God. As Orin Starn notes in the introduction to the English edition, "If a single theme runs through the tale, it is the almost magical capacity of certain institutions and ideologies to shape lives. Gavilán . . . shows how dangerous it can be to subsume one's own will to any greater crusade. Yet this book is not some simple morality play about the hazards of groupthink. Gavilán also conveys the attractions and sometimes joys of comradeship, purpose, and belonging for a meaning-seeking and social species like ours, no matter what the larger cause may be."[59]

Soldier is an appropriate term to use in the title of Gavilán's memoir, for it is the only identity that remains fixed in this text. As a soldier, Gavilán had very little room for independent thinking or individual desire in any of these institutions, which might in part explain that while he lived these experiences, he writes from a distance, as though he were a fly on the wall observing himself and others; his individual identity is subsumed to that of these organizations. This distance might also be a legacy of the traumatic experiences that he enacted on others and had enacted on him.

Though violence is everywhere in this book, it is nowhere in detail. It is often just lightly touched on in passing: his witnessing and participating in the burning of villages and the stoning of his countrymen while a member of Shining Path; his awareness of the rape of prisoners and the extrajudicial killings while a member of the Armed Forces. Gavilán uses words sparingly in general in this text, and his succinct narration of specific acts of violence are among the most parsimonious passages. He tends to reserve detail for describing nature, the lyrics of songs, or his constant hunger. For Vargas Llosa, Lurgio Gavilán's lapses into descriptions of nature are "like a delicate poem in the middle of an apocalypse": "the plants, the trees, the ravines, the rivers, blow a fresh breeze in the middle of such pain and misery."[60] One gets the impression of Gavilán as a singing, hungry, nature-loving adolescent, not entirely aware of the turmoil around him.

The style of the Spanish original, which employs passive voice extensively, leaves a distance between violent acts and the author's agency; thus several commentators were reluctant to name Gavilán a "perpetrator." The youth of the author at the time of the events described also mitigates against such a labeling. Degregori wrote that Gavilán "tells everything, almost everything, but without getting lost in the most brutal stories," and Vargas Llosa observed that Gavilán "was witness and maybe complicit."[61] In the English version, perhaps because of the English language's aversion to the use of passive voice, Gavilán's complicity and agency in the violence are much starker than in the Spanish version, though his sense of remorse is no more or less evident in either. In both versions, he writes from a distance, where he condemns the acts of violence and suffering experienced by others.[62] Furthermore, in both versions, his narration is surprisingly free of politics or at least of solid political convictions as he slides from one identity to another, from one historic moment to another, seemingly without realizing their importance.[63] Vargas Llosa commends Gavilán for his simple and direct writing, "his obvious sincerity and moral cleanliness, his lack of pretension and his poise, for the simplicity and freshness by which he has written."[64] Yet for another contemporary *testimoniante*, the historian José Carlos Agüero, Gavilán's is a literary voice, one that allows the adult author to write as a child and thus distance himself from taking responsibility for his cruel acts and from the suffering of others that he witnessed. But it was also a voice that had the potential to be heard by the public at that moment "because Lurgio's discourse, the child *senderista*, the adolescent military, the young priest, and the adult anthropologist, is the type of discourse that a sector of the population was waiting for, and above all [a voice] from Ayacucho."[65] But it is Gavilán's past as a preadolescent *senderista* that seemed to captivate the audience the most, not his years of military service.

Gavilán's Decade in the Army

The public reception of *Memorias de un soldado desconicido* has tended to focus mostly on Lurgio Gavilán's experience as a child soldier in Shining Path, the first of his three identities prior to entering academia. For instance, in the prologue to both the Spanish and the English editions, Carlos Iván Degregori writes that one of the contributions of Gavilán's book is that it "helps to humanize the members of Shining Path."[66] Similarly, at a presentation held at the IEP on December 11, 2012, to discuss Gavilán's book and at a colloquium on January 24, 2013, that also included discussions of the Army's *En honor a la verdad*, the panelists spoke almost exclusively about his participation as a child in Shining Path or compared the book with other *senderista* cultural works at the time.[67] This attention to Gavilán's years as a member of Shining Path probably has much to do with when the book was published, the entry onto the political scene in 2012 of a new actor, MOVADEF, and the perception that youth needed to learn "that true justice" could not be found "at the end of a barrel."[68] But the story is just as much about Gavilán's time as a Franciscan novice and as a member of the Armed Forces—indeed perhaps even more so the latter, for it accounted for nine or ten of the seventeen years (1983–99) of the conflict covered by his testimony.[69]

Yet Gavilán's account, while perhaps "humanizing" Shining Path, does the contrary for the Army, an institution that is depicted as cruel and lawless except for a few individuals such as the lieutenant known as Shogun. As Vargas Llosa notes, "The savagery is no less [than that of Shining Path] among the soldiers fighting terrorists. Human rights do not exist for the forces of order nor are the most elementary laws of war respected. Prisoners are executed almost immediately, except in the case of women, because these were taken to the barracks to cook, wash clothes and are raped every night by the troops, before killing them."[70]

Gavilán describes the ill treatment of local communities, the forced disappearance of suspected *senderistas* and torture, and the wall of denial that family members faced when they came looking for loved ones held at the Army base. Among the many crimes and human rights violations described by Gavilán, the treatment of female Shining Path prisoners stands out, not just because of its savagery but also because of the uncharacteristic detail and space that Gavilán dedicates to it; his revulsion for the way these women were treated is evident. When he arrived at the base in San Miguel in March 1985, four *senderista* prisoners were already in sexual and domestic enslavement (a crime similar to that for which Guatemalan soldiers were convicted in February 2016 and for which Peruvian soldiers also stand accused). Gavilán states that when an inspection was announced for the military base in June 1985, "they decided to kill all of us who had been taken prisoner." Gavilán and the lover of the base commander were saved, but the remaining female prisoners were killed. He describes the horrific incident: "Around twelve that night they took the women out to the parade ground where we always lined up. All of us had to witness their execution. The grave was already dug. Two shots sounded in unison and the women fell over, dead. Now it was not because they had committed an error, but because the inspection [by superiors] was coming and it was better to make them disappear" (50–51).

When Gavilán returned from a few months of convalescence in 1993, he noticed a shift in the way that the Army treated the locals, from brutality and disdain to a kinder engagement, and the Army was now more diverse, with recruits and soldiers from Andean regions (whose inhabitants had previously been barred from admission because they were considered *terrucos*). He notes that this change was reflected in the lyrics of Army chants: "The songs we once sang as we ran through Huanta's streets had changed. No longer did we say: 'Terrorist / if I find you / I will eat your head,' but [we now sang] 'Good day / the soldiers of Peru salute you" (60–61).

The Gray Zones:
Writing *los Buenos y Los Malos*

Gavilán's book has often been commended for bringing to light the gray zones of the conflict, the blurring of the dichotomies by which the actors were subsequently viewed. Having transitioned from one armed band to another, Gavilán speaks from firsthand experience, from within the organizations rather than from outside, about what Shining Path and the military were like. Thus, Gavilán can "know" in a way that few others could. For the military, this lack of direct knowledge was one of their key criticisms of the CVR: the commissioners had not been in the conflict zones and thus could not possibly have known what it was like.[71] The Armed Forces cannot make this criticism of Gavilán. It is precisely because Gavilán is an insider that his testimony is potentially damaging to a more positive, heroic image of *los buenos militares* present in the other military memory works produced since the CVR, such as *En honor a la verdad* and Carlos Freyre's *Desde el Valle de las Esmeraldas*.

We can get a sense of the military's response to Gavilán's memoir from the comments Gavilán received at the colloquium dedicated to his book and from those of the CPHEP's *En honor a la verdad*, for which Carlos Freyre had been the principal writer. On a warm, late afternoon in January 2013, members of Lima's academic circles, the Armed Forces, and the general public filled beyond capacity the IEP's auditorium. There to discuss Gavilán's book were established Peruvian historians and anthropologists; there to discuss *En honor a la verdad* were General Marco Merino, Major Carlos Freyre, and Lieutenant Carla Granados, the historian Lourdes Medina (a civilian member of the CPHEP), and the historians Lourdes Hurtado and Antonio Zapata, all of whom had personal or professional ties with the military. Video and photographs of the event also show several members of the military in the audience. Although both discussions were on the agenda that afternoon, they were placed in separate sequential panels, and few of those present discussed both works. An important exception was the presentation by General Merino, who acknowledged Gavilán's memoir, comparing it to both *En honor a la verdad* and the fiction of Carlos Freyre:

> I was fortunate to read the book *Memorias de un soldado desconocido*. Greetings to the author [Merino nods to Lurgio Gavilán]. Thank you for your *testimonio*. One can read this book quickly, in a few days; its contribution is very agile and fresh, even when there are episodes, phrases that are painful.
>
> You will also find some of this in our book [*En honor a la verdad*] because we recount through art and not just through investigation; [you will find it] as well through the art of the novels published by Major Freyre [e.g., *Desde el Valle de las Esmeraldas*]. Similarly, [you will] find episodes of lives lived. Applying [the methods of] microhistory, we put the lens close to an individual and then magnified out, attempting to understand what happened in a zone, in a region, in a period, and how everything kept changing and changing in variety [*variando*]. Another important aspect of our Army, or your Army, of the Army of Peru is that it has the same years of history as the republic and has lived [through] a series of facts and events that have been horrible. [But the Army] has the virtue of constantly learning, making changes, renewing itself, never staying in the before, in the error, but always looking forward."[72]

By comparing Gavilán's autobiography with *En honor a la verdad* and the fictional works by Freyre, Merino suggests a fruitful juxtaposition that I attempt to make use of in this chapter: to compare the content and framing that compose their narratives of the Armed Forces during the conflict years. In the parallel lives of the contemporaries Freyre and Gavilán, we can learn much about the personal trajectories of male Peruvian youth, defined by geography, class, ethnicity, and age. Freyre, the son of a military man, could choose to attend the military academy of Chorrillos; his future lay in entering the officer classes. Gavilán, while having some choice—he could have chosen not to join Shining Path at a young age and waited to enter the armed conflict as a military conscript—faced much more limited options. His age, ethnicity, and location made his dramatic and tragic early life seem normal, at least to him and probably to other male youth around him. In the words of the film *Vidas paralelas*, Freyre and Gavilán were united in the conflict, at times fighting on opposite sides and at other moments on the same side, a conflict that was lived among "brothers of race and culture," but it was precisely the difference in their "race and culture" that led to their different lives.

Despite the different trajectories of Freyre and Gavilán, their work similarly suggests the fluidity of identity within the conflict, thus challenging the binary logic that frames much of the public dialogue over the past, and they do so as military insiders. This fluidity stands in contrast to the more solid identities and subjectivities that are present in *En honor a la verdad*. Yet while Freyre's book may muddy some binaries at the core of the Army's self-conception (order/chaos, hierarchy/egalitarian, and good/bad), Gavilán completely places in question the image of the Army presented in *En honor a la verdad*: of order, of respect for human rights, and importantly the cultural integrity of the Army, that is, its honor.

In the twenty-five pages dedicated to the almost ten years that he lived in barracks, Gavilán decimates the heroic and honorable image of state security forces depicted in other military cultural interventions I discuss in previous chapters. Originally as a captured Shining Path prisoner, then as a young conscript, then as an enlisted soldier, Gavilán saw with his own eyes, and at times experienced in his own flesh, the comportment of the Army: sloth, bribery ("because [the] own officers' promotions depend upon it"), theft, rape, kidnapping, forced disappearances, sexual enslavement, prostitution, drugs, staged confrontations with Shining Path to justify the corpses of prisoners, executions, abuse of power, and endemic abuse within the military corps (especially of recruits). Stripped of any utopian dream of social justice that had undergirded his participation in Shining Path, the events Gavilán describes while in the Army are written as pure brutality, without any lofty ideals. While Carlos Freyre's novel had done much to construct an image of the Army as respecting local populations, of defending the town and the "*Constitución*," all of this is placed in question by Gavilán's testimony.

Beyond casting doubt on the legality and humanity of the Armed Forces' actions, Gavilán's description of Shining Path also shatters the image of Shining Path as a worthy adversary, one that Freyre's protagonist struggled to defeat. Gavilán and his column were young, poorly equipped, illiterate, with no training, and undernourished often to the point of near starvation. As Peruvian political scientist Alberto Vergara asks, "How precarious must the state have been to stagger before a famished guerrilla? Or, rather, did the state never stumble but rather the senderologists imagined a formidable enemy where none existed?" Ultimately, after reading Gavilán's book, Vergara had the impression that it was "a war between hungry and needy soldiers on both sides."[73]

Gavilán's account of his years on military bases does not shy away from documenting laziness, malfeasance, crimes, and human rights violations. He names names, at least the pseudonyms by which perpetrators were known, location, and rank: his captain, who fell in love with a prostitute; a Captain

Braulio who used drugs and sexually abused his subordinates; the presence of officers Shogun and Savage stationed at a military base where sexual and domestic enslavement were practiced; a Commander Baquéton, who "liked" a reenlisted sergeant, "known by the name of Centurión." "[He] [Centurión] was feared by everyone in Shining Path and by the peasant militias. They said he was a real assassin. He liked hanging the prisoners upside down and shocking them with electricity" (52).

The potential exposure of military men in this account is real. It is not difficult to track through the Internet the pseudonym of Centurión to an actual person, and following this lead, one quickly reaches through association the top of the military establishment, including a former minister of the interior and presidential candidate in the 2016 elections, Daniel Urresti. Centurión was the alias given to Johnny José Zapata Acuña, who was accused of being responsible for twenty-three deaths in communities near where Gavilán was stationed.[74] Zapata Acuña was also implicated in the death of journalist Hugo Bustíos while under the command of Urresti (alias "Arturo"), who was at the time a captain and chief of intelligence for the infamous military base of Castropampa.[75] In his memoir, Gavilán remembers Castropampa in the lyrics of a song: "It is raining in Castropampa. / At the base where I live / are the bloodthirsty ones. . . . We will destroy where they live / and cut their throats. / To Castropampa you will go" (49, 57).

Who are the *buenos* among the *malos* is far from clear in Gavilán's memoir. By comparison, Freyre's novel noticeably separates the heroes from the villains, despite moments of confusion, of blurring, of *fratricida*. For Freyre, the soldiers are portrayed unquestionably as *los buenos* in his novel, in *En honor a la verdad*, and in the film *Vidas paralelas*. All three of these cultural interventions were produced at the time of ongoing human rights prosecutions and in response to negative images of the military circulating in the media and in artistic representations. For instance, *Vidas paralelas* was made for a Peruvian audience and seemed to be quite a blockbuster. Yet the film not only addressed a national audience but also came to speak to an international one, one that had earlier accorded great acclaim to Claudia Llosa's film *La teta asustada* (The milk of sorrow, 2009, renamed *Fausta* for international distribution). This film follows the life of a young woman who is the product of a gang rape of her mother by the military. It was likely in response to the international success of *La teta asustada (Fausta)*, awarded the prestigious Berlin Golden Bear for Best Foreign Film, that the rector of the Universidad Alas Peruanas and other members of the Armed Forces decided to promote their own film at international festivals, where they spoke to foreign audiences about *Vidas paralelas*, the conflict, and the CVR.[76] By producing a film and disseminating it, the rector and his men were actively promoting their cultural memory product as well as engaging and expanding the memory market for it. One wonders what their response will be to the film adaptation to Lurgio Gavilán's book.

Beyond the impact of Gavilán's memoir and its film adaptation on the public's imagination, his account also has concrete juridical ramifications. Gavilán was courageous to put in print memories that place him as witness to events that could be useful to human rights prosecutors. While Freyre changed the names and locations in his novel *Desde el Valle de las Esmeraldas*, in part because of the ongoing trials at the time,[77] Gavilán, whose book claims veracity as an "autobiography and anthropology of the violence," did not. Gavilán used the pseudonyms assigned during the conflict, as was the practice for both Shining Path and the military. Yet these pseudonyms do not assure anonymity against prosecution.

Perhaps Gavilán was unaware of the potential personal and juridical ramifications of his book. In an interview with Javier Torres in December 2012, he did not seem to understand why his account might upset the military, and why his military "father" might be angry with him for his account.[78] He had acknowledged in his memoir that "with a mother's tenderness the military and then the Franciscans took me in" (77). In an interview that was excerpted in the Army magazine *Revista actualidad militar*, Gavilán's gratitude is expressed in the article's title, "El Ejército me dio alimento y educación" (The Army gave me food and education).[79] Though his time as a member of Shining Path is only alluded to in the article, his life in the military is highlighted: "Ten of the best years of his life were spent serving the patria, after having taken the wrong path." The Army was not only a home but also a family for the young Lurgio: "The Army gave him bread and a roof, and gifted him a father, brothers, an education and much more." The article ends by reminding the readers of Gavilán's debt to the Army: "He does not stop thanking the Army because now he is academically disciplined, thanks to the training he received in the barracks." Gavilán may have come to realize only later that his very damning portrayal of the military put him at odds with his former brothers in arms.

The term *guerra fratricida* and the changeable identities present in both Gavilán's and Freyre's accounts probably more accurately reflect the various subjectivities and experiences of those caught up in the war than a narrative that structures the conflict between heroes and *buenos* against villains and *malos*. The notion that adversaries were brothers on the battlefield, fighting together and against each other, of the same origin (Peruvian), and even moving from one camp to another present in the works of Gavilán and Freyre undermine the dichotomies central to the heroic narrative present in the various cultural interventions studied in the previous chapters.

Yet this blurring also distorts another important category in post-CVR Peru, that of the "victim." In the CVR's report, the victim was presented as seemingly *pueblos ajenos* (foreign towns) within Peru, and the profile was "campesinos, pobres, [y] indigena" (peasants, poor and indigenous).[80] In the works of Gavilán and Freyre, this distance collapses: they are at times brothers in arms but also brothers, to an extent, in their suffering. Gavilán's primary identity in his memoir is that of an Andean child and adolescent. Because of his age, Gavilán represents the permissible victim. Freyre also claims victimhood for his main character, Lima-born Leoncio from the middle class: years of war have affected him and other soldiers who lost their lives or were physically or mentally harmed, and, worse still, the transitional justice outright victimized them. As studied in the next chapter, the Army may claim and present its own victimization that came to engulf the nation, not only through film and written words but through other means, such as museological exhibitions, that came to show how they were harmed by the conflict but also to write about their victimization in Peru's era of human rights.

4

Military Curations in the Turn to Human Rights Museology

In his pioneering work *Memorial Museums*, Paul Williams maps out what he has identified as a boom that began toward the end of the last century in a new commemorative form for societies to remember their tragic national histories: the memorial museum. The memorial museum combines the already-amalgamated functions of monuments (which traditionally aim to glorify the past by making war both noble and uplifting) and of memorials (which signify loss and mourning) *with* museums (whose standard role is to collect, preserve, exhibit, and teach the past through objects, art, and testimonies). Williams lists the many museums dedicated to troubling national pasts, starting with the Hiroshima Peace Memorial Museum in Japan (1955) to the National September 11 Memorial and Museum in New York (2014). All the museums he studies share certain characteristics: they are dedicated to providing a place for remembering crimes against humanity; they are addressed in part to those affected by these crimes; and several of them emerge out of recommendations from truth commissions or human rights organizations, once countries have segued from these difficult pasts. They are also all spaces that promote memory against the corrosion of time and respect for human rights. With time they have given rise to yet another museological form, that of the human rights museum,[1] a shift that mirrors the ascendancy of human rights as a global discourse.[2]

Peru has also participated in this memorial museum boom. In the period during the Peruvian truth commission's investigation and the following decade, there has been much public debate over creating a national memory museum, what eventually took shape as the LUM (the Spanish acronym for the Place of Memory, Tolerance, and Social Inclusion). Indeed, building a memory museum was one of the earliest initiatives proposed by human rights groups, and it was supported by the CVR in its recommendations for symbolic reparations. Organizations such as "Para que no se repita" (In order to not repeat) proposed a "memory avenue" in the Campo de Marte (Martian Fields) to link the memorial El Ojo que Llora (The Eye That Cries) with a museum and educational center that in turn would house the CVR's visual account of the conflict, the photography exhibit *Yuyanapaq: Para recordar* (In order to remember). In the regions hardest hit by the violence, *casas de memoria* also emerged: the Asociación Nacional de Familiares de Secuestrados, Detenidos y Desaparecidos del Perú (ANFASEP, National Association of Kidnapped, Disappeared, and Detained Relatives of Peru) constructed a museum above its community center and kitchen and also beside a memorial park, and at least six other "houses of memory" were erected elsewhere in the department of Ayacucho.[3]

Yet as Williams notes, there is an inherent contradiction in memorial museums between the "reverent remembrance" attributed to memorials and the "critical interpretation" that museums are meant to provide. The "uneasy coexistence" of these two functions results in memorial museums finding themselves "instantly politicized."[4] Questions over whose memories will be housed, how they will be displayed, and what are the narrative threads that might unite the different stories and objects prove thorny. So too in Peru. The importance of participating in the debates about how and what to exhibit from the past did not escape members of the political elite or the Armed Forces who spoke out vociferously against the construction of a memory museum once the German government offered a donation of some $2 million dollars in 2009. What was once simply a civil society initiative of the "caviars" risked turning into a state project. Several members of the Alan García government (including the president himself) opined that the money could be better used for development works rather than museums. The head of the Ministry of Defense, Rafael Rey, stated, "If I have people who want to go to the museum but don't eat, they are going to die of starvation. . . . There are priorities." He also questioned whether such a museum would be objective in its evaluation of the Armed Forces. Some members of the military proposed opening their own memory museum instead.[5]

Yet the military did not need to construct any new museums because it already had some. In addition to the more traditional museums, such as the

Navy Museum in Callao (whose focus is specifically on naval history up to the early twentieth century and is a destination for foreign tourists and schoolchildren alike), two other museums run by state security forces are advertised as "open" to the public: the Dirección contra el Terrorismo (DIRCOTE, National Police Terrorism Unit) museum and the Armed Forces' Monument to the Heroes of Chavín de Huántar.[6] And despite their early reservations about a national memory museum, when invited to discuss the LUM's museological script, ten representatives of the Armed Forces and the National Police agreed to participate in a consultative forum. This chapter examines the content and story line of these two military exhibition spaces as well as analyzes the negotiation between the LUM curatorial team and security forces over how military memories should be curated in the era of human rights museology.

To date, the two military exhibition spaces studied here differ from most memorial museums and sites that have been the focus of previous scholarship, a tendency that reflects the predominance of human rights memorial museums and the research interests of scholars within memory studies. Most museums considered are state-sponsored or grassroots initiatives that build on former sites of detention, torture, and disappearance. For instance, Villa Grimaldi in the outskirts of Santiago, the Escuela Superior de Mecánica de la Armada (ESMA, Navy Higher Mechanics School) on the banks of the La Plata River in Buenos Aires, and the Departamento de Ordem Política e Social (DOPS, Department of Political and Social Order) police station in downtown São Paulo are all sites that are sacred because of their connection with these countries' violent histories. They escaped from becoming ruins because human rights and survivor groups have worked to appropriate and assign new meaning to them.[7] These sites are public memorials to mourn the past with clear pedagogical aims of teaching the history to avoid repeating it and to instill human rights values in present-day visitors. In Peru, there is as yet no such site, though grassroots groups have managed to have part of the grounds of the Army headquarters and detention center in Ayacucho, known as Los Cabitos Number 51, assigned to them for the creation of a memory sanctuary. The LUM is the first and only state-sponsored site to remember this past for the entire country, yet it resides on a former garbage dump in a middle-class neighborhood of Lima that has no link to the period of violence.[8] In its artificial location, the LUM is more similar to the Chilean memory museum, though the latter is much more easily accessible by public transportation.

Memorials and museums that are resignified and reappropriated former traumatic sites call attention to the crimes committed and are themselves evidence of these crimes. In the case of DIRCOTE and Chavín de Huántar, these museums are located within institutional branches of the security forces. They are not intended as symbols of repression (though some might interpret them as such) or as evidence of past wrongdoing. Indeed, quite the opposite. Thus, while most academics have considered how "memory entrepreneurs" attribute meaning to post-trauma sites in a pejorative way (shaming the state for the crimes committed), the museums studied here are the result of memory entrepreneurs attributing positive meanings to these sites and in so doing returning to (or retaining) the earlier traditional role of monuments and museums as celebrating the nation and its heroes.

One reason to focus on exhibition spaces is to consider the importance of curating and presenting the past in the form of a display and the implicit pedagogical aims of such endeavors. We often think of museums as educational tools and accord a certain kind of legitimacy to them. But a quick overview of North American museums reveals that there is no specific process of accreditation: one can erect a museum on any theme and call it such. So while one may find prominent museums such as the Canadian Museum for Human Rights or the United States Holocaust Memorial Museum, one can also find the Creation Museum in Kentucky, where Adam and Eve–like wax figures stand near that of a tyrannosaurus. How "knowledge" is curated tells us much about who has done the arrangement, the politics within which the curators are embedded, and indeed the curators' perception of the past or at least the version of the past that they wish to present to the public and have carry into the future. That is, we can learn much about state actors' memories from the way they have chosen to curate the past.

Curating Police Memories: DIRCOTE's Museum

Upon hearing the news, on the twenty-year anniversary of Shining Path leader Abimael Guzmán's capture, that the DIRCOTE had a gallery dedicated to Shining Path's "People's War" against the Peruvian state and DIRCOTE's role in combating that "war," I went to visit the museum in late October 2012.[9] DIRCOTE is a special intelligence group within the National Police that is best known for having captured Guzmán on September 12, 1992. The museum, located in the National Police buildings in the center of Lima, is not exactly "open" to the public, but after some effort, I was granted entry with my colleague, historian Ricardo Caro.

We were given a tour by a colonel who had been a student at the University of San Marcos in the 1970s, a university remembered for its Shining Path presence, where he had studied psychology and from which he later entered into DIRCOTE.[10] The colonel was informally attired, congenial in his manner, and I felt rather disoriented, having to undo some of my preconceived expectations. He brought us to a seminar room with a door in the corner, removed a set of keys from his pocket, unlocked the door to the exhibition rooms, and began the tour by telling us *his* story. In total he spent nearly two hours with us, not once indicating he was in a rush or that we and our questions were a nuisance. I asked the colonel if I could take photographs. He looked at me a bit sternly and said, "One or two." Nevertheless, he let us photograph most of the museum.

The colonel reminisced about his fellow students of the era, reflecting on youth who are by nature revolutionary, wanting to change the world: "They [*sanmarquinos* of the past] wanted to make things better but were led astray," he surmised. When asked about campesinos, from his view, they were "brainwashed." The colonel gave the impression that he wanted to understand the other students' motivation to follow Shining Path. Yet he did not link this motivation to questions of poverty, inequalities, oppression, state incompetence, or other factors, just a general revolutionary spirit that Shining Path was able to harness with its propaganda. He used the metaphor of religion as a means to explain the success of Shining Path: "It was like a religion, and even in prison, they [those imprisoned as *senderistas*] didn't let it go because it gave them meaning." He brought up young people involved with the MOVADEF as present-day equivalents to the youth of his era, with the difference that today's youth "are all on Facebook and Twitter." At times his description of the past conflated with the present, making it hard for me to follow when he was talking about "back then" versus "now."

Visiting this museum without the colonel would have been a very different experience, and for me it would have been difficult to understand the objects with their limited signs. Yet one probably cannot visit the museum without a guide. Indeed, the guide was perhaps there to make sure that we properly interpreted the exhibition. The colonel appeared concerned that the colorful paintings and handcrafted objects on view might have the power to make people sympathetic to Shining Path. He pointed to one painting of healthy farmers and armed insurgents basking in the radiant light of the sun crowning Guzmán's head as they marched to victory over the Army, the president, and Yankee turncoats. He remarked, "These beautiful images inspire one to the revolutionary project," adding, "But then, you have to see the final product." He reminded us of the bombed buildings of Tarata Street, the result of a Shining Path attack on an affluent neighborhood in Lima in July 1992 that brought the war to the doorstep of middle-class Peruvians; photos documenting the attack were posted on movable display boards at the exhibit's conclusion.

Above these photographs of Shining Path attacks hangs a sign warning that "a people who forget their history are doomed to repeat it."

The exhibition space consists of two medium-sized rooms with glass cases and dividing boards. Inside the display cases and attached to the walls were some 1,200 objects presently held in "custody," implying that the objects would one day be returned to their owners once they had been tried in the courts, served their sentences, and been released. As most of the objects in this museum were made by *senderistas* imprisoned in El Frontón, Lurigancho, and Santa Bárbara prior to 1986, it is unlikely that they are all alive to reclaim their work. In that year, state troops descended on the Shining Path pavilions in these prisons to quell an uprising. Hundreds of prisoners died, of which many were seemingly executed after they had surrendered.

The objects on display are of a wide variety: paintings, large hanging carpets, small pieces of hand-carved jewelry, carved stone and wood, engraved leather, *retablos* (wooden triptych boxes), a boxed set of silverware covered by a red felt cloth decorated with the symbols of Shining Path (the hammer and sickle), a hand-carved chess set, woven baskets with inlaid pictures depicting various scenes of Sendero Luminoso attacks and *vivas*. At the entrance to the first room hangs a painting of Abimael Guzmán teaching at the "Primera Escuela Militar" (First Military School), where he gave his famous "We Are the Initiators" speech. The color of Shining Path, red, predominates throughout the exhibition.

These objects show the intimate workings of Shining Path ideology and relationships. They also hint at how DIRCOTE viewed its adversary. Though few and succinct, some labels or tombstones provide insight into DIRCOTE's interpretation of the exhibition pieces. For instance, one label indicates that the objects enclosed in the glass cases were "embossed in leather with subversive motifs made by inmates in different prisons of the Republic [accused of] the Crime of Terrorism and given to the Sendero Luminoso directorate during the celebration of events and dates significant for that organization." By including in the exhibition space Guzmán's library and by carefully spacing his personal affects for clear viewing (his glasses, canes, pens, and papers) and those of his first wife, Augusta La Torre Carrasco (her jewelry, wigs, and cigarette cases), we learn about the worthy adversaries that DIRCOTE succeeded in bringing down. Guzmán's doctoral dissertation is positioned front and center with the cover indicating the title (about Kantian theories of space), and the second volume is opened to a page for the visitor to read. Facing his possessions, leaning toward a shelf full of handmade weapons (some by the MRTA), stands a creepy wax reproduction of Guzmán with wild hair and dressed in striped prison garb (figure 4.1). This figure is one of the few objects that appear to have been constructed specifically for this exhibition space.[11]

Figure 4.1. A wax figure of Abimael Guzmán on display in the DIRCOTE museum; this would have been a familiar image to many because it portrays him as he looked after his capture, when he was presented before the Peruvian media in a cage. (Photograph by author)

These personal possessions from the owners' lives prior to capture and the objects acquired while in captivity remind visitors that they are viewing the spoils of war. Take, for instance, the placement of a famous photograph of Guzmán mourning the death of his first wife. In the original photograph, above Guzmán hangs a Shining Path flag with written dedications and an embroidered tapestry of a phoenix. Now in the DIRCOTE museum, this flag and embroidery hang opposite the photograph (figure 4.2). This juxtaposition of the photograph with this same flag and tapestry on the facing wall makes clear to visitors that what they are seeing is not just Shining Path propaganda art but their private lives and the success of DIRCOTE in invading and pillaging from them.

That all these objects, crafts, and artwork—essentially war booty collected from 1980 to 1992—are on display (some with small labels) in glass cases with locks or carefully hung on the walls, spaced to allow for viewing, and with a few additions such as photographs and the wax figure of Guzmán, suggests that deep thought went into the exhibit's curation. The order of the exhibition presents a story line of revolutionary zeal that descends into horror: from the

Figure 4.2. First room in the DIRCOTE museum, October 2012. Note flag on the left and the phoenix embroidery in the center. They are positioned facing a photograph of Guzmán mourning his first wife in a room where they originally hung. (Photograph by author)

bright, hopeful (though often violent) imagery of the art and crafts produced by imprisoned *senderistas* one moves through the dénouement of the death of Guzmán's wife and the capture of Guzmán, marked by their personal objects, and ends with images of the destruction wreaked by Shining Path, in photographs of bombed cars and buildings and strewn bodies. While not overtly heroic because of the focus on Shining Path artwork and artifacts, the exhibition clearly celebrates the successful capture of Guzmán by the National Police as a turning point in the conflict; thus the DIRCOTE exhibition of this past concludes with Guzmán's downfall in 1992. That is, the narrative is one in which the National Police saved the nation from Shining Path's leader.

We have to remember that DIRCOTE is presenting its institutional memory of the conflict. Yet DIRCOTE does not represent the armed state actors' memory as a whole, and indeed, DIRCOTE might be using this museum as a means to speak not only outside its walls to Peruvian society at large and schoolchildren too young to remember but also internally within the Armed Forces as well. The capture of Guzmán did much to repair the pride of the National Police, having been replaced by Belaúnde by the Armed Forces to address the Shining Path threat. Furthermore, the next generation of service-men and women pass through this gallery as the space is used to teach DIRCOTE recruits and other members of state security forces about the conflict.[12] And as Ricardo Caro has noted, DIRCOTE may need this museum not only to keep alive memories of Shining Path but also to keep active the reason for DIRCOTE's existence within the National Police, a poor sibling within the state's security apparatus.

The DIRCOTE museum is a small, simply organized space. The scale of the exhibition is meager compared to the grandiose efforts to reproduce the Chavín de Huántar Operation in the military academy in Chorrillos. This modest scale may have something to do with the actual event, in which DIRCOTE captured Guzmán without Fujimori's involvement or his knowledge until the operation was complete. In contrast, Fujimori placed himself front and center of the successful 1997 Chavín de Huántar Operation. Reproductions through media coverage of the time and in the years following (though more muted once he was placed in jail) show Fujimori as the commander in chief, in charge, and in control of the situation. Renditions of Chavín de Huántar are numerous, and the museum is only one of many interventions to keep this event in the public's imagination, despite the controversy over its resolution.

Reenacting the Heroism of the Peruvian Armed Forces: Chavín de Huántar

In an operation named after one of Peru's most ancient archaeological sites, President Alberto Fujimori ordered a commando team to launch an attack to free the remaining seventy-two hostages, after they had been held by the MRTA for nearly four months in the Japanese ambassador's home. At 3:23 p.m. on April 22, 1997, loud subterranean explosions rang through the quiet neighborhood of San Isidro, followed by gunfire. Soon afterward, the hostages crept along the tiled patio of the ambassador's house to the safety of awaiting soldiers. After about half an hour, the duration of the operation, the commando team gave signs and shouts of victory. In total, two military men and one hostage lost their lives (the latter died on the way to the hospital). Not a single one of the fourteen hostage takers survived the assault. It was this unequal ratio of survivors and dead that places in question the heroism of the Operation Chavín de Huántar, for it raises the question of whether the hostage takers had been extrajudicially executed. Some of the released hostages, including a former head of DIRCOTE, later testified to having witnessed the surrender of some MRTA captors who were subsequently found dead.

The publication *Operación militar del rescate de rehenes "Chavín de Huántar"* by the CPHEP clearly frames this rescue mission as heroic, one that should be remembered by the nation in a positive light. Indeed, the operation does inspire awe: the ingenuity to carve out undetected tunnels under the residence, a microphone hidden in former admiral Luis Giampietri's guitar case (sent through the Red Cross by his wife to play and keep the hostages' spirits high), and the bravery of the 142 commandos. With such a real story, a minor industry of revisiting this operation emerged after 1997: studies, reports, published memoirs, television documentaries (for instance, *Al final del tunel* [At the end of the tunnel]), a fictionalized miniseries (*Los rehenes* [The hostages]), and an international best seller by American author Ann Patchett (*Bel Canto*). Even a computer game, or training program, "Universal Soldier Project," was created in 2011.[13] As stated in the prologue to *Operación militar*, "the operation and its completion have served as an example to other military forces for planning and tactics of special forces but [are] also an example of bravery, wit, and tenacity."[14]

In April 2012 a series of events, editorials, interviews, a Facebook page ("I support the Chavín de Huántar commandos"),[15] and publications emerged to mark the rescue's fifteenth anniversary. These homages, however, should be understood not only within the context of national pride about this operation but also in light of the controversy over the deaths of the MRTA hostage takers. The case of Chavín de Huántar had come before the court of the Inter-American Commission on Human Rights (IACHR) because some of the dead MRTA family members sought a hearing outside Peru after the military tribunal had absolved state agents of any wrongdoing.[16] This anniversary homage came four months after the IACHR had requested Peruvian courts to investigate the case,[17] a decision that prompted the Armed Forces, the government, and prominent public figures to rally in support of those accused.[18] A few days after the IACHR announcement, President Humala stated that the commandos involved would be decorated with honors in recognition of their bravery. He also promised them legal support for their defense.[19]

Thus on April 22 (the day of the operation), 2012, Cardinal José Luis Cipriani, who had acted as the mediator between the government and the MRTA during the hostage crisis, held Mass and asked those in attendance to pray on behalf of the survivors and the fallen.[20] Earlier that same week, in Congress Keiko Fujimori, along with Cipriani and Giampietri, organized a commemoration of the Operation Chavín de Huántar and paid tribute to the 140 commandos who were present. Fujimori expressed her concern about the possible reorganization of terrorism and reiterated her support for the valiant rescue in 1997, which "has given a great instruction from which all military schools learn." In his speech, Giampietri—himself involved in another case before the IACHR for the summary execution of El Frontón prisoners—criticized

Figure 4.3. Japanese residents of Lima watching the Chavín de Huántar reenactment, Chorrillos, April 2012. (Photograph by REUTERS/Pilar Olivares)

Figure 4.4. Chavín de Huántar reenactment, April 2012. (Photograph by REUTERS/Pilar Olivares)

NGOs that "defend the interests of the neutralized terrorists." Giampietri further requested greater financial oversight of NGOs that "seek to tarnish the reputation of the Armed Forces."[21]

Perhaps the most excessive and exuberant manifestation of a range of events reinforcing the heroic myth of the Chavín de Huántar Operation was a historical reenactment of the original operation. On the grounds of the military school in Chorrillos, to the south of Lima, the replica of the ambassador's home that had been used to train commandos for the original operation was converted into a stage. Here soldier-actors reenacted the operation, an homage presided over by the minister of defense, before a group of commandos and some former hostages; the president of congress; the commanding generals of the Army, the Navy, and the Air Force; and members of Lima's Japanese community (figure 4.3).[22] Bombs exploded, grenades were thrown, and guns fired (figure 4.4). Commandos entered the building, hostages were returned to safety, and soon the commandos could be seen victoriously celebrating in the fashion of the real event, as a Reuters photographer in 2012 documented. Only the hostage takers seemed to be missing from the photographic records of the reenactment.[23]

Visiting Chavín de Huántar

In the year prior to the fifteenth anniversary of the Chavín de Huántar Operation, García had named April 22 "The Day of Military Courage" to commemorate the brave actions of the military during the conflict and in particular this operation.[24] On the grounds of the First Special Forces Brigade of the Chorrillos Military Academy, the replica of the ambassador's home was officially converted into the "Monument to the Heroes of Chavín de Huántar," open to the public and tourists.[25]

Encouraged by this announcement, I visited the site on November 11, 2014, with a Spanish colleague and historian, Raúl Hernández Asensio, after confirming the opening hours on an official tourism website and phoning ahead.[26] However, gaining entry to the museum proved difficult. When we arrived at the appointed time one morning at the gate of the Chorrillos Military Academy, no one seemed to know what to do with us. After making several phone calls, speaking with soldiers of different rank, and showing our passports and stating repeatedly the purpose of our visit, we were assigned a cadet who walked us to the monument.

The walk from the entrance gate to the monument entailed passing through two security checkpoints and took some twenty minutes along a dusty dirt road that followed the edge of a high wall on one side and open fields on the other. The young soldier-in-training walked wordlessly ahead of us. He seemed stiff and serious. After a period of silence, I asked him if he played soccer in the nearby field; he said that they trained there. Suddenly smiling and more relaxed, he started to tell us about how hard the training was, having to climb walls, hang from bars, go along ropes, and so on. But in order to advance—that is, to merit the next level of insignia for one's wool cap—a soldier had to succeed in completing the course in under 4 minutes. I asked him how long he took; 3.36 minutes, he replied, pointing to his cap.[27] We asked the cadet, while we continued our walk, if many visitors came to the museum. He said not really, just groups of dignitaries once in a while, like the "group of *chinos* who came from Japan." Then he told us the story of the famous operation.

Once we arrived at the museum, we were met by Major Miguel Angel Velezmoro Rojas, now retired; according to his card he was the "Director, Museo de la Pacificación Nacional 'Chavín de Huántar'" (Museum of the National Pacification, 'Chavín de Huántar,' yet another name for the site). He told us that he himself had participated in the rescue and was on the terrace where the "most important hostages" were released. Major Velezmoro explained to us how the replica had been built quickly, in forty-five days, and told us briefly about the groups of commandos who had participated in the attack. He placed the hostage taking in the larger scenario of the internal conflict, which according to him cost twenty-five thousand lives, and stated that "Fujimori had the certainty" to give the order to attack. "Unfortunately, Fujimori is in prison for reasons not related to the operation," he explained.[28]

The major walked us quickly through the entrance to a back room where food supplies would have been kept in the original residence. The room instead housed chairs positioned in rows facing a large projection screen. He told us to feel free to take photographs during our visit and that he would arrange for us to have a DVD of the operation upon our departure.[29] He then left us in the care of a young female soldier who showed us three short videos about the operation.[30]

After the third video, a different female cadet took us on a tour of the building. We started in the back of the house where the MRTA had played indoor soccer, *fulbito*. Our guide asked us if we wanted a tour "with details." We said yes. So she started with describing the party at the Japanese ambassador's home, and how the MRTA managed to get in, driving around in an ambulance and then bursting through the neighboring wall shared by an NGO. She explained that the television channel Canal 5 had filmed their *telenovela* series *Rehenes* (Hostages) in this replica, and that the Association of the Friends Chavín de

Figure 4.5. A mannequin on the staircase representing MRTA's Nestór Cerpa at the Chavín de Huántar Museum. (Photograph by author)

Huántar holds a ceremony every April 22 to which they "invite everyone," have food and refreshments, and perform a reenactment that lasts about five minutes, using smoke canisters for effects and firing "real guns, but not within the house, but outside to give the appropriate sound effects."[31]

In her description, the guide wove together the real and the manufactured. She explained that this was a replica of the original house but that the damage was genuine, since a bomb in their practice preparing for the actual operation was too strong, so they inadvertently made a real hole in the replica's ceiling. Still on the main floor, the guide took us to a room where, neatly displayed in a case, were actual MRTA weapons, backpacks (filled with the original MRTA clothing), and baseball hats. Everything was clean. While climbing the winding stairs leading to the second level, the guide recounted that this was where the head of the MRTA, Nestór Cerpa, had been killed, since he had gone up to look out the staircase window when he heard a police helicopter.[32] To represent the MRTA leader, a larger-than-life mannequin stands with his face covered by a bandana, beside a photo of two MRTA corpses (figure 4.5). I asked the guide what had happened to the MRTA hostage takers. She replied, "*Todos fallecieron*" (they all died) and provided no further explanation.

On the top landing, we had paused to view a series of photographs when the cadet who had shown us the films came and interrupted our guide.[33] She informed her colleague of the arrival of some eighty Marine cadets. It seemed that this was an unexpected visit. Our guide told the new guide to take over but not to forget to give us "lots of details." Before she left, she agreed to let me take their photograph together. The two young soldiers-in-training posed and smiled for the camera.

Smoothly picking up where her colleague had left off, the second guide led us through several more rooms.[34] As we walked down a long hallway, I asked the cadet how she had become a guide for the museum. She said that she was sent over from the First Special Forces Brigade and told to read CPHEP's book on the Chavín de Huántar rescue, from which she learned the story. (She would have been a toddler at the time of the rescue.) The guide then repeated that this operation had been "the most successful in the world because all the hostages made it out alive." She clarified that the one who did die, did so later, from a heart attack "because he was old." (She did not seem aware of any controversy over how justice Carlos Gusti Acuña died and who might have benefited from his death).

Suddenly, the guide's tone became livelier. She began recounting to us the dramatic events surrounding the death of Commando Jiménez—one of the two commandos killed in the operation. He had been trying to remove a hostage when he was shot in the back by a "*delincuente terrorista*" (terrorist delinquent); she pointed to another armed MRTA mannequin at the end of the hall, wearing rain boots on his feet and a bandana over his face. Despite being shot, Jiménez was still alive. An MRTA member then threw a homemade grenade down the hall. There was much smoke, and one could not see well. The other commando kicked it away, but as he did so, it exploded, and this is how he lost his leg, and Jiménez his life.

At this point, a third guide, a soldier bearing the rank of a *técnico* (technician), came quickly down the hallway and told our guide that she was needed to help with the visiting cadets. He then continued the tour and told us the exact same story again, almost word for word, thus giving both Raúl Asensio and I the impression that the soldier-guides had learned a kind of script. While the second guide had spoken quite excitedly at times (such as when she described Jiménez's death or how Giampietri had hid a beeper in his pants), and the first guide was engaging and informative, our third guide put on a theatrical performance. He acted out the scenes for us, crouching like a commando in the hallway, pointing an imaginary gun, and making gunfire sounds. He played both the roles of the "*delincuente terrorista*" at the end of the hall, shooting Jiménez, and he played Jiménez falling to the ground.

Unlike the previous guides, who were students in the military academy of Chorrillos, he was a professional soldier (hence his title, *técnico*) in his mid-forties, and he probably remembered the dramatic events of the time. A few years earlier, he had served for a year in VRAEM, where the military is fighting against narcotraffickers. During that time, seventeen soldiers had been killed, though none from his troop; after that year, he was asked if he would like to return to VRAEM, and he said he would prefer a transfer. He then went to Lima and joined the tank division in Rimac. After this service, Major Velezmoro brought him to the museum, where he also takes care of ammunition. He confessed, "When I arrived here [at the museum] and saw the garden, I thought I had died in the VRAEM and been reborn in paradise."

Creating "Cultural Magic" through Guides and Objects

The *técnico*'s performances and dynamic tour livened what was otherwise a fairly dull museum. More importantly, he and the other guides, like the colonel in the DIRCOTE museum, were necessary to provide the context and meaning of the space and objects housed there. Most of the rooms were empty or sparsely filled. The only rooms with detailed descriptions were the entry hall with some standing poster boards and a front room where some logistical diagrams and a miniature model of the house were displayed. The guides, thus, are crucial to the narration in DIRCOTE and Chavín de Huántar for reasons shared with human rights memorial sites and museums, such as Robben Island in South Africa or ESMA in Argentina; the limited objects, photographs, panels and labels cannot be relied on to represent the past as the curators might wish. Yet the guides, despite their shared function, differ. In some human rights memorial sites and museums, the guides are sometimes former inmates or human rights workers.[35] In DIRCOTE and Chavín de Huántar, our official guides were either men who had participated in the conflict as part of the security forces (the colonel was a student who had joined DIRCOTE, Major Velezmoro was one of the commandos, and the *técnico* had fought in the subsequent protracted drug conflict) or soldiers too young to remember the conflict and indeed because of their sex could not have participated prior to 1997, when the Armed Forces began accepting female recruits. The young, female faces of the official guides present a very different image to that of a military man from the previous generation.

The objects and visual images in both the DIRCOTE and the Chavín de Huántar museums would have been less meaningful without the narration of the guides. Nevertheless, these objects play a key role in establishing the truth value or authenticity of the narrative and the sites. The DIRCOTE artifacts produced by Shining Path inmates and the objects confiscated at the time of Guzmán's capture were all war booty that proved the National Police had helped save the nation. For the Chavín de Huántar museum, the objects— guns, backpacks, and reading materials of the MRTA and personal possessions of the two fallen commandos (Jiménez and Valer), who are remembered in individual display cases—further help to establish the replica as authentic. Since the original house had been demolished, this replica is all that remains of the operation. Thus the few objects and images have the task of conjuring the "cultural magic" of freezing a moment in time and making this site "secular sacred," in the sense of directly linking it to the dramatic and traumatic events of those months that were abruptly brought to a close one afternoon nearly two decades ago (the "frozen in time" effect more so than the "sacred").[36] In what was a partial attempt to create the effect of the "real," the different guides reminded us of which parts of the replica were actually used in the final operation, for instance, that explosives had been tested during preparations for the rescue, leaving holes in the replica, or that the tunnels underneath the museum grounds had actually been used in training for the successful operation.

The role of objects in the Peruvian military exhibition spaces discussed here is interesting to compare to that of memorial museums more broadly: in memorial museums dedicated to victims of atrocity, the victims are "object poor" precisely because perpetrators sought to destroy evidence. These objects are thus important proof of what happened, especially in the face of debate and denial of the historical record.[37] Because much debate continues in Peru about what transpired, who was responsible, and what reparations are to be made (and to whom), the objects in the security forces museums examined here similarly are presented as "evidence," but one that advances a contested narrative, for instance, as proof of the heroism of the Peruvian Armed Forces rather than proof of atrocity.

Narrating an Old Script in New Times

Both of these exhibition spaces—DIRCOTE and Chavín de Huántar—narrate from specific institutional memories of the state's victory over terrorism. For DIRCOTE, it was the tireless effort over many years that led to the culminating moment of Guzmán's capture. The objects in the museum and the narration stop at this moment in time. No subsequent history is told, nor is the fate of the imprisoned Shining Path members whose artwork fills these two rooms. It is telling that this artwork all dates from around the time of the fifth anniversary of the launch of Shining Path's "Guerra Popular," for by the time of the sixth anniversary many of these inmates would have died in the state's response to the prison uprising. Nor does the exhibition explain why this story of Guzmán's capture is so important for the National Police, an event that did much to reclaim their pride in combating Shining Path. For Chavín de Huántar, the guides told stories of the Armed Forces' ingenuity (the tunnels being quietly built, the hidden microphone, etc.), of their sacrifice (the deaths of two commandos and the wounding of others), of commanding officers proud to have served with their brave subordinates, and of their success in freeing all the hostages alive (except for one who they remember as old and not having died under their care).

The triumphant script of these state security museums harks back to an earlier role of memorial spaces that praised the heroism of soldiers, while teaching that war was both noble and tragic. That is, they employ a museology that reinforces positive national narratives. Yet these stories were told and displayed at a time when this nation-rallying myth was being undermined by an active judiciary that had ensnared several of the state actors mentioned in the two tours,[38] and in a context of human rights groups pushing for a victim-based museology, that is, museum spaces dedicated to the stories of those who suffered from, rather than perpetrated, the violence.

In their focus on a singular point of view or perspective (that of the heroes), these state security museums are more representative of previous generations of museology than of contemporary ones. They do not reflect the new museological turn of the last decades that seek not only an expansion of the audience but also a democratization of the kinds of stories, whose stories, and how they are told. Today's museums attend to a much more diverse constituency of museumgoers, and the focus of these museums in general (not just memorial or human rights ones) reflect this diversity.[39] This diversity of public and a multivocality of stories are absent from DIRCOTE and Chavín de Huántar.

Yet the curators of state security exhibitions are also aware of the changing times and the political uses of museums as a means to influence the public's perception of the past. That museums can be used as tools to mute or evade politically sensitive "truths" is not specific to the state security exhibitions studied here: even laudatory museums such as the U.S. Holocaust Memorial may inadvertently silence other genocides; memorials such as the Kigali memorial center may hide ethnic diversity and exclusion, or ambition museums such as the Canadian Museum for Human Rights may dilute the meaning of human rights by excessive expansion of the term.[40] But what is particularly striking in the case of these two museums of the Peruvian security forces is that the heroic narrative and its display are throwbacks to the era of select experts and authorities yet mixed with a desire to appear welcoming. By making what are essentially institutional museums originally intended for the internal training of National Police and Armed Forces cadets into museums "open" to the public, the Armed Forces are tapping into the perceived cachet of museums as cultural interventions with potential social and political impact beyond their institutions. Furthermore, they are using culture (here the museum) as a means to efface the violence associated with these institutions and sites.[41]

However, these museums are not quite engaging the public. The difficulty to gain entry suggests a reluctance to be fully accessible, and thus they are only partially open spaces.[42] They are, after all, situated in an active police station and a military school. Even when visitors manage to gain entry, these spaces are not entirely friendly to the public: the limited signs explaining the objects, photographs, and rooms; the low-quality videos; and the expectation that the visitor will be satisfied by simply looking at the objects in glass cases. There is nothing interactive in the displays: no video screens (outside the initial film screening in the Chorrillos museum), no tablets to touch, no special lighting, and no recorded testimonies. The weapons and personal artifacts (such as the MRTA reading materials and backpacks) on display are all very clean, stripped of their potential impact as "authentic."[43] The guns are so restored and polished that they do not look real. The only objects made for these exhibition spaces, beside a series of the gray and white charcoal serial drawings in Chavín de Huántar, are mannequins: one of Guzmán in DIRCOTE and two MRTA members in Chavín de Huántar—both more reminiscent of nineteenth-century British wax museums than part of our newer range of museological strategies. They were probably added to these spaces to fill perceived gaps in the narration or to reinforce aspects of the story. Raúl Asensio noted how Chavín de Huántar was a museum *"poco profesional,"* and not because Peru does not have experience with museums. Peru's archaeological museums are world class: three dimensional displays, videos, lights, touchscreens, and sound effects. But the curatorial endeavors studied here are stuck in an earlier era of museums and curatorial practices. Is this because the curators do not have access to new museological approaches, or because they are not interested in them, or because they do not have resources dedicated to them? Perhaps it is some combination of these factors. Despite innovations in international forms of memorialization, armed state actors' projects are throwbacks to an earlier age of monumentality and museological methods that promote the heroism of state actors from a singular perspective, that of the victors. That is, armed state actors go against newer memorialization strategies and goals that present more complex narratives of the past and that seek greater inclusivity.

Bringing Military Memories
into the New Museology

Whatever the reasons for the no-frills museology of the DIRCOTE and Chavín de Huántar exhibits, the state-sponsored memory museum LUM brings the Armed Forces into this new museological era—with its international architectural contest, use of interactive technologies, and shift to museum spaces as places of diversity and accommodation. When the LUM project became official in 2009, members of the political elite and the Armed Forces did not wish to enter this new era: they pointed to the architecture and gadgets as evidence of the "caviars" behind the project and to the subject matter of the LUM—what became part of the museum's title of "memory, tolerance, and social inclusion"—as themes that rang too closely to those of the Peruvian truth commission.

Originally conceived by private citizens and NGOs as a place to exhibit victims' memories of the war, including the CVR photography exhibition *Yuyanapaq*, the museum became a state project after the German government made a donation for its construction. The then-president, Alan García, originally rejected the donation, but after the intercession of Mario Vargas Llosa, he accepted.[44] García named Vargas Llosa as the head of a high-level commission in charge of erecting the LUM, a post he held until 2010, when he stepped down in protest over a law that if introduced would have granted de facto amnesty to soldiers and police who had committed human rights abuses (Legislative Decree 1097). Subsequently, the commission had two directors, including the jurist and former president of the Inter-American Court of Human Rights Diego García Sayán (referred to on the ADDCOT website as "caviar #2").[45] Unable, it seemed, to agree on a curatorial script during the early stages of the project, the proponents of a national memory museum worried that unlike Argentina's ESMA, which could remain empty of objects yet still be full of memory because of its direct link with the past, Peru's museum would succumb to political fighting over its content, a building empty of memory and objects or too full of meaningless items.[46] With time, however, the concern shifted to that of a museum too full of objects, which were potentially too meaningful.

In the spirit of inclusiveness and awareness of a myriad of experiences and a plethora of truths, the LUM's director, Denise Ledgard, and members of the curatorial team, Ponciano del Pino and José Carlos Agüero, invited interested parties to discuss the museum's script in November 2013 as part of a "participative process": victims from Ayacucho, Lima, and Satipo (Asháninka), victims and family members from Peruvian security forces, artists, journalists, human rights workers, functionaries, members of the business community, and the Armed Forces and the National Police (but not Shining Path or the MRTA).[47] These workshops shed light on the different points of tension among these stakeholders over the potential content and narration of the national memory museum.

When the ten members of Peruvian security forces sat down with the LUM team to discuss the curatorial script in late November at the Army base El Pentagonito in a dark, wood-paneled room that exuded formality, their stance as saviors and the message of their heroism so prominently displayed in DIRCOTE and Chavín de Huántar softened.[48] Though the conversation at first was stiff, a bout of laughter eased the tension. At the close of the nearly three-hour workshop, General Marco Merino stated his commitment to participating in the LUM, "so that we have a beautiful Place of Memory," a glowing endorsement of the project and its importance.[49]

Yet for this space to be "beautiful," it was made clear in this first meeting that it must include military memories.[50] While some participants made remarks that sounded inflexible, such as "[The LUM] has to show exactly what we want," or insisted that what they were engaging in was "*combate de la memoria*" (memory combat), for the most part those present seemed willing to debate both the content and the form that the curatorial script would take. While far from adopting a conciliatory tone, the representatives of the Armed Forces and the National Police mostly did not opt for an openly confrontational one either. This is surprising considering that the script being discussed— prepared by the earlier curatorial team of Karen Bernedo and Miguel Rubio, who had been abruptly removed from the project—firmly placed the security forces in the role of "perpetrators," which could have potentially led to a fairly closed response on their part. Yet when presented with a possible room titled "Pepetradores" (Perpetrators), the Armed Forces personnel actively opposed the name but not their inclusion in such a room; rather, they advocated incorporating into the room politicians and the media as well. The LUM team were themselves uncomfortable with aspects of the script that had been precirculated to all the workshops' participants.[51] For instance, the LUM director, Ledgard, said that perhaps *perpetrators* was not the best term, to which one general responded, "Not at all."[52]

The choice of terms was a sticking point in the meeting.[53] In addition to their unhappiness with *perpetrator*, the participants also questioned the use of the term *internal armed conflict*, which they suggested replacing with *war against terrorism* or a vaguer *period of violence*. They expressed concern over the word *disappearance*, for they rejected the claim that the Armed Forces employed disappearance as a tactic, and they wanted assurance that the visitors to the LUM would be informed that their "institutions have held a position that condemns [disappearance], and this position distances them from this type of practice."[54] Furthermore, they opposed having the abuses that the Armed Forces committed framed as "systematic"; however, they did agree to acknowledge in some form their role in the violence. All their preferred terms distanced the curatorial script from the CVR's *Final Report*.

Another tension over the curatorial script involved the presentation of objects. According to one member of the National Police, the narration spoke to the heart and not to the mind, "exploiting emotions" rather than educating visitors on "the context of this phenomenon of violence." His complaint, echoed by others, was that the script was overwhelmingly victim focused, *"un discurso sumamente victimizante."* What he and his colleagues proposed instead was having more text ("rational and objective" information) and fewer objects and testimonies in order to dampen the emotional charge of the script as thus prepared.[55]

Yet this wish to move away from provoking emotional response through objects and stories was contradicted by other suggestions. In the workshop, the participants all agreed on the importance of placing military objects on display and providing military testimonies. This request showed their awareness of the role of objects and testimonies as witnesses, and that objects acquire a life that represents those absent.[56] Take, for instance, the discussion over a room titled "Ofrenda" (Offering), in which the clothing of the dead would have been displayed, an exhibition technique that draws on a traditional Andean practice of mourning (the *pachavela*).[57] The Armed Forces representatives expressed their desire to also have their clothes on display, not just those of highland victims.

In contrast to the prominent heroic narratives of the DIRCOTE and Chavín de Huántar exhibitions, the shift by armed state actors to a narrative of *their* victimization stands out. In discussions with the LUM team, the Armed Forces' participants wished to highlight not only their bravery and their strategic skills (they mentioned the importance of including the capture of Guzmán and the Chavín de Huántar operation not as "strokes of luck" but as illustrative of their ability to effectively combat the Shining Path threat) as well as their suffering. Such a turn suggests that once they became aware of their inability to propagate a straightforward heroic narrative in this new wave of human rights museology, Armed Forces' participants worked on creating a narrative of their own victimhood, which would elicit sympathy from the visitor. This shift from heroes to victims is important, for not only does it lessen their culpability by placing the military within the broader "grammar of violence" that encompassed Peru, but it also overlaps their memory of heroism with that of human rights groups' memories of victimization.[58]

After many starts and stops over nearly seven years, changes in the direction and staff, and some eleven million dollars, the LUM finally opened its doors to its permanent exhibit on December 18, 2015.[59] President Humala gave an inaugural address to those in attendance, where he reminded the audience that he too had lived "in the flesh" the violence and from which he could recount many memories (*"podía dar sin número de recuerdos"*). He officially endorsed the space, stating that "justice is important for reconciliation," and that "this place [the LUM] should unite us [Peruvians] through the notion that we should *never again* return to this type of terrorist activities, we must settle with the past, and we must *remember* so as *not to repeat* history. We should strengthen our democracy, democratic values. And we should work with a new mentality, an Armed Forces that looks to the future, that acts with transparency and that is able to account for each act done."[60]

Visiting the LUM over a year following its inauguration, I noted that the curators had made adjustments to the museological script discussed in the workshops. The exhibition remains predominantly oriented toward how the conflict was experienced by those who suffered most, the three-quarters of victims who were non–native Spanish speakers (as illustrated in one of the first rooms dedicated to the Asháninka peoples and to the communities of Uchurracay and Putis) and the hundreds of thousands of Peruvians displaced. However, at least on the surface, the exhibition appears to have heeded several of the concerns raised by the military consulted yet without presenting the Armed Forces as unproblematically heroic.[61]

The narrative threads that spread over the three floors of the exhibition represent the strengthening of institutions and democracy, empowerment through education, and resistance (to the Shining Path and state violence) by Peruvians as a whole. The exhibition begins with the image of a woman voting; thus the visitor learns that the 1980s elections were not just the moment when the Shining Path launched its "People's War" but also a return to democracy and the first time illiterate women could vote.[62] After providing a timeline of the main events from the military revolutionary government of the late 1960s to the transitional government of Valentín Paniagua in 2000, the first section is dedicated to "La violencia y el ámbito educativo" (The violence and the educational setting), which displays photographs, testimonies, and school textbooks from the conflict era as well as an art installation of damaged school desks. The theme of learning is also extended to the military: one centrally situated panel has the title "La lucha contra el terrorismo estuvo marcada por un lento aprendizaje" (The [military's] battle against terrorism was marked by the slow [process of] learning). The second floor turns to civilian resistance and contribution to bringing the conflict to an end and to the military defeat of Shining Path and the MRTA. The main exhibition culminates with the return to democracy in 2000 and societal efforts at accountability and remembrance. Just prior to the exit on the third floor is a last area, titled "Ofrenda," though the space has no victims' clothes on display as suggested in the original script discussed in the consultative workshop.[63] Rather, there is a mural representing Peru's Amazonian region and an oval-shaped exhibition space with a video projection of urban scenes and names of victims (presumably culled from the Single Victim Registry).

Throughout the exhibition are reminders of harm done to Peruvians by armed groups, subversive and state. In regard to the role of the Armed Forces in the conflict, the LUM exhibition can be read on two registers: as heroes (the sacrifices made by and successes attributed to the Armed Forces) and as perpetrators (the human rights violations committed by them). In the case of the latter register, one of the three emblematic cases described in depth in the LUM is that of Putis. It is a story that is impossible to tell without including the merciless act perpetrated by the Armed Forces: the massacre of communities seeking state protection. To help recount the massacre, the curators use a child survivor's drawings and children's clothes found in a mass grave (figure 4.6). Elsewhere in the exhibition, a re-creation of an exhumation of a mass grave and description of La Hoyada on the Cabitos military base in Ayacucho also point to extrajudicial killing and to the act of disappearing individuals. Near the end of the exhibition space, in a separate room, an entire wall is embossed with victims' statements of sexual abuse and torture; all but three of these acts are attributed to members of the Armed Forces. Even though at first glance the panel dedicated to the evolving tactics of the Armed Forces (gently described as "a slow [process of] learning" rather than the easing of systematic violence) might appear too light on the military, the curators' presentation of the military is more negative on closer inspection. Hanging next to this text is an enlarged photograph of the municipal stadium in Huanta, the location of a Marine base and clandestine torture center (as noted in small print in the accompanying didactic label). Similarly, while a panel about Chavín de Huántar heralds this successful operation as "recognized the world over as a strategic model for hostage rescue," the curators also included a paragraph on the judicial proceedings over the possible extrajudicial killing of MRTA hostage takers.

Despite the nuanced and at times more overt critique of the Armed Forces, the heroism and sacrifice by Peru's security forces are also prominently displayed on a series of panels dedicated to their "fundamental role in the defeat

Figure 4.6. Children's clothes exhumed from the clandestine mass grave in Putis, donated to the LUM by the president of the Victims' Association of Putis. (Photograph by author).

of Shining Path and the MRTA" alongside efforts by civil society: one on the Chavín de Huántar operation, one on the capture of Guzmán, and two on civic works provided to affected communities. As explained on the first panel in this section, "the Forces of Order and civil authorities sacrificed life and suffered grave harm in combating them [Shining Path and the MRTA]." This panel reproduces the last sentence of *En honor a la verdad*: "The Peruvian Army condemns acts against the law committed by certain members of the Armed and Police Forces who acted individually and not as part of a policy of extermination [*política de exterminio*] dictated by some military hierarchy."[64]

The suffering of the state armed actors and their families is advanced in the section titled "Una persona, todas las personas" (One person, all people), a title that equates these individuals' harm with that of Peruvians as a whole (figure 4.7). Four out of eighteen life-size touch screens are dedicated to members of

Figure 4.7. Screens suspended at eye level play testimonial excerpts from Peruvians affected by the conflict. (Photograph by author)

security forces and their families who recount their experiences: the widow of an Army soldier (featured on the cover of *En honor a la verdad* with his troop just prior to his death), a disabled soldier, a former member of the police (who became a well-known quechua-blues rock star), and the sister of a fallen police officer. The testimonies recounted avoid easy compartmentalization of these individuals or their loved ones as "perpetrators." Situated at eye level with the museum visitor, these testimonies are very moving. The soldier tells visitors of how folly and a desire to stay with his friends led him to join the Army at a young age, a decision that changed tragically his life's trajectory. The former police member recounts the inner dynamics within the Police (such as masculinity, fear, and competition). At one moment, he becomes so overwhelmed by his memories that he leaves the screen, returning with a deeply distraught expression on his face. In both of these testimonies, the suffering of the individuals is apparent. Yet it is difficult to interpret the inclusion of these testimonies as entirely exculpatory, for while the individual's experiences are distressing, the acts by members of their institutions are also condemned. For just a few feet from the testimony of the disabled soldier and the former police officer are the testimonies of a woman who was raped by police officers when a teen and of a woman whose son was last seen being taken away by Army soldiers to Los Cabitos. Disconcertingly, by placing these individuals together—whether members of the institutions that perpetrated crimes or those who were victimized by them—creates a kind of equivalency between these individuals' suffering and victimhood. That the expansive category of "victim" is accepted uncritically by some visitors is made apparent by the two walls covered with Post-it note messages from schoolchildren to those whose testimonies are reproduced in the room: they are all "heroic" in one way or another for having overcome severe hardship.

Overall, the LUM's exhibition seems to neither directly confront the role of the Armed Forces nor advance an exonerating narrative. However, at the time of the opening of the LUM, a short-term concession was made to the Armed Forces that granted them one of the four temporary exhibition spaces at the end of the permanent exhibit.[65] Thus, alongside the victim-based narrations of ANFASEP and the museums of Huancavelica and of Junín, the Armed Forces were given an empty space in which to display their own curation, a task undertaken by members of the CPHEP. It was a prime location, for it was the last exhibition space just prior to the building's exit; thus its content had the last word. The space was uncluttered, with only a few objects, such as an improvised bomb and a portion of a downed helicopter that led to the deaths of those on board. Titled *La Búsqueda de la Paz en una Gran Tiniebla* (The search for peace in a large mist), the exhibit relied heavily on text and even more so on images to present the narrative of the sacrifice made by "young men with limited resources," who suffered "hunger, violence, confusion, ambushes, mutilation, and the pain of their own dead," and who had been sent by the state to defend "constitutionally" the nation in this "unconventional war." One whole wall of the small exhibition space was covered by a single image: that of a young soldier in a body bag (figure 4.8). Beside the photograph was an excerpt from *En honor a la verdad* that states that the blame is not theirs alone but to be shared by all of society (discussed in chapter 2).[66]

Thus the image that the Armed Forces chose to project in their exhibition space was that of their sacrifice and of their own victims. This portrayal of their victimhood went beyond the LUM's more nuanced narrative that tries to display their heroism while acknowledging wrongdoing. This small, contained exhibition curated by the military was placed beside that of the regional museums dedicated to highland victims; the placement oddly juxtaposed the memories of the victims of state agents and Shining Path aggression with that of their state aggressors' victimization. In so doing, the Armed Forces situated themselves like all Peruvians in their shared experience of the violence, a narrative that counters the historic past and that helps legitimize state armed forces in democracy and in the era of human rights. Thus, the Armed Forces' display also repeated one of the LUM's overarching narrative threads: "one person, all people."

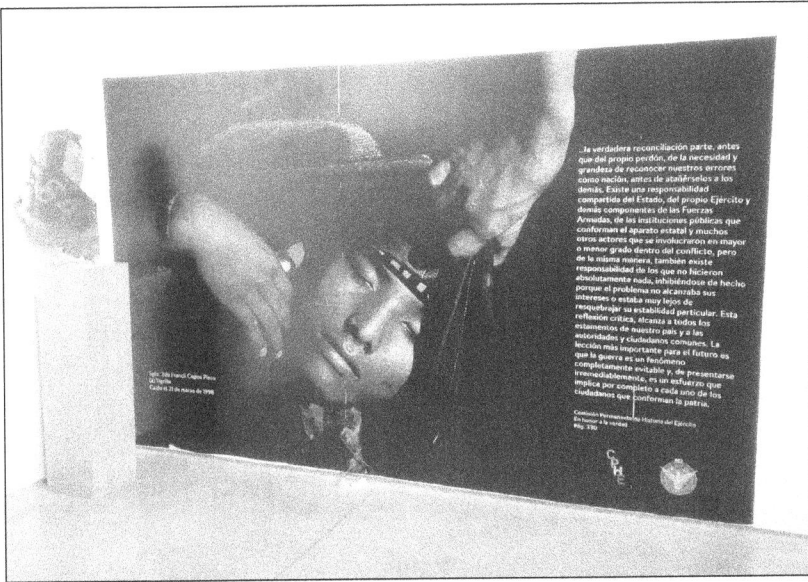

Figure 4.8. The Armed Forces' temporary display in the LUM, February 2016. (Photograph by Carlos Bracamonte)

The task before the LUM was daunting: to craft a curation that incorporated the many different requests of the stakeholders into a single script on which all could agree.[67] The LUM curatorial team attempted to situate itself between Peru's two entrenched memory camps (the human rights and the heroic camps), while also opening up to other stakeholders (such as the business community, journalists, state functionaries, and artists). The team did not wish to be seen as a "next step" after the CVR to avoid the earlier contested responses to the CVR. Rather, the curators envisioned the LUM as a space that emerged from the CVR's work yet was independent from it.[68] Nor did the curators wish to be seen as pandering to conservative sectors or the Peruvian Armed Forces.[69] Indeed, the LUM's final script does not refer to either the term *internal armed conflict*, used in the CVR's *Final Report*, or *war against terrorism* used by the military. Rather, this period is referred to as "*los años de violencia*" (the years of violence) and "*el ciclo de violencia política*" (the cycle of political violence), as though it had been a natural disaster that swept the nation.[70]

The Peruvian Truth and Reconciliation Commission plays a very discrete role throughout the museum. It is only referenced directly a few times: such as in the very first introductory panel, on a timeline, in a description of the exhumations, and in the last room, "Iniciativas de Verdad, Memoria y Justicia"

(Memory, Truth and Justice Initiatives), where there is a panel dedicated to the CVR as one "initiative" among others, and where nearby eight of the nine volumes of the *Final Report* are on display. Despite its subtle presence, the CVR provided much of the chronological narrative and statistics cited in the LUM, such as three-quarters of the victims as non–native Spanish speakers, the 600,000 displaced, and the 40 percent of the victims who came from Ayacucho. Yet, the descriptive panels do not indicate the CVR as the source for these numbers. And, beyond the short mention of 69,280 as the number presented by the CVR ("based on a statistical projection" and that there is "no official definitive number"), at no point is the public reminded "40 percent" of what number. The same introductory panel notes that several years after the CVR, the Single Victims Registry had counted 31,972 cases with first and last names, and that "this number, however, did not include dead subversives." It is this number that the museumgoers are reminded of near the exit, that over 30,000 "people who died have been identified to date," rather than the more than 69,000 stated by the CVR.[71]

Furthermore, even though the CVR's photography exhibition *Yuyanapaq* was key to the emergence of the LUM, since it had stirred the German government to offer the original donation, only a panel with two photographs from the exhibition are on display. The sparing text accorded to the *Yuyanapaq* exhibition seems to contradict the small tombstone that states that "*Yuyanapaq* was an important milestone in our collective memory."[72] The absence of the *Yuyanapaq* photographs is purportedly because of insufficient space in the vast museum. Most likely, however, the LUM wishes to distance itself from the controversies provoked by *Yuyanapaq*, especially the critiques in 2003 that it did not show enough of the suffering of the nation's heroes.

The implicit curatorial efforts to downplay the role of the CVR in its own trajectory and to present the LUM as an objective pedagogical space have reaped limited success. While the LUM has managed to keep its doors open despite a precarious budget, the Armed Forces and some political elite remain disturbed by the museum's content. The lengths to which some will go to discredit the LUM are revealing of their deep displeasure. In May 2019, the former head of the Armed Forces, Congressman Edwin Donayre, disguised himself as a Colombian victim of that country's Armed Forces who was unable to speak. With helpers, he recorded a guided tour. After releasing an edited video of this tour, Donayre accused the guide of inciting terrorism ("apología al terrorismo"), and the widely circulating video implied that the LUM was a space sympathetic to Shining Path.[73]

❧

The Turn to Human Rights Museology

In this fraught, politicized space over a contested history, the LUM curatorial team had clear pedagogical objectives that situated its project between memorial and human rights museums: the curation looks to the past in hope of learning from it but also to the future in hope of realizing citizenship rights for all. This aspiration to learn from the past with the aim of furthering an inclusive society invites the "uneasy coexistence" of "reverent remembrance" and "critical interpretation" identified by Paul Williams, one that is perhaps necessary and unavoidable.[74] This "uneasy coexistence" is what comes most to the fore in the LUM's interactions with the Armed Forces, for while the former wished to interpret and teach the past, the latter wished to honor the nation and its heroes. Still, by engaging with armed state actors, the LUM opened up the possibility for a dialogue with the Armed Forces, inviting them to enter the era of multivocality and inclusiveness in the military's own curations.

Despite the differences of Peru's main memory camps, which the LUM attempted to house, all seem to agree that the past must not be forgotten. The sign at the exit of the DIRCOTE museum states, "a people who forget their history are doomed to repeat it," a similar affirmation invoked by military personnel in attendance at the LUM forum and made by the CVR in its *Final Report*. Yet the past that they wish not to repeat and the past they evoke are different. For the CVR and human rights groups, the past to be remembered is the racism, marginalization, and violence inflicted by Shining Path and the state, and the abuse of fundamental rights suffered by Peru's most vulnerable citizens and their endurance and ongoing demands for social redress. For some conservative sectors, the past to be remembered is much less complicated: the serious terrorist threat of Shining Path and the heroism of state security forces. Theirs is the narrative of the war years as displayed in DIRCOTE and Chavín de Huántar museums: it seeks to reaffirm the armed state actors without reforming security institutions or seeing beyond their triumph. For human rights groups, what is not to be repeated are past injustices and the root causes of poverty and exclusion that lay the groundwork for continued discontent; for state security forces, Shining Path is not to be repeated. Indeed, these two memory camps display two very distinct tales of "Never Again." The challenge for the LUM is to navigate between these two tales, while incorporating many other voices of the past and future generations into their curation. This complex task of providing a space for "uneasy coexistence" in Peru's polarized memorial landscape is one that if not done carefully risks not only distorting the past but putting in peril the LUM's future prospects.[75]

5

Captive to History

Military Memories and Censorship in Public Spaces

The theater La Plaza was an unlikely place in November 2014 to stage the play *La cautiva* (The captive), which looks back on the conflict that claimed the lives of some sixty-nine thousand Peruvians, mostly rural and of indigenous descent. The theater is situated in the modern, luxury, sea-view shopping center Larcomar in the Miraflores neighborhood of Lima, a location that evokes not the violence of the past but rather Peru's later economic boom. Yet this is where such a play should be performed, for this is the public who ought to be reminded of the recent past. When the head of the CVR, Salomón Lerner, asked how so many people could die and disappear without "anyone missing them," he pointed to a double scandal: the first scandal was the large-scale assassination, disappearance, and torture; and the second was the indolence, ineptitude, and indifference among those who could have prevented this humanitarian catastrophe from happening.[1] *La cautiva* succeeded in capturing both elements of this scandal, for it attracted the attention of the Armed Forces and appealed to the imagination of Lima's well-off, who had seemed unaware or indifferent to the scale of the conflict. Because of its portrayal of the former, in the months following the opening, the playwright, the theater director, and the actors all came under suspicion of DIRCOTE, the National Counterterrorism Directorate, for "apology/incitement of terrorism" (*apología al terrorismo*), a charge that could have led to years of imprisonment for those involved in the play.[2]

One of the more expected forms of the Peruvian Armed Forces' interventions in the public arena is an effort to control what is said and how, suppressing uncomfortable "truths" about Peru's conflict in the public domain, that is, censorship. Yet that censorship in its crude and overt forms should continue to take place after the democratic transition is perhaps surprising. The overt tactics of authoritarian censorship might morph into social amnesia or the silencing of taboos, but open censorship goes against the core principles of transitional justice.[3] In addition to the establishment of a truth commission to study the period from 1980 to 2000, other steps were taken in an effort to consolidate the return to democracy: reforms were made in the electoral bodies and the judiciary, Peru returned to the Inter-American Court of Human Rights, and the government undertook efforts to foster greater openness, including the introduction of the Law on Transparency and Access to Public Information.[4] Nevertheless, remnants of the previous practices of curbing public debate carried over to the new era. In this chapter, I present specific examples of censorship in the cultural realm (rather than traditional media communications of radio, television, and printed press), most of which emerged at the behest of state security forces, though they may not be the product of a coherent plan or strategy. My argument is that in addition to introducing and presenting information in the public sphere as shown in other chapters here—such as books, literature, film, and museum exhibitions—the military is also circumscribing what is permissible to circulate in cultural realms. That is, if we envision museums, memory books, memorial sites, and the like as forms of *writing* about the past, we might also consider censorship as a form of *editing* this past.

Caricatures and Exhibitions: What May One Draw and Display?

On the eve of the opening in June 2007 of an exhibition of works by artist Piero Quijano at the Casa Museo de Mariátegui in Central Lima, the Instituto Nacional de Cultura del Perú (INC, National Institute of Culture) removed three drawings at the behest of the commanding general of the Peruvian Army, Edwin Donayre. The INC justified its decision as an act not of "censorship" but rather of establishing the "parameters of good sense."[5] All the works on display had been previously published in Peruvian newspapers, hence the exhibit's title, *Dibujos en prensa 1990–2007* (Drawings in the press, 1990–2007). Yet the three offending images later came to mark the limit of "good sense" in what may be publicly displayed, despite their previous circulation. One drawing implied that the historic site of Manchu Picchu was up for sale to foreign investors; another showed Alan García with a campaign pin embossed with "TLC [tender loving care] and I'll give you a baby." (TLC refers to the trade agreement signed with the United States and the baby conceived with an American citizen.) It was the third drawing, however, that provoked the most

Figure 5.1. Quijano's "Iwo Jima." (His pseudonym is Martín Ikeda, hence the signature on the image.) (Art by Piero Quijano)

controversy in the subsequent days and may have been the piece that led to the censorship of the exhibit, called informally Quijano's "Iwo Jima" (figure 5.1).

This drawing took as its inspiration the famous Pulitzer Prize–winning photograph by Joe Rosenthal of five American marines and one navy corpsman raising the flag of the United States on Mount Suribachi on the island Iwo Jima on February 23, 1945, an event that signaled the first Allied victory on Japanese soil. It is possibly the most reproduced photograph of all time. The iconic image later served as the model for the U.S. Marine Corps War Memorial in Arlington, Virginia, and has become synonymous with American heroism in various conflicts dating back to the Revolutionary War of 1775.

In his reworking of Rosenthal's photograph, Quijano took the silhouetted form captured in the photograph and in the memorial, yet cast doubt on the heroism of the Peruvian armed state actors portrayed. Four Peruvian soldiers hold a large machine gun with a bayonet fixed to the muzzle, with which they

Captive to History

pierce the body of an Andean man who lies splayed on the ground. The plaque on Quijano's imagined memorial reads "The Nation to Its Heroes," in imitation of the Arlington memorial. Yet Quijano takes up the patriotism evoked by the Arlington memorial, which reads "Uncommon Valor was a Common Virtue," in an ironic way. While the Arlington memorial commemorates American soldiers' heroism dating back to the Revolutionary War, Quijano similarly points to the valor (or rather the lack thereof) of Peruvian soldiers, perhaps dating back to the War of the Pacific, which has meant the repeated oppression of Peruvian highland peoples.

The organizers of the exhibition in the Casa Museo de Mariátegui probably intended to elicit a reaction from the public when they chose this image for their publicity posters, thus bringing attention to a less than favorable depiction of the military's heroism; yet they may not have anticipated that a leading general and public figure such as Donayre would direct the INC to censor the exhibit or that the minister of defense during the second García presidency, Allan Wagner, would also speak out against the exhibition. Wagner argued that the INC had removed these drawings because they had been taken out of their original context. Apparently this specific drawing, Quijano's "Iwo Jima," had first appeared in an article about the CVR. Because the drawing was detached from this article and placed in the context of an exhibition, Wagner was concerned that it gave "the impression that this behavior by Armed Forces [was] permanent and continuous, which [he knew] not to be the case."[6] That is, the image implied systematic human rights abuses by the Armed Forces, a finding of the CVR that the military hotly contests.[7] Even the president of the republic felt compelled to enter into the melee, stating that the INC had not exercised censorship "but rather something different" since the artist's work was not prohibited throughout the country, just in this specific space. However, García inveighed, "One cannot allow the Peruvian Armed Forces to be insulted in a public space, and I personally would not allow it either. Now, you have the street, you have your home, there are thousands of exhibition galleries everywhere, you have the newspaper *Perú21* to publish in, but in public spaces, to allow one to harm the Armed Forces, to me this seems, frankly, unbearable. I have seen the caricature, and it seems to me shameful."[8]

Of course, art censorship is not specific to Peru, nor is it new. According to historian Robert Goldstein, in revolutionary France authorities feared the power of images because even though much of the population was illiterate, *la plèbe* could nevertheless interpret visual imagery. Thus a French minister warned that "engravings and lithographs act immediately upon the imagination of the people, like a book which is read with the speed of light; if it wounds modesty or public decency the damage is rapid and irremediable."[9] This fear of the corrupting power of images was such that even though print censorship officially ended in 1822 in France, censorship of caricatures lasted until 1881 and of theater until 1906, only to be replaced afterward by censorship of the cinema.[10]

Modern-day governments have similarly recognized the usefulness of active censors for maintaining social stability and moral norms both under authoritarian regimes and during subsequent democracies. For instance, in June 1997 the supreme court in Chile maintained a ban on the Canadian-U.S. film *The Last Temptation of Christ*, which offended some conservative Catholics, despite the many years that had passed since the Pinochet dictatorship. It took a ruling by the Inter-American Court of Human Rights for the ban to be lifted and for Chile to review and amend its constitutional laws on censorship.[11] Caricatures in particular are designed to contest power, poke fun at the political order, and find humor in the intolerable and injustices; thus they continually face potential backlash from the political establishment.[12] As Leigh Payne has written of political caricatures, such humor can be unsettling for both authoritarian and postauthoritarian governments: "Humor speaks a truth silenced by official channels. It raises a mirror on society that reflects an image very different from the one promoted by the old authoritarian order and its transitional successor."[13]

Peru has a long track record of censorship of the arts. Censorship may have its roots in the nineteenth-century rise of satirical caricatures (a trend echoing contemporary French newspapers), what historian Mario Lucioni refers to as "combat comics" ("*historietas de combate*") in newspapers. They appeared and disappeared sporadically because of state censorship and returned at moments of peace.[14] Theater also reached the censors: President General Manuel Odría (1948–56) closed down a play by Juan Rivera Saavedra, one of Peru's most celebrated playwrights. In this play, *Los profesores* (The teachers, 1958), Rivera recounted the story of teachers driven insane by the insufficiencies of the education system who devised a plan to murder the minister of education.[15] Decades and several military governments later, censorship, state-induced and self-inflicted, was common enough to provide sufficient works for an exhibit in Miraflores, Lima, in 2012 dedicated solely to art that had been removed from view between 1980 and 2010, *Vigilar y castigar: Breve historia de la censura del arte en el Perú* (To watch and to punish: A brief history of censorship in Peru).[16]

In his study of the history of the caricature in Peru, sociologist Carlos Rodrigo Infante Yupanqui sees caricatures as emerging at moments of political tensions and openings, moments in which the caricature is "quintessentially another space where one can order and reorder power dynamics." In his interviews with Peru's best-known caricaturists, Infante notes in particular the

Captive to History

political opening afforded by the scandal of the *vladivideos* showing high-level corruption, after which political drawings increased in Peru's official press. However, even then their creators faced impediments to their political expression. For instance, the caricaturists felt that they still could not attack Fujimori directly in this new opening, so instead they went after Montesinos. According to caricaturist Eduadro Rodríguez ("Heduardo"), "The most intense moment was when things started to fall apart quickly in the last years of *fujimorismo*. We knew that where we [now] could inflict harm was on Montesinos."[17]

With the fall of Fujimori and the return to open elections, Quijano and others were able to publish images, more widely, at least for a time, that would offend the political elite. This might explain in part why the initial publication of Quijano's "Iwo Jima" in a newspaper at the time of the CVR did not initially provoke controversy. The Peruvian press in general was filled with such caricatures challenging Fujimori and the military, and the latter were publicly shamed by the *vladivideos* that showed their complicity in Fujimori's web of corruption. The subsequent controversy surrounding Quijano's "Iwo Jima" a few years later might signal that by 2007 the Armed Forces had already begun to recover from their shame and was striving to protect their image, and as Víctor Vich has noted, displaying the offending caricature in an "official museum" (and a "place of authority") seemed inappropriate in a way that the earlier venue of a newspaper was not.[18]

While authoritarian regimes may practice censorship through laws that curtail expression or through more physically direct means (like threats, kidnapping, torture, forced emigration, and disappearance), in transitional justice processes free speech is supposed to replace authoritarian silencing.[19] For instance, previous censorship laws may be repealed and replaced by others that seek greater openness and transparency, such as through the implementation of freedom of information (FOI) legislation. While only one country in Latin America had such FOI legislation in 1985 (Colombia), with the wave of democratization in the region, by 2011 thirteen others did.[20] Peru passed its own FOI law in 2002. Notwithstanding the return to democracy and an initial expressed will to greater accessibility, formal and informal censorship continued even in the absence of specific censorship laws. Indeed, subtle silencing and muting may be integral to how democracies function. Censorship emerges to maintain "decency" when works offend moral boundaries (such as the display of nudity) or religious sensitivities, or to circumscribe political commentary on issues such as failed state projects, state violence, or collusion in environmental degradation.[21]

The decision to remove artistic representations of the internal conflict, like that of Quijano's "Iwo Jima," may come at the request of government or state officials as well as from private organizations and individuals. Thus, perceived acts of censorship do not necessarily originate with state agents, though the state may be accused of having "censored" works, for at times it is difficult to identify who formally requested a work's removal. Indeed, censorship might also serve as publicity for the artists and the venues exhibiting potentially controversial matter, thus allowing for the possibility of false claims or exaggeration of censorship. Furthermore, as elsewhere in Latin America, self-censorship may be at work, especially among organizations that depend on state publicity contracts, so as to avoid more serious problems with the government and sponsors (what historian and journalist Juan Gargurevich refers to in his study as "publicity boycotts").

Controlling public depictions and portrayals in the arts is distinct from censorship of traditional media in that it does not necessarily involve overt top-down control. During the years of the military government (1968–80), the freedom of the press was circumscribed by efforts to co-opt the media (television, radio, and print) within the state. To this end, Gargurevich notes three stages: the first was the closing of the daily newspapers *Expreso* and *Extra*; the second was their later expropriation along with key radio and television stations through the introduction of the General Law of Telecommunications; and the third was the introduction of a state-controlled national press that in turn weakened traditional media and their owners. One of the first acts by President Belaúnde upon the return to democracy was to restore these companies to their original owners. Nevertheless, Belaúnde and his successor, García, kept the state unit in charge of information created during the years of the military government—though the name changed with each new government—thus the state had its own media channels: state newspapers (for example, *El Peruano*, *La Crónica*, and *La Tercera*), radio (for example, *Radio Nacional* and *Radio La Crónica*), and television (for example, *Canal 7* and *Noticias Andina*).[22] After the "self-coup" in 1992, Fujimori introduced new measures to control the press, which largely relied on the use of bribes and the explosion of Fujimori-condoned "*chicha* press" (sensationalistic newspapers). Indeed, the heads and representatives of newspapers and radio and television stations can be seen accepting money in the *vladivideos*. On the occasion when bribes, threats, or publicity boycotts did not succeed in subordinating the head of the television station *Canal 2*, the government stripped its owner of his Peruvian citizenship and sold the company to minority stockholders. The transitional government of Valentín Paniagua attempted in 2001 to break the concentration of the media in so few hands and to prosecute the heads of the main television stations who had colluded with the Fujimori government. A ruling by the Inter-American Court of Human Rights returned *Canal 2* to its owner, once again a Peruvian citizen.[23] Yet the media remains prone to monopolies: in 2013 80 percent of Peruvian print media formed part of the *El Comercio* group, and most of the radio and television stations belonged to four families.[24]

Censorship is orchestrated not necessarily from the top of the administration but by individuals related to them who take it upon themselves to try to close down or black out negative portrayals. Take, for instance, the impromptu closing of a small installation in the central square of Huánuco in August 2011. Here the Defensoría del Pueblo and a group called Colectivo Post CVR displayed some images taken from a traveling version of the CVR's photography exhibition *Yuyanapaq* to mark the eight years since the truth commission's *Final Report*. A selection of the exhibition had been developed into laminated photographs on boards (ca. 90 cm x 50 cm), and they were displayed on stools on the edge of the plaza. The photographs were not new; they had been taken during the years of conflict, and some had been reproduced in newspapers then and later. Yet these photographs still managed to stir the public: two members of the police radio patrol ransacked the exhibit. A representative of the Defensoría del Pueblo present at the time, Claudia Vega, described how one of the policemen had shouted, "Whose photos are these?" and had accused her of being an apologist for terrorism. Despite showing the policemen their permit to display the photographs in the public plaza, the policemen threw the photographs on the ground, in front of a surprised group that had gathered on the spot. "They had a menacing attitude," Vega recalled. Later, a major from the radio patrol sent someone to the local offices of the Defensoría del Pueblo with his apologies for the disturbance.[25]

It is sometimes hard to determine who removes specific images and why they offend and to identify who benefits from such censorship. This is the case with the exhibition curated by Peruvian visual artist Karen Bernedo that was sponsored and supported through funds earmarked for symbolic reparations by the executive secretary of the Comisión Multisectorial de Alto Nivel (CMAN, High-Level Multisectorial Commission), a commission appointed by the Ministry of Justice and Human Rights.[26] Works from Bernedo's exhibit were removed after complaints were made to the ministry on the day of the opening. On her Facebook page, Bernedo notes the irony of the Ministry of Justice censoring its own exhibition. The traditional media then picked up the story as one of censorship.

This exhibition, *20 años de la historia en el Perú* (20 Years of History in Peru), consisted of several illuminated display boards in an open-air plaza in Villa El Salvador. The display was meant to mark the twentieth anniversary of the capture of Abimael Guzmán as well as to pay homage to María Elena Moyano (a former deputy mayor of the district who had been killed by Shining

Path), the people who had courageously participated in the Walk for Peace in Villa El Salvador in 1992, and the victims of the Tarata bombing (a Shining Path attack in the affluent neighborhood of Miraflores). Just hours after the inauguration of the exhibition—attended by the deputy minister of human rights and access to justice, the mayor of Villa El Salvador, and the sister of María Elena Moyano (a congresswoman from Fujimori's party, Martha Moyano)—twelve pieces were removed, apparently by order of the justice minister.[27]

The seemingly disparate choice of images removed makes it difficult to discern the reasons that the exhibition was censored: press archives, graphics by Álvaro Portales, comic strips by Juan Acevedo and Jesús Cossio, and one piece from Mauricio Delgado Castillo's project "A Day in Memory."[28] Since a main theme of the exhibition was the twenty years since Guzmán's capture, curator Bernedo had been expecting problems from the political wing of Shining Path, MOVADEF, a group that "is very strong in Villa El Salvador."[29] Rather, it was the Ministry of Justice that complained. Perhaps some pressure to remove images came from Martha Moyano, who had expressed her discontent at the time of the inauguration over the use of the word *violence* instead of *terrorism* in some of the descriptions attached to the works. Indeed, Martha Moyano and others have used the image and memory of her sister, María Elena, for competing political ends.[30] As a *fujimorista*, Moyano might also have been offended by Delgado's piece, which suggested that Alberto Fujimori captured Guzmán not to end subversion but rather for electoral gain.

Yet the other images removed do not easily fall into the logic of suppressing public condemnation of Peru's political elite. Rather, the works by cartoonists Jesús Cossio (figure 5.2) and Juan Acevedo (figure 5.3) were openly critical of Abimael Guzmán and Shining Path. In Cossio's short comic, he mocks Guzmán's dogmatism, tracking Guzmán's aging political discourse that concludes with his shouting, "Everything but [a presidential] pardon is illusion." Similarly, Acevedo questions Guzmán's confused thinking, which ends with Guzmán transforming his famous dance of "Zorba the Greek" into a Mexican *ranchera*.

In a filmed conversation posted on the Internet, Cossio and Acevedo try to understand why images critical of Guzmán and Shining Path would be censored.[31] If censorship is to protect the state's interests, they pondered, it seemed impossible to them that the Ministry of Justice would remove artwork that mocked Sendero Luminoso. "Perhaps they made a mistake and they didn't read the comic strips," and thus, they thought the images were "apologetic [of terrorism]." "Everything is possible in the world of bureaucracy," surmised Cossio. Yet making fun of Guzmán has long been a means to respond to

Figure 5.2. Comic by Jesús Cossio illustrating Guzmán's ideological transformation over the years. (Art by Jesús Cossio)

Figure 5.3. Juan Acevedo's comic, published originally in *Perú21*, also makes humor from Guzmán's discourse. (Art by Juan Acevedo)

Shining Path's dogmatism: the figure of Guzmán is important not only in the iconography of Shining Path but also in political humor that attempts to upend Shining Path ideology (as in the case of Cossio) or to display the inadequacies of the state's response to its threat.[32] Nevertheless, to draw Guzmán or any image from Shining Path's pantheon poses a risk, even if it is meant as a joke: artist Alfredo Márquez was sentenced to twenty years in prison for having painted a Warholesque image of Mao with lipstick before a backdrop of a repeating image of incarcerated Shining Path members. As Juan Acevedo remarked in response to the censorship of his own comic, such a disproportionate response based on a misunderstanding reflects a continued "lack of calmness" among government officials. Cossio added it might yet be worse because such censorship denies MOVADEF sympathizers the opportunity to learn what Shining Path thought and who they were, and thus lessen their appeal to poorly informed youth.

Cossio and Acevedo might be correct that state officials misunderstood what their works meant or that they had simply made an ill-calculated response. Yet when placed in the larger context of censorship in Peru's democracy, this particular event falls into a larger trend. Members of Peru's state institutions may simply be fearful of *any* mention of the past, even when Shining Path is criticized, as in the case of Cossio's and Acevedo's drawings. This concern over the power of Shining Path ideology and imagery (such as the objects housed in the DIRCOTE museum discussed in the previous chapter) as well as portrayals of the less-than-heroic acts of the Armed Forces was not isolated to an occasional act of inexplicable censorship but occurred when a growing number of cases against military men were before the Peruvian judiciary and reflect the rising political aspirations of the Armed Forces.[33]

Censorship occurred to protect the image of the Armed Forces as military men enter the political mainstream or wish to maintain their position. This may explain why a small sculpture that had been on display in the Ayacucho museum of disappeared family members (ANFASEP) since 2005 suddenly received attention ten years after its installation. In early April 2015, some Peruvian newspapers reported that two members of congress, Carlos Tubino and Daniel Mora—both with personal links to the Armed Forces—criticized a sculpture that they deemed inappropriate for public display. (Tubino, of Keiko Fujimori's political movement Fuerza Popular, was a retired admiral, and Mora, originally of Alejandro Toledo's Perú Posible, was a military officer and formerly the minister of defense under Humala.) The sculpture depicts a soldier kicking a campesino (or pushing him with his foot), while he points a double-barreled gun at the two campesinos (figure 5.4). On the ground lies a sobbing woman holding on to the soldier's leg, presumably begging him to

Figure 5.4. Sculpture in ANFASEP's Museo de la Memoria, Ayacucho. (Photograph by Markus Weissert)

release her loved ones. From Tubino's perspective, the small sculpture "depicts the Armed Forces as violators of campesinos' rights; it is a very hard and strong [*dura y fuerte*] image, one that does not deserve to be there or exhibited." Similarly, Mora stated that the piece showed only one side of reality, and that if "excesses" had been committed by the Armed Forces, this did not mean that all military men behaved so. Mora was concerned that the sculpture gave the impression that they [the museum curators and caretakers] "do not know that the Forces of Order combated terrorism and that they fought for a democratic government. [This sculpture] makes the Army look bad." The ANFASEP president, Adelina García, was surprised by the sudden criticism from "some *señores* who did not live the violence." She stated, "I lived the violence and this is why this [sculpture] has been on exhibit since 2005." ANFASEP had never been questioned about this piece previously, even though other military men and members of congress had visited the museum, and even though the German president Joachim Gauck had come to the museum in March 2015 accompanied by a Peruvian state entourage.[34] Indeed, compared to the even more violent portrayal of the military and much larger mural outside the museum for all passersby to see, this small sculpture, situated in a wall nook and behind glass, seems rather insignificant.[35]

The controversy around the play *La cautiva* is another conspicuous example of the still-strong social and political prohibition against public mention of the human rights abuses committed by the Armed Forces. The reaction to this play by state security forces and government spokespeople at the end of 2014 demonstrated that more is at stake than simply a lack of reading and calmness, an overreaction, or the use of politically opportune moments. Rather, there seems to be a concerted effort by individuals within the Armed Forces to circumscribe public discourse over Peru's contested past, including when this public comes from the "integrated society" that had earlier permitted the double scandal described by Salomón Lerner in his delivery of the CVR's *Final Report* in Lima.

The Use of "Apology for Terrorism" as a Means to Censor the Past

La cautiva, as staged in the theater La Plaza, takes place in one room: a morgue in the city of Huanta in highlands Peru, in the mid-1980s after the military had been installed to address the threat of Shining Path.[36] In the opening scene, a doctor sits in a corner reading a paper and listening to the radio, while his young assistant prepares a naked body for an autopsy. On the radio, the news broadcasts the latest confrontation between Shining Path and the military. The doctor, from Lima, rants for a while and then rises to list the possessions of the cadaver, a young marine: his clothes, a lollypop, and a letter from his mother. The bruised body lies inert as they clean it. Afterward, they place the corpse into a drawer of the too-full morgue, which is soon to receive many more bodies, according to the news. To save space, they lay the marine in the same drawer as the body of a *senderista* whom the assistant had similarly prepared earlier. The doctor places the arm of the *senderista* over the marine so that they both fit into the drawer and to prevent the marine from rolling out: "*como novios*" (like lovers); he smirks, thus sexualizing their corpses and equating two forces—that of the state and of Shining Path.

In a dark corner lies another body, now next in line, that of a young girl, "with the face of an angel," notes the doctor. The doctor leaves the assistant to prepare her for an autopsy while he goes off to eat. This is the heart of the play: the assistant hears the girl's story, even though she is dead, the story of what happened to her and her family, and he helps her to find solace so that she can die in peace and make the transition to the hereafter.

The assistant and the cadaver introduce themselves: Mauro and María Josefa. While Mauro thinks he has lost his mind and is angry with the girl for having broken the solitude of his job and the certainty that comes with working with dead bodies, he cannot get María Josefa to keep silent. She will not let him return to the tranquility of his work. María Josefa's story is one of horror: the young girl had been captured when the Army came to her house; they killed her parents (elementary school teachers who espoused Shining Path ideology of a more equal, just society); and they took the young girl as captive and war booty.[37] Her post-mortem wish is to eat breakfast again with her *abuela*, to finish school, to dream of her sweetheart Esteban, and to turn fifteen and celebrate her coming of age. As she oscillates between her truncated life's trajectory and the reality of her brutal death, Mauro's resistance crumbles, and he accepts the necessity of imagination. When María Josefa remarks that she is thirsty, he takes in his hands pure water from the Andean mountaintops and offers her a drink. Though complaining of no glass, she accepts the water from his empty hands and quenches her thirst. An agreement is struck: they will imagine together.

Mauro asks María Josefa to sleep a little while so that when she awakes she will be ready for the day of her fifteenth birthday. She agrees. While sleeping he cleans her, preparing for the autopsy, yet washing away the sins committed against her. He then dresses her in the clothes of an earlier corpse, one who must have been a bride killed on her wedding night. When María Josefa awakes, Mauro pretends to be her grandmother getting her ready for the big day. María Josefa puts on the wedding dress (marked with faded bloodstains) and listens to Mauro-the-grandmother's stories of her birth. Excited, they prepare for the festivities. The sounds outside the morgue are incorporated into their role-playing: it is Semana Santa (Holy Week). Indeed, it is Holy Friday, the day when Jesus dies and thus cannot witness what takes place on earth. There is no protective saint.[38] Mauro then transforms into María Josefa's fancy, Esteban, and he takes her on innocent and awkward adventures of young love. Their happiness is interrupted by the noises from outside that can no longer be held at bay. There is a loud knocking at the morgue's door. The door flies open, and in comes the local Army base captain—the man who had killed the girl (figure 5.5). Mauro whispers to María Josefa that the man is a mythical figure here to bless her on her *quinceañera*. But no, he is here to rape her, soon to be followed by his subordinates. When the captain lies on top of the body, shuddering with passion, Mauro stabs and kills him with a knife. This is the play's culminating moment.

The next scene has all the dead of the morgue waking up and reenacting, through a kind of dance, the battle between Shining Path and the state (represented by the *senderista* and the soldier, who have climbed out of the drawer) over possession of the pueblo (María Josefa). At one point, María Josefa appears

Figure 5.5. María Josefa, Mauro, and the Army base commander in *La cautiva*. (Photograph by Carlos Galiano and provided by La Plaza Theater)

like the Virgin Mary in a Holy Week procession. This otherworldly scene of flowing movement ends abruptly: the doctor has returned to the morgue and seeing the Army captain dead, and Mauro with a knife in hand, accuses Mauro of "being one of them," a *senderista*. The doctor runs out quickly to tell others. Mauro then kills himself. Now dead, he can join María Josefa, who agrees to take him with her to the New Huanta, a beautiful place of bright, pure light. The play ends thus.

In its cast of characters, *La cautiva* sticks closely to the different historical personages who also emerged in the CVR's account: the doctor who represents "*Lima de espaldas*" (Lima with its back turned away); the *senderista* (both in María Josefa's portrayal of her fanatical father espousing dogmatically their fight for a more just society and in the dance of the resurrected young *senderista*); the Army captain's drunkenness, vulgarity, and brutality; and María Josefa, the pueblo caught between two fires, whose youthful innocence makes her a victim, one upon which all Peruvians can agree.

Mauro is perhaps the least stereotypical character in this play in the sense that there seems to be little historical precedent from which to draw upon, yet it is this very character who brings this past into the present. Mauro's initial inaction, his lack of courage, his preference to be in the company of the

Captive to History

nonspeaking dead are shattered when he agrees to imagine with María Josefa. He finds courage, so much so that he defends her dead body and takes his own life, though in so doing recognizes himself as "guilty" (for he killed the Army captain). As Luis Alberto León, the playwright, said in an after-play forum, "Mauro is what Peru should have been but was not."[39]

But how to reach this Peru, the *limeño* audience of the comfortable classes ("integrated society") who like Mauro at the beginning of the play were silent, and who despite a decade since the truth commission still claim not to have known or just recently know? They are the many "doctors" of Lima who, as in the play, turned their backs during the violence of the 1980s and 1990s. How to get them to come and see this play? Could this play reach them in a way that the CVR did not, teach them to be more empathetic, like Mauro? Signs with María Josefa's sad face crowned in white advertised the play on the corners of Lima's posh neighborhoods. Literary and art-scene luminaries promoted the play in flashy announcements posted on the Internet, in newspapers and magazines, and on TV programs, and the play was sponsored in part by Starbucks.

The director of La Plaza Theater clearly attempted to reach out to this "unknowing" (or "not wanting to know") public. In a discussion between the author, León, and the director, Chela De Ferrari, De Ferrari stated that for her it was important that this work, the first Peruvian work she had produced, take place in her theater: "I know that part of our public thinks that it is unnecessary, harmful, *even dangerous*, to speak of these years. And I have spoken with well-intentioned individuals, but I believe that these are thoughts that do not permit us to grow. How can we progress if we are not able to examine one of the most difficult moments in our history? If we do not speak of these years, our thoughts will end up frivolous." Indeed, it seems that both the director and the author wanted to take members of their social class on a journey similar to the one they themselves had made the previous decade when they came to realize how dreadful the conflict had been. For De Ferrari, her play was "a small symbolic reparation for all that I did not do before. For some time, I have asked myself how could this happen? Where was I during this? What was my responsibility in all this?"[40]

Indeed, her peer group was the public—affluent *limeños*—who attended *La cautiva* (tickets cost around sixty soles, approximately twenty USD). During the play, the audience laughed at times, perhaps a nervous response to the drama unfolding. A couple sitting in front of me used the darkness to exchange small kisses, and only some in attendance stood up for an ovation of this work, though critics called it the best Peruvian play of 2014. The distance between the audience and the historical protagonists as well as between the location of the performance and the place where the violence occurred was reinforced by the actors' use of *castellano quechuizado*, a Spanish filled with Quechua words and rhythm. Each Thursday after the play, a public forum was held where audience members could ask questions of the director, the author, the actors, and the research assistants. And while it was encouraging to hear a public dialogue over this past—at least from the third of the audience who chose to remain—it also showed the limits of engagement. Along with questions such as "What was I doing during the conflict?" were comments such as "Thank you for opening my eyes"; both echo sentiments that were expressed in page after page of the comment books of the CVR's photography exhibit *Yuyanapaq*, the visual accompaniment to its *Final Report*, ten years earlier.[41]

Once eyes are open, is one's vision changed? How does one bring this knowledge into the present in a way that does not reify or entrench the positions over the past? As De Ferrari and León discussed, "if we are unable to review this past, and try to understand what happened . . . and to recognize ourselves as a society, the inequality will continue to live, and the horror be born."[42] Their concern was prescient. For while the play is oddly frozen in a faraway past—Ayacucho in the 1980s—the legacies were still very much present when the play was performed. In the months following the play, the head of DIRCOTE, the head prosecutor for anticorruption and antisubversion (*procurador* Julio Galindo), and the minister of the interior launched an investigation into *La cautiva* as a potential "incitement of terrorism," a crime that carries a possible prison sentence of up to twelve years, for its portrayal of the Armed Forces and Shining Path.[43]

The particular scenes in *La cautiva* that caught the attention of the heads of several state units, including the then-minister of the interior, Daniel Urresti, were the ones that depicted *both* the Armed Forces and Shining Path. According to the official DIRCOTE report of December 29, 2014, which reached the media (with the word *secret* stamped on top), an active colonel had filmed with his cellphone the performance and the after-play discussion the previous month.[44] Based on this recording, DIRCOTE concluded that the play might constitute an "incitement of terrorism." Excerpts of the play's text were reproduced in the report, phrases such as "Long live the Communist Party!," "Long live the armed battle!," "Long live President Gonzalo!" (a reference to the Shining Path leader), followed by the singing of the *senderista* song "The Hymn of the Guerrillero." The report quoted actor Carlos Vitrio, who played the doctor, as saying in the after-play forum that the Armed Forces had never apologized nor accepted their responsibility for their acts of violence.

The key concern over this work, expressed in the opening paragraph of the "secret" document, was that *La cautiva* presented the systematic violation of human rights by the forces of order and that the play "surreptitiously revealed Shining Path objectives." The scenes that potentially disturbed the colonel in

Captive to History

the audience were the act of putting the corpse of the young soldier and that of the *senderista* in the same morgue drawer and the portrayal of the Army base captain as a cruel and abusive man who committed necrophilia. In a long scene, the Army base commander describes his own victimization, the trauma that he has suffered after witnessing Sendero Luminoso's brutality toward communities.[45] Despite the playwright's efforts to humanize the captain (at the urging of the producer), his story of suffering seems far from justifying his own actions as a victimizer and moral deviant.[46]

Though no censorship laws are presently on the books in Peru, the "*apología al terrorismo*" in Peru's penal law may be invoked in their absence. Just days prior to the breaking news about the investigation into *La cautiva*, the minister of interior also closed an art exhibition, titled *En su nombre* (In your name), produced by prisoners incarcerated for being members of Shining Path. This focus on curtailing performance and visual art suggests that the Ministry of the Interior, the Office of the Prosecutor for Anticorruption and Anti-Subversion, the Armed Forces, and the National Police considered themselves as having a wide mandate when assuring that Shining Path does not re-emerge or use cultural venues as forums for its proselytizing. As Urresti stated, "apología al terrorismo" is an investigative tool, though perhaps not one as unbiased as he suggests.

> DIRCOTE is very professional in preventing Shining Path from returning and has the right to do all the investigations it wants. . . . When the PNP [Peruvian National Police, of which DIRCOTE forms a part] [intervene], they are not judging. For this there are courts, the Public Ministry, and the Judiciary. If the Public Ministry presents a complaint, I invite it to consider [the art] as an *apología* [incitement of terrorism]. The police have the obligation to investigate everything. The police don't have an opinion, and nor do I. They do this without prejudice. Calm down; [there is] no reason to be disturbed [*No se alboroten, no hay por qué*].[47]

Narrowing What Integrated Society Sees

In her analysis of cultural memory production in post-transition Argentina, Nancy Gates-Madsen points to the empty spaces, ellipses, and unspoken words about state terrorism in various cultural texts despite the decades that have passed since a military junta governed. During the military regime, bystanders chose not to perceive what was taking place, referring to disappearances, death, and torture under their breath as "*por algo será*" (there must be a reason). The deadened sensibility of fellow citizens' ability to see (or "percepticide," to repeat Diana Taylor's term) continued after the transition.[48] Some topics still remain too difficult to broach for individuals and for society. These silences are sometimes public secrets and sometimes private, and they are all by choice, not the result of authoritarian laws that mute their expression.[49]

Moreover, though governments may shed their former authoritarian censorship laws, other laws that hinder the freedom of speech may persist, beyond the unspoken taboos that suppress expression. In Peru, one of these laws is the *"apología al terrorismo,"* which originated in a series of antiterrorism legislation put forward by Alberto Fujimori that was declared unconstitutional by the Constitutional Court in 2003.[50] Article 7 of Fujimori's decree, however, was salvaged and reintroduced as a subsequent paragraph (Legislative Decree 924) added to the penal code. To be enforced, the law requires that the "incitement" (or "apology") be in reference to an act of terrorism or by an author or participant who has been charged for terrorism.[51] If found guilty, the sentenced individual may face from six to twelve years of imprisonment, and if the apology took place through social media or other Internet means, from eight to fifteen years. This legislation, along with attempts to introduce a Peruvian variant of "Holocaust denial" laws (Ley de Negacionismo, "Law of Negation" proposed in 2012), means that there is a thin tightrope to traverse when broaching the subject of the internal conflict.[52] The fear that an act, a word, a work, a performance, or the like might be considered a possible incitement of or apology for terrorism or a possible qualification or justification of Shining Path limits what one can publicly exhibit and say about the past. One needs to carefully consider whether to portray Shining Path or the Armed Forces, for portraying either risks the cultural producer running afoul of the censors, or worse, facing a criminal sentence. Thus cultural producers might prefer to make only vague illusions to uncomfortable truths, such as Peruvian military collusion with Fujimori, or implicitly draw parallels between the military's behavior in democratic Peru and that of their counterparts in Southern Cone dictatorships.[53]

Yet censorship does not necessarily function as the censors intend. Much like vandals who have repeatedly sought to silence public memories of the conflict's victims, whose names are engraved in the over thirty thousand rocks of the memorial El Ojo que Llora (The Eye That Cries), when censors seek to prevent the diffusion of opinions, they may end up unintentionally sparking debate, if not generating free publicity for the offending works.[54] Thus Quijano's cartoon drew a much greater public when it was shown again in a larger retrospective in an independent gallery just days after the censorship; Bernedo's exhibition, which would have otherwise reached a very limited local population, made it into major newspapers; the LUM received a boom of visitors after Donayre's "exposé"; and *La cautiva* had a second run with free admission at the LUM.

Figure 5.6. Caricature by Carlín (Carlos Tovar) of the antiterrorist prosecutor Julio Galindo stating that he will have to investigate the police officer for having repeated a pro-*senderista* slogan. It was originally published in *La República*. (Art by Carlos Tovar)

By highlighting these examples of silencing art, I do not intend to give the impression that artistic representations of Peru's internal war face censorship in general. Indeed, caricaturists continue to make fun of both the military and the political elite. For instance, in the days following the investigation into *La cautiva* as an incitement of terrorism, the caricaturist Carlos Tovar (Carlín) published in the newspaper *La República* a caricature of the then-antiterrorist prosecutor Julio Galindo in conversation with a Peruvian police officer. Galindo tells the officer that he will have to investigate him for having repeated the phrase "*viva el president Gonzalo*" (long live president Gonzalo) (figure 5.6). Similarly, the theater troupe Yuyachkani has been an outspoken critic of many governments, as well as of Shining Path and the Armed Forces during the conflict.[55] As far as I know, none of its works has been censored.[56] Nor has the Micromuseo of Gustavo Buntix faced overt condemnation for its series of exhibitions that relate to the conflict, including a show dedicated to the work of Ricardo Wiesse on the Cantuta massacre committed by the government-sponsored paramilitary squad Grupo Colina (one of the charges for which Fujimori was incarcerated).[57] The mural graphically portraying the brutality of the Armed Forces still covers the walls of the ANFASEP museum in Ayacucho.

What made it possible for these works to escape the censor, yet not *La cautiva*, might have something to do with the audiences they reach: in the case of Yuyachkani's performances on a fixed stage, they tend to speak to spectators already sympathetic to their views, people whom the political elite and the Armed Forces would consider the "caviar."[58] However, *La cautiva* succeeded in reaching a different audience beyond the caviar who previously had not acknowledged or did not wish to acknowledge the different actors, including state actors, who had participated in the violence. The play received their critical acclaim.[59] That is, *La cautiva* reached members of "integrated society" who had turned their backs during the conflict (an audience that had previously suffered from "percepticide"). This time it was members of the previously "not seeing" integrated society who came to the defense of those involved in *La cautiva*, by invoking the right of artistic freedom—the right to fictionalize military abuse. Once they cried out, the case against *La cautiva* was dropped after ten stressful days for the playwright, the producer, the actors, and the theater staff.

In this debate over the limits of what a play could present (and to whom), integrated society was reminded of what remained taboo. Thus, when Chela de Ferrari proved correct in her fear that broaching the past might be "dangerous," or when Cossio worried that mocking a public enemy might be interpreted as an "apology for terrorism," or Quijano found his drawings removed years after their first publication, they all experienced the limits of what could be comfortably expressed in public. Despite the transition to peace and democracy, the risk remains: by opening one's eyes and recognizing the historical past, one may be held captive in its wake or cut by the censor.

In August 2017 even the LUM fell victim to what many might see as the censor's scissors. On the morning after the inauguration of a temporary exhibition involving thirty-six artists, *Carpeta Colaborativa: De Resistencia Visual, 1992–2017* (Collaborative folder: Visual resistance, 1992–2017), the minister of culture, Salvador del Solar, and his chief of staff, Denise Ledgard, responded to complaints by a Congress member of Keiko Fujimori's party (Fuerza Popular) who stated that it was "anti-Fujimori." The exhibition treated 1992 as a pivotal year in the conflict (Fujimori's self-coup, the death of activist Pedro Huilca, the Cantuta massacre, the capture of Guzmán, the Shining Path Tarata attack, and the murder of activist Moyano) but examined its broader political legacies.[60] Del Solar, who was known for his film about a former army soldier turned taxi driver haunted by his memories, *Magallanes* (2014), and Ledgard, who had previously been director of the LUM and who had largely brought the permanent exhibition to fruition, were now on the "other side of the desk." Indeed, less than two years before, prior to their posts in the ministry, both del Solar and Ledgard had signed the January 12, 2015, letter "En defensa de *La cautiva*" (In defense of *La cautiva*), which states that "we consider that this [DIRCOTE] investigation [into *La cautiva*] emerges from a profound lack of understanding of the role of culture as an agent of reflection and to raise awareness of the community, and that it is an attack on the liberty of expression."[61]

Seemingly distant from his earlier concern over the freedom of artistic expression, del Solar requested the resignation of the then LUM director, Guillermo Nugent, for exhibiting this show in a state museum. According to del Solar's Facebook post, this was not a case of censorship. Rather, del Solar stated that Nugent had not respected his mandate to foster the LUM as "a space in which all Peruvians can get closer to the delicate theme of memory with an open mind, and as much as possible, without feeling attacked, excluded, or inclined to reject the idea of visiting, to anticipate or assume the predominance of a single vision or a political position over others." From the minister's perspective, this artistic exhibition was biased and the director should not have shown it. Though the director resigned, the exhibition remained in place, and visitors were invited to see it in order to judge for themselves. This contradiction of condemning the exhibition while promoting it was apparent to some who participated in social media debates. Yet a warning was clear to most: the LUM director was censored for having put it on display.

Conclusion

The Army's Dirge and Countermemorial Resurrection in the Era of Human Rights

El Ejército unido a la historia
por fecunda y viril tradición,
se corona con lauros de gloria
al forjar una libre nación.

Evocando un pasado glorioso
del Incario su antiguo esplendor,
Ayacucho, Junín, Dos de Mayo
libertad conquistó con valor
Zarumilla, La Breña y Arica
gestas son que a la historia legó
Bolognesi ¡oh, sublime soldado!
por patrono ejemplar te aclamo.

Las fronteras altivo defiende
cual guardián del honor nacional
de su pueblo recibe las armas
y es bastión de justicia social.
Soy soldado que en filas milito
y un deber tengo yo que cumplir,
a la patria vivir consagrado
y por ella luchar a morir.

The Army united to history
by fertile and virile tradition,
is crowned with laurels of glory
by forging a free nation.

Evoking a glorious past
of the Inca's ancient splendor,
Ayacucho, Junin, Dos de Mayo
freedom conquered with courage.
Zarumilla, La Breña, and Arica
deeds that are bequeathed to history
Bolognesi oh, sublime soldier!
I hail you as an exemplary patron.

The borders he proudly defends
like a guardian of national honor
from his people he receive the arms
and is bastion of social justice.
I am a soldier who in these ranks militate
and I have a duty to fulfill,
to live dedicated to the homeland
and to fight to the death for her.

n the hymn of the Peruvian Army, "El Éjercito unido a la historia," the history of the nation and that of the Army are one.[1] The chorus repeats throughout the song that "the Army [is] united to history." That this hymn predates the conflict is a clear reminder that the participation of the Peruvian Armed Forces in contemporary debates over the nation's past is not a new engagement. Indeed, the Army has long considered itself integral to that history and the nation. What ties the Army to the republic and its people is a sense of common descent from an Incaic past and their courageous battles for independence and against foreign occupiers; the Army is bound to the nation by the duty to protect the "national honor," to be a "bastion of social justice," and "to fight to the death" for the nation. Though rooted in nineteenth-century notions of a shared national history and imagined community, this hymn, adopted in 1973, emerged in the years of strong nationalist sentiments of a military government, that of General Juan Velasco Alvarado. Though most of the themes and historical moments evoked by the hymn predate the military regime, they also continue into the present day as Army men and women raise their voices in unison, singing to their patron Bolognesi and to their nation.

Yet the Army's patriotic hymn came to sound more like a dirge in the wake of the scandals that embroiled the Armed Forces with the fall of Alberto Fujimori's government in 2000, of the CVR's findings in 2003 that not only were the Armed Forces and National Police responsible for some 36 percent of the killings and forced disappearances, but at certain times and places this violence equaled systematic abuse of human rights, and of the subsequent legal prosecutions against those military personnel responsible for corruption and crimes against humanity that locked even the most mighty behind bars by 2009. "El Éjercito unido a la historia" transformed into a funereal song in the era of human rights, sung solemnly for a dead, past time when the Army was seen as a bastion of social justice, the defender of the nation, an honorable institution.

The Army's narrative used to be entwined with the *gran relato* (grand story) of the nation, but with the lengthy conflict with fellow citizens, the CVR's findings, and the sentencing of military men, the Army became decoupled from the nation, for the heroes were no longer immaculate, and their errors were apparent to many. While the military had inflicted violence on citizens previously and had through most of Peru's republican history defended the interests of the oligarchy, the Revolutionary Government of the Armed

Forces of the late 1960s nurtured a vision of the Army as *del pueblo*, of the people. Yet years later, emerging from the conflict of the 1980s and 1990s, the Army was a battered and morally demoralized institution, whose link to the common citizen seemed remote, even though it had been victorious in the battle against Shining Path. As the soldier studying in the human rights program at the Universidad Católica del Perú tried to remind me, "Senorita Doctora, no olvide usted que había buenos militares también." But in the memory landscape right after the transition and the CVR, as well as during the trials, it was hard to see who those "good military" might have been.

In the more than ten years since the CVR issued its *Final Report*, the Armed Forces (the Army in particular) did much cultural work to improve their image, to draw the public's attention to the "*buenos*," and to narrate a different version—their version—of what took place. The Armed Forces argued that for various reasons the CVR got it wrong (the commissioners were biased, absent, did not interview military members, and, as outsiders, could not possibly understand the honor of these institutions); they explained that the human rights violations and crimes against humanity were "errors" by individuals, produced in moments of distress, and the product of "excesses"; they exhibited the suffering of their own members and the great sacrifices they had made; they pointed to their own heroism; and, at times, they hinted at contrition. Yet there were also members of the Armed Forces and those close to them who displayed little remorse and belligerently continued to insist that they had saved the nation and to deny wrongdoing and human rights violations.

Though the trials are ongoing and the whiff of foul play still surrounds individual members of the military, the military seems to have managed to rebuild its public image nonetheless, and military men have returned to the political stage as electoral candidates, congressmen, and even president. That is, the Army's efforts to repair its image—which employed many cultural works along with other more formal, institutional venues—succeeded not only in reattaching the Army to the body politic but also in shifting the content of Peru's memory debates. The Army's memory production in the wake of its shame has done much to restore its earlier sense of honor and self by improving how the military is perceived from both within and without the institution. The dirge "El Éjercito unido a la historia" has transformed into a ballad of resurrection and redemption. In the decade and more since the CVR, many events point to this narrative shift: for instance, the 2011 election of Ollanta Humala as president despite rumors of human rights violations; the 2015 LUM script, which highlights the Armed Forces' sacrifice, heroism, and efforts to learn how to confront Shining Path; and the nearly unanimous decision to honor the Chavín de Huántar commandoes in Congress "as heroes of democracy" on April 17, 2017, in anticipation of the twenty-year anniversary of the rescue.[2]

"El Éjercito unido a la historia" reminds us not only that the Army has an already-entrenched sense of history and its place in it but also that the Armed Forces' participation in the realm of public culture is nothing new. The military's use of culture is not a recent tactic for public persuasion. As noted in the introduction, in Peruvian towns and cities, military memories were already deeply etched into urban topography. In addition to the many monuments to military heroes (especially those of independence and the War of the Pacific), the streets themselves are military memorial sites. From large boulevards to small streets, the urban landscape bears the names of the nation's military heroes (such as Bolognesi, Miró Quesada, Pardo). That in 1986, at the height of the conflict with Shining Path, a statue was erected in tribute to Andrés Cáceres (who led an unsuccessful resistance campaign against nineteenth-century Chilean occupiers) in the middle-class Lima neighborhood of San Isidro tells us that the Armed Forces have always wielded "soft" power in the form of urban beautification and planning (figure C.1), what we might consider careful curations to evoke a shared glorious past. Cityscapes are themselves memoryscapes of national histories, a material culture erected on the streets and etched into monuments, the product of top-down efforts by municipal and national governments to build a sense of common heritage, a common identity.[3]

This sense of a common identity is deeply held by many Peruvians, for military culture is passed on through education and military service. Generations of schoolchildren have been taught to admire the nation's military heroes. Thousands of conscripts and *licenciados* (graduates) returned to their homes after the internal armed conflict. They participate in civic festivities, dressed in military regalia and marching in military style. Civilians also imitate military culture by the purchase of clothes that resemble those of enlisted men and women.[4] As one rural participant in a parade explained, "We are dressed like the military, because we are Peruvians."[5] This broader military culture in Peruvian society helps explain why Peruvians mimic the military (in parades, in clothing and the like) and why Peruvians (especially in rural regions) might join the military (as a path to social mobility and because of a sense of national pride) and later return to their communities as *licenciados* or former *ronderos* expecting recognition for their role in defeating Shining Path.

🝆

Figure C.1. A memorial to Cáceres erected in San Isidro (Lima) in 1986. (Photographs by author)

War, triumph, resilience, conflict, "these are the stuff of national histories," writes anthropologist Sharon Macdonald, and for much of the nineteenth and twentieth century they were seen as signs of "a country's achievements." Yet more recently such glorious pasts for many countries are "understood as a reason for regret": colonialism is no longer envisioned as bringing unquestioned good to dependent peoples but is now considered a shameful past; battles once trumpeted as triumphs are now quiet "sources of embarrassment."[6] But this shift from earlier honor to present-day regret is fairly recent for many countries (my own included), and it is in this shifting yet overlapping terrain of a nineteenth-century conception of nation and the twenty-first century discomfort over a "difficult heritage" that the Peruvian Armed Forces find themselves caught by history. For with the turn to transitional justice and human rights, the Armed Forces find that their past actions are not understood as honorable or noble, even though they won the battle against Shining Path. Further compounding this problem of being both caught and tied to history—the nation and the military—is that this difficult heritage resides in living memory as opposed to faraway acts.

Despite an awareness that times have changed, much of the means by which the military understands and cares for this past in its curatorial efforts are stuck in the older museological and monument-building era of the unproblematic good of nation building, and how they envision themselves and their role in the nation is still framed by the chorus of the Army's hymn of "united to history" by honor. Thus, a key tension in contemporary memory battles in Peru is between the more traditional modes of nation building through public space (such as memorials, monuments, and museums) and the content of these spaces, which in the era of human rights makes the pasts they represent far from noble. The military counters this ignoble perception by returning to earlier methods and practices of nation building, but it does so employing the language, lexicon, and tools of the more recent memory and transitional justice discourses as a means to repackage the historical content.

The epitaph to the Army's report *En honor a la verdad* concluding section, which includes the "Lessons Learned," is an example of such use of memory and transitional justice discourse: "The space of memory is thus an arena of political struggle that is frequently conceived in terms of a struggle 'against oblivion': remember so as not to repeat. These slogans, however, can be tricky. [Slogans such as] 'memory against forgetting' or 'against silence' hide an opposition between distinct, rival memories (each one with its own forgetfulness). This is, in truth, 'memory against memory.'"[7] That the Peruvian Army would choose to cite Elizabeth Jelin's important distinction—that what is at work in post-conflict societies is not necessarily memory countering silence or oblivion but rather memories in competition—suggests an awareness by members of the Armed Forces not only of the stakes involved in nurturing and advancing their memories in the public sphere but also of the field of memory studies.[8] That is, they are aware of the memory market as both a battlefield and an academic field.

In coining the expression the *justice cascade* to describe the reverberation of human rights prosecutions as a global norm, political scientist Kathryn Sikkink focused on the tireless work of NGOs, activists, lawyers, and judges who formed local and international human rights community. Rebecca Atencio reminds us that we must also pay attention to the interplay between culture and transitional justice mechanisms to understand how these new norms take root.[9] Yet such efforts to produce new norms fall not solely into the camp of human rights advocates and cultural producers but also into the camp of state agents and negationists who seek to assert pro-military memories that deny the historical past. The same lexicon and narrative structures that organize and disseminate these new norms may come into play but with a twist when used by armed state actors. Several key terms and phrases emerge repeatedly in their writings—*truth, para no olvidar, justice, victims, reconciliation,* and *human rights*—but they mean something different when coming from regime insiders: *not to forget* the terrorist threat; *never again* Shining Path and inept governments; the lack of *justice* that incarcerates heroic soldiers who fought to save the nation and democracy; they are the *victims* first of Shining Path violence and later of a vengeful democracy at the hands of the caviar Left, which threaten the possibility of reaching reconciliation; and the related abuse of their *human right* to forget and their right to fair judgment based on the rules at that time. These terms are all key concepts in transitional justice processes to which military men find themselves vulnerable, yet they are also the same concepts that these military agents employ in their cultural memory production so as to shift the public debate over the past. As Ann Burlein has written of the religious right in the United States, "Such memories are *counter* not because they are foreign to the mainstream, but because they draw on mainstream currents in order to redirect their flow."[10]

The military and its memory producers are mindful of the turn to human rights and its international resonance. Again and again this notion (if not necessarily the term) turns up in their fictional and nonfictional accounts: they define the term *human rights*, they negate having systematically violated them, and they ask, somewhat rhetorically, about the respect of their own human rights, which have come under attack after the transition. In the latter use of the concept, the Army shifts itself from perpetrator to victim, again a movement

Figure C.2. The memorial to the Armed Forces' fallen personnel during the years of violence in the main military base (El Pentagonito) in San Borja, Lima. (Photograph by author)

that takes a mainstream current and redirects the flow. Along with the rise in human rights discourse has come the expansion of victims groups considered as socially legitimate. Thus the military lays claim to its human rights and subsequently its victimhood.[11]

Take, for instance, memory sites. The practice of naming victims is an often-used means of symbolic reparations. One of the few national sites for remembering the victims of the internal conflict is El Ojo que Llora (The Eye That Cries), erected by a consortium of NGOs and citizens in 2005, which is situated in a locked garden within Lima's Campo de Marte (Martian Fields), (which, coincidently, is not far from where the annual Military National Parade is often held). Though the monument is somewhat difficult to reach, it is a site for remembering the dead *and* for contesting the past, as evinced through the site's repeated defacement.[12] El Ojo que Llora was not, however, Lima's first memorial to commemorate the internal armed conflict's dead. The military had also turned to naming the dead in stone while Fujimori was president, years before El Ojo que Llora. In a quiet part of the central military base, El Pentagonito, not far from the one-story barracks of the CPHEP, sits a massive monument, a series of slabs that create a curved wall of names (figure C.2).

The naming of the fallen soldiers harks back to a traditional form for commemorating their sacrifice for the greater national good. Yet the Pentagonito's memorial does not evince the same opening to egalitarian inclusiveness as El

Figure C.3. The memorial to the Armed Forces' fallen personnel during the years of violence in the military headquarters in San Borja, Lima. Note in the lower center that Fujimori's name and the date were removed from the memorial despite the quote that came from his dedication ("that my words are for those who put aside their interests, and devoted themselves to the nation with the greatest cost of their lives"). (Photograph by author)

Ojo que Llora, not simply because it excludes nonmilitary victims but also by the ordering of those named. In their shared sacrifice, the military's victims reflect the hierarchical and ethnic divisions of the Armed Forces. Each slab is organized by division within the Armed Forces, year of death, rank, and name. This organizational structuring illuminates the ethnic and class divisions within Peru's security forces: most of the names engraved into the slabs are those of members of the National Police and the Army, fewer to members of the Marines, and only a handful to members of the Air Force.[13] The whiter, the wealthier, the fewer the names. The memorial also marks erasure of inconvenient memories: Fujimori's name was removed from his dedication of the monument (figure C.3).

These hierarchical divisions are more than organizational schemes for memorializing the dead; they also show real divisions and tensions within the Armed Forces, which do not share a homogenous version of the past. Not only have *fujimorista* memories been physically erased, but the Marines, the Air Force, and the *ronderos* are shown as secondary to the victory. It is the Army and the National Police that suffered the most casualties, and it is mainly their members who face trials and long sentences. This may, in part, explain why most of the cultural works that I have discussed here were produced by the Army and not by the Marines or the Air Force.

A key tension in contemporary memory battles resides within the Armed Forces, and particularly within the Army branch. The Army has its own institutional memories that do not necessarily map onto those of the Marines, for instance. Furthermore, while the Army's hymn harks back to a collective memory—an Incaic past, a courageous struggle for independence, the War of the Pacific—these themes of honor and duty in defense of the nation are placed in question by the very acts that the soldiers committed or were asked to participate in during the confrontation with Shining Path. The individual memories of soldiers do not necessarily correspond with their group's collective memory, as dissident voices make clear, like those of the rank and file who testified before the CVR, and like some who chose to publish their own story, such as Jesús Sosa and Lurgio Gavilán.

Nor does the next generation of soldiers, the men and women who have joined the military since the end of the conflict and after Fujimori, identify with this past.[14] Anthropologist Máximo Badaró, in his insightful study of the Argentine military, employs the metaphor of a soldier's backpack (*mochila*) to describe the relationship of the newer generation of soldiers to the institution's shameful past. All recruits receive a backpack as part of their equipment and provisions, and while they are obligated by the state to wear this backpack, it does not belong to them but remains the property of the Army. So too this past: the soldiers of the newer generation carry the weight of this past, but they do not own it.[15]

Curating this past in order to lighten this *mochila* is part of the work performed by the Armed Forces' memory entrepreneurs. We cannot necessarily attribute intentionality or point to a single meeting when a plan was hatched to boost the military's image, but the Armed Forces' memory interventions do correlate with a spirit of the times, a memory boom that began with human rights groups and NGOs and was then picked up by the Armed Forces. Peru's military is not unique in trying to restore and remake itself after a prolonged conflict; many other post–Cold War militaries have recounted their past in a transitional justice present (as was the case for other historical defeats, such as

Napoleon's exile in Elba or the US army after Vietnam). For instance, the Argentine military exhibits many of the same trends and reformulations of the past, and it too uses human rights tools and vocabulary, though it did so earlier and over a longer period of time than Peru.[16] Colombia seems to have inspired some Peruvian military cultural productions, in particular General Edwin Donayre's book *El silencio de los héroes*.[17] Among Latin American militaries, Guatemala is probably the most active in attempting to advance a counternarrative to the 1998 UN-mandated truth commission, giving rise to a subfield in military historiography that has developed in tandem with the judicial proceedings against military men (cases such as Ríos Montt, Dos Eres, Plan de Sánchez, and Sepur Zarco), a field that is supported by private universities, individual academics, and veterans' associations.[18] In Peru, these memory entrepreneurs include very public figures such as General Edwin Donayre and General Daniel Urresti and organizations such as ADDCOT, the CPHEP, the Universidad Alas Peruanas (which is behind much of the production of the cultural works examined here), and the Asociación Civil Patria, which facilitates legal counsel for accused military men.

Yet another layer of memory entrepreneurs work outside the limelight toward improving the military's image and restoring its supposed earlier honor. In my study of military memories in Peru's public sphere, I have noted a network of memory entrepreneurs, composed of individuals who attempt to bring the Armed Forces', especially the Army's, version of the conflict into the public realm and Peru's memory debates through different cultural texts.[19] Many of these memory entrepreneurs come from this newer generation of military personnel, who are obliged to carry the military's backpack yet do not claim ownership. I have had the opportunity to speak with some of these individuals, who act as guides in museums or as functionaries of the state and the Army, a few with military rank. I have not sought out anyone who does not already hold a public function. They have engaged the public through workshops, presentations, televised interviews, or published memoirs. None of them fit the image of a hard military man with a shady past. Indeed, most were not directly involved in the conflict, some are women, and all seemed genuinely concerned about their institutions' role in the violence. They are, of course, the Army's public face and have either selected themselves for these posts or have been selected for their abilities, including their interpersonal skills.

The Army may have brushed itself off, regrouped, and returned to the fold of democracy, but there are still some dispirited members among its ranks. When I asked one young soldier what it was like to be a female in the military, she said that she was proud of being part of the Army. She followed this statement by saying that when she walks through villages wearing her uniform, people greet her warmly. But when in Lima, she is sometimes coldly asked how she could possibly join an institution that committed such violence, especially against women. Her answer to such a question expressed a hope that her presence and that of other women in the Army would prevent it from happening again. "It's complicated," she said.

This idea that the past is complicated is at the heart of the supposed paradox of perpetrators and victims that several military members raised with me. They ask how could it be that soldiers inflicted harm on people like themselves? That the social, ethnic, and geographical profiles of the victims and the perpetrators were so similar aligns with the two central narratives within the Army's reformulation of the past: that members of the Armed Forces too were victims (as represented, for instance, by the wall-sized photograph of the dead soldier in a body bag on temporary display at the LUM, figure 4.8), and that the Army is of the people; as in the hymn, they are united by a common history.

Speaking with soldiers of this newer generation and with some from the previous generation, I got the sense that they see themselves as different from the Armed Forces of the conflict years, but that they are the legacy of Velasco that had been pushed to the margins by the hardliners and has since returned. Thus, when in Carlos Freyre's novel *Desde el Valle de las Esmeraldas*, the main character, Leoncio Goicochea, is asked by a committee of officers why he wishes to join the Army, Leoncio is flooded with thoughts of wanting to serve his country but utters only one word, "Velasco" (95). Similarly, the many reminders in the military accounts of the Army's civic works during the conflict liken the Army's position to that of Velasco's era of great public projects. While to the readers and recipients of these cultural products, such focus on civic works might pale in comparison to the violence perpetrated, we must remember that what military memory producers are projecting is what they want to be remembered for. The silences in their cultural interventions are thus many.

While some of the military's claims may be factually wrong and morally offensive, it is still important to take them on their own terms, for by listening to them unimpeded (but with discernment) we can enter into their world and better understand the memories that they are putting forth and their reasons for advancing them. Researching and writing this book have not been easy, for I have found myself attempting to untangle my own sort of knot, bound by the desire for accountability and the wish to avoid providing a platform for repackaged military claims while also arguing for the importance of taking these tailored memory products seriously. That is, in this book I wanted to understand and respond to the request by the military student studying human rights "to not forget the *buenos militares*."

Yet this in itself—the obscuring of the distinction between the "*buenos*" and "*malos*"—already indicates that a cultural shift has taken place in how Peruvians view the past. That the Armed Forces can claim their own victimization and argue the shared responsibility of all society in the violence in a national place of memory (the LUM) means that the Armed Forces have successfully curated a past that is much less damning than that presented in the CVR's *Final Report*. That a former military man stained by rumors of human rights violations may become president, and that others with similar charges also aspire to lead the country, and that many others may publicly claim their heroism and self-sacrificing patriotism while downplaying or remaining silent on their own crimes, means that the military has overcome in part its negative national image and resurrected itself in Peru's democracy. Perhaps we should not look to the past as having "*buenos*" and "*malos*," for despite the dichotomy, there is a blurring of the actors and an effacement of their actions and intentions. Yet we should also be cautious about accepting too readily the gray zones. While a clear divide between the conflict's victims and perpetrators was not necessarily fixed, there are still "victim victims" and "perpetrator perpetrators," no matter how the past is spun or sung in the aftermath.[20]

Notes

Introduction

1. Kirsten Weld notes a tendency in Latin American studies to treat the term *historical memory* as shorthand for the "historical memory of political violence" from the Cold War era that is constantly "threatened by the flattening power of neoliberalism and the legerdemain of the perpetrators of past violence." Weld, "Writing Political Violence," 175–76.

2. Several scholars of memory have warned of this potential to abuse memory, such as Todorov in *Mémoire du mal*; Ricoeur in *Memory, History, Forgetting*; and Jelin in *State Repression*.

3. By *armed state agents* or *actors*, I mean the Peruvian National Police (which in 1988 combined three earlier branches) and the Peruvian Armed Forces (made up of the Air Force, the Navy, the Army and special forces); I am not taking into consideration the state-supported civil defense groups (rural peasant patrons and self-defense committees). Among these armed state actors, this book focuses mainly on that of the Army branch, largely because much of the cultural work produced comes from Army personnel and affiliated organizations. I argue in this book that this production is in part a response to judicial proceedings against members of the Peruvian security forces, in particular the Police and the Army. As the Marines are becoming increasingly exposed for the past crimes, in particular the case of Manta and Vilca, they may also come to produce more cultural interventions.

Please note that I have chosen to capitalize *Armed Forces* and their branches. Though this is not common practice in English, it reflects the Spanish-language practice as well as clearly identifies them as specific actors within the conflict. I use the term *Armed Forces* most often in reference to the Army, the Navy, and the Air Force, and at times fold into this term the National Police as well though technically they stood apart as separate entities within the state security forces.

4. Regional studies into the roots of Shining Path argue for different factors for this initial support and its subsequent loss, thus providing a more complex picture of

the dynamics in play. See La Serna, *Corner of the Living*; Heilman, *Before the Shining Path*; and del Pino, *En nombre del gobierno*.

5. Kruijt and Tello, "From Military Reformists," 44.

6. Ibid., 60n43. According to the Comisión de la Verdad y Reconciliación (CVR), 24 percent of national territory was under a state of emergency in 1988. CVR, *Informe final*, vol. 2, 279n41.

7. For a description of the Peruvian CVR, its mandate, its origins, and its findings, see González Cueva, "Peruvian Truth"; Root, *Transitional Justice in Peru*, esp. chap. 4; Milton, *Art from a Fractured Past*, 4–7; Hayner, *Unspeakable Truths*, 35–39.

8. The Peruvian Truth and Reconciliation Commission gave the specific figure of 69,280 as an estimate for the dead and disappeared caused by the internal armed conflict, based on statistical equations used in Guatemala and Kosovo. The range is between 61,007 and 77,552. See CVR, *Informe final*, annex 2, 13. On the number of women and children affected by the violence, see CVR, *Hatun Willakuy* (this abbreviated version of the report was published in Spanish in 2004 and in English in 2010 and 2014; all pages cited here are from the 2014 English version), 284, and on internal refugees, see CVR, *Hatun Willakuy*, 285.

Note that although an English translation of the original, full-length report, *Informe final*, has not been published, I have chosen to reference it in the text as *Final Report* for the sake of simplicity and to distinguish it from generic references to a "final report."

9. Civil defense groups are grouped with unknown actors for 7 percent. These percentages come from CVR, "Conclusiones generales del Informe finale de la CVR," and from CVR, *Informe final*, vol. 2, 232. There is some minor variation among these numbers even within the *Informe final* depending on the dataset analyzed (see Annex 2: 13, 17). In the CVR's abbreviated English version of its findings, *Hatun Willakuy*, the violence committed by state agents (the Armed Forces and police) is grouped with self-defense groups and paramilitary to account for 37 percent of deaths and disappeared, of which the Armed Forces were responsible for a little more than three quarters of the cases. CVR, *Hatun Willakuy*, 12–13. The CVR's *Hatun Willakuy* also states 6.6 percent for police forces and 28.73 percent for the Armed Forces. CVR, *Hatun Willakuy*, 187; Milton, *Art from a Fractured Past*, 28n39.

10. CVR, *Hatun Willakuy*, 6–7, emphasis mine.

11. Ibid., 7.

12. Drinot, "For Whom the Eye Cries," 26.

13. Jorge Ortiz Sotelo, "Some Lessons from Peru's War against Terrorism" (presentation, Université de Montréal, March 19, 2009), and email correspondence, March 22, 2009. This historian later went on to write a lengthy chapter on the Marine's participation in the conflict in his history of the Marines, *Acción y valor*.

14. This student was most likely referring to the 1970 earthquake in Huaraz.

15. As Ortiz Sotelo stated, "[We need to go] beyond the issue of heroes and villains." Email correspondence, March 22, 2009.

16. Indeed, development work might be considered the "soft power" of counterinsurgency efforts followed by or used in tandem with "hard power" counterinsurgency

tactics of the Cold War. Grandin discusses the link between these two forms of counterinsurgency, military force and military-led development, in *The Last Colonial Massacre*. On the link between developmental projects and authoritarianism in Bolivia, see Field, *From Development to Dictatorship*. I thank Kevin Gould for his discussion of these two prongs of counterinsurgency approaches, one that scorches the earth and the other that plants on it. In Peruvian studies, scholars have studied the shifting between these two tactics in counterinsurgency, including the incorporation of *rondas* and civic action programs into the "developmental" approach (see, for instance, chapters by Jo-Marie Burt, Ponciano del Pino, Carlos Iván Degregori, Enrique Obando, and José Luis Rénique in Stern, *Shining and Other Paths*).

17. Quoted in Degregori, "Heridas abiertas, derechos esquivos," 84–85. Unless otherwise indicated, all translations are mine.

18. Drinot, "For Whom the Eye Cries," 17–18.

19. Obando, "Civil-Military Relations in Peru," 388.

20. Quoted in Toche, *Guerra y democracia*, 63. The historian Carlos Contreras poses the question of who would make the ideal soldier in an opinion piece written at the time of the possible introduction of a lottery system for conscription in 2013. He concluded that those who do not wish to be soldiers—pacifists, intellectuals, and defenders of human rights—would make good soldiers since they would not abuse the civilian population, and perhaps not even *senderistas* once captured, and thus would have saved the nation a truth commission. Contreras, "¿Quién quiere ser soldado hoy?"

Mandatory military service was in place in Peru until 1999, when Fujimori introduced a law to convert the military to a fully voluntary force, a decision upheld by García during his second mandate. Humala unsuccessfully attempted to modify the service in late 2012 and 2013 (through decree) by introducing a lottery system of two-year mandatory military service during times when volunteers were insufficient to meet the Armed Forces' needs. If implemented, the lottery would have drawn names of male youth from the ages of eighteen to twenty-five years old who had no physical or mental impediment, were not enrolled in a university program, and were unable to pay a fine for not complying (1850 nuevos soles or half of a tax payment, *"una unidad impositiva tributaria"*). The proposed project was blocked by the Defensoría del Pueblo (Ombudsman of Peru) and by challenges to the constitutionality of the fine (a ruling of the Constitutional Court). Rocío La Rosa, "¿Vuelve el servicio militar obligatorio en el país?," *El Comercio*, March 22, 2013, http://elcomercio.pe/politica/gobierno/gobierno-anuncio-sorteo-cumplir-servicio-militar-obligatorio-noticia-1553578; "TC declara inconstitucional multa de la Ley del Servicio Militar," *El Comercio*, May 23, 2014, http://elcomercio.pe/politica/justicia/tc-declara-inconstitucional-multa-ley-servicio-militar-noticia-1731611.

21. A young person might voluntarily join the Armed Forces for several reasons: during the conflict years, the conflict itself pushed young men to join because they had lost family members or because of fear. Other factors possibly motivating youth to join that continue to the present day are a desire to escape family pressures, economic vulnerability, limited future prospects, and the ambition to get an education. These

motivations are expressed in a series of interviews conducted in 2011 by Gerardo Alberto Arce with some two dozen youth who had served in the 1990s. Arce, "Licenciados," 70–72. Cecilia Méndez refers to Andean campesinos as the "dorsal fin" of the Army from the era of the *caudillos* of the nineteenth century through the twentieth. Méndez, "Las paradojas del autoritarismo," 18.

22.   Other cases are mentioned in CPHEP, *En honor a la verdad*, 64.

23.   On abuses within the military, see Ricardo Uceda, "Por qué desertan los reclutados a la fuerza," *La República*, June 17, 2013, http://www.larepublica.pe/17-06-2013/por-que-desertan-los-reclutados-a-la-fuerza.

In addition to vague references to abuses committed against young conscripts mentioned in Arce, "Licenciados," such acts of violence are also noted in Lurgio Gavilán's memoirs (discussed in chapter 3) and in an interview with "Pancho," a former conscript, poor and poorly educated, in Starn, Degregori, and Kirk, *Peru Reader*. Seeing photographs of the era, one is struck by how young some of these soldiers were. Conversations with the anthropologist María Eugenia Ulfe in June 2012.

24.   That the typical victim and typical foot soldier should come from the same demographic is noted by both members of the military and human rights groups with whom I have spoken. Yet the emphasis placed on this "paradox" is tellingly different: for the military, this shared demographic is introduced into a conversation as a means to question the CVR's findings. That is, how could someone inflict this supposed violence on their own (the implication being that they did not). By contrast, human rights workers bring up this paradox as an unresolvable moral question: how could they do this to their own? This demographic similarity between foot soldier and victim was made apparent in the moving account of the Guatemalan conflict by Rigoberta Menchú. She tells of an event when her indigenous, peasant community captured a young soldier, and the mothers of the community asked him "how he could possibly have become a solider, an enemy of his own race, his own people, the Indian race. [Their] ancestors never set bad examples like that." Menchú, *I, Rigoberta Menchú*, 138. Indeed, that there is a perception of a paradox suggests the need to study further the history of the military in rural regions. As historian Cecilia Méndez notes, "The relationship between the military and campesinos is central to whichever attempt to understand the political history of Peru." According to Méndez, such in-depth studies of this relationship have not taken place because of the "compartmentalization" of research into "rural society, civil society, military, state and ethnicity as separate themes." Méndez, "Las paradojas del autoritarismo," 18.

25.   This statement is not meant as a criticism of scholarly works on the period of the Peruvian internal conflict as a whole. Rather, this impression dates from the early years following the CVR, through my attendance at different events related to the developing field of memory studies. In part, this tendency to consider Peruvian security forces as like those of Southern Cone countries was simply the result of the extant literature at the time, which was produced largely by scholars working on Argentina and Chile. Much of the language and theory for studying Peru's internal armed conflict derives from this literature, such as the important works by Elizabeth Jelin and Steve Stern and the generation of scholars who came out of the Social Sciences and Research

Council (SSRC) training and research projects that they led with Carlos Iván Degregori and Eric Hershberg. But also, as Peruvian sociologist Javier Pizarro Romero notes, there is a tendency among educated civilian circles more broadly in Peru ("un discurso letrado civil") "to construct the military as a homogenous group and a natural enemy of civilians." Pizarro Romero, "La construcción de la identidad," 310.

26. See Hershberg and Agüero, *Memorias militares*. Toche similarly points to a gap in extant literature of studies into "the changes and continuities of the military's political attitude." Toche, *Guerra y democracia*, 20. Pizarro Romero, as part of his undergraduate thesis, argues that studies need to move beyond seeing the military as a "homogenous group" and as the "natural enemy of civilians and to investigate how the police and military represent themselves. Pizarro Romero, "La construcción de la identidad," 312–14.

27. Many of the artistic representations—such as paintings, drawings, wooden triptychs (*retablos*), film, and song—studied by the contributing authors in *Art from a Fractured Past* point to this abuse of human rights by state agents. Milton, *Art from a Fractured Past*.

28. For instance, Leiby's careful efforts to recode the CVR's statistical findings indicate an underestimation of the Armed Forces' abuses, in particular sexual violence. Leiby, "Digging in the Archives." The CVR's report does provide statistical information on nonfatal human rights violations though these were not included in their overall number. See, for instance, figure 10 on arrests and torture as well as forced disappearances and extrajudicial executions: CVR, *Hatun Willakuy*, 32.

29. Much has been written on Latin American waves of military regimes. Among the classical texts, see O'Donnell, *Modernization and Bureaucratic Authoritarianism*; Rouquié, *L'État militaire en Amérique latine*; Vayssière, *Les révolutions d'Amérique latine*; and Stepan, *Rethinking Military Politics*.

30. Toche argues that this image of the Armed Forces as "guard dogs of the oligarchy" was "as entrenched as it was fallacious," in that they did not work simply as a function of the oligarchy. Rather, because their role had become one to protect not just the nation's borders but also "order," the Armed Forces in fact maintained the status quo, to their own detriment (Toche, *Guerra y democracia*, 98–99).

31. The events surrounding Sánchez Cerro's assassination remain unresolved. It is unclear if his assassin acted on behalf of the American Popular Revolutionary Alliance (Alianza Popular Revolucionaria Americana, APRA), independently, or with the help of the subsequent president, General Óscar Benavides. Antonio Zapata, "¿Quién mató a Sánchez Cerro?," *La República*, May 5, 2010, http://cdn8.larepublica.pe/columnistas /sucedio/quien-mato-sanchez-cerro-05-05-2010. Sánchez Cerro helped to consolidate a Fascist party (1931–33), el Partido Unión Revolucionaria; though it had little direct contact with the Italian, German, or Spanish Fascist parties, it was influenced by their political ideology, especially by that of the Italians. Molinari Morales, "El Partido Unión Revolucionaria."

32. Antonio Zapata, "El general de la alegría," *La República*, October 30, 2013, http://cdn8.larepublica.pe/columnistas/sucedio/el-general-de-la-alegria-30-10-2013.

33. Hurtado, "Velasco," 183–84.

34. Kruijt and Tello, "From Military Reformists," 35.

35. Vayssière, *Les révolutions d'Amérique latine*, 210.

36. After Velasco (1968–75) was deposed, General Francisco Morales Bermúdez (1975–80) steered the Revolutionary Government away from his predecessor's reformist projects.

37. Hurtado, "Velasco," 322–24.

38. See, for instance, Seligmann, *Between Reform and Revolution*; Rénique, *La batalla por Puno*; Kruijt and Tello, "From Military Reformists"; Aguirre and Drinot, *Peculiar Revolution*.

39. It was not until after World War II that the United States came to influence the Peruvian Armed Forces. However, the number of US official advisors was never large. Kruijt and Tello, "From Military Reformists," 30–31. On training of Peruvian military personnel in the infamous School of the Americas (SOA), which reached its peak in the 1970s, anthropologist Leslie Gill writes that despite Velasco's "warm relations" with the Soviet Union, of the 1,820 Peruvians trained at the SOA between 1970 and 1975, 62 percent were sent by Velasco, and 38 percent by his more "U.S.-friendly" successor, Morales Bermúdez. Gill, *School of the Americas*, 80–81.

40. Toche, *Guerra y democracia*, 91.

41. Ibid., 87–90. On the current account of events, see Zapata, "¿Quién mató a Sánchez Cerro?"

42. Quoted in Toche, *Guerra y democracia*, 88.

43. Later important studies into the Peruvian military include Masterson, *Militarism and Politics*; and Kruijt, *Revolution by Decree*.

44. For instance, Hurtado, "'Unido a la historia.'"

45. These fields of study are listed as part of a course offered at the Pontificia Universidad Católica del Perú, "I Curso Internacional de Introducción a la Historia Militar," in August 2013. See http://facultad.pucp.edu.pe/letras-ciencias-humanas/no ticias-y-eventos/eventos/cursonuevahistoriamilitar/.

46. For example, Huapaya Amado, "Militares en la décima"; Mendoza Policarpio, "El film 'Alerta en la frontera.'"

47. Méndez and Granados, "Las guerras olvidadas del Perú."

48. On the literature on the Revolutionary Government of the Armed Forces, see Aguirre and Drinot, *Peculiar Revolution*. Several chapters in this volume study the military's culture and self-presentation, in particular chapters by Carlos Aguirre, Charles Walker, and Lourdes Hurtado.

49. Toche, *Guerra y democracia*, 17–19. Other works that address the military and its mentality are Masterson, *Militarism and Politics*; Villanueva, *Cien años*; and Rodríguez Beruff, *Los militares y el poder*.

50. Méndez, "Las paradojas del autoritarismo," 17–34; Granados, "El desfile," 45.

51. Toche, *Guerra y democracia*, 37–34.

52. Ibid., 39.

53. Quoted in ibid., 150.

54. Ibid., 149–60; Granados, "El desfile," 24–28; see also M. E. García, *Making Indigenous Citizens*.

55. Toche does not state that the premilitary education was suspended, but this is the implication here. Toche, *Guerra y democracia*, 158.

56. Since the transition in 2000, the minister of education has three times (in 2006, 2007, and 2011) passed resolutions to prohibit the use of the classroom for the preparation of military parades (and the use of military clothing and replicas of arms) in favor of celebrating "national independence with more civic and democratic events." Granados, "El desfile," 107–8.

57. Ibid., 108.

58. Toche, *Guerra y democracia*, 14.

59. Root, *Transitional Justice in Peru*, 67.

60. For example, General Rodolfo Robles, who according to Kruijt and Tello represented the Velasco-inspired army personnel, had been vocal in his criticism of Montesinos and Hermoza and leaked the involvement of the Colina Group in the Cantuta massacre. This led to his expulsion from the Armed Forces and Peru. In 2000 he returned to Peru from exile in Guatemala. Kruijt and Tello, "From Military Reformists," 49, 57, 63n91.

61. According to Fernando Rospigliosi and Carlos Basombrío in April 2001, the transitional government retired fifty Army generals, twenty Navy vice and rear admirals, and fourteen Air Force generals, all who had signed their support of the 1992 coup. Cited in Arce Arce, "Fuerzas Armadas," 29.

62. Hermoza Ríos was charged with illegal enrichment, human rights violations, abuse of power, and drug trafficking. Generals José Villaneuva Ruesta and Walter Chacón Málaga were also charged with illegal enrichment, corrupting government officials, bribery, and illicit arms deals. Root, *Transitional Justice in Peru*, 66–67.

63. Ibid. Despite the public shaming of corruption and criminal networks, these practices are still present in the forces of order, for instance, over the illicit sale of gasoline in 2006. (Donayre was sentenced in April 2019 for his role in the "Gasolinazo" scandal.) To cite another example, in November 2014 a retired colonel of the National Police, Benedicto Jiménez, who had helped to capture Abimael Guzmán, was caught while in flight to avoid prosecution for his participation in an expansive web of corruption and narcotrafficking. While in handcuffs, he reminded the public that he was a "hero of the nation," a sentiment reiterated by some Facebook users. The possibility that one can be a crook and a hero at the same time as long as the latter is framed within Cold War rhetoric is a legacy of the conflict years.

64. According to Root, the proposed cuts amounted to $424 million. Root, *Transitional Justice in Peru*, 68.

65. In the time from the transition in 2000 to the 2016 elections, nine of the twenty-nine interior ministers have been retired police generals (except for one who was still active and one Army general).

66. Bryan Villacres, "Guión de impunidad: Amador Vidal, 'Ojos de Gato,' ahora 'duda' sobre sus declaraciones sobre la participación de Daniel Urresti en crimen de Bustíos," *Revista Caretas*, October 30, 2015, http://www.caretas.com.pe/Main.asp?T=3082&S=&id=12&idE=1232&idSTo=0&idA=73570#.VjjCkb8eWHk. Some Internet commentators, such as "Kurundanga," view Urresti's presidential bid as a means to

prevent his incarceration. Mario Mejía Huaraca, "Caso Bustíos: Jueces viajarán a Huanta para una inspección," *El Comercio*, March 3, 2016 http://elcomercio.pe/politica /justicia/caso-bustios-jueces-viajaran-huanta-inspeccion-noticia-1883727. An opinion piece published in the *New York Times* suggested that Urresti might govern from prison. Sonia Goldenberg, "Peru's Possible Prison President," *New York Times*, February 1, 2016.

One example of Urresti's very public role: Urresti participated in a game show titled *The Value of Truth*, in which the interviewer asks the contestant a series of questions. If the contestant tells the truth—measured by a polygraph prior to his or her performance on the televised show—and is declared "*Verdad*" by a large sign and dramatic tone, the contestant wins almost US$15,000. In this game, Urresti denied giving orders to kill the journalist or of ever having killed anyone. He went home all the richer (money he planned to put toward his presidential campaign), though he faced condemnation from the courts for having spoken publicly about an ongoing trial. "El Valor de la Verdad," YouTube, February 6, 2016, https://www.youtube.com/watch?v= TZE1buogghE&spfreload=10.

67. Stern, *Remembering Pinochet's Chile*, 120–24.

68. The memory knot has strong historical and social connotations in Peru: the Incaic *quipus*, or cords, consisted of mnemonic knots and remain socially relevant today for symbolic purposes. This discussion of Stern's "memory knot" in the Peruvian context is originally from Milton, "Defacing Memory," 193–95.

69. I borrow this term from Alex Wilde, who used it to describe the reemergence of memories despite societal silence in the years following Pinochet. Wilde, "Irruptions of Memory."

70. MOVADEF seeks recognition as a legitimate political party and amnesty for all who committed crimes during the conflict. Like the other two camps discussed here, MOVADEF also uses cultural means to promulgate its memories in public spheres. By attending and disrupting conferences and cultural events and employing various social media, MOVADEF advances a narrative that seems to follow the earlier Shining Path script of antigovernment, antipolitical parties, and anti-NGOs. Though far from reaching the same level of public engagement as the salvation/heroic and human rights memory camps described here, first-generation Shining Path memories are still in circulation (noted in Renzo Aroni Sulca, "La memoria subversiva de la 'guerra popular' de Sendero Luminoso" [presentation, International Congress of Americanists, July 20, 2012]). Nonetheless, because they did not live during the conflict years, MOVADEF's largely young members are resignifying past violence to fit the present day and in so doing are able to provoke reactions from the highest levels of government. For instance, the Peruvian congress created a program called "Terrorism Never Again" for teaching Peru's recent past and for fostering democratic sentiments among adolescent and university students (Macher, *¿Hemos avanzado?*, 164–65). An important and thoughtful contribution to bringing Shining Path memories into public debate is José Carlos Agüero's *Los rendidos*.

71. The addition of the umbrella group Frente Amplio (Wide Front) in the 2016

presidential elections and its positive results suggest that the Left can coalesce into a sustainable political movement.

72. Degregori, "Heridas abiertas, derechos esquivos," 76.

73. Burt, *Political Violence*, esp. 145–55; Coletta Youngers, *Violencia política*.

74. Milton, "At the Edge," 13–15.

The media's reporting on the CVR is worthy of study. We must remember that the media were also undergoing a "transitional period," and probably uncertain about the new rules of the game. The CVR's *Informe final* held the limelight for a relatively short time after its publication. Indeed, it may have spurred more debate prior to its actual publication (Root, *Transitional Justice in Peru*, 90–97). After the release of the *Final Report*, newspapers and the media quickly turned to issues of the nation's economy. Salomón Lerner has remarked on the difficulty of getting the media to engage with the CVR's findings (personal communication, October 22, 2012). Based on his observations during the Toledo and Humala governments, economist Herbert Morote describes a more orchestrated campaign by the media against the dissemination of the CVR's findings in his damning but insufficiently annotated book, *¡Todos contra la Verdad!*

75. Not just the political Right but also the Left questioned the CVR's statistical findings: Rendón, "La polémica sobre las cifras."

76. According to Martín Tanaka, "If you are a *fujimorista* you support authoritarianism, human rights violations, and you buy the whole package, while a doctrinaire liberal may be in agreement with Fujimori's economic reforms but feel that everything was done badly: authoritarianism, control of the media, [and] human rights crimes." "Los dos derechas," *Revista Domingo (La República)*, January 15, 2012, http://archivo.larepublica.pe/15-01-2012/las-dos-derechas.

77. "A Public Talk by Keiko Fujimori," Harvard University, September 30, 2015, http://drclas.harvard.edu/keiko-fujimori-2015.

78. "Keiko pide reparationes para familias de militares," *El Comercio*, January 11, 2016, http://elcomercio.pe/politica/elecciones/keiko-fujimori-pide-reparaciones-familias-militares-noticia-1870142?ref=nota_politica&ft=mod_leatambien&e=titulo.

79. "Keiko miente por congraciarse con militares que su 'api' dejó," *El Comercio*, January 12, 2016, http://elcomercio.pe/politica/elecciones/keiko-miente-congraciarse-militares-que-su-api-dejo-noticia-1870438?ref=nota_politica&ft=mod_leatambien&e=titulo. It should be noted that in the same article, the technical secretary of the Consejo de Reparaciones (the organization in charge of reparations) is cited as stating that the fallen state agents are already on its list, of which 73 percent have received reparation payments.

80. Here Obando's succinct chapter "Civil-Military Relations in Peru" is helpful for it clearly describes the internal divisions not only within the Peruvian Armed Forces but also within the Army itself, especially during the Bélaunde and García governments, when the hardliners came to a position of dominance, pushing out the remnants of the *velaquista* contingent within the Armed Forces. These memories emerge again in the post–Shining Path period, as becomes apparent in my reading of CPHEP, *En honor a la verdad* (see chapter 2).

81. Kruijt and Tello use the term *institutionalists* to describe Velasco-inspired military personnel. Kruijt and Tello, "From Military Reformists."

82. This internal discord became very public in the last year of Ollanta Humala's presidency as he placed members of the generational cohort of his brother Antauro, and those who were in his own graduating class from the Chorrillos military academy, in prominent government and military positions. In so doing, he was chided for not respecting the tradition within the military of rewarding high-ranking officers with such posts. While not illegal, this action elicited the rancor of more-senior military personnel. Gustavo Gorriti, "De Acensos y Golpismos," *Revista Caretas*, October 30, 2015, www.caretas.com.pe/Main.asp?T=3082&id=12&idE=1232&idSTo=512&idA=73551#.VjjEJ78eWHk.

83. Degregori, "Las heridas abiertas, derechos esquivos," 79. Maxwell Cameron argues that the release of these videos (rather than the fraudulent elections of 2000 or the mass mobilization of the March of Cuatro Suyos) are what ultimately brought down the Fujimori government, for once the videos became public, their blackmail potential was lost. As a result, the videos made public what many already knew (the nefarious web of the media, business, and public officials, including the Armed Forces) and caused an irreparable rift between Fujimori and his advisor. When Montesinos fell, Fujimori most likely calculated that despite his ongoing popularity, without Montesinos's network of control, which "maintained internal cohesion through coercion, bribery and blackmail" (286), Fujimori would be unable to govern. Cameron likens Fujimori to Macbeth, but rather than being a tragic figure, Fujimori was simply pathetic (290), and his fall was "a result of inevitable internal tensions within the regime given the massive concentration of executive power" (272). Cameron, "Endogenous Regime Breakdown."

84. González, "Peruvian Truth and Reconciliation Commission," 71–75. The Armed Forces high command gave a press conference after the release of the videotape in which they "asked for the understanding and forgiveness of Peruvians." Root, *Transitional Justice in Peru*, 67. Importantly, this apology concerned their subordination to Fujimori and their support of his self-coup, while stating their objection to human rights investigations. It was not an apology for having committed human rights violations.

85. Public shaming might be the only outcome for many of the accused: only 2 percent of the denunciations received by the prosecutor general (Ministerio Público or Public Ministry) reached sentencing; among these 187 cases from 2006 to 2012, 121 were acquitted and 66 convicted. Burt, "Paradoxes of Accountability," 161. According to the statistics compiled by the Peru Human Rights Trial Project, twice as many former state agents accused of grave human rights violations have been acquitted than convicted in Peru. Of the more than 2,880 cases before the Public Ministry, mostly from Ayacucho, more than half have been shelved largely because of insufficient information or documentation about the perpetrators, a problem exacerbated by the Armed Forces' unwillingness to provide necessary documentation or claims that such documents do not exist. Burt and Cagley, "Access to Information"; Burt "Paradoxes of Accountability," 159.

There is another serious obstacle to bringing cases forward: victims access the legal system with difficulty, since only some 30 percent have legal counsel (Macher, ¿Hemos avanzado?, 160), yet defense lawyers for military and police officers accused of human rights violations are paid by the state. In addition to the acquittals, the closing of cases, and the general torpidity of the judicial system, there are efforts to undermine the judiciary through changes to the terms governing the circumstances in which cases can be tried and in the kinds and length of sentences served, and in the very language used for the crimes committed. In addition to the 2010 failed bid to pass a legislative decree that would have granted amnesty to individuals being processed in Peruvian courts for human rights violations, in 2012 attempts were made to reduce the charges against those responsible for the Barrios Altos massacre, changing crimes against humanity to the much lighter charge of homicide.

86. In May 2016 a journalist from *El Comercio* interviewed General José Williams Zapata, who led the campaign to release the hostages held by the MRTA and was later acquitted in September 2016 for his role in the Accomarca massacre for lack of evidence. The interview concerned the newly formed Asociación Civil Patria, described as "a civilian initiative, not political," "to defend Police and Armed Forces facing trials, which they consider unjust since they violate their human rights." Williams Zapata served on the organization's board. "Williams Zapata: El afán es defender a militares procesados," *El Comercio*, May 19, 2016, http://elcomercio.pe/politica/actualidad /jose-williams-zapata-afan-defender-militares-procesados-noticia-1902692.

87. The National Intelligence Service was formed in the 1970s, bringing together under the same roof the intelligence of Army, Navy, Air Force, National Police, and civil services. The powers of the SIN expanded greatly under Montesinos's direction, and included internal spying on its members. Kruijt and Tello, "From Military Reformists," 50–52, 59n17.

88. César Campos, "Fuerzas Armadas y Policiales del Perú: 'En honor a la verdad,'" *El Diario Expreso*, December 1, 2010, http://www.generacion.com/usuarios/41638 /fuerzas-armadas-policiales-peru-en-honor-verdad.

89. Kruijt and Tello, "From Military Reformists," 56.

90. Ollanta Humala's brother Antauro is serving a nineteen-year sentence for having led another unsuccessful revolt in 2005, this time against Toledo, under the *indigenista* banner of "ethno-cacerisme."

91. Kruijt and Tello, "From Military Reformists," 57.

92. Pizarro Romero, "La construcción de la identidad," 312–14.

93. Kruijt and Tello, "From Military Reformists," 57. This nostalgic support for Velasco is something I also noted in my interviews with military personnel in November 2014 in the Army headquarters of El Pentagonito. Even the architecture of El Pentagonito harks back to this earlier era. Many also spoke favorably of the nineteenth-century hero Cáceres.

94. Ibid.

95. In this letter, Arias Graziani expresses his concern that the CVR's report "produces in some way, a negative perception of the forces of order, which, as has been

proven, is not true. Furthermore, individual responsibility must be clearly differentiated from the institutional responsibility suggested by the [CVR]." For Arias Graziani, the number of victims according to the CVR is a projection, not "a proven truth," and the roots of the conflict lie not in Peru's history of inequality and racism but in Shining Path ideology. CVR, *Informe final*, vol. 8, 267–70.

According to one story published in *Perú21*, Arias Graziani officially broke his silence (again) nine years after the CVR, claiming that the commissioners were biased against the military and wrong in their finding of nearly seventy thousand dead and disappeared. He stated that twenty-five thousand was a more accurate figure. He clarified that he was alone among the commissioners in holding this opinion. "Informe fue sesgado y antimilitarista," *Perú21*, February 27, 2012, http://peru21.pe/2012/02/27/actualidad/informe-fue-sesgado-y-antimilitarista-2013577.

See also the video "La Verdad del Comisionado Luis Arias Graziani," YouTube, February 27, 2012, https://www.youtube.com/watch?v=yP2KomHH4hs. The two comments attached to the video are interesting: one commentator states that Grau, one of Peru's key national heroes, taught human rights; another commentator states that Arias Graziani was a member of the elite, with no connection to the conflict, and was "perversely used" by the CVR.

96. The CVR presented forty-three cases to the prosecutor general (Ministerio Público) that were ready for prosecution in addition to four cases that it had previously presented. The total number of cases for immediate action were thus forty-seven. In the *Final Report*, another seventy-three cases were listed for further investigation but not for immediate response. González Cueva, "Peruvian Truth and Reconciliation Commission," 70, 87, 91n7, 93n38; Burt, "Paradoxes of Accountability," 153.

The Defensoría del Pueblo (ombudsman) played an important role in these and other cases of human rights violations. The Defensoría del Pueblo was established in 1993 as an autonomous state institution to defend citizens' rights. It does not have legislative powers but rather assembles information and makes recommendations that are then presented to the appropriate authorities and institutions. One of the tasks of the Defensoría del Pueblo is to track the implementation of the CVR's recommendations. On its mission, see "Quiénes somos: Nuestra institución," http://www.defensoria.gob.pe/defensoria.php.

97. Burt, "Paradoxes of Accountability."

98. On the project, see ibid., 158–59, 171n12, n13; for its findings, see http://rightsperu.net/; see also Collins, Balardini, and Burt, "Mapping Perpetrator Prosecutions."

99. Burt, "Paradoxes of Accountability," 161, 171n15.

100. Ibid., 159–60.

101. Ibid., 163. For example, the court's ruling in 2009 on the Los Laureles case of forced disappearance pointed to this trend of reversal of previous advances in human rights trials. The court absolved military chiefs for lack of material evidence and direct links to the crime.

102. Salvi, "Slogan 'Complete Memory.'" For more on Argentina, see also Salvi, *De vencedores a víctimas*; Badaró, *Militares o ciudadanos*; and Robben, *Political Violence*.

103. Hershberg and Agüero, *Memorias militares*, 1–34.

104. It is important to note that this interview would have taken place years before the Kirschner-era memory boom. Payne, *Uncivil Movements*, 51–52, 58–59, 252n16. Similar repackaging by former state and paramilitary combatants has been noted by anthropologists Winifred Tate and Leslie Gill, including the Italian suit and tie. Tate, "From Greed to Grievance" and *Counting the Dead*; Gill, *School of the Americas.* Such refashioning also has implications for the meaning and use of the term *victim*, a category that has changed over the many years of violence in Colombia. See Nicolás Rodríguez, "La naturalización de la violencia." Other examples of perpetrator discourses can be found in Payne, *Unsettling Accounts*, discussed here in more detail in chapter 1.

105. Gill, *School of the Americas*, xviii.

106. Tate, *Counting the Dead*, esp. chapter 7, 276–77.

107. Some political scientists describe the Fujimori regime as "electoral authoritarianism." According to Maxwell Cameron, "the Fujimori regime had two faces: a popular and effective president on the one hand, and a corrupt government within the government, on the other. Put slightly differently, the political system, especially post-1992, was built on a combustible mix of formally democratic institutions—above all elections—and the erosion of the separation of powers. Elections without the separation of powers might be an apt characterization of 'delegative democracy.' However, once the checks and balances inherent in a presidential democracy are eroded past a certain point, one is more apt to speak of 'electoral authoritarianism.' The line between delegative democracy and electoral authoritarianism is drawn when the minimal conditions necessary to guarantee that elections are free and fair are no longer present." Cameron, "Endogenous Regime Breakdown," 288. Another term is *competitive authoritarianism*: Levitsky and Way, "Elections without Democracy."

On the discrediting of the Left during the Fujimori regime, see Burt, *Political Violence*; and Youngers, *Violencia política.*

108. Giampietri, *Rehén por siempre*, 169.

109. Ulfe and Milton, "¿Y, después de la verdad?"

110. "Ejecutivo plantea hasta 8 años de cárcel para quienes nieguen terror senderista," *La República*, August 29, 2012, http://www.larepublica.pe/29-08-2012/ejecutivo-plantea-hasta-8-anos-de-carcel-para-quienes-nieguen-terror-senderista.

111. Nelson Manrique, "Que incluye a todos," *Diario La Primera*, August 24, 2012, www.diariolaprimeraperu.com/online/politica/que-incluya-a-todos_118547.html.

112. The model here is most likely Germany's laws about Holocaust denial. The twenty-eighth of August is also the date that marks the return of Tacna to Peru in 1929 (after the Chilean annexation during the War of the Pacific) and thus is a national holiday. Congress adopted a modified version of Humala's proposal. See *La República*'s article "Ejecutivo plantea hasta 8 años."

113. Burt provides similar examples in "Paradoxes of Accountability."

114. As Jelin notes, memory entrepreneurs emerge from different ideological positions. She cites the example of the political Right in Chile, *State Repression*, 34. On the

memory battles over the last decade, see Huber and del Pino, *Políticas en justicia tran-sicional*; and Milton, "Truth Ten Years On."

115.   For instance, several of the chapters in Aguirre and Drinot's *Peculiar Revolution* describe the Velasco era as that of "military self-fashioning," such as the use of the image of Túpac Amaru as an endogenous national hero (as opposed to the foreign libera-tors of San Martín and Bolívar).

116.   "El país tributará homenaje a los héroes de la democracia," *El Peruano*, April 1, 2007.

117.   I wish to recognize the strong Canadian presence within these extractive companies and the unyielding stance of Canadian governments to sanction or curtail their practices abroad, despite demands at home to do so. See Grinspun and Shamsie, "Canadian Re-engagement in Latin America."

118.   This heart-wrenching reality of the destruction and lost hopes because of the war, and of the complexity of continuing violence after the war, is made evident in McAllister and Diane Nelson, *War by Other Means*. See also Franco, *Cruel Modernity*.

119.   I thank Steve Stern for underscoring the importance of including the hyphen in terms such as *post-atrocity* and *post-Shining Path*. For Stern, "the hyphenate form also is useful because it underscores that we are dealing with a kind of paradoxical hybrid of temporalities: 'post' the times of atrocity, yet a continuing presence of the past that makes the atrocity both a living legacy in the present, and a referent of things that happened in the past." Personal communication, June 6, 2013.

120.   Regarding the military's undemocratic history, see Toche, *Guerra y democracia*, 20. For rumors of Armed Forces' negotiations, see Nicolás Lynch, "¿Cuál es el peligro contra la democracia?," *Otramirada*, *Infodiario* 669, September 17, 2015.

121.   Payne, *Uncivil Movements*, xviii–xix.

122.   Ibid., xix.

123.   Indeed, the Peruvian political elites can take and leave the CVR at their bidding. In their initial rejection of Ollanta Humala, they used the CVR to justify their condemnation of him as a "human rights violator," yet later when he had adopted a more conservative approach, their position softened. Because of Humala's failure to stymie human rights trials, some members of the Armed Forces view him as a "traitor." These observations are based on my reading of the Peruvian press, a conversation with the political scientist Alberto Vergara (June 21, 2015), and from Vich, *Poéticas del duelo*, 123–28, especially his analysis of a particular political caricature by Carlín that depicts the head of Peru's most influential television channel asking his secretary to get him a copy of "this excellent report" of the CVR so that it might be used to bolster the human rights abuses attributed to Humala. His secretary appears surprised since he had earlier described the report as "Marxist garbage" to be thrown away.

124.   One of the requests within the military establishment is the right to vote, as argued by the president of the Universidad Alas Peruanas, Fidel Ramírez Prado, in his book *El voto de los militares*, 12.

125.   Payne offers the following definition of uncivil movements: "Uncivil move-ments are political groups within democracies that employ both civil and uncivil

political action to promote exclusionary policies. They resemble other political groups—for example, political parties, interest groups, social movements, counter-movements, and authoritarian movements. Indeed, uncivil movements form, participate in, and evolve into and out of these other types of political groups at different times." *Uncivil Movements*, 1.

126. For instance, the trials during civilian governments of military men for murder and disappearance during Peru's conflict have not led to a version of Argentina's Carapintada uprising (that is, a band of military generals who attempted coups against the government in response to the trials). While the coups were not successful, the Carapintada did succeed in having the trials ended and the officers exonerated. They then transformed themselves into a political party known as MODIN (Movement for Dignity and Independence) (Payne, *Uncivil Movements*, xvii–xviii). No such political party has emerged in Peru, though associations have formed that seek to protect members of the military establishment and the reputation of the Armed Forces, such as ADDCOT, ADOGEN, and Asociación Civil Patria. See also Bakiner, *Truth Commissions*, 137, 261n97.

127. Payne, *Uncivil Movements*, xxiv. Upon reflecting why members of these uncivil movements would agree to interviews with Payne, she concludes, "These informants wanted to talk and I wanted to listen. And I was perceived by them (because of my identities) to be a less biased listener than others. These movements generally get bad press. Indeed, because they don't like their public image, they try to avoid the media. But they believe in their mission, and they want to tell their side of the story." Ibid., xxvi.

128. This meaning of *curation* comes from Erica Lehrer and my introduction to a volume on new museological and memorial practices. Lehrer and Milton, "Witnesses to Witnessing," 4. The notion of "difficult knowledge" has its roots in the work of educational theorist Deborah Britzman, *Lost Subjects*.

129. See the author contributions in my edited volume *Art from a Fractured Past* for a sense of the variety of cultural engagements. See also Saona, *Memory Matters in Transitional Peru*; Vich, *Poéticas del duelo*; Lambright, *Andean Truths*; and some of the chapters in del Pino and Yezer, *Formas del recuerdo*. For an interesting twist on how art may speak about or silence past violence, see González Castañeda's study on the secrets that are hidden in the Sarhua artform of the *tabla*, *Unveiling Secrets of War*.

130. Atencio, *Memory's Turn*, 5–7. Argentina and Chile have a long tradition of cultural engagement with "truth" debates. See, for instance, the pioneering works of Jelin and Stern and more recently Gómez-Barris, *Where Memory Dwells*; Lazzara, *Chile in Transition*; Gates-Madsen, *Trauma, Taboo, and Truth-Telling*.

131. Jelin notes the importance of certain social actors as "emprendedores de la memoria," a phrase that somewhat infelicitously has been translated as "memory entrepreneurs." This translation comes from Jelin, *State Repression*, 33. There is no adequate equivalent in English for Jelin's phrase "emprendedores de la memoria." The translation as "memory entrepreneurs" places too much emphasis on the economics or marketing of memory with innuendos of financial benefits and connotes an impresario,

while not placing sufficient emphasis on the stakeholder aspect connoted in the original Spanish, which could include public and social projects. On how memory may indeed be marketed for financial gain or for repackaging of the past, see Bilbija and Payne, *Accounting for Violence*. Bilbija and Payne further add to the mix of potential uses by memory makers "the commercialization of memory of atrocity," which "opens up the possibility for the promotion of memory goods without a political message." Bilbija and Payne, *Accounting for Violence*, 10–13.

Chapter 1. Military Memory Books

1. Atencio, *Memory's Turn*, 5–8.

2. Cueto had a similarly themed novel (*La pasajera*, 2015) made into a feature-length film (*Magallanes*, 2014). The film's director, Salvador del Solar, was named minister of culture in December 2016. Roncagliolo published *La pena máxima* in 2014.

3. The titles mentioned in this chapter are not intended as a complete list but rather as examples of the kinds of stories that are in circulation. For literary scholars interested in literature about and produced during and after the conflict years, see Faverón Patriau, *Toda la sangre*; de Vivanco Roca Rey, *Historias del más acá* and *Memorias en tinta*; and Ubilluz, Hibbett, and Vich, *Contra el sueño de los justos*.

From 2013 to 2015, many fictional films and documentaries focused on the conflicted past came to the cinemas, including *NN* (2014) by Héctor Gálvez, *Magallanes* (2014) by Salvador del Solar, *Dibujando memorias* (2015) by Marianne Eyde, *Viaje a Tombuctú* (2013) by Rossana Díaz Costa, *Caminantes de memoria* (2014) by Heder Soto Quispe, *Tempestad en los Andes* (2014) by Swedish director Mikael Wiström, and *Te saludan los cabitos* (2014) by Spanish director Luis Cintora. Several new novels were also published, for instance: Pita's *El rincón de los muertos*; Pérez's *Criba*, winner of the 2014 Petroperú prize "Premio Copé International"; and Cisneros's *La distancia que nos separa*.

4. Some of the fictional works written during the conflict from the perspective of armed actors are Vargas Llosa's *Death in the Andes* (Spanish edition, 1993) (in addition to his earlier novels involving the character Peruvian Army captain Pantaleón Pantoja); Rada's *Senderos de sangre*, from the perspective of a fictional *senderista* (1995), and Luís Baldoceda's 1989 work, *Confidencias de un Senderista: Juicio popular*, a forty-one-page comic based on the account of an incarcerated Shining Path militant, which was circulated principally in highland towns. In the post-CVR literature boom, some of the few books that offer a military perspective are the character of Cubo in L. F. Cueto's *Ese camino existe* and Cisneros's autobiographical novel, *La distancia que nos separa*, about his father, who was minister of the interior during the government of Morales Bermúdez (and thus an earlier period). The question of the children of the "perpetrators" also emerges in recent works, including Renato Cisneros's and Alonso Cueto's novels (the latter entirely fictional); Agüero's *Rendidos* (2014) offers insights into his childhood with *senderista* parents and on contemporary Peru; and Martínez Garay's series of short stories, *Mano poderosa*, in which the main character, "Hugo Martínez Garay,"

reflects on his past and present. In one story, he recounts hearing of the CVR's investigation of his father, a former commanding general in Ayacucho, while the author himself worked for the commission.

5.   The use of the term *unsettling* is a nod to the study by Payne of perpetrators' public "confessions," *Unsettling Accounts*. Despite being potentially disturbing, as Peruvian scholar Renzo Aroni has remarked, "Armed actors need to be explored more. Studies tend to focus on the victims and not on the perspective of real [*carne y hueso*] perpetrators." Quoted by Jacqueline Fowks, "La nueva mirada de Perú a la guerra," *El País*, August 28, 2015, http://cultura.elpais.com/cultura/2015/08/28/actualidad /1440788832_365049.html.

6.   Gálvez Olaechea (MRTA) also wrote *Desde el país de las sombras*.

During the conflict years and after, Shining Path literature circulated somewhat clandestinely, often in facsimile copies; for instance, the two volumes of *Memorial de trincheras: Testimonios de prisiones* (Memorial from the trenches: Prison testimonies) and *Memorial de trincheras: Testimonios de la guerra popular* (Memorial from the trenches: Testimonies from the popular war) printed in 2015 (no indication of publisher) and a series of short stories by *senderistas* incarcerated in the Canto Grande prison, Grupo Literario Nueva Crónica, *Camino de Ayrabamba y otros relatos* (The New Chronical Literary Group, Ayrabamba path and other stories) (Lima: Canta Editores, 2007).

7.   Steve Stern has noted the importance of cultural interventions as "formulas" for forgetting, for laying the past to rest, often associated with the interest of the state, conservative sectors, and security forces as well as possible "wedges" for furthering remembrance that align with the calls for accountability pertaining to victims and human rights advocates. In his study of memory politics in Chile, Stern refers to written interventions in the context of transitional Chile as "memory books," whether they are favorable or critical of key junctures in the past. Stern, *Reckoning with Pinochet*, 222, 453n18.

8.   I do not have a complete list of the post-CVR memory books, fictional or nonfictional. However, based on my efforts to track down this literature, I have the impression that books by regime insiders and armed state actors fall mainly in the genre of nonfiction. There are exceptions, of course. In chapter 3, I discuss Carlos Freyre's *Desde el Valle de las Esmeraldas*. Another novel written by a former army lieutenant is *El pecado de Deng Xiaoping: La guerra de los tenientes* (2010) by Claudio Montoya Marallano. This work was a limited edition originally "for friends, colleagues, and family," one of whom handed a copy to the journalist Gustavo Gorriti. Gorriti noted the importance of this novel in providing insight into the experiences of young officers and soldiers, the ones who fought the war, while the command kept their distance. Gorriti expressed hope that others would follow suit and provide their accounts. Montoya's book was originally published in 2008 in Spain, but an electronic version of the book, under the title *La Guerra de los tenientes: Memorias de la guerra con Sendero Luminoso*, was later made available on the Internet. Gustavo Gorriti, "La Guerra de los Tenientes," *Caretas*, no. 2131, May 27, 2010, http://www.caretas.com.pe/Main.asp?T=

3082&idE=880&idS=301#.VipNt78eWHk. In 2016, another book written from a soldier's perspective was self-published: Luis Cárdenas Cruzado, *Lágrimas de un soldado*. Books by regime insiders published prior to the CVR include former commanding general in Ayacucho Clemente Noel, *Ayacucho, testimonio de un soldado* (Lima: CONCYTEC, 1989).

9.   The focus here is on books written by individuals or groups related to state security forces. Several books by journalists also uncover the past, for example, Jara's *Ojo por ojo*; Roncagliolo's *La cuarta espada*; and Uceda's *Muerte en el Pentagonito*.

10.   Several of these books are published by ADDCOT, http://defensoresdela democracia.org. The group was vocal during the transition and following the CVR but is no longer active. Its former president, Brigadier General Wilfredo Mori Orzo, was sentenced in September 2016 for his participation in the Accomarca massacre in 1985. He became a fugitive. In 2007 ADDCOT published *Injusticias contra los que combatieron y derrotaron a los terroristas (1980—2000)*. Retired military man turned author José Cabrejos Samamé (*La verdad sobre Accomarca*) was also accused by Telmo Hurtado of having stood with his arms crossed as he witnessed the extrajudicial killing of fifteen detainees in the Army headquarters Los Cabitos. "Telmo Hurtado acusa a ex jefes militares de participar en matanzas de campesinos," *La República*, December 20, 2012, http://larepublica.pe/20-12-2012/telmo-hurtado-acusa-ex-jefes-militares-de-partici par-en-matanzas-de-campesinos.

Another member of ADDCOT and its published authors, Brigadier General José Valdivia was accused in 2015 of instigating the Cayara massacre. Henry Campos, "Juicio por caso Cayara empieza la próxima semana," *Diario16*, February 27, 2015, http://diario16.pe/noticia/58032-juicio-caso-cayara-empieza-proxima-semana.

11.   I want to thank Jo-Marie Burt and the members of the Human Rights Trials in Peru Project for tracking the trials and efforts at accountability. See Burt, "Paradoxes of Accountability," for these early efforts and the subsequent years. In her chapter, Burt writes, "Perhaps this is [the] real challenge for transitional justice theory: rather than the current focus on understanding the 'impact' of transitional justice on 'democracy' or 'human rights' in an abstract way, we need to better understand, through grounded contextual and historical analysis, how politics fundamentally shapes the terrain upon which those seeking truth and justice think and act and struggle to achieve those objectives, and how others, sometimes successfully, and sometimes not, seek to obliterate it." Burt, "Paradoxes of Accountability," 169.

12.   For instance, Giampietri cites "25,000 Peruvians who had lost their lives" in *41 Seconds to Freedom*, 185; and Fournier states 26,000 in "*Feliciano*," 236.

13.   According to an interview with Giampietri, a Japanese translation was made available in 2008, though I have not found any confirmation of this publication. "El Rehén victorioso," *Juez justo: Revista de investigación, denuncia y actualidad* 2, no. 14 (2011): 4–7. This magazine had just emerged the year prior to the interview. The magazine's title, *Juez justo* (Fair judge), implies a response to the denunciations after the CVR. The magazine's director was Benedicto Jiménez, a retired colonel of the National Police involved in the capture of Abimael Guzmán, who was later imprisoned

for money laundering and conspiracy. He was further accused of using this publication to defame authorities who had investigated his co-accused, Rodolfo Orellana, while lauding more docile magistrates. The magazine folded. "Benedicto Jiménez dice que no tiene dinero para pagar abogado," *El Comercio*, December 10, 2014, http://el comercio.pe/politica/justicia/benedicto-jimenez-dice-que-no-tiene-dinero-pagar-abo gado-noticia-1777561?ref=flujo_tags_6128&ft=nota_2&e=titulo.

14. Giampietri, *41 Seconds to Freedom*, 178.

15. Ibid., 181.

16. Giampietri, *Rehén por siempre*, 2nd ed. (2012), 19, emphasis mine.

17. In addition to overturning the first Bélaunde government and the repression of Apristas (including its founder), according to the historian Pablo Macera the anti-Aprista sentiment was so great in the 1930s that "it was part of the education of the cadets in military school, and constituted one of the key cohesive factors among the armed forces." Cited by Vayssière, *Les révolutions d'Amérique latine*, 210.

18. Giampietri, *Rehén por siempre*, 175.

19. Montesinos's most recent publication is *Operación militar Chavín de Huántar: Con el terrorismo no se negocia*, published in time for the twentieth anniversary of the hostage release.

20. According to an article in *Caretas*, the magazine attached to *El Comercio*, a 2014 superior court decision ordered the transfer to a local penitentiary of several high-profile *senderista* and MRTA inmates (Polay, Ramírez, Rincón, and Cárdenas). This sentence, warned the author, might open a Pandora's box, for other inmates could also benefit from this precedent. Enrique Chávez, "El desalojo de la base," *Caretas*, March 20, 2014, 16–18.

21. "Para un autodenominado 'revolucionario' el tiempo es distinto que para quien no lo es." Montesinos, *Sin Sendero*, 13.

22. Ibid.

23. Álvarez Sotomayor, *Un soplón llamado Valdimiro*, 232, emphasis mine.

24. Ibid., 20. Álvarez's account traces the life of Montesinos from childhood until his imprisonment and recounts how he was introduced to Fujimori during his presidential campaign by Loayza, whom Montesinos later pushed out of favor. *Un soplón llamado Valdimiro*, 232.

25. A. García, *El mundo de Maquiavelo*.

26. Fournier, *"Feliciano,"* back cover.

27. The congressman Alfredo González Salazar's book, *Caso Leonor La Rosa: Historia de una mentira* (The case of Leonor La Rosa: History of a lie), was published in 2006 by the UAP (and launched in the presence of its rector Fidel Ramírez Prado). Press release from the Congreso de la República, July 3, 2006, www2.congreso.gob.pe/Sicr /Prensa/heraldo.nsf/NotDia/02d4b30b0725b0e605257120007b614b?OpenDocument.

28. Donayre, *El silencio de los héroes*, 234.

29. Ibid., 257.

30. Promotional materials and from a report in Radio Programas del Perú (RPP), "General Edwin Donayre presentará su libro 'El silencio de los héroes,'" June 26,

2009, http://www.rpp.com.pe/2008/2009-06-26-general-edwin-donayre-presen
tara-su-libro-el-silencio-de-los-heroes-noticia_190968.html.

31. Personal conversation with Lourdes Medina, June 1, 2015.

32. His book was probably part of his political campaign as well as a response to
the active judiciary against former soldiers. Donayre ran as a candidate in the October
2014 regional elections in Ayacucho and came in second place, very close to the winner,
another Quechua speaker rumored to have narcotrafficking connections. Indeed,
when I originally tried to obtain a copy of his book, it was unavailable because Donayre
had taken all the copies to Ayacucho to distribute prior to the elections. I was able to
obtain the book once the elections were over. Donayre was elected to the Congress of
the Republic in the 2016 elections.

33. Hurtado, "Velasco," 179–80.

34. Donayre, *El silencio de los héroes*, 11.

35. CVR, *Hatun Willakuy*, 6.

36. Donayre, *El silencio de los héroes*, 231–32.

37. Burt, "Paradoxes of Accountability," 162. Subsequent court rulings (such as
the ruling in 2014 on Pucará and 2016 on Accomarca) suggests that this tendency to
exonerate the higher-ranking military men at the expense of those following orders is
not quite so stark. In October 2014 three generals were sentenced to twenty years in
prison along with eight other military men (and one civilian) sentenced to nineteen
years for participating in the killing of eight civilians in the region of Pucará in 1989.
"Poder Judicial condenó a 20 años de cárcel a militares por matanza en Pucará," *Perú21*,
October 8, 2014, http://peru21.pe/politica/poder-judicial-condeno-20-anos-carcel-mili
tares-matanza-pucara-2200678.

38. This is not the only scandal that might have contributed to Donayre's early
retirement. Donayre, along with forty-two other members of the Armed Forces, faced
charges for having stolen and sold fuel destined for internal military use in 2006, while
he served as head of the Army.

39. The video was posted under the name of "peruanobienperuano" on YouTube,
July 15, 2009, https://www.youtube.com/watch?v=SoxH82W2hvA.

40. Donayre, *El silencio de los héroes*, 241.

41. Ibid., 244.

42. Ibid., 232.

43. Ibid., 241.

44. Ibid., 237.

45. On the honor/shame complex and honor as virtue and social precedence, see
Stern, *The Secret History of Gender*, ix–xi, 13–14.

46. Fournier, *"Feliciano,"* 14.

47. Ibid., 237.

48. "'Feliciano' pidió perdón al Perú por los crímenes de Sendero Luminoso,"
Perú21, http://peru21.pe/politica/feliciano-pidio-perdon-al-peru-crimenes-sendero-lu
minoso-2123725. Perhaps Óscar Ramírez Durand's admiration for Fournier was genuine.

Ramírez came from a military family; he is the son of an Army general and a cousin to Montesinos.

49. Fournier, *"Feliciano,"* 232.

50. Ibid., 230–231. According to Fournier's website, he authored two books, both of which have the term *verdad* in the title (the other is *Tiwinza con zeta*, about the border conflict with Ecuador), and he participated in four other publications.

51. Boesten, *Sexual Violence*, 32–33. Only Jesús Sosa spoke specifically about rape in his conversations with Uceda. Sosa explained to Uceda that rape was permitted as a means to reduce "any administrative risk" that might have occurred if the soldiers' desires were not met. Uceda, *Muerte en el Pentagonito*, 122. Sosa later stated that he did not know these conversations would be published.

52. Franco, *Cruel Modernity*.

53. Henríquez and Mantilla, *Contra viento y marea*, 91. Cited in Boesten, "De violador a marido," 98. As Boesten notes the woman's and her family's honor could be restored through marriage to her aggressor, thus leading to the domestication of this crime.

54. Race, class, and gender dynamics in Peru exacerbated widespread sexual violence against Andean women and girls by the Armed Forces, and a normalization of this violence made it difficult for women to speak about these abuses. Despite the 538 cases documented by the CVR and another 16 cases for which the evidence had been gathered (these low numbers suggest the difficulty of speaking directly about sexual violence), none had come to trial, meaning the perpetrators of such acts were exempted from punishment in peacetime. Boesten, *Sexual Violence*, 5. In July 2016 the case of sexual abuse and crimes against humanity committed against over a dozen women from Manta and Vilca began preliminary hearings against fourteen accused military officers.

55. Citation from a colonel's testimony before the CVR, in Boesten, *Sexual Violence*, 30.

56. Fournier, *"Feliciano,"* 236.

57. Ibid., 238.

58. Efforts to undermine the significant scope of the CVR team's investigation serve to reduce the CVR's *Final Report* to a "version," "opinion," or "interpretation," rather than the product of facts and research. The CVR sought testimonies from members of the Armed Forces, both high-ranking and lower-level military personnel. These interviews are included in the nine-volume report and in the CVR archives.

59. According to one YouTube commentator, Graziani had been "perversely used" by the "caviars and communists," and "he was disloyal to his comrades in arms, the Army," for having participated in the CVR. The commentator described Graziani as an "old man who had not fought in any war," "who never fired a shot in his life," and came from the "Velasco era." "Ex-miembro CVR Graziani desmient conclusiones de CVR," YouTube, February 27, 2012, https://www.youtube.com/watch?v=yP2KomHH4hs.

60. Fournier, *"Feliciano,"* 238.

61. Ramal, *La paz*, 13.

62. Ibid., 144.

63. Ibid., 103 and 170.

64. It may be that this assertion comes from the CVR's projection that if the deaths and disappearances in Ayacucho had taken place at a similar level across the nation, the number of dead Peruvians would have reached 1.2 million. CVR, *Hatun Willakuy*, 12.

65. See, for instance, his table of "Terrorist and Counter-Terrorist Actions, 1980–2000." Fournier, *"Feliciano,"* 231. It should be noted that these authors were not trained in the social sciences and humanities and therefore might not understand the importance of citing their sources. However, the publisher ought to have known, especially in the case of the academic press of the Universidad Alas Peruanas. In order for military personnel to ascend in their careers, they must seek higher education in institutions such as UAP or the Center for Advanced Military Studies (Centro de Altos Estudios Militares, CAEM), where they might have been exposed to citation practices.

66. Morán, *Complot contra los militares*, 9.

67. Ibid., 17.

68. Listed in his bibliography are five titles dedicated to religious topics (including works by Thomas Aquinas and Saint Augustine), four titles on military topics, four on recent events in Peru, General Clemente Noel's memoir, the Peruvian Constitution, and works such as *La oscura verdad sobre George Soros* (The dark truth about George Soros), a title Morán presents as proof of a global conspiracy of international NGOs.

69. Morán, *Complot contra los militares*, 56.

70. Ibid., 21. Indeed, nearly a whole page dedicated to Chavín de Huántar is placed in bold text. The section title is "Chavín de Huántar, ni siquiera los héroes pueden salvarse" (Chavín de Huantar, not even heroes can save themselves). Ibid., 146.

71. In the section "Testimonio para la historia," Morán draws lessons from Argentine admiral Emilio Massera's trial, in which "those military leaders who defeated subversion now [sat] on the bench of the accused." According to Morán, Massera states that "history" would make it so that his children and grandchildren would "pronounce with pride the name that [he had] left them." Ibid., 132–33.

72. Ibid., 239. General Carlos Tafur Ganoza spoke publicly in favor of amnesty for military personnel charged with human rights abuses, including those indicated by the CVR. "No fue error firmar Acta de sujeción," *La República*, March 2, 2006, http://larepublica.pe/02-03-2006/no-fue-error-firmar-acta-de-sujecion.

73. Universidad Alas Peruanas, "Nota de prensa," http://www.uap.edu.pe/noticias/nota%20de%20prensa%20de%20la%20biblioteca%20de%20chorrillos.pdf.

74. Noticiero Masónico Internacional del Perú, "El M.R.H. Luis F. León Pizarro G.M. de la Gran Logia Patriótica del Perú realizando la presentación del Coronel Pablo Moran R. en la Conferencia Magistral: Falacias de la C.V.R.," May 22, 2015, http://www.noticieromasonicoperuano.blogspot.com/2015/05/el-mrh-luis-f-leon-pizarro-gm-de-la.html.

75. The case of Lurgio Gavilán complicates easy categorization. See chapter 3 for further discussion. Confessions and remorse did occur in interviews before the CVR, for instance, in the interviews with MRTA members Peter Cárdenas Schulte and Alberto Gálvez Olaechea and Shining Path member Óscar Ramírez Durand "Feliciano." CVR, "Sesiones públicas de balance y perspectivas," June 10, 2003, http://www.cver dad.org.pe/apublicas/sesiones/sesion10a.php. Silva Santiesteban describes the perform-ance of remorse by "El Brujo," a member of the state security forces who committed human rights abuses. He also expresses his anger with and frustration against his superior officers. *El factor asco*, 176–81.

76. Uceda, *Muerte en el Pentagonito*, 12. Cited also by Silva Santiesteban, *El factor asco*, 100.

77. Silva Santiesteban, *El factor asco*, 176–81; Franco, *Cruel Modernity*, 103–4. The specific call to vigilante justice referred to here is that of President Belaúnde when he publicly commended Huaychao residents for having killed some *senderistas*. This praise at the highest level of government could have been interpreted by others as linking patriotism and the defense of the nation with extrajudicial killings, not only by military personnel but also by Peruvians more broadly. The president's remarks may have played a role in the death of the journalists in Uchuraccay who were killed by villagers who possibly mistook them for *senderistas*.

78. The Colina Group member with the pseudonym "Montfort," after a French saint for the marginalized, is recorded as stating, "This act of removing them from Huachipa, burning them and burying them again, seems to me monstrous. No matter how much a terrorist. I cannot sleep thinking that God will not forgive us for this." Uceda, *Muerte en el Pentagonito*, 474–75.

79. Jesús Sosa, "Sin Remordimiento," interview with Mabel Huertas, for program *Día D*, Canal ATV, November 25, 2007, www.youtube.com/watch?v=ZGIa_10Z-rY. All quotes in this paragraph are from this interview.

80. Center for Justice & Accountability, "Telmo Hurtado Testifies to Cover-Up of Accomarca Massacre in Peruvian Court," April 9, 2012, http://www.cja.org/article .php?id=1080; http://peru.com/2012/04/09/actualidad/otras-noticias/telmo-hur tado-me-pidieron-hacerme-loco-no-implicar-altos-oficiales-noticia-57773; "Telmo Hurtado admite participación en masacre de Accomarca," YouTube, April 9, 2012, www.youtube.com/watch?v=-kgkT-RthoM.

81. Hurtado was sentenced in September 2016 to twenty-three years in prison along with nine other military men: Lieutenant Juan Rivera Rondón for twenty-four years, General Wilfredo Mori Orzo for twenty-five years, Colonel Nelson Gonzales Feria and Colonel Carlos Pastor Delgado Medina for twenty-five years, and five others for ten years. The tribunal absolved General José Williams Zapata for lack of evidence.

82. Franco, *Cruel Modernity*, 102.

83. Sosa, "Sin Remordimiento," interview with Mabel Huertas.

84. This notion of bare-bones democracy and tolerance for undemocratic measures was held by many. As the political scientist Maxwell Cameron notes, "Failure to appre-ciate this lesson [from the Fujimori regime] entails a major risk: that we may ignore

the fact that a substantial number of Peruvians supported an autocratic president *not in spite of* his repeated violations of fundamental rights and freedoms but *because* such violations were believed to be necessary to create a stronger, more 'authentic' democracy. This sentiment, rooted in the catastrophic experience with democracy in the 1980s, is what generated both the popularity of Fujimori and the public's tolerance for Montesinos, and this sentiment did not disappear with the collapse of the regime." Cameron, "Endogenous Regime Breakdown," 288–89.

85. "Por primera vez: Ex militar pide perdón a familiares de desaparecidos," *La República*, April 21, 2013, http://larepublica.pe/21-04-2013/ex-militar-pide-perdon-fa miliares-de-desaparecidos; "Ayacucho: Ex militar pide disculpas a campesinos por de-saparecer a sus familiares," *Publi.metro*, April 21, 2013, http://publimetro.pe/noti cias-de-collins-collantes-guerra-37896.

86. Fujimori publicly asked for forgiveness in October 2012 by way of a painting done while in prison, called by some the "self-portrait of sorry" (*autoretrato de perdón*). Upon closer inspection of the small print on the painting, however, one sees that he asked forgiveness not for what he had done but for what he had not managed to complete while in government.

87. In comparison, 3,800 copies of Cipriani's *Doy fe* were printed.

88. Montesinos's second edition of *Sin Sendero* (2011) did not get much mention in Peruvian newspapers. *El Diario Correo* announced that his lawyer, Estela Valdivia, would represent him at the book launch. The article does not mention his present in-carceration but states that he would soon undergo an operation due to health prob-lems, thus suggesting the latter as a reason for his absence at the event. "Montesinos presenta libro 'Sin Sendero. Alerta Temprana II," *El Diario Correo*, October 27, 2011, http://diariocorreo.pe/politica/montesinos-presenta-libro-sin-sendero-alerta-tem prana-ii-484592/. His 2016 two-volume account of the Chavín de Huántar operation got a bit more coverage. It took place in a Lima hotel, where he was again represented by lawyers who held out for viewing the originally hand-written manuscript. In Valdivia's remarks she stated that this book was published through proceeds of the sales of his previous books (he owes money to the Peruvian state). "Vladimiro Mon-tesinos: Así fue la presentación del libro del ex asesor," *Perú21*, January 24, 2017, http://peru21.pe/actualidad/vladimiro-montesinos-asi-fue-presentacion-libro-ex-ase sor-2268728.

89. Donayre was accused of reproducing sixty-five photographs and testimonies from an earlier Army publication, *El precio de la paz*, apparently produced by the Army in 2008 with the help of the CPHEP team, while Donayre was commanding general of the Army. "Acusan a Edwin Donayre de plagiar libro," TV Perú, http://www.tvperu.gob.pe/informa/elecciones2016/acusan-edwin-donayre-de-plagiar-libro; "Edwin Donayre: Otro plagio en APP," Foros Perú, http://www.forosperu.net/temas /edwin-donayre-otro-plagio-en-app.871161/.

90. "Clemente Noel, ex jefe político militar de Ayacucho, murió con orden de captura," *La República*, March 6, 2005, http://larepublica.pe/06-03-2005/cle mente-noel-ex-jefe-politico-militar-de-ayacucho-murio-con-orden-de-captura.

91. Hurtado and Sosa both named Martin Rivas and Hermoza Ríos. Hurtado also named Mori. One of the "hooded" judges ("*juez sin rostro*," or faceless judge) spoke publicly about his experiences in an interview, but his remarks on the whole justified the system, put in place by a decree law (25475) from May 1992 to December 1997 that kept magistrates anonymous. "Un ex juez sin rostro da la cara para contar su experiencia," *El Comercio*, April 3, 2013, http://elcomercio.pe/peru/lima/ex-juez-sin-rostro-da-cara-contar-su-experiencia-noticia-1558691.

92. Uceda interviewed "Montfort" while in prison. Rather than the possibility of a reduced sentence for naming others involved, in particular, his superiors, Montfort stated that he would not name them: "Acá vamos a sacar la cara por el Ejército" (we are going to be sacrificed for the Army). Uceda, *Muerte en el Pentagonito*, 477. Hurtado's declarations before the court contradicted the defense's arguments that the massacre resulted from the excesses of an individual, unbeknown to the command, and that indeed his testimony "corroborated the systematic crimes against humanity committed by the state." Jo-Marie Burt and Kristel Best Urday, "De confesiones y culpas," *Retablo*, June 20, 2012, www.noticiasser.pe/20/06/2012/contracorriente/de-confesiones-y-cul pas-el-juicio-por-el-caso-accomarca.

Indeed, Hurtado's statements were damning. His superior officer, Mori, was sentenced to twenty-five years in prison. In trial statements in 2012, Hurtado directly accused Mori not only of issuing the orders but also of shirking his responsibility in recognizing his role. Hurtado stated before the court, "It's time already, General Mori, for you to accept your responsibility for the things that happened. The officers ordered it and permitted it. You have to tighten your belt because in your unit you permitted illegal procedures, and things happened because you ordered them." See *La República*'s article "Telmo Hurtado acusa."

93. Payne, *Unsettling Accounts*, 104.

94. Jelin, *State Repression*, 35–36.

95. Stern, *Remembering Pinochet's Chile*, 106–7, 110–11.

96. Gates-Madsen, *Trauma, Taboo, and Truth-Telling*.

97. Kimberly Nance notes, however, that the *testimonio*, no matter how moving, may not ultimately provoke the reader to actively condemn or intervene, thus contravening the original goal of the genre. Nance, *Can Literature Promote Justice?*, 23–31.

98. Atencio, *Memory's Turn*, 38.

99. I received this book in Montreal, Quebec, in March 2016.

Chapter 2. The Army's Memory Entrepreneurs and Their Truth Report

1. Although originally published in October 2010, *En honor a la verdad* reached wider distribution only in April 2013. All citations here are from the 2012 edition of *En honor a la verdad* unless otherwise noted.

2. Comisión Permanente de Historia del Ejército del Perú (CPHEP), *Operación militar*. This publication involved much of the same investigative team (not including

General Marco Merino) as *En honor a la verdad*, yet it is a less developed and researched report, consisting of 162 heavy, high-gloss pages with little print but many photographs.

3. CPHEP, *En honor a la verdad*, 5.

4. Ibid.

5. Brigadier General Marco Merino, "Introduction," in *En honor a la verdad*, 7.

6. Ibid., 8.

7. I am uncertain how unique the CPHEP is among Latin American Armed Forces; some other Latin American militaries have branches (such as the Chilean Army) whose members include history buffs. Both the Ecuadoran and the Salvadoran armies have historical commissions; the latter has a truck with its logo on it. Other militaries may also have historical commissions. According to one CPHEP member, Peru's Army seems unusual in employing a team of civilians with degrees in history who work with professionally trained historians who are military personnel. Personal communication with Lourdes Medina, July 1, 2015.

8. CPHEP, *Compendio*, 290–91.

9. The Navy's Instituto de Estudios Histórico-Marítimos del Perú (Institute for the Study of Peruvian Marine History), founded at the same time as the CPHEP, similarly studies its institutional history and includes some prominent academics with doctoral degrees. They have not engaged twentieth-century topics as far as I have been able to ascertain. I have not found any information indicating that such a group was formed for the Air Force.

10. Kruijt and Tello, "From Military Reformists," 37 and 49.

11. Personal communication with Brigadier General Marco Merino, July 9, 2015.

12. The commission was called the National Commission for the Sesquicentennial of Peruvian Independence. Aguirre, "The Second Liberation? Military Nationalism and the Sesquicentennial Commemoration of Peruvian Independence, 1821–1971," in Aguirre and Drinot, *Peculiar Revolution*, 27–29.

13. As a sign of their renewed efforts, in 2005 the CPHEP completed the fifth volume of the Historia del Ejército del Perú series, which focuses on the nineteenth century.

14. Personal communication with Lourdes Hurtado, July 7, 2015.

15. There may also have been a desire among Army personnel to "put themselves at the same level" as the Navy, which is typically considered the more "professional" (*más calificados*) of the two institutions, according to historian Antonio Zapata. Personal communication with Antonio Zapata, July 10, 2015.

16. For instance, both the Universidad Nacional Mayor de San Marcos and the Pontificia Universidad Católica del Perú (PUCP) established a program by which members of the Armed Forces and National Police may take courses at these universities. Personal communication with PUCP professor María Eugenia Ulfe, July 6, 2015; "Convenio entre UNMSM y Ejército del Perú impulse estudios postgrado," November 8, 2010, http://www.unmsm.edu.pe/noticias/ver/1302.

17. The military pays the salary of recruits who simultaneously seek higher educational degrees.

18. The CPHEP investigative team for *En honor a la verdad* was also headed by three brigadier generals, who "supported the research." Personal communication with Lourdes Hurtado, July 7, 2015.

19. See the CPHEP Facebook page, www.facebook.com/ComisionPermanente DeHistoriaDelEjercitoDelPeru. In addition to the Facebook page, the CPHEP has a blog, though it is not up to date. See http://cpheperu.wix.com/blog-de-la-cphep.

20. Among its publications cited in a promotional pamphlet of the CPHEP since the transition are *Compendio*, *Evolución histórica de los uniformes*, *Historia de unidades*, *Historia de la Escuela Técnica*, and *Historia de la aviación*.

21. Brigadier General Merino was in the same graduating class as Antauro Humala and among the ten from this class who were promoted by Ollanta Humala in 2013. "19 generales de la promoción Humala asumen mandos de grandes unidades EP," *La República*, January 1, 2013, http://larepublica.pe/06-01-2013/19-generales-de-la-pro mocion-humala-asumen-mandos-de-grandes-unidades-ep.

22. Carlos Freyre wrote a biweekly report for the Instituto de Defensa Legal (Institute for Legal Defense, IDL).

23. Personal communication with Lourdes Medina (July 1, 2015) and Antonio Zapata (July 10, 2015). See also Zapata, "En honor a la verdad."

24. Personal communication with Major Carlos Freyre, February 19, 2016. According to Antonio Zapata, he was invited to a meeting by members of the Armed Forces sometime in 2007 or 2008 in which he was asked his opinion if such a book might be a good idea. In retrospect, he saw this question as emerging from the impact that the CVR was having on the Armed Forces: a negative perception in public debate that positioned the Armed Forces along with Shining Path as human rights abusers, and by then a series of trials against its members were under way. Personal communication with Antonio Zapata, July 10, 2015.

25. Personal communication with Lourdes Medina, July 1, 2015. Gloria Cano from APRODEH also confirmed that *En honor a la verdad* was cited vaguely by Army personnel in their legal defense, without making specific references to the content. Email communication, November 3, 2015.

26. I thank Rebecca Atencio for drawing my attention to the Orvil project. Personal communication, December 1, 2016. See also "Jornais revelam conteúdo de livro secreto de Exército," *Vermelho*, April 15, 2007, http://www.vermelho.org.br/noticia /15526-1. The entire 953 pages can be viewed at http://www.averdadesufocada.com /images/orvil/orvil_completo.pdf. According to fellow researchers Claudio Barrientos, Francesca Lessa, and Valentina Silva, there seems to be no comparable document produced by the Chilean, Argentine, and Uruguayan armies. Personal communication, November 8–9, 2016.

27. I thank historian Antonio Zapata for this insight into the Libros Blancos. Personal communication with Antonio Zapata, July 10, 2015. See also Toche, *Guerra y democracia*, 182.

28. César Campos, "Fuerzas Armadas y Policiales del Perú: 'En honor a la verdad,'" December 1, 2010, www.generacion.com/usuarios/41638.

29. While *En honor a la verdad* was supposed to be distributed free of charge to interested parties, I know of at least two members of human rights organizations who bought their copies. Most, however, had been given the book.

30. According to the authors, the leader of each base and patrol had to regularly submit a patrol report, an *informe de patrulla*. These reports were collected by the operations officers and used to prepare summaries and intelligence reports. This measure was introduced to improve control over the troops. Yet a footnote states, "The conservation of official documents such as these has been very deficient. Twenty-six years after the beginning of the war, almost none of the documents of this type exist, because each battalion administered itself, and each determined its own fate. Particularly for units that moved from one place to another and those that participated in the Cenepa conflict of 1995, the possibility of passive archival documents is practically nil." CPHEP, *En honor a la verdad*, 65n139.

31. According to Gloria Cano, despite requesting specific documents mentioned in *En honor a la verdad*, APRODEH had not been given access to any of them. The Army replied that it did not have them, not even the yearly report of the Army (*Memoria anual del Ejército*) that the CPHEP had used for their book. Email communication, November 3, 2015. On the failure of the Armed Forces to provide requested documentation, including sources cited in *En honor a la verdad*, see Burt and Cagley, "Access to Information," 84.

32. This might explain in part why when I originally heard about *En honor a la verdad* in 2011, I was unable to locate a copy, in addition to the fact that it had a much smaller print run.

33. I was told this story about the soldier in the center of the photograph by at least three different people in the military. One person told me that a widow, upon seeing the cover, came to the CPHEP to identify him as her husband. The widow's testimony is included in the LUM exhibition section "Una persona, todas las personas," discussed in chapter 4.

The differences between the 2010 and 2012 versions seem fairly minor. For instance, in the section "Lessons Learned" in the 2012 version, the book states that the Armed Forces' entry into the conflict had been planned by Shining Path "*un hecho previsto*" (*En honor a la verdad* [2012], 329)—as part of "its strategy to take power" instead of the earlier "*una previsión*," "forecast" (*En honor a la verdad* [2010], 333).

34. Personal communication with Lourdes Medina, July 8, 2015.

35. "Sofía Macher: "Me opuse a llevar a militares a las audiencias de la CVR," *Perú21*, September 10, 2012, http://peru21.pe/politica/sofia-macher-me-opuse-llevar-militares-audiencias-cvr-2041549.

The CVR did not have a specific *audiencia pública* (public hearing) with members of the Armed Forces or the National Police (though some chose to participate in the other *audiencias públicas*). It was decided at the time not to hold a public hearing for armed state actors because some of the commissioners, including Sofía Macher, felt that doing so would risk giving an open microphone to the Armed Forces. Such a public platform might have undermined the spirit of the CVR, which was meant as a forum and opportunity for victims to recount their experiences. In the 2012 interview, Macher stated that the CVR ought to have held an *audiencia pública* for the Armed Forces in the spirit of reconciliation. She imagined that the participants would have probably caught themselves in their own fabrications. Personal communication with Sofía Macher, June 7, 2015.

Macher's remarks were reduced by others to her having stated that the CVR had not consulted the Armed Forces at all. In many of my interviews and in much of the material I have read, this claim was repeated, always with the aim of casting doubt on the CVR's findings and highlighting its limitations and bias. In one example, Keiko Fujimori surprised the audience at her Harvard University lecture in the fall of 2015 by making some mildly positive statements about the work of the CVR. Accused of turning into a "caviar" and risking division within her own political party, Fujimori reminded audiences back home that the CVR, though an important first step, had not taken into consideration the opinions of the Armed Forces and National Police. "La CVR tuvo un sesgo al no considerar opinión de FF.AA. y PNP," *El Comercio*, October 5, 2015, http://elcomercio.pe/politica/actualidad/keiko-fujimori-cvr-tuvo-sesgo-al-no-con siderar-opinion-ffaa-y-pnp-noticia-1845999?ref=nota_politica&ft=mod_leatam bien&e=titulo.

In an attempt to limit the harm done by this misinterpretation of Macher's comments and to make clear that the CVR did indeed consult the National Police and the Armed Forces, Dr. Salomón Lerner responded in "El papel de las Fuerzas Armadas: Recordando el Informe Final de la CVR," October 6, 2015, http://idehpucp.pucp .edu.pe/comunicaciones/notas-informativas/el-papel-de-las-fuerzas-armadas-recor dando-el-informe-final-de-la-cvr/.

It is important to note that some military members, of course, recognize that the CVR did include military testimonies but that these were "insufficient." See, for instance, the presentation by Brigadier General Marco Merino at "Diálogos por la paz y la memoria: Fuentes y testimonios para la reconstrucción de la guerra reciente: *Memorias de un soldado desconocido* y *En honor a la verdad*," IEP, Lima, January 24, 2013, https:// www.youtube.com/watch?v=IZX-4UxnXk8.

36. Indeed, researchers have used these testimonies, for instance, Pizarro Romero, "Ni héroes ni enemigos."

37. CPHEP, *En honor a la verdad*, 194, 103.

38. Kruijt and Tello, who conducted interviews with retired officers in the late 1990s, similarly note the ill-preparedness of the Armed Forces, as well as their reluctance, to engage with Shining Path. "From Military Reformists," 44.

39. CPHEP, *En honor a la verdad*, 164.

40. Ibid., 331.

41. Personal communication with Lourdes Medina, July 8, 2015; Merino, "Introduction" in *En honor a la verdad*, 7.

42. In the acknowledgments, the CPHEP thanks the following institutions, thus

giving readers some indication of the location of the written sources and published works: Biblioteca Nacional del Perú, Centro de Información para la Memoria Colectiva y los Derechos Humanos (the archive of the CVR's documents); Biblioteca del Congreso; Archivo Central del Ejército; Archivo de la Oficina de Asesoría Jurídica del Ejército; Centro de Estudios Histórico-Militares del Perú; Biblioteca del Centro de Altos Estudios Nacionales; and Biblioteca de la Escuela Superior de Guerra. CPHEP, *En honor a la verdad*, 4.

43. For instance, Merino cites historians José Luis Igue, Jesús Cosamalón, and Paulo Drinot in his introduction.

44. Antonio Zapata, presentation at "Diálogos por la paz y la memoria: Fuentes y testimonios para la reconstrucción de la guerra reciente: *Memorias de un soldado desconocido y En honor a la verdad*," Instituto de Estudios Peruanos (IEP), Lima, January 24, 2013, https://www.youtube.com/watch?v=IZX-4UxnXk8.

45. CPHEP, *En honor a la verdad*, 54.

46. Ibid., 37–38.

47. Tucked away in the footnotes is the fact that this meant only 1,754 people (probably based in Lima) had made such a statement. Ibid., 42, 42n80.

48. Ibid., 33, n54, n55.

49. Zapata, "En honor a la verdad."

50. CPHEP, *En honor a la verdad*, 96.

51. CPHEP, *En honor a la verdad*, 96–97.

52. In addition to unnamed "Official Documents of the Army," this section also cites José Cabrejos Samamé's *La verdad sobre Accomarca*, published by ADDCOT in 2006. Samamé, formerly chief of the Joint Command's "Estado Mayor" and thus advisor and second to General Nicolás Hermoza Ríos ("División Blindada," *Revista Caretas*, May 30, 1996, http://www.caretas.com.pe/1416/mdf/mdf.htm), was forced into retirement in 2010. He died in May 2014 while head of ADOGEN, one week after providing testimony against his will. According to one blog, the prosecution did not heed the medical advice that Cabrejos was too ill to attend, and the stress from this experience led to his death. The posting is titled "Another Victim of Hate," in the blog by "Politically Incorrect," https://victorrobles.wordpress.com/2014/05/27/la-muer te-del-general-cabrejos/#more-2567.

53. A similar analysis of this "closed defense" and the basing of the CPHEP version on 2009 interviews and testimonies of military personal (in some cases men who would later face criminal charges) could be made of the CPHEP coverage of the Cayara case and the Cenepa War.

54. Zapata, "En honor a la verdad." That *En honor a la verdad* is specifically focused on the Army's participation in the conflict might explain why the role of *rondas* in the pacification received little mention. CPHEP, *En honor a la verdad*, 30–32, 319–20. A CPHEP project was apparently under way in 2015 to write the history of the *rondas*' participation in the conflict. Personal communication with Lourdes Medina, July 8, 2015.

55. Burt and Cagley, "Access to Information," 84.

56. At least one of the CPHEP historians did not consider Donayre's book a serious academic study and would have preferred not to have participated in it. There is some confusion over whether this research was done for *El silencio de los héroes* or another 2008 Army publication, *El precio de la paz*. I have not been able to locate this book or publishing information. It is mentioned in a denunciation for plagiarism against Donayre. "Edwin Donayre: Otro plagio en APP," Foros Perú, http://www.forosperu.net/temas/edwin-donayre-otro-plagio-en-app.871161/.

57. Personal communication with Lourdes Medina, July 8, 2015. In her presentation at the IEP, Medina positioned herself and colleagues as part of those years. Having studied for degrees at the Universidad de San Marcos between 1977 and 1990 and then entering the Armed Forces as associates (*socios*), she considered them "witnesses to before and after the war." Lourdes Medina, presentation at "Diálogos por la paz y la memoria: Fuentes y testimonios para la reconstrucción de la guerra reciente: *Memorias de un soldado desconocido* y *En honor a la verdad*," Instituto de Estudios Peruanos (IEP), January 24, 2013, https://www.youtube.com/watch?v=IZX-4UxnXk8.

58. Personal communication with Brigadier General Marco Merino, July 9, 2015.

59. Medina presentation at "Diálogos por la paz y la memoria."

60. Personal communication with Lourdes Medina, July 8, 2015.

61. Merino presentation at "Diálogos por la paz y la memoria."

62. Personal communication with Lourdes Medina, July 8, 2015.

63. The coding of the testimonies makes it difficult to ascertain the number of participants. Assuming that each code represents a single individual, after repeated numbers are removed, there are seventy-one distinct testimonies, out of a total of eighty-two (seven start with code TO/TC, fifty-six start with EO/EC, fifteen are named interviews, and four are unnamed interviews). In addition, two interviews come from Donayre's *El silencio de los héroes*; to the fifteen named interviews, one could add the testimony of Tarcila Rojas Huamán taken from Donayre, *El silencio de los héroes*. CPHEP, *En honor a la verdad*, 113n243.

64. Citing historian Lewis Taylor, the CPHEP state that the military was considered the invading force and Shining Path the "local team." The CPHEP authors imply that because of the *sinchis*' use of "indiscriminate force against citizens," highland peoples "hated" soldiers. CPHEP, *En honor a la verdad*, 51.

65. In his testimony before the CVR, Huamán more clearly explained that this "bread strategy" was meant to win over the local population, which needed to be not "reconquered" but "conquered" by the state since the state had never been there in the first place. Huamán described bringing large quantities of bread to communities, inviting older women to gather so that they could fill up their *polleras* (skirts) with bread, followed by the men, with whom he would then converse. News of the distribution of bread spread swiftly so that "the other towns knew that when the helicopter arrived it came with bread, thus facilitating the counterstrike." Defensoría del Pueblo, transcription of interview with Adrián Huamán Centeno, caja 4, núm. 46, cantidad 3, April 3, 2003. This positive association contrasts greatly with the fear of helicopters

depicted in post-CVR artwork and accounts. Milton, *Art from a Fractured Past*, 43–44; Cecconi, "Dreams, Memory, and War."

66. CPHEP, *En honor a la verdad*, 58.

67. Ibid., 57.

68. Ibid., 58.

69. Ibid., 57.

70. In his interview with the CVR, in response to the question of whether Huamán had received complaints about rape or sexual abuse by soldiers, marines, or police, he responded, "No, in this case, the campesinas are very modest [*recatadas*]." While he recognized that there were cases of rape—"by the police"—he stated that the women, being modest, would not openly denounce such abuse. He turned the conversation quickly to "some shameless individuals [*unos cuantos sinverquenzas*] who fell into corruption." Defensoría del Pueblo, interview with General Adrián Huamán Centeno, 29. On the continued impediments for testifying to rape in post-CVR Peru, see Boesten, *Sexual Violence*, esp. 104.

71. CPHEP, *En honor a la verdad*, 58.

72. Ibid.

73. Ibid., 60.

74. Ibid., 57.

75. The term *systematic* is used many times in the CVR's abbreviated version of its final report, *Hatun Willakuy*, in reference to both Shining Path and the Armed Forces. In reference to state agents, for instance, "the systematic and widespread use of these methods constituted grave crimes against humanity which are condemned by Peruvian and international law" (29); 1983 and 1984 are referred to as years in which the state agents committed "widespread and systematic human rights abuses in the Ayacucho region" (64); a section has the title "the political-military commands: systematic, generalized patterns of human rights violations" (193); and two conclusions also point to systematic practices (number 55: "the CVR affirms that at some places and moments in the conflict, the behavior of members of the armed forces not only involved some individual excesses by officers or soldiers but also entailed generalized and/or systematic practices of human rights violations that constituted crimes against humanity as well as transgressions of the norms of international humanitarian law," 337; number 84: "the CVR has established that both the creation of the political-military commands and the intervention of the armed forces were carried out without civilian authorities taking necessary preventive measures to protect the fundamental rights of the population. This resulted in numerous violations of human rights being carried out in a systematic and/or generalized manner," 341).

76. CVR, *Hatun Willakuy*, 47. On the period of Huamán as a "reformer," see Kruijt and Tello, "From Military Reformists," 44.

77. CPHEP, *En honor a la verdad*, 71.

78. The commanding generals in Ayacucho—Noel, Huamán, Mori, and Juan Antonio Gil Jara—correspond to the period that the CVR identified as the "militarization of the conflict," from January 1983 to June 1986. According to the CVR, "This

phase of the militarization produced massive human rights abuses attributed to the security forces, such as the massacre in Socos (Sinchis of the former Civil Guard, November 1983), Pucayacu (Navy, August 1984), Putis (Army, December 1984) and Accomarca (Army, August 1985). The PCP-SL also committed some of its worst atrocities during this period, such as the massacres in Lucanamarca and Huancasancos (April 1983)." CVR, *Hatun Willakuy*, 48.

79. Burt, *Political Violence*, 58.

80. Obando, "Civil-Military Relations in Peru," 389. Helpful in understanding how the Armed Forces could both be "pro-development" and use "hardline" tactics is Obando's chapter in Stern's *Shining and Other Paths*. He clearly describes how the *velasquistas* (using a win-the-heart-and-mind approach) lost ground within the Armed Forces to the conservative hardliners (dirty war approach), the latter having the support of civilian authorities. Throughout the Belaúnde era and into Gracía, the *velasquistas* would emerge in important positions within the Army only to be replaced because their ideas of economic development as an approach to resolving the conflict were deemed too costly. This explains why there were openings and moments of more progressive relationships between the Army and local populations that would suddenly close shut. Ideologically, the Left wing within the military further lost credibility as an unsustainable discourse in the face of terrorism from the left. Obando, "Civil-Military Relations in Peru," 388–89.

81. Ibid., 388–89.

82. CPHEP, *En honor a la verdad*, 31.

83. When García fired high-ranking military leaders for having covered up the Accomarca massacre, the Armed Forces refused to perform their duties in the southern Andes for some nine months, thus allowing Shining Path to regain its foothold, an act that brought the government to heel. Burt, *Political Violence*, 63.

84. Obando, "Civil-Military Relations in Peru," 389.

85. CPHEP, *En honor a la verdad*, 164.

86. Ibid., 165–66.

87. According to Burt, this correlated to one-third of national territory under military control. Burt, *Political Violence*, 168–69. According to *En honor a la verdad*, 44.27 percent of the population was under a state of emergency or 22.14 percent of national territory in 1995. Their source for these numbers is Nicolás Lynch's *Una tragedía sin héroes*, whose information is from yet another source. CPHEP, *En honor a la verdad*, 286. The CVR only provides numbers up to the year 1989; in 1988, 24.14 percent of national territory was under a state of emergency. CVR, *Hatun Willakuy*, 188.

88. Burt, *Political Violence*, 166–69; Obando, "Civil-Military Relations in Peru." Burt argues that rather than considering the 1992 *autogolpe* the result of a political impasse, it should be understood as a plan hatched early on by Fujimori and Montesinos to centralize power in the executive in order to subordinate democratic institutions. This "authoritarian consensus" necessitated the participation of the Armed Forces, which in return gained control over counterinsurgency and guaranteed impunity. Burt, *Political Violence*, 169–71. On this alliance, see CVR, *Hatun Willakuy*, 208–18;

on Fujimori's use of decrees, see CVR, *Hatun Willakuy*, 228–31. Antonio Zapata has referred to the period of successive hardliners who rose to the top as "regressive selection," whereby those with the greatest propensity to envision their position as a sinecure for self-aggrandizement aligned with the position of civilian government. Personal communication with Antonio Zapata, July 10, 2015.

89. CPHEP, *En honor a la verdad*, 309–10.

90. Zapata, presentation at "Diálogos por la paz y la memoria."

91. CPHEP, *En honor a la verdad*, 5.

92. The commanding general of the Army, Ricardo Homero Moncada Novoa, dedicated the 2012 book to the honor of those who defended the nation and to the truth necessary for "solidarity and fraternity." Ibid., 3.

93. Ibid., 312. While the Human Rights Trials in Peru project has tried to obtain specific numbers of denunciations and trials, and the status of both, it would have been clear to the Armed Forces that the case universe was much larger than the original number of CVR cases. Burt and Cagley, "Access to Information," 80–82.

94. In the case of the latter, the authors see history as holding the potential to absolve the Army of wrongdoing. CPHEP, *En honor a la verdad*, 313.

95. Ibid.

96. Ibid., 66.

97. Ibid., 295–300, 311–13.

98. Ibid., 33.

99. Ibid.

100. By linking the umbrella group CNDDHH as one of these "façade organizations" ("*organismos de fachada*"), the authors of *En honor a la verdad* must have considered most human rights NGOs in Peru to be ideologically sympathetic to the cause of Shining Path. CPHEP, *En honor a la verdad*, 33.

101. CPHEP, *En honor a la verdad*, 50 (emphasis mine).

102. The website of the Peruvian Army offers a lengthy "Code of Honor" that guides the conduct and orients the identity of its individual members. Point number 4 of the code states, "I AM A MAN OF HONOR, my word is Truth, Commitment and Guarantee, my Conscience has no price and Justice is my aspiration" (capitalization in the original). Ejército del Perú, "Codigo de honor," http://www.ejercito.mil.pe/index .php/nosotros/277-codigo-de-honor.

103. CPHEP, *En honor a la verdad*, 295.

104. Ibid., 297.

105. Ibid., 51n93. Perhaps it was the implementation of these basic criteria and their diffusion that saved the young Lurgio Gavilán, discussed in chapter 3, who was taken as a prisoner rather than being killed.

106. Ibid., 65.

107. Ibid., 64–65.

108. Ibid., 298.

109. Ibid., 295.

110. Ibid., 313.

111. According to Jo-Marie Burt, there is no equivalent in English to *autoría mediata*, which is usually translated as "perpetration by means." It refers to those who have ultimate authority and command of decision over an "organized power apparatus." Burt, "Paradoxes of Accountability," 157, 170n10. The Army's concern about the charge of *autoría mediata* is stated in *En honor a la verdad*, 312.

112. Several military personnel told me that the Army had asked for forgiveness in *En honor a la verdad*. I appreciate Lieutenant Carla Granados for indicating to me the sections that were considered as such in *En honor a la verdad*. Personal communication, November 17, 2015.

113. CPHEP, *En honor a la verdad*, 305.

114. The fate of these victims was thus not the consequence of Peruvian history or society. As such, the authors do not adopt the CVR's argument that the conflict was the product of historical injustices that led to 75 percent of victims being non–native Spanish speakers.

115. CPHEP, *En honor a la verdad*, 306.

116. Ibid., 305.

117. Some examples of errors cited are improper burials (which gave outsiders the impression of extrajudicial killings) and the policy of punishing soldiers who had committed some infraction by sending them to yet more remote areas, which was later seen as a "tremendous error." Ibid., 309, 307.

118. Ibid., 311, emphasis mine.

119. Ibid., 330.

120. The CVR uses the term *genocide* not in reference to the actions of the Armed Forces but rather to describe Shining Path's incursions into Asháninka territory, which led to the destruction of indigenous communities. CVR, *Hatun Willakuy*, 65.

121. CPHEP, *En honor a la verdad*, 331.

122. The latter point is also made by Antonio Zapata in his presentation at "Diálogo por la paz y la memoria."

123. These and other cases before the Peruvian judiciary are discussed in Burt and Cagley, "Access to Information," 84–86.

124. Putis is mentioned only once in *En honor a la verdad* as the location where a military base was established in May 1985. This footnote states that prior to this date "no base operated in this population." The dates are important to note, for the inference here is that the Army cannot be held responsible for the deaths and the mass graves later found, despite evidence to the contrary. CPHEP, *En honor a la verdad*, 95n192.

125. María Eugenia Ulfe and Vera Lucía Ríos, "Diálogos para la paz y para la memoria," *NoticiasSER.pe*, January 30, 2013.

126. See Gonzalo Portocarrero's remarks during the question-and-answer period at "Diálogos por la paz y la memoria: Fuentes y testimonios para la reconstrucción de la guerra reciente: *Memorias de un soldado desconocido y En honor a la verdad*," IEP, Lima, January 24, 2013, https://www.youtube.com/watch?v=UDVv8BMRUrk.

127. Emilio Camacho, "El infante que contaba historias," *La República*, March 17, 2013, http://larepublica.pe/17-03-2013/el-infante-que-contaba-historias.

128. Another, similar dialogue took place on April 29, 2016, but between released "political prisoners of indirect *sendero* affiliation" and three members of the Peruvian Army, including a retired general, to which historian Antonio Zapata had been invited. The event was organized by the former prisoners. At this event, Zapata described three positions being discussed: that of the Army (represented by the military men present), that of Shining Path (represented by the prisoners), and that of the CVR (to which Zapata was tasked with representing). From Zapata's description, the conversation did not go into detail. Each "camp" described the general lines of its position, yet the fact of holding such an event was significant. As Zapata wrote, it was "an unexpected dialogue." Antonio Zapata, "Un diálogo inesperado," *La República*, May 4, 2015, http:// larepublica.pe/impresa/opinion/764792-un-dialogo-inesperado.

Chapter 3. *Guerra fratricida*

1. Lurgio Gavilán and Carlos Freyre almost share a birthday; both were born in 1974, just days apart, though Gavilán's exact year of birth is uncertain, a consequence of his socioeconomic and geographical origins. Gavilán, *When Rains Became Floods*, 112n19.

2. It was not until late in the first decade of the twenty-first century that the region came to be referred to as the VRAE, and then later VRAEM, after the rivers that make up the region.

3. Freyre started writing for the IDL in 2014, by invitation of Gustavo Gorriti. Carlos Freyre, "¿Irías a rescatalo?," *Diarios de guarnición*, https://idl-reporteros.pe /irias-a-rescatarlo/. Prior to *Desde el Valle de las Esmeraldas*, Freyre published short stories and two other novels (*La muerte de Giuseppi Bari*, 2003; *Huayna Quiya o el capitán enamorado de la luna*, 2005). He subsequently published *El fantasmocopio* (2010), *El semental* (2012), and *El ultimo otoño antes de tí* (2015). Biographical information about Freyre was gathered from a variety of sources: Hugo Martínez Garay's "Héroes y villanos"; Internet sources (articles, Facebook postings, and YouTube videos); and personal conversations with Freyre.

4. Gavilán was incorporated into the Army prior to the 1993 decree law that made legal this earlier practice.

5. What is perhaps less fair to Gavilán is my focus on the chapter in his autobiography that deals with his years in the Army. Gavilán did not intend for his book to be read in this way. Indeed, the narrative is such that his different experiences led him to (and were perhaps atoned for by) his joining the Franciscans and the closing of the circle when he returned to his natal lands as a social anthropologist.

6. For instance, author Hugo Coya's prologue to *Desde el Valle de las Esmeraldas*.

7. Freyre, *Desde el Valle*, 178. Further citations of this work are given parenthetically in text.

8. While military spokespersons and others have equated the CVR with *sendero*, this is one of the few instances that I have noticed where the military likens itself to Shining Path.

9. Kruijt and Tello describe the Armed Forces' reluctance to fight against the guerrilla movements of the 1960s because they "had to fight adversaries who were not really enemies" and they shared an understanding of the insurgency's causes as rooted in Peruvian social and economic underdevelopment and the political system's inadequacies: "it was just a matter of time before a new wave of guerrilla led rebellion would sweep the country." Kruijt and Tello, "From Military Reformists," 38.

10. Description taken from the DVD cover. The scene where Sixto Caya and Felipe Cano promise to be brothers to each other takes place early in the film, while a Guzmán-like character is in the village espousing the need to create a new society. Felipe cements the bond by giving Sixto a small image of the Virgin Mary, to which Sixto responds, "She is just like your mother."

11. Almost half the book takes place in and around "Constitución." The main character refers to the area as the Emerald Valley, but the larger region is supposedly Suinabeni. Suinabeni is most likely a name invented by the author that refers to Somabeni in the VRAEM. The soldiers in the photograph on the front cover of *En honor a la verdad* (2012) were stationed in the area of Somabeni. According to the author, he has changed the names of some but not all of these communities. Conversation with Carlos Freyre (via Skype), February 19, 2016; CPHEP, *En honor a la verdad*, 246.

12. CPHEP, *En honor a la verdad*, 21.

13. Lladó, *Vidas paralelas*, closing text.

14. In the film *Vidas paralelas*, a female character, Bertha, portrays a character similar to Chola Bonita.

15. The author presents Chola Bonita as a mother in Peru's diverse nation, of the next generation. When Elías barges into Chola Bonita's house to confront her about a recent ambush, he encounters her calmly seated near her two sleeping sons, the younger one who had "coppery skin and coarser hair and who had trouble breathing" and the older boy who had features of the "coast" and "could have passed for a son of [his]" (151). It is the only place in this novel where the readers encounter this younger set of brothers (one of indigenous descent and the other of Spanish or mestizo descent), products of the previous generation's fratricide, and we do not find out what happens to them, this next generation. This theme of two "races" fighting on opposite sides is more obvious in the film *Vidas paralelas*. In the film, the Sixto Caya character has more Andean features, and Felipe Cano more costal features, a difference also indicated by their last names.

16. When they get news of Muca's betrayal, a soldier says to Elías, "Muca went back, Comrade Elías," meaning that she had returned to the side where she had originated and also implicating Elías by using the term *comrade*. The patrol later replaces Muca with another dog, which they give the same name (114).

17. Even Guzmán is portrayed fairly lightly, as an overweight, middle-aged philosopher, who was a misguided person (*un ser equivocado*) (91).

18. One blogger seems to consider real the person who is supposedly interviewed: Elton Honores, *Illuminaciones*, June 11, 2011, http://eltonhonores.blogspot.it/2011/06/carlos-enrique-freyre-desde-el-valle-de.html. Though readers may think that Freyre is

the main character, he has stated that he is not. Personal communication with Carlos Freyre (via Google Hangouts), February 17, 2016.

19. Martínez Garay, "Héroes y villanos," 6.

20. In addition to the places already mentioned, Freyre was sent to the following locations: Huancané (Puno), Pampas (Huancavelica), on the frontier of Ecuador, in Apurímac and Chungui. As an example of the remoteness of the places he has traveled, he mentions "Wawa Wasi," a name given by the military to this village because of the kidnapped and orphaned children. Personal communication, February 27, 2016.

21. On camaraderie, Freyre writes, "We ate together, without following the old distinction of hierarchical rank so present in the military academy and in troop battalions; we shared bedding and mosquito nets, cutlery, and discomforts of home remedies. We listened to the music out the force of habit, and I laughed at their jokes and listened to their absurd stories of love, sex, passion and the reasons why they served in the Army." Freyre, *Desde el Valle*, 69. In our interview, Freyre also spoke of the stories and superstitions of the men under his command. Many of these young soldiers came from rural regions and from the zones in which they were stationed. Personal communication with Carlos Freyre (via Skype), February 19, 2016.

22. Personal communication with Carlos Freyre, February 27, 2016.

23. Personal conversation with Lourdes Medina, July 1, 2015.

24. But as Hugo Martínez argues, it is a discourse resting on certain binaries that become blurred over the course of the novel, such as the military/civilian binary mirroring that of order versus chaos. Yet the military was poorly prepared to enter the war, and the training that it had was not as useful as the knowledge of lower-ranking and more local personnel, such as Saldaña, who advised Elías to adopt the dog Muca. Nor does the Army appear particularly well organized since the numbers of confrontations with Shining Path mentioned in the book were only slightly more than the accidental confrontations with other patrols. Martínez Garay, "Héroes y villanos."

25. A notably violent series of incursions in the central jungle region was the 1994 Operation Aries, which "led to the highest death toll of the entire conflict," and might be the inspiration for Freyre's description of Elías's last confrontation. CVR, *Hatun Willakuy*, 235–36.

26. Indeed, in his public interview with "Noticia Rebelde," Freyre describes Shining Path members as individuals who chose the wrong path. "Carlos Freyre, el mayor del Ejército que se dedica a la literature en el VRAEM," YouTube, November 29, 2015, https://www.youtube.com/watch?v=NJlVdODI5Do.

27. There is no mention of rape in the film *Vidas paralelas*, except for an oblique reference that is turned into a joke. In the film, when the main character arrives in the highlands, he complains of the cold temperature, to which a soldier replies that he should find a pair of "*cholas*" to keep him warm. When the protagonist looks confused, the soldier explains that he means some "hot water bottles," thus implying not local women. The CVR reports 83 percent of rapes were committed by state armed forces, 11 percent by Shining Path or the MRTA, and 6 percent by unknown actors. CVR, *Informe Final*, vol. 6, 278.

28. Boesten, *Sexual Violence*, 115–16.

29. Because of the paragraph spacing, it is unclear if Leoncio is speaking directly to Isolina or if these are his inner thoughts.

30. Diaries may work against military personnel. For instance, the discovery in 2001 of the intelligence agent Fabio Urquizo Ayma's (also known as "Agent Carrion") personal diary provided information useful to prosecutors. In his diary, he describes his participation in the killing of fourteen people. See Burt and Cagley, "Access to Information," 82.

31. I think that the female prosecutor in the film was meant to remind viewers of Cristina Olazábal, a lawyer engaged in human rights prosecutions.

32. Yet despite these many cultural products that take the internal armed conflict as their subject, Freyre most likely sees himself not as an *emprendedor de la memoria* but rather as someone who actively pursues writing alongside a military career. He has written on many themes, only some of them military. His other military works are about the era of the War of the Pacific: a coffee-table book published by Telefónica, *Cáceres* (2014), and a screenplay for the film *Gloria del Pacífico* (2015), both in collaboration with the CPHEP. Freyre has described himself as a "neoliberal writer," writing out of enjoyment but also for the market as a means to gain extra income. In this vein, his 2015 publication, *El ultimo otoño antes de tí*, is a love story between an octogenarian man and an adolescent girl. He subsequently submitted a vampire story to his publisher.

33. Personal communication with Carlos Freyre, via Skype, February 18, 2016.

34. Emilio Camacho, "El infante que contaba historias," *La República*, March 17, 2013, http://larepublica.pe/17-03-2013/el-infante-que-contaba-historias.

35. Personal communication with Carlos Freyre, via Skype, February 18, 2016.

36. Please note that in this chapter, I refer to Gavilán's *When Rains Became Floods* as a *testimonio*, autobiography, and memoir. I am aware than in literary studies these are separate but related genres. I do not make a distinction in this chapter, since both authors and critics have used these three terms interchangeably.

37. Mario Vargas Llosa, "El soldado desconocido," *El País*, December 16, 2012, http://elpais.com/elpais/2012/12/13/opinion/1355421080_101974.html.

38. The proposed title for the film by Luis Llosa and screenplay by Mario Vargas Llosa was "Tatuajes en la memoria" (Tattoos of memory). Fernando Vivas, "Vida de Lurgio Gavilán llega al cine con guión de Vargas Llosa," *El Comercio*, February 8, 2015, http://elcomercio.pe/luces/cine/vida-lurgio-gavilan-llega-al-cine-guion-mario-vargas-llosa-noticia-1790121.

39. As Javier Torres stated in his interview with Gavilán, it was the first time this history was told from the perspective of someone who "had directly participated in it." Interview by Javier Torres, "Lurgio Gavilán en *El Arriero*," YouTube, December 13, 2012, https://www.youtube.com/watch?v=E_MIFZocyI4.

40. Just before its publication in Peru, rumors circulated of a "senderista memoir" by a young Ayacuchan anthropologist studying for his master's degree in Mexico City. That few people seemed to have a clearer sense of the memoir's scope and who its

author might in part have been because many in human rights circles were mourning the illness and death of Carlos Iván Degregori, who wrote the prologue to the book prior to his passing. This information is based on my own observations at the time.

41. Vivas, "Vida de Lurgio Gavilán."

42. Vargas Llosa, "El soldado desconocido."

43. Gavilán's book, and the dialogue it has opened up, made possible publication of other personal accounts, such as Agüero's *Los rendidos*.

44. It should be noted that Lurgio Gavilán authored his own testimony, whereas in the case of Rigoberta Menchú and Domitila Barrios, their testimonies were mediated by anthropologists. A third means of bringing testimonies to print is through a more horizontal collaboration, such as Rosa Isolde Reuque Paillalef and Florencia Mallon in *When a Flower Is Reborn*. On the testimonial of Luz Arce, see Lazzara, *Luz Arce and Pinochet's Chile*. Ishmael Beah's memoir is *A Long Way Gone*. The photograph on the cover of the English edition, which shows the young Gavilán dressed in his Army uniform, presents the book as a military *testimonio*. This choice of cover art situates Gavilán's memoir in a small but important genre of child-soldier testimonies.

45. Gavilán, *When Rains Became Floods*, 2. Further citations of this work are given parenthetically in text.

46. Degregori wrote in the endnotes to his prologue that Gavilán's case was not unique (107n5). Indeed, Gavilán's own brother switched sides: after completing his obligatory military service, he joined Shining Path (16).

47. Gavilán uses the term *normal* to describe the acts of violence committed by Shining Path and the Armed Forces (including the abuse of young recruits) in his interview with Beto Ortiz on the morning TV program "Abre los ojos." "Exsenderista, exsoldado y exfranciscano: La asombrosa vida de Lurgio Gavilán, "Abre los Ojos," YouTube, January 29, 2013, https://www.youtube.com/watch?v=dvE9jh_BcQA.

48. Interview with Javier Torres, "Lurgio Gavilán en *El Arriero*."

49. *"Asombrosa"* (amazing) is featured in the title of the interview between Beto Ortiz and Lurgio Gavilán. Javier Torres remarked in his interview with Gavilán that *limeños* tended to see the internal political conflict as "*blanco y negro*." "Lurgio Gavilán en *El Arriero*."

50. Vargas Llosa, "El soldado desconocido."

51. Carlos Iván Degregori, "Surviving the Flood: The Multiple Lives of Lurgio Gavilán," in Gavilán, *When Rains Became Floods*, xi.

52. *"Instituciones totales"* (total institutions) was the term Degregori used to describe Shining Path, the Army, and the Catholic Church, and it was picked up by Gavilán and others in their discussion of the Spanish version of his book. Degregori, "Prólogo," in Gavilán, *Memorias de un soldado desconocido*, 13.

53. Degregori, "Surviving the Flood," xi, 107n4.

54. Indeed, Peruvian TV journalist Beto Ortiz in his interview with Gavilán also questioned how the transition could be so quick, but Gavilán responded that the change from *senderista* to soldier was from one day to the next: "Sí, el día siguiente," he

was a "cabito," a term for the young captured *senderistas* who became soldiers. "Abre los ojos" interview, "Exsenderista, exsoldado y exfranciscano." Javier Torres similarly questions the suddenness of the transition, yet Gavilán also states that it was from one day to the next. Interview with Torres, "Lurgio Gavilán en *El Arriero*."

55. CPHEP, *En honor a la verdad*, 254, 246.

56. Interview with Torres, "Lurgio Gavilán en *El Arriero*."

57. It is confusing that Gavilán refers to the Army base in Huanta by the same name as the one in Ayacucho (44). Gavilán even refers to it as Los Cabitos N°51, perhaps because he also spent time there. Los Cabitos N°51 in the departmental capital was the center of command for the Armed Forces and was used for clandestine detention. Here detainees were interrogated, tortured, and executed; some disappeared; and the bodies of others were cremated, as charged in the Los Cabitos case that began in 2005 and reached a ruling in 2007, convicting military men for the 1983 mass killings.

58. Pajuelo, "Reseñas al libro," 68. This article was based on the 2012 IEP presentation discussed below.

59. Orin Starn, "Introduction," in Gavilán, *When Rains Became Floods*, xxi.

60. Vargas Llosa, "El soldado desconocido."

61. Degregori, "Surviving the Flood," xi; Vargas Llosa, "El soldado desconocido."

62. Similarly, Alberto Vergara has noted, "Even though we could assume that having participated in this savage violence for one or the other side leaves traumatic traces, regrets, and guilt, it is certain that it is difficult to identify them in this narration." Vergara, "Esperando un guion."

63. Gavilán consistently argued in his book in favor of the vulnerable, the discriminated, and the abandoned, as noted by Jacqueline Fowks in her 2012 IEP presentation: Pajuelo et al., "Reseñas al libro," 76. The lack of a specific affinity by members to either Shining Path or the Army is also noted in *En honor a la verdad*: "As one saw earlier, it was not strange that Shining Path members infiltrated the ranks of the Army in order to obtain relevant information or to steal weapons. Sometimes the opposite happened: soldiers passed into the ranks of terrorists, and then as if by magic, reappeared in other Army units. They passed their lives fighting, without any apparent direction." Quotation taken from one of the gray-shaded pages, which might be an extract from an interview: "Document Number 11: A Senderista Looks for Protection," CPHEP, *En honor a la verdad*, 254.

64. Vargas Llosa, "El soldado desconocido."

65. Agüero, *Los rendidos*, 73.

66. Degregori, "Surviving the Flood," xi.

67. Pajuelo focused almost exclusively on Shining Path and the participation of children and adolescents in the war; he argues that Gavilán's memoir helps readers to understand the "other side"; María Eugenia Ulfe places Gavilán's memoir in the context of two other "senderista memory productions" in the same year, 2012: the documentary films *Sibila*, about the widow of José Arguedas, Sibila Arrendondo; and Andrés Mego's *Aquí vamos a morir todos*, about Julio Yovera, who survived El Frontón

in 1986. Ulfe writes that "together these three stories give us an intimate look into the lives of those about whom we know little: the subjectivity of actors in the internal armed conflict, the 'marked ones,' that do not form part of the Single Victims' Registry [Registro Único de Víctimas, a registry for reparations], but are nonetheless present." Ulfe in Pajuelo et al., "Reseñas al libro," 72–73. A video of the IEP presentation in December 2012 on Gavilán's book is available at http://iep.org.pe/noticias/libro-me morias-de-un-soldado-desconocido-de-lurgio-gavilan-se-presenta-en-el-iep/.

Two exceptions were the January 2013 presentation by Cecilia Méndez, in which she described the origins of the idea to present the two works together (Gavilán's and the Army's), and a text by Fernando Calderón that was published with the other reviews as part of "Reseñas al libro." In her presentation at "Diálogos por la paz y la memoria," Méndez specifically discussed state actors' violence, focusing for a few minutes on the rape of Shining Path prisoners. The mention of this part of Gavilán's book may explain some comments made later at the same colloquium by Major Freyre about the rape of domestic workers in upper-class *limeño* households that goes unacknowledged by society (Méndez's presentation is available at https://www.youtube.com/watch ?v=8gK71AxaEyo; Freyre's presentation is available at https://www.youtube.com /watch?v=IZX-4UxnXk8). Calderón in his essay reflects on Gavilán's memoir from his own perspective as the son of a military man who grew up in the 1990s. For Calderón, Gavilán's book allowed him to see a different side of Shining Path than the one he had learned as a child—that its members were "monsters." Gavilán introduced Calderón to Shining Path's early ideas of social justice as well as to the violence committed by the Armed Forces. Calderón noted the violence committed by the Armed Forces as recounted by Gavilán but also pointed to their suffering and sacrifice. He expressed hope that Gavilán's book would inspire members of the Armed Forces to also "tell us their own story." Calderón in Pajuelo et al., "Reseñas al libro," 77–79.

68. Vargas Llosa, "El soldado desconocido."

69. There is a discrepancy concerning how many years Gavilán was a member of the Army. He was captured in March 1985 at the age of fourteen. According to his memoir, he left the Army in 1995, and in an interview with *Revista actualidad militar*, he stated that he left at the age of twenty-four. Orin Starn writes in the introduction (xix) that Gavilán was in the military for seven years. Perhaps Starn was referring just to his time served once Gavilán started his obligatory military service. While male youth were obliged to serve when they turned eighteen, in practice boys also served at sixteen. In the above-mentioned interview, Gavilán was said to have begun obligatory military service at eighteen. The difficulty over dates is further complicated by discrepancies in Gavilán's year of birth.

70. Vargas Llosa, "El soldado desconocido."

71. For instance, Calderón writes about the CVR: "Among Army officials, I have frequently heard them question a priori the report of the Truth and Reconciliation Commission that those who composed it were not there during the period of violence. For many military and police, the proximity to death and the consequences of this

state of mind are not transmissible life experiences; [they are too] difficult for others to understand." Calderón in Pajuelo et al., "Reseñas al libro," 78–79.

72. Freyre, presentation at "Diálogos por la paz y la memoria," https://www.you tube.com/watch?v=IZX-4UxnXk8. Cecilia Méndez also spoke about both works: https://www.youtube.com/watch?v=8gK71AxaEyo.

73. Vergara, "Esperando un guion."

74. Centurión is also mentioned in the interviews of Andean women by Robin Kirk and Dorothy Q. Thomas on the case of Chilcahuaycco, the massacre of the twenty-three community members on September 21 and 22, 1990. Kirk, *Untold Terror*, 36. Gavilán's statement "that the sergeant ended up being condemned to death by a military tribunal because he killed an entire community" is incorrect. Zapata died in 2010 from an illness. IDEPUCP, "Seguimiento de casos judicializables presentados por la CVR," January 2010, http://idehpucp.pucp.edu.pe/images/docs/cuadro_de_ casos_cvr_enero_2010.pdf.doc, and "Seguimiento de casos de violaciones de Derechos Humanos," http://idehpucp.pucp.edu.pe/seguimiento/casos/seguimiento-de-ca sos-cvr/. On the relationship between Zapata Acuña and Urresti, see "Fiscalía dispone exhumar fosas de campesinos asesinados en Ayacucho," *RPP Noticias*, April 24, 2011, http://rpp.pe/peru/actualidad/fiscalia-dispone-exhumar-fosas-de-campesinos-asesina dos-en-ayacucho-noticia-358773; and "'No estuve presente en la muerte del periodista,' dice acusador de Urresti," *La República*, July 13, 2014, http://larepublica.pe/13072014 /no-estuve-presente-en-la-muerte-del-periodista-dice-acusador-de-urresti.

75. Fernando Rospigliosi, "Opinion: 'Carlos' y 'Arturo,'" *El Comercio*, July 6, 2014, http://elcomercio.pe/opinion/mirada-de-fondo/carlos-y-arturo-fernando-rospiglio si-noticia-1740911.

76. In the screening I attended as part of an Ibero-Latin American film festival in Montreal in June 2011, the rector of the UAP stated to the audience during the discussion period that *Vidas paralelas* was meant to tell the "other side of the story," that is, the story not told by other films, the "pro-senderista films," and the truth commission. In reference to the truth commission, the rector said, "CVR members have been very similar in ideology to Shining Path," and he stated that in 2011 the NGOs were "Shining Path" ("*son senderistas*"). The rector went on to inform the audience, made up mostly on non-Peruvians, that thousands of military men were languishing in prison while the terrorists were being let out. Milton, "Parallel Lies?"

77. Personal communication with Carlos Freyre (via Skype), February 19, 2016.

78. Gavilán responded to Torres's question: "I am not sure [if he would be angry], but I am very grateful to him, to the Army, and to the lieutenant in particular." Interview with Torres, "Lurgio Gavilán en *El Arriero*." After the book's publication, Gavilán posted on the Internet a letter to Shogun that went unanswered.

79. I received a copy of this article from Lurgio Gavilán but have not been able to obtain the original publication information. Interview with Torres, "Lurgio Gavilán en *El Arriero*."

80. CVR, *Hatun Willakuy*, 14, 352.

Chapter 4. Military Curations in the Turn to Human Rights Museology

1. Barbara Kirshenblatt-Gimblett identifies the emergence of "museums of conscience" as a turn in museum practices to scrutinize more closely both shameful national histories and the role of museums in these histories. Kirshenblatt-Gimblett, "Museums as Catalyst." As of 2008, several museums formed an association called the Federation of International Human Rights Museums (FIHRM). See Fleming, "Human Rights Museums." Orange and Carter distinguish between human rights museums (such as the Canadian Museum for Human Rights) and those that display human rights along with other topics. Orange and Carter, "'It's Time.'"

2. See Cmiel, "Recent History of Human Rights"; Moyn, *Last Utopia*; and Stern and Straus, "Embracing Paradox," among others.

3. At the time of his investigation (2010), Weissert had identified seven "*casas de memoria*"; since then some have closed, and others in varying forms have opened. Weissert, "Entre dos fuegos." More than a hundred memory sites have been erected in Peru since the CVR; see Reátegui, Barrantes and Peña, *Los sitios de la memoria*.

4. A memorial is "seen to be, if not apolitical, at least safe in the refuge of history"; a museum, by contrast, "is presumed to be concerned with interpretation, contextualization, and critique." Williams, *Memorial Museums*, 8.

5. Ulfe and Milton, "¿Y, después de la verdad?"; "Rafael Rey desconfía de la imparcialidad del Museo de la Memoria," *Perú21*, December 17, 2009, https://peru21.pe /noticia/382798/rafael-rey-desconfia-imparcialidad-museo-memoria. Rey continued to express doubts years later: "Lugar de la Memoria es insulto al Perú," *Cronología Política del Perú*, March 21, 2015, http://cronologiapoliticadelperu.org/2015/03/21 /lugar-de-la-memoria-es-insulto-al-peru/.

6. Another military museum is housed at the Base Infantería de Marina in Ancón. When I went there in 2014, I was not granted access. Indeed, if I had been granted access, I would most likely have been the museum's first "tourist." Karen Bernedo and Miguel Rubio both visited as part of their preparation for the LUM script. Personal communication with Karen Bernedo, November 15, 2014.

7. On memory and ruins in Chile, see Richard, "Sites of Memory, Emptying Remembrance"; and in Ayacucho, see Bayers, "'Words of the Dead.'"

8. According to one account, the first state-funded memory museum was opened on June 2, 2014, in Huancayo, Junín. "Se inaugura el Lugar de la Memoria en Junín," PUCP, http://idehpucp.pucp.edu.pe/comunicaciones/notas-informativas/se-inau gura-el-lugar-de-la-memoria-en-junin/.

9. The following information comes from my field notes of the visit, dated October 26, 2012. A more detailed description of this visit (with more photographs) is provided in Milton, "Curating Memories."

10. The colonel's entry into DIRCOTE could have followed a trajectory that overlapped his studies with his work, for it is said that DIRCOTE placed spies among the students.

11. The layout of the exhibit differed slightly when Víctor Vich, Javier Torres, and Jesús Cossio visited (on two separate occasions). Earlier a final room showed photographs of Shining Path attacks and housed Guzmán's library. This room was apparently under renovation when we visited, which may explain why Guzmán's books were piled in the middle of the second room. Personal communications with Vich, Torres, and Cossio, October 2013.

Anthropologists María Eugenia Ulfe and Vera Rocío visited the DIRCOTE museum shortly after my visit. At that time, the mannequin of Guzmán was placed in a cage. On their analysis of this exhibition space, see Ulfe and Rocío, "Toxic Memories?"

12. Personal communication with DIRCOTE entrance attendants and guide. Author's field notes, October 2012.

13. This program started as a thesis project from the software engineer faculty of a Peruvian university, La Universidad Peruana de Ciencias Aplicadas (UPC). According to one of the developers, "this project looks to simulated [sic] the rescue operation to maintain the history live [sic] and pay a tribute to all the soldier [sic] who participated in the operation." Carlos Castañeda, "Project: Soldado Universal behind the Real History," Epic Games, January 21, 2011, http://forums.epicgames.com/threads/760094-Project-Soldado-Universal-behind-the-real-history.

14. CPHEP, *Operación militar*, 7.

15. The first commentary on this Facebook page reads: "We are all against terrorists, but few have the courage to confront it. We support our heroes against the CIDH and the unjust process that it is opening." See the About page at www.facebook.com/yoapoyoaloscomandoschavindehuantar.

16. The CIDH announced its ruling in June 2015 on the case of one dead MRTA member: while recognizing extrajudicial death, the court stated that attributing guilt was nearly impossible. The court did, however, argue that the NGOs that brought the case before the court should have their legal expenses compensated, a decision that the Humala government outright rejected. Both pro-military groups and human rights organizations claimed the ruling as a "victory."

17. "Aprovechando heroísmos," editorial, *El Comercio*, March 11, 2012, http://elcomercio.pe/opinion/1385819/noticia-editorial-aprovechando-heroismos.

18. "Perú homenajea militares que liberaron rehenes en sede japonesa hace 15 años," April 20, 2012, RNW Latin America, http://www.enlatino.com/peru-homenajea-militares-que-liberaro.

19. "Gobierno condecorará commandos," *Perú21*, January 5, 2012, http://peru21.pe/2012/01/05/actualidad/gobierno-condecorara-comandos-2006221. The motion to honor the commandos as "heroes of democracy" passed in Congress on the eve of the twentieth anniversary of the operation.

20. "Cardenal Cipriani pidió orar por los caídos y rescatados en Operación Chavín de Huántar," *El Comercio*, April 22, 2012, http://elcomercio.pe/actualidad/1405130/noticia-cardenal-cipriani-pidio-orar-caidos-rescatados-operacion-chavin-huantar.

21. "Comandos de Chavín de Huántar fueron homenajeados en el Congreso de la

República," *El Comercio*, April 17, 2012, http://elcomercio.pe/actualidad/1402947/no ticia-comandos-chavin-huantar-fueron-homenajeados-congreso-republica.

22. "Gobierno rindió homenaje a comandos Chavín de Huantar," *El Comercio*, April 20, 2012, http://elcomercio.pe/politica/1404201/noticia-gobierno-rindio-home naje-comandos-chavin-huantar.

23. This reenactment was staged again in January 2014 before the IACHR judges, who had been invited to watch the military's version of the operation. See Milton, "Curating Memories," on how this may have lent not only a sense of legitimacy to the military's version but also one of authenticity to the site.

24. This was only one of García's efforts to pay homage to the Armed Forces. After the IACHR ruling over Castro Castro, García introduced a *decreto supremo* (supreme decree) ordering that the members of the Armed Forces and the National Police who died because of the violence were to have their names published in the state newspaper *El Peruano* as "new heroes of the nation" and that the streets in Peru's cities that were presently designated by numbers be replaced with the names of these "heroes." "El país tributará homenaje a los héroes de la democracia," *El Peruano*, April 1, 2007.

25. "Turistas podrán visitar réplica de residencia japonesa donde se ensayó rescate de rehenes," *El Comercio*, February 12, 2010, http://elcomercio.pe/politica/413943 /noticia-turistas-podran-visitar-replica-residencia-japonesa-donde-se-ensayo-res cate-rehenes.

26. When I wrote an earlier version of this chapter (Milton, "Curating Memories"), I had not yet visited the site myself, so I relied on the account of a Peruvian blogger, "Javi," who wrote an extensive description of his visit to the monument in September 2006. Javi270270, "Visita al monumento: Museo heroes de Chavín de Huánter," February 12, 2010, http://javi270270.blogspot.com/2010/02/visita-al-monumento-mu seo-heroes-de.html.

According to a tourism website, the site is "an establishment with cultural objectives under the administration of the Peruvian Army." "Museo del Ejército Contemporáneo Chavín de Huántar (FF.AA. del Perú)," http://turismoi.pe/museos/museo-del-ejer cito-contemporaneo-chavin-de-huantar-ff-aa-del-peru.htm.

27. With his promotion, the soldier received a better salary, some 200 soles (65 USD) a month.

28. Major Velezmoro's clarification is interesting, for it may imply that one could be jailed for reasons linked to this operation. If so, this was the only suggestion during our tour of a potential legal problem with the operation. It was one of the few times that Fujimori was mentioned during our tour.

29. Major Velezmoro's invitation to take photographs of whatever we wanted was in response to my description of the reason for our visit, that I was writing an academic text on military museums and memories. I thank Major Velezmoro and the museum guides for the tour and their assistance.

30. The films were of very poor quality, the images distorted, yet they were subtitled in English, which suggests a potentially international audience for the museum. The first video narrated the rise of Shining Path and the terrorism in the 1980s; then a new

strategy developed by the Armed Forces resulted in the arrests of top *senderistas*, including Guzmán. In regard to the hostage situation, the film identified two strategies: the first was to seek a "peaceful solution" (the film shows images of people dancing in front of the ambassador's residence), and the second was a "military solution" (the film showed images of training, scaling walls, building a model, digging tunnels, all with heroic music playing in the background). The film did not mention any dead hostage takers. The film ended with a voice stating, "The Peruvian right to live in peace."

The second video showed clips from the rescue operation and reenactments mixed with original footage. The third video gave the testimonies of surviving commandos and from the families of the fallen soldiers. The commanding officer, José Williams Zapata, gave thanks for having had the opportunity to lead these men. In 2005 Williams Zapata was accused of having ordered the Accomarca massacre, but he was later acquitted.

31. They used the replica to stage the reenactments in front of the building (even demolishing it a few times), but subsequently they came to worry about the building's stability, so now they perform only in the back. Note, however, that when the IACHR judges came to Chavín de Huántar in 2014, the reenactment took place in the front and lasted fifteen minutes, which meant that the organizers did their best to show the court their version of the operation. Personal communication with an anonymous person who was present at the IACHR visit, November 17, 2014.

32. According to the guide, the National Police had not been informed of the operation, which is why Cerpa was not blown up in the library as the Special Forces had planned. Throughout the tour, our different guides indicated to us when the operation did not go as planned and why, usually because of someone else's fault. There is apparently a debate about whether Cerpa's corpse and another body were actually found on the staircase or placed in the stairwell to improve the photo shoot done later of Fujimori's tour that same evening. Milton, "Curating Memories."

33. The photographs displayed different moments and actors in the hostage crisis: the early part of the first evening, the release of most of the hostages, the Canadian diplomat and Cardinal Cipriani, who served as negotiators. According to the guide, the latter had been chosen "because he was neither in favor of or against terrorism." The guide pointed to another photo in particular, one of three MRTA members with guns and bandanas covering their faces. She noted that the one on the left was a woman, but that "she had cut her hair short so as to seem like a man." Both of the female guides in the Chavín de Huántar museum wore military clothes and had long hair pulled back into ponytails.

34. One of these rooms displayed photographs of the commandos in operation (including a later group photo in which the director, Major Velezmoro, was smiling). Another room contained several flags, one for the Army, one for Peru, one for Operación Chavín de Huántar. Our guide explained to us the symbol of Operación Chavín de Huántar: Chavín in the middle, encircled by the sword of the Army, the anchor of the Navy, and the wings of the Air Force—but she noted that the latter did not participate in the operation. A similar comment about the limited participation of the Air

Force was made by a member of the Peruvian Army during my visit to the monument to the fallen in El Pentagonito; it is suggestive of the divisions within the Armed Forces and how the Army—more of the *pueblo*—sees the Fuerzas Aéreas, whose personnel comes predominantly from the upper class.

35. In the case of the DOPS (the police station of the Department of Political and Social Order in downtown São Paulo, Brazil), Atencio did not have a guided tour. However, the play that had been staged there, *Lembrar*, had actors who took on different roles at various moments, including the detainers, and positioned visitors as detainees. Atencio, *Memory's Turn*, 108–15.

36. "Cultural magic" is from Stern, *Remembering Pinochet's Chile*, 123; "secular sacred" is from Williams, *Memorial Museums*, 44.

37. Williams, *Memorial Museums*, 25.

38. Of the different state actors directly mentioned during the two tours, several are serving sentences or have been accused of crimes: Montesinos, Fujimori, Hermoza Ríos, Benedicto Jiménez, and Williams Zapata. Giampietri was also involved in another case before the IACHR.

39. See Patterson, "Teaching Tolerance," and Simon "Afterword," on pedagogical challenges in museum spaces; see Karp et al., *Museum Frictions*, on democratization of museums.

40. See Conley-Zilkic, "Rights on Display"; and Sodaro, "Politics of the Past." These are my observations of the CMHR.

41. I borrow this observation from Rebecca Atencio, who notes in her chapter on the DOPS how "culture" is used to erase the location's violent past. Atencio, *Memory's Turn*.

42. Human rights museums and memorials might be similarly difficult to access, since many are geared mainly for prearranged group visits.

43. Raúl Asensio noted that perhaps the cleanliness of the objects had something to do with military culture, rather than museological awareness, since in the museum director's office was a sign reminding employees that "the office should be kept clean."

44. Mario Vargas Llosa held a meeting with the commanding general of the Peruvian Army, Otto Guibovich, afterward, which resulted in the general expressing more positive opinions of the project. "El Ejército apoya la construcción de un museo de la memoria," *Perú21*, March 31, 2009, http://peru21.pe/noticia/266964/ejercito-apoya-construccion-museo-memoria. When Guibovich was replaced, this warming to the museum seemed to cease.

45. The presence of García Sayán as head of the LUM would have underscored for some members of conservative sectors the roots of this museum emerging from *los caviares*. See ADDCOT, "Caviar N°2: Diego García Sayan," December 9, 2012, http://www.defensoresdelademocracia.org/index.php?option=com_content&task=view&id=101&Itemid=53.

46. Ulfe and Milton, "¿Y, después de la verdad?"

47. The LUM seems unique among memorial museums in consulting such a wide

spectrum of stakeholders. Most museums, such as the Museo de Memoria in Chile, consulted human rights and victim groups but not to my knowledge the military or the business elite.

48. This description of the workshop is based on conversations with Ponciano del Pino and from del Pino and Agüero, *Cada uno*, 170–84.

49. Del Pino and Agüero, *Cada uno*, 184. Marco Antonio Merino is an Army general (General de Brigada) as well as a historian (his undergraduate degree in history is from the Universidad Católica del Perú). He participated in *En honor a la verdad* (discussed in chapter 2).

50. The LUM went on to hold several other consultations with members of the Armed Forces.

51. Personal communication, Ponciano del Pino, June 8, 2015.

52. Del Pino and Agüero, *Cada uno*, 176.

53. This discussion of these terms illustrates well what Stern refers to as the working out of memory knots and the knots in the throat. See discussion in the introduction.

54. Del Pino and Agüero, *Cada uno*, 178. It is interesting to note how vehemently the participants rejected this practice—while not acknowledging that they caused disappearances, they are acknowledging that it was morally wrong.

55. Ibid., 175, 181.

56. Memorial museums rely heavily on these "witnessing objects" and on their value in the mythmaking process, but such uses reduce the life lived and the object to the moment of suffering (Williams, *Memorial Museums*, 31).

57. Williams would classify these objects as "hot," since they are emotionally charged. He differentiates between "hot" and "cold" objects. The former call out to the visitor from the past and "can be made to speak emotionally due to their high capacity for personification"—he gives the example of a bar of soap with "I love you" written on it and the scratching on the wall left by prisoners. Cool objects are ordinary objects without emotional appeal that explain what took place; "they provide a visual 'hook' that might assist visitors in recalling the story." Williams, *Memorial Museums*, 33–34.

58. Drinot, "For Whom the Eye Cries," 26.

59. Around 80 percent of the money for the LUM's construction came from the international community. Jacqueline Fowks, "Perú ajusta cuentas con su pasado con el Lugar de la Memoria," *El País*, June 5, 2014, http://internacional.elpais.com/interna cional/2014/06/05/actualidad/1401975407_788874.html.

60. "Ya están abiertas las puertas del Lugar de la Memora en Miraflores," *Perú21*, December 18, 2015, http://peru21.pe/actualidad/ollanta-humala-inaugura-lugar-memo ria-2234664. For his entire speech, see "Presidente Humala inauguró el Lugar de la Memoria," December 17, 2015, http://www.youtube.com/watch?v=dLuDEv-baaI.

61. Please note that this description and observations are based on my visit to the LUM in early May 2017 and on a tour with one of the curators, historian Ponciano del Pino, in November 2014 while the space was still empty.

62. Del Pino described this narrative thread to me during our tour of the LUM in November 2014.

63. Elsewhere in the museum there is a solo-standing square room covered with glass cases into which families of victims are invited to place their loved ones' possessions.

64. CPHEP, *En honor a la verdad*, 331.

65. I did not see this temporary exhibit that was installed for eight months. The description here is based on photographs provided to me by Carlos Bracamonte from his visit on February 21, 2016.

66. CPHEP, *En honor a la verdad*, 330. See above, pp. 95–97.

67. For Ponciano del Pino, the challenge was not only to produce an inclusive script but also to incorporate the script effectively into the architecture of the museum. The architectural space is beautiful, tucked into the hillside made of the same pale grey-brown color as the earth, and at the time of day when I visited on November 7, 2015, with stunning light radiating off the ocean below. The building is filled with many windows permitting much light and vast open spaces, and the team had to devise ways to carve the space into smaller exhibition sections that permitted the planners to follow a coherent narrative up several levels, a trajectory that would also allow them to follow a narrative line of "from darkness to light."

68. Denise Ledgard's remark in del Pino and Agüero, *Cada uno*, 172. The title of the LUM book alone indicates the team's hope to be inclusive ("To each, a place of memory").

69. Indeed, Ponciano del Pino seemed aware prior to the inauguration that the LUM might not succeed in pleasing either the human rights community or the Armed Forces, for the former felt that victims' stories should be displayed alone, and the military would most likely be upset with the inclusion of references to brutality, corruption, and subsequent judicialization for crimes against humanity. Personal communication, November 7, 2014. My sense from other conversations in 2017 (with a former marine, active military personnel, and members of human rights NGOs) was that both "sides" of the memory camp do indeed criticize the LUM, yet those within the human rights movements recognize the importance of the space for gatherings and education despite what they saw as limitations in the curatorial script.

70. In Andean tradition, one accompanies by candlelight (*velar*) not the clothes of the disappeared but the clothes of the dead. Personal communication with Ponciano del Pino, June 8, 2015. The term *la violencia* allowed the curators to use one term uniformly throughout the exhibition space. Some specific events, however, are referred to as "terrorist acts" in the exhibition. Personal communication with Ponciano del Pino, April 13, 2016.

71. García Sayán stated that the decision to avoid giving a specific number was a conscious one. In regard to the CVR, he stated it was one source of information, "but not the only one." Jacqueline Fowks, "Perú ajusta cuentas con su pasado con el Lugar de la Memoria," *El País*, June 5, 2014, http://internacional.elpais.com/internacional /2014/06/05/actualidad/1401975407_788874.html.

72. The *Yuyanapaq* exhibition, now at the National Museum on a multiyear lease, drew nearly 239,000 visitors from 2004 to 2013 (Macher, *¿Hemos avanzado?*, 166).

73. As of May 2019, the video ("Congresista Donayre denuncia apología al

terrorismo en el LUM," www.youtube.com/watch?v=Fl3EUou78z4) had been viewed more than nine thousand times.

74. Williams, *Memorial Museums*, 8.

75. At the very end of writing this book, a controversy struck over the LUM's inclusion of a temporary exhibition, *Carpeta Colaborativa: De Resistencia Visual, 1992–2017* (Collaborative folder: Visual resistance, 1992–2017), which was deemed by some as "biased," "too one-sided," and too "anti-Fujimori." According to the minister of culture, Salvador del Solar, such an exhibition risked making possible the accusation that the LUM was a biased institution ("the worst harm that could be done"). See documents collected by Roberto Bustamante, "La crisis del LUM: Un museo virtual," https://www.flickr.com/photos/elmorsa/sets/72157687817231686; and "Salvador del Solar cede a la presión fujimorista y obliga a renunciar a director del LUM," *La República*, August 20, 2017, http://larepublica.pe/politica/1076150-salvador-del-so lar-cede-a-la-presion-fujimorista-y-obliga-a-renunciar-a-director-del-lum.

Chapter 5. Captive to History

1. Lerner Febres, "La entrega del *Informe final* en Lima," in his *La rebelión de la memoria*, 147–48.

2. There is no adequate equivalent in English for "*apología al terrorismo*." "Incitement of terrorism" is not quite the right translation since it suggests the active encouragement of certain acts. "Apology" is the literal translation. The actual law also includes an element of "denial."

3. On social amnesia, silencing, and perduring taboos after the transition in Argentina, and after the memory boom of 1995, see Nancy Gates-Madsen's insightful analysis of cultural texts, *Trauma, Taboo, and Truth-Telling*. Surprisingly little has been written on enduring forms of censorship after transitions from authoritarianism to democracy. For instance, in the three-volume work of Stan and Nedelsky, *Encyclopedia on Transitional Justice*, censorship does not figure among the entries or in the index.

4. Burt and Cagley, "Access to Information," 78–79.

5. "Bákula reitera que no hubo censura contra dibujos de Piero Quijano," *Perú21*, July 12, 2007, http://peru21.pe/noticia/85589/bakula-reitera-que-no-hubo-censura-con tra-dibujos-piero-quijano.

6. "Wagner justifica la censura a Piero Quijano," *Perú21*, July 7, 2007, http:// peru21.pe/noticia/78878/wagner-justifica-censura-piero-quijano.

7. Yet the military may have just made matters worse, for as Rocio Silva Santisteban noted, if they had just left the exhibit alone, these caricatures would likely have gone unnoticed by the Peruvian press and indeed by most Peruvians. Because of this controversy, however, more visitors ended up viewing the controversial images through media reproductions and in the independent gallery that went on to host intact the exhibition. Rocio Silva Santisteban, "Quijano y la censura," *La Insignia*, July 1, 2007, www.lainsignia.org/2007/julio/cul_002.htm.

8. Cited in Vich, *Poéticas del duelo*, 206.

9. Goldstein, "Editor's Preface," 1.

10. Ibid.

11. Catalina Botero Marino and Michael J. Camilleri underscore the importance of the Inter-American Court of Human Rights in the repeal of authoritarian censorship laws, though they note that other extant laws may continue to suppress freedom of speech. In Peru, one of these laws is the "*apología al terrorismo*" put in place during the Fujimori years, abolished in 2003, only to reappear in an amended form. Botero and Camilleri, "Freedom of Expression."

12. Infante Yupanqui, *Poder, tensión y caricatura*, esp. 274–78, 310.

13. Payne, "Humor that Makes Trouble," 68, 72.

14. Lucioni, "La historieta peruana."

15. This play is mentioned in a short film by a group called Presencia Cultural on censorship of art in Peru, "CensurARTE: Casos de censura en el arte," April 3, 2007, http://www.dailymotion.com/video/x1m9jn.

16. Among the works present in the retrospective *Vigilar y castigar* was a piece by Jorge Miyagui: a reddish orange kimono on which he had silkscreened the faces of Fujimori, Montesinos, Cipriani, and Martín Rivas (representatives of the state, the church, and the Armed Forces). On the shoulders of the kimono sits a mirror with the message "*silencio complicita*" (complicit silence) that reflects the face of the spectator, most likely a member of the Japanese-Peruvian community who would have come to visit the exhibit. The work, *Kimono para no olvidar* (Kimono so as not to forget) was intended to draw attention to "the submissive, complacent and shameful attitude of the Japanese-Peruvian community in the face of the crimes of Fujimorismo." The Japanese-Peruvian cultural center chose not to display the piece with the other kimonos that formed the original exhibition, thus perhaps confirming Miyagui's initial concern. See "Arte censurado: 'Es una prepotencia pensar que el cuerpo humano tiene algo que no se pueda mostrar,'" *La Mula*, August 2, 2012, https://lamula.pe/2012/08/02/arte-censurado-es-una-prepotencia-pensar-que-el-cuerpo-humano-tiene-algo-que-no-se-pueda-mostrar/harrylee66/. This was not the first time that Miyagui's work was censored; in 2002 his paintings that criticized the press were removed from a contest sponsored by Peru's telephone company (Concurso de Artes Plásticas de Telefónica del Perú). See "Caso censura Telefónica Jorge Miyagui en Hildebrandt 2002," June 29, 2012, www.youtube.com/watch?v=zhcvsumLgXA; and El Sr. Miyagui Contraataca, "Caso Censura Telefónica Jorge Miyagui en Entre líneas 2002," July 2012, http://jorgemiyagui.blogspot.ca/2012/07/caso-censura-telefonica-jorge-miyagui.html.

17. Discussion between Infante and Rodríguez, San Barolo, November 2007, reproduced in Infante, *Poder, tensión y caricatura*, 276.

18. Vich, *Poéticas del duelo*, 206.

19. Andrés Avellaneda distinguishes between these two types of authoritarian censorship: official and subtler unofficial forms. *Censura, autoritarianismo y cultura*, 10.

20. Burt and Cagley, "Access to Information," 76–77, 93n4.

21. While not meant as an exhaustive list, the following cases give a sense of the diversity of topics that may provoke censorship. For instance, in a case of censorship

for reasons of "decency" because of sexual content, the Asociación Cultural Peruano Británica attempted to censor the 2009 theater piece *La habitación azul*. The theater director eventually dropped the project. See "Rechazo a censura en el Británico," *La República*, June 6, 2009, http://www.larepublica.pe/06-06-2009/rechazo-cen sura-en-el-britanico. On questions of nudity, Diego Lama had a photograph removed from the Exposición BOLD in April 2007, at the request of the hosting institution, the Casa Goyeneche. The offending photograph showed a naked, obese Afro-Peruvian woman. See "La ira del poder: 30 años de censura," *La Mula*, July 25, 2012, https:// dinosauriosdelaton.lamula.pe/2012/07/25/la-ira-del-poder-30-anos-de-censura/ceci liapodesta/. On religious sensitivities, after protests from neighbors of San Isidro and some representatives of the Catholic Church, the Municipality of San Isidro closed Cristina Planas's 2008 exhibition *La migración de los santos* in the Galería Vértice. The artist had made kitsch portrayals of local patron saints Sarita Colonia, Santa Rosa, San Martín de Porres, and Señor de los Milagros. See Tomacini Sinche López, "La Santa Polemica," November 3, 2008, http://escuela-de-marte.blogspot.ca/2008/11/la-sanata-po lemica-por-tomacini-sinche.html. Planas's work again faced protests in 2012. See "Miraflores: Despiden a director de sala cultural ante críticas a exposición artística," *La República*, October 19, 2012, http://www.larepublica.pe/19-10-2012/miraflores-despi den-director-de-sala-cultural-ante-criticas-exposicion-artistica. Artist Natalia Iguñiz's works have been removed from galleries, and in one case the streets, for provoking "problems with certain people," including at one point the Archbishop of Lima, and another time the president of Congress and the Commission for Women and Human Development. See Ann Kaneko, *Against the Grain*. Censorship on questions of the environment include a group of cinema directors who were denounced in 2012 for their environmentalist documentaries, in particular a film that showed the pollution of potable water because of extractive industries. See "Perú: Denuncian censura de docu mentales sobre conflictos ambientales en evento oficial," Servindi, July 9, 2012, http:// servindi.org/actualidad/67897; and "Cine, agua y censura," https://es.scribd.com /doc/99246279/Cine-Agua-y-Censura. Jaime Miranda considers the removal of his Monument in Honor of Truth for Reconciliation and Hope in the dark of one early morning in May 2010 to also be an act of censorship. Personal communication with Jaime Miranda, July 10, 2015.

22. Gargurevich, "Los medios masivos," 12, 18–19.

23. Ibid., 23.

24. "Grupo *El Comercio*: Un pulpo de los medios de comunicación," *Revista IDEELE*, no. 234 (November 2013), http://revistaideele.com/ideele/content/grupo-el-co mercio-un-pulpo-de-los-medios-de-comunicaci%C3%B3n.

25. Jeremías Godoy, "Policías atacan muestra fotográfica Yuyanapaq," *Diario Correo*, August 25, 2011, http://diariocorreo.pe/ultimas/noticias/EPENSA-031179 /edicion+huanuco/policias-atacan-muestra-fotografica-yuyanapaq.

26. Personal communication with curator Karen Bernedo, May 22, 2015.

27. Cecilia Podestá, "Ministerio de Justicia censura obras que critican a Abimael," *Diario16*, October 22, 2012, http://diario16.pe/noticia/19931-ministerio-de-justicia-cen sura-obras-que-critican-a-abimael.

28. Photographs of the empty laminated display boards may be viewed at Yanina Patricio, "Censura en muestra fotográfica de Villa el Salvador," October 20, 2012, http://blog.yaninapatricio.com/censura-en-muestra-fotografica-de-villa-el-salvador/.

29. Personal communication with curator Karen Bernedo, May 22, 2015.

30. In her work, artist Natalia Iguiñez attempted to overcome these uses of Moyano to uncover the original person. Rodríguez Ulloa, "Artist Archives." On the different uses of María Elena Moyano, see Burt, "Accounting for Murder."

31. Conversation, "Juan Acevedo y Jesús Cossio hablan sobre la censura en Villa El Salvador," October 22, 2012, https://www.youtube.com/watch?v=se2guɪlkɪZM. In this video, Acevedo reads a letter from CMAN explaining that they had removed some of the images because of complaints in order to determine whether the complaints were valid and that once they had concluded that they were not offensive, they returned the images to the exhibition.

32. Vich analyses a specific cartoon published in 1983 that questions the government's control of the growing threat of Shining Path: Guzmán is portrayed as shaving President Belaúnde while the latter wonders, "Where on earth is Guzmán hiding?" Vich, *Poéticas del duelo*, 118–19.

33. In addition to what appears to have been increased censorship of creative interventions, Burt and Cagey note as well that by 2013 the FOI legislation faced many impediments, in particular, the unwillingness of the Armed Forces to provide the information requested by prosecutors, thus effectively blocking transparency and accountability. Burt and Cagley, "Access to Information."

34. "Congresistas critican esta escultura en museo de Ayacucho," *El Comercio*, April 6, 2015, http://elcomercio.pe/peru/ayacucho/congresistas-critican-esta-escul tura-museo-memoria-ayacucho-noticia-1802250.

35. A similar small ceramic depicting the abuse of *campesinos* by members of the Armed Forces was also on display at the Huanta museum. My thanks to Markus Weissert for sharing both images with me.

36. This description draws from my review written in consultation with María Eugenia Ulfe, who had attended the premier, and Karen Bernedo, who attended with me. Milton, Ulfe, and Bernedo, "Review: *La Cautiva*."

37. While not stated explicitly in the play, the story of the character María Josefa is one that has been described both by the CVR and academics: the rape of Andean women and girls by the state agents. See, for instance, Boesten, *Sexual Violence*; Theidon, *Intimate Enemies*; and Leiby, "Digging in the Archives."

38. I thank María Eugenia Ulfe for her observation of the significance of the Holy Week setting.

39. Yet this resolution is unsettling for it suggests that the way out of the quagmire of the violence was possible only through further acts of violence. Furthermore, Mauro's death poses a conundrum in the script: If he dies, who will tell us of María Josefa's tale? Who will testify on her behalf? For León, this obligation is now the audience's. In this way the audience also becomes a witness and fulfills a societal debt indicated by the CVR: that so many died in the internal conflict, yet Lima did not know, for that

lack of willingness to observe and for the lack of witnesses and of tangible evidence of their existence, let alone their deaths. These victims thus became Peruvian citizens in the act of the audience's recognition of their once having been alive. Personal communication with Luis Alberto León, July 9, 2015.

40. Conversation between Chela De Ferrari and Luis Alberto León, printed in the promotional booklet for the play (emphasis mine).

41. On the comment books for the CVR's exhibition *Yuyanapaq*, see Milton and Ulfe, "Promoting Peru," 212–17.

42. Conversation between Chela De Ferrari and Luis Alberto León, printed in the promotional booklet for the play.

43. Galindo was eventually dismissed from his post as antiterrorism attorney (*procurador*), and in the newspaper accounts at the end of his term, readers were reminded that he had been "criticized for his attempt to denounce the theatre piece *La cautiva* for incitement of terrorism. He later dropped these efforts because he did not have proof of the accusations for not having seen the piece performed." "Gobierno finaliza nombramiento de Julio Galindo como procurador antiterrorismo," *La República*, June 7, 2015, http://larepublica.pe/politica/5966-gobierno-finaliza-nombra miento-de-julio-galindo-como-procurador-antiterrorismo.

44. Taken from documents reproduced in Giovanna Castañeda, "Tienes que leer lo que dice el documento de la investigación contra 'La cautiva,' que está avalando el ministro Urresti," *Útero*, January 12, 2015, http://utero.pe/2015/01/12/tienes-que-leer-lo-que-dice-el-documento-de-la-investigacion-contra-la-cautiva-que-esta-avalando-el-mi nistro-urresti/.

45. This scene may come directly from the drawings of Edilberto Jiménez, published in his collection *Chungui*, thus transforming a visual testimony into the play's fictional account. Jiménez's *Chungui* was for sale at the theater.

46. Personal communication with Luis Alberto León, July 9, 2015.

47. Urresti quoted in Castañeda, "Tienes que leer."

48. Diana Taylor, *Disappearing Acts*, esp. chapter 5.

49. Gates-Madsen, *Trauma, Taboo, and Truth-Telling*.

50. The original legislative decree (Decreto Legislativo) 25475, Article 7, reads: "It shall be punishable with imprisonment of no less than six nor more than twelve years, when through any public means one makes an apology for terrorism or for the person who had committed it. The Peruvian citizen who commits this crime outside the territory of the republic, in addition to the custodial sentence, will be sanctioned with the loss of Peruvian nationality." Decreto Ley no. 25475, http://idehpucp.pucp.edu.pe /images/docs/terr_d_ley_25475.pdf.

51. Decreto Legislativo no. 924, http://idehpucp.pucp.edu.pe/images/documen tos/normas/decreto_legislativo_924_apologia_al_terrorismo.pdf.

52. The law proposed in 2012 (on the day of the ninth anniversary of the CVR's *Final Report*), Ley de Negacionismo (Law of Negation), if adopted, would have allowed criminal sentencing and imprisonment for up to eight years of anyone who placed in question, downplayed, or attempted to justify the violence committed by Shining

Path. Congress adopted a modified version. "Ejecutivo plantea hasta 8 años de cárcel para quienes nieguen terror senderista," *La Republica*, August 29, 2012, http://www .larepublica.pe/29-08-2012/ejecutivo-plantea-hasta-8-anos-de-carcel-para-quie nes-nieguen-terror-senderista.

53. Here I am referring to an art exhibit in Miraflores of works by Peruvian artist Rudolph Castro, *Sesenta y dos horas de viaje, ciencuenta y nueve años en el sur*, which displayed objects and images from Uruguay, Paraguay, Chile, Argentina, and Brazil, all participants in the Condor Operation. While no explicit reference is made to Peru in the exhibit, visitors did note Peru's absence in their remarks in the exhibition comment book.

54. Milton, "Defacing Memory."

55. *La cautiva* is very different in style from the works of Miguel Rubio and Yuyachkani, the theater troupe best known for addressing the internal conflict and sociopolitical themes in general. Though the creators consulted Rubio, *La cautiva* differs in particular because of its more traditional dramaturgy and a clear, singular narrative line. Yet the influences of Yuyachkani on *La cautiva* are apparent in the use of Quechua and in a dance sequence that Ana Correa, a member of Yuyachkani, helped choreograph. *La cautiva* is also reminiscent of Claudia Llosa's film *Madeinusa* (2005): it is set in the Week of Semana Santa, María Josefa is dressed as the bridge/Virgin Mary, and it uses Andean songs.

56. Yuyachkani might have eluded overt censorship because of the troupe's ability to transform itself and its projects (to street theater, for instance). Personal communication with Soccoro Naveda, Yuyachkani's manager, June 2, 2015.

57. Buntix did, however, leave the country during the Fujimori government, in response to fears over the reaction to his work.

58. This latter comment refers to pieces that take place within Yuyachkani's theater. Their street theater and traveling performances, for instance, reach a much more diverse public, and indeed, one raison d'être for Yuyachkani is public engagement and education with popular classes. These mobile forms of theater are more difficult to censor. On Yuyachkani, see Taylor, *The Archive and the Repertoire*, ch. 7.

59. This argument is somewhat similar to Vich's explanation for why Quijano's caricature produced controversy once shown in an official museum. As this theater in Larcomar was a "place of authority," it was unacceptable to denigrate the Armed Forces. Vich, *Poéticas del duelo*, 206.

60. The curator of this exhibit was Karen Bernedo, the same curator who had earlier exhibited in Villa El Salvador an artistic retrospective twenty years after these events. The LUM exhibition of twenty-five years since 1992 was funded by the Coordi-nadora Nacional de Derechos Humanos and the Goethe Institute-Peru. For Facebook and other posts cited here, including Ledgard's statement on "the other side of the desk," see documents collected by Roberto Bustamante, "La crisis del LUM: Un museo virtual," https://www.flickr.com/photos/elmorsa/sets/72157687817231686; and "Salvador del Solar cede a la presión fujimorista y obliga a renunciar a director del LUM," *La Républica*, August 20, 2017, http://larepublica.pe/politica/1076150-salva dor-del-solar-cede-a-la-presion-fujimorista-y-obliga-a-renunciar-a-director-del-lum.

61. "En defensa de *La Cautiva*," January 12, 2015, https://www.scribd.com/doc/252826620/La-Cautiva.

Conclusion

1. The hymn's music and lyrics were by Pedro Schmitt Aicardi. See "Himno del Ejército del Perú," http://www.deperu.com/abc/himnos/989/himno-del-ejercito-del-peru.

2. These rumors of human rights violations in Madre Mía and subsequent bribing of witnesses returned to haunt Humala in April 2017. Karem Barboza Quiroz, "La fiscalía reabrió la investigación del Caso Madre Mía," *El Comercio*, May 13, 2017, http://elcomercio.pe/politica/fiscalia-reabrio-investigacion-madre-mia-implicaba-ollanta-humala-434267.

The vote in Congress naming the commandoes as "heroes of democracy" was ninety-five votes in favor, nine against, and three abstentions. Within a week, fourteen members of Congress from different political affiliations signed a motion to also honor Luis Giampietri, Juan Luis Cipriani, and Francisco Tudela with "Defenders of Democracy" medals for their involvement in the Chavín de Húantar operation. "Proponen dar 'Medalla al Defensor de la Democracia' a cardenal Cipriani," *Perú21*, April 25, 2017, http://peru21.pe/politica/proponen-entregar-medalla-al-defensor-democracia-cipriani-giampietri-y-tudela-2279179.

As a further indication of improved public perception of the Armed Forces, in an opinion poll after the devastating flooding in regions of Peru in March and April 2017, the public found the Peruvian Armed Forces and National Police response to the disasters much more "*destacado*" (outstanding) than that of the national government (54, 38, and 20 percent, respectively). "La reconstrucción de PPK," *Opinión data*, no. 218 (April 17, 2017): 4. Public perception of the Armed Forces may also have improved as a consequence of the Odebrecht scandal, which implicated four former presidents as well as Keiko Fujimori (the latter placed in preventive prison). Her father, Alberto Fujimori, remains in prison.

3. Macdonald, *Difficult Heritage*, 2.

4. Informal street vendors sell camouflage uniforms that closely imitate the ones issued by the Armed Forces. These clothes have emblems and different insignia that indicate different divisions within the Armed Forces, such as the Escuela de Comandos, which is the most prestigious unit of the Army's Special Forces. Granados, "El desfile," 102–3.

5. Ibid., 99.

6. Macdonald, *Difficult Heritage*, 2–3.

7. CPHEP, *En honor a la verdad*, 329.

8. The authors, however, incorrectly credit this idea to Kimberly Theidon. Ibid.

9. Sikkink, *The Justice Cascade*; Atencio, *Memory's Turn*, 20–22.

10. Burlein, "Counter-memory on the Right," 215–17.

11. As Greg Grandin and Kenneth Cmiel note, many on-the-ground actors and scholars evoke the concept of "human rights," yet what they mean differs, not just

across time but within contemporaneous moments. Grandin, "Human Rights and Empire's Embrace"; Cmiel, "Recent History of Human Rights."

12. Milton, "Defacing Memory."

13. A wall is also dedicated to the *ronderos*, though the list of names is very incomplete. From 1991 to 2009, only forty-eight dead *ronderos* are named.

14. While fighting continues, especially in the VRAEM, resulting in the tragic headlines of yet more fallen soldiers, the conflict in the twenty-first century is largely seen as separate from that of the 1980s and 1990s, for instance, in the case of the ten soldiers and civilians killed in an ambush on April 9, 2016, in the VRAEM. "Se confirman muerte de 10 personas en ataque terrorista en Vraem," *El Comercio*, April 11, 2016, http://elcomercio.pe/peru/vraem/vraem-confirman-muerte-diez-personas-ataque-ter rorista-noticia-1893147?ref=nota_peru&ft=mod_leatambien&e=titulo.

15. Badaró, *Historias del ejército argentino*, 174–76.

16. Ibid., esp. chap. 6.

17. Apparently, the Colombian Armed Forces and Defense Ministry plan to build the largest military theme park in the Americas, eleven hectares, not far from Bogotá, where visitors can learn military history from the country's independence "to the civil wars" "through simulation, heightened reality, holograms, monuments, and interactive screens." "Colombia tendrá el parque temático militar más grande de América Latina," *El Mundo*, June 23, 2015. Colombia may also be learning from the Peruvian experience of erecting a memory museum and the importance of having a military voice in the design and curation. José Antequera, "La batalla por la memoria del Ministerio de Defensa," *El Espectador*, April 17, 2017.

18. I thank historian Marc Drouin for summarizing for me the military's response since the 1994 truth commission (Commission for Historical Clarification). Personal communication, December 1, 2016. One such private university is Universidad Francisco Marroquín, and an example of an academic who advances a negationist position is Carlos Sabino in his book *Guatemala: La historia silenciada* (Guatemala: The silenced history).

19. It should be noted that the Armed Forces do not necessarily have to work too hard to have their view asserted in the public sphere since there are civilians who speak as though they were part of the military, individuals such as Martha Moyano, Julio Galindo, Juan Jiménez (who launched the "Todos contra el Terrorismo" campaign, which brought together the ministries of defense, education, and culture), and some media communicators. Take, for instance, journalist Umberto Jara's book, *Secretos del Túnel*, reissued in 2017 in commemoration of twenty years since the successful Chavín de Huántar operation, after apparently having successfully sold "over thirty thousand copies." He bemoans that the commandos have had to "wage battle in inhospitable politicized trials" and that organizations such as APRODEH, whom he accuses of having received funds from "terrorist delinquents," are particularly active in "persecuting" the commandos. Jara, *Secretos*, 190. I thank Iris Jave for this insight.

20. Sociologist Gonzalo Portocarrero's comments at the January 24, 2013, IEP event "Diálogos por la paz y la memoria," https://www.youtube.com/watch?v=UDVv 8BMRUrk&nohtml5=False.

Bibliography

Agüero, José Carlos. *Los rendidos: Sobre el don de perdonar*. Lima: IEP, 2015.

Aguirre, Carlos. "The Second Liberation? Military Nationalism and the Sesquicentennial Commemoration of Peruvian Independence, 1821–1971." In *The Peculiar Revolution: Rethinking the Peruvian Experiment under Military Rule*, edited by Carlos Aguirre and Paulo Drinot, 25–48. Austin: University of Texas Press, 2017.

Aguirre, Carlos, and Paulo Drinot, eds. *The Peculiar Revolution: Rethinking the Peruvian Experiment under Military Rule*. Austin: University of Texas Press, 2017.

Alarcón, Daniel. *Lost City Radio*. New York: Harper Collins, 2007.

———. *War by Candlelight*. New York: Harper Collins, 2005.

Álvarez Sotomayor, Eduardo. *Un soplón llamado Vladimiro Montesinos: Biografía no autorizada de un traidor de la patria*. Lima: E. Álvarez Sotomayor, 2008.

Arce Arce, Gerardo Alberto. "Fuerzas Armadas, Comisión de la Verdad y justicia transicional en el Perú." *SUR- Revista internacional de derechos humanos* 7, no. 13 (2010): 27–49. http://www.corteidh.or.cr/tablas/r26955.pdf.

———. "Licenciados: Testimonios acerca del servicio militar en el Perú." In *Juventud y género en las Fuerzas Armadas: Una mirada desde las regiones*, edited by Ana María Tamayo Flores, Eduardo Toche Medrano, Gerardo Alberto Arce, Jefrey Gamarra Carrillo, Marco Antonio Vélez Fernández, and María Fernanda Castro Rivas, 69–83. Lima: Instituto de Defensa Legal, 2012.

Asociación Defensores de la Democracia Contra el Terrorismo (ADDCOT). *Injusticias contra los que combatieron y derrotaron a los terroristas (1980—2000)*. Lima: ADDCOT, 2007.

———. *Omisiones a la verdad ¿Y la reconciliación?* Lima: ADDCOT, 2003.

Atencio, Rebecca J. *Memory's Turn: Reckoning with Dictatorship in Brazil*. Critical Human Rights. Madison: University of Wisconsin Press, 2014.

Avellenada, Andrés. *Censura, autoritarismo y cultura: Argentina 1960–1983*. Buenos Aires: Centro Editor de América Latina, 1983.

Badaró, Máximo. *Historias del Ejército Argentino, 1990–2010: Democracia, política y sociedad*. Buenos Aires: Edhasa, 2013.

————. *Militares o ciudadanos: La formación de los oficiales del Ejército Argentino*. Buenos Aires: Prometeo Libros, 2009.

Bakiner, Onur. *Truth Commissions: Memory, Power, and Legitimacy*. Pennsylvania Studies in Human Rights. Philadelphia: University of Pennsylvania Press, 2016.

Bayers, Richard. "'Words of the Dead': Ruins, Resistance, and Reconstruction in Ayacucho." In *Telling Ruins in Latin America*, edited by Michael J. Lazzara and Vicky Unruh, 147–61. New York: Palgrave Macmillan, 2009.

Beah, Ishmael. *A Long Way Gone: Memoirs of a Boy Soldier*. New York: Sarah Crichton Books, 2007.

Bilbija, Ksenija, and Leigh A. Payne, eds. *Accounting for Violence: Marketing Memory in Latin America*. Durham, NC: Duke University Press, 2011.

Boesten, Jelke. *Sexual Violence during War and Peace: Gender, Power, and Post-Conflict Justice in Peru*. New York: Palgrave Macmillan, 2014.

Botero Marino, Catalina, and Michael Camilleri. "Freedom of Expression in Latin America: The Inter-American Human Rights System." *ReVista: Harvard Review of Latin America*. Spring/Summer 2011.

Britzman, Deborah. *Lost Subjects, Contested Objects: Toward a Psychoanalytic Inquiry of Learning*. Albany: State University of New York Press, 1998.

Burlein, Ann. "Counter-Memory on the Right: The Case of the Focus on the Family." In *Acts of Memory: Cultural Recall in the Present*, edited by Mieke Ball, Jonathan Crewe, and Leo Spitzer, 208–17. Hanover, NH: University Press of New England, 1999.

Burt, Jo-Marie. "Accounting for Murder: The Contested Narratives of the Life and Death of María Elena Moyano." In Bilbija and Payne, *Accounting for Violence*, 69–97.

————. "The Paradoxes of Accountability: Transitional Justice in Peru." In Stern and Straus, *Human Rights Paradox*, 148–74.

————. *Political Violence and the Authoritarian State in Peru: Silencing Civil Society*. New York: Palgrave Macmillan, 2007.

Burt, Jo-Marie, and Casey Cagley. "Access to Information, Access to Justice: The Challenges of Accountability in Peru." *SUR International Journal on Human Rights* 18 (2013): 75–95.

Cabrejos Samamé, José. *La verdad sobre Accomarca*. Lima: ADDCOT, 2006.

Calderón, Fernando. "Reseñas al libro 'Memorias de un soldado desconocido' de Lurgio Gavilán (IEP-2012)." *Argumentos: Revista de análisis y crítica* 7, no. 1 (2013): 65–79.

Cameron, Maxwell A. "Endogenous Regime Breakdown: The Vladivideo and the Fall of Peru's Fujimori." In *The Fujimori Legacy: The Rise of Electoral Authoritarianism in Peru*, edited by Julio F. Carrión, 268–93. University Park: Pennsylvania State University Press, 2006.

Cecconi, Ariana. "Dreams, Memory, and War: An Ethnography of Night in the Peruvian Andes." *Journal of Latin American and Caribbean Anthropology* 16 (2011): 401–24.

Cipriani Thorne, Juan Luis. *Doy fe: Un testimonio sobre la crisis de los rehenes en la residencia del embajador de Japón.* Lima: Planeta, 2012.

Cisneros, Renato. *La distancia que nos separa.* Lima: Planeta, 2015.

Cmiel, Kenneth. "The Recent History of Human Rights." In *The Human Rights Revolution: An International History,* edited by Akira Iriye, Petra Goedde, and William I. Hitchcock, 27–52. New York: Oxford University Press, 2012.

Collins, Cath, Lorena Balardini, and Jo-Marie Burt. "Mapping Perpetrator Prosecutions in Latin America." *International Journal of Transitional Justice* 7, no. 1 (2013): 8–28.

Comisión de la Verdad y Reconciliación del Perú (CVR). *Informe final.* 9 vols. Lima: CVR, 2003. http://www.cverdad.org.pe.

———. *Hatun Willakuy: Abbreviated Version of the Final Report of the Truth and Reconciliation Commission, Peru.* Lima: CVR, 2014. http://www.ictj.org/sites/default/files/ICTJBookPeruCVR2014.pdf.

———. *Hatun Willakuy: Versión abreviada del Informe Final de la Comisión de la Verdad y Reconciliación, Perú.* Lima: CVR, 2004.

Comisión Permanente de Historia del Ejército del Perú (CPHEP). *Compendio de la historia general del Ejército del Perú: 3,000 años de historia.* Vol. 2. Lima: Oficina de Información del Ejército, 2001.

———. *En honor a la verdad: Versión del Ejército sobre su participación en la defensa del sistema democrático contra las organizaciones terroristas.* 2010; Lima: CPHEP, 2012.

———. *Evolución histórica de los uniformes del Ejército del Perú, 1821–1980.* Lima: CPHEP, 2005.

———. *Historia de la aviación del Ejército.* Lima: CPHEP, 2010.

———. *Historia de la Escuela Técnica del Ejército.* Lima: CPHEP, 2007.

———. *Historia de unidades del Ejército del Perú.* Lima: CPHEP, 2001.

———. *Operación militar de rescate de rehenes Chavín de Huántar: Versión oficial del Ejército del Perú.* Lima: CPHEP, 2010.

Conley-Zilkic, Bridget. "Rights on Display: Museums and Human Rights Claims." In Stern and Straus, *Human Rights Paradox,* 61–80.

Contreras, Carlos. "¿Quién quiere ser soldado hoy?" *Ideele Revista* 229 (May 2013): 21.

Cueto, Alonso. *La hora azul.* Lima: Peisa, 2005.

Cueto, Luis Fernando. *Ese camino existe.* Lima: Ediciones Copé, 2012.

Degregori, Carlos Iván. "Heridas abiertas, derechos esquivos: Reflexiones sobre la Comisión de la Verdad y Reconciliación." In *Memorias en conflicto: Aspectos de la violencia política contemporánea,* edited by Raynald Belay, Jorge Bracamonte, Carlos Iván Degregori, and Jean Joinville Vacher, 75–85. Lima: Embajada de Francia en el Perú, IEP, IFEA, Red para el Desarrollo de las Ciencias Sociales en el Perú, 2004.

———. *How Difficult It Is to Be God: Shining Path's Politics of War in Peru, 1980–1999.* Edited by Steve J. Stern. Madison: University of Wisconsin Press, 2012.

Dellepiane, Carlos. *Historia militar del Perú.* Lima: Librería y imprenta Gil, 1931.

del Pino, Ponciano. *En nombre del gobierno: El Perú y Uchuraccay: Un siglo de política campesina.* Lima: La Siniestra Ensayos, 2017.

del Pino, Ponciano, and José Carlos Agüero, eds. *Cada uno, un lugar de memoria: Fundamentos conceptuales del Lugar de la Memoria, la Tolerancia y la Inclusión Social.* Lima: LUM, 2014.

del Pino, Ponciano, and Caroline Yezer, eds. *Formas del recuerdo: Etnografías de la violencia política en el Perú.* Lima: IEP, 2013.

Denegri, Francesca, and Alexandra Hibbett, eds. *Dando cuenta: Estudios sobre el testimonio de la violencia política en el Perú (1980–2000).* Lima: PUCP, 2016.

de Vivanco Roca Rey, Lucero. *Historias del más acá: Imaginario apocalíptico en la literatura peruana.* Lima: IEP, 2013.

———, ed. *Memorias en tinta: Ensayos sobre la representación de la violencia política en Argentina, Chile y Perú.* Santiago de Chile: Ediciones Universidad Alberto Hurtado, 2013.

Donayre Gotzch, Edwin. *El silencio de los héroes.* With Hilda Balbín Alcócer. Lima: UAP, 2009.

Drinot, Paulo. "For Whom the Eye Cries: Memory, Monumentality, and the Ontologies of Violence in Peru." *Journal of Latin American Cultural Studies* 18, no. 1 (2009): 15–32.

———. "Remembering Velasco: Contested Memories of the Revolutionary Government of the Armed Forces." In *The Peculiar Revolution: Rethinking the Peruvian Experiment under Military Rule,* edited by Carlos Aguirre and Paulo Drinot, 95–119. Austin: University of Texas Press, 2017.

Faverón Patriau, Gustavo, ed. *Toda la sangre: Antología de cuentos peruanos sobre la violencia política.* Lima: Grupo Editorial Matalamanga, 2006.

Field, Thomas C., Jr. *From Development to Dictatorship: Bolivia and the Alliance for Progress in the Kennedy Era.* Ithaca, NY: Cornell University Press, 2014.

Fleming, David. "Human Rights Museums: An Overview." *Curator: The Museum Journal* 55, no. 3 (2012): 251–56.

Fournier Coronado, Eduardo. *"Feliciano": Captura de un senderista rojo, la verdadera historia.* Lima: n.p., 2002.

———. *Tiwinza con zeta: Toda la verdad.* Lima: Fimart, 1995.

Franco, Jean. *Cruel Modernity.* Durham, NC: Duke University Press, 2013.

Freyre, Carlos Enrique. *Desde el Valle de las Esmeraldas.* Lima: Estruendomudo, 2011.

Gálvez Olaechea, Alberto. *Con la palabra desarmada: Ensayos sobre el (pos)conflicto.* Lima: Fauno Ediciones, 2015.

———. *Desde el país de las sombras.* Lima: Sur, Casa de Estudio del Socialismo, 2009.

García, Alan. *El mundo de Maquiavelo.* Lima: Editora Matices, 2004.

García, María Elena. *Making Indigenous Citizens: Identities, Education and Multicultural Development in Peru.* Stanford, CA: Stanford University Press, 2005.

Gargurevich Regal, Juan. "Los medios masivos de información en el Perú, 1980–2012." *Conexión: Departamento de Comunicaciones de la PUCP* 1, no. 1 (2012): 11–31.

Gates-Madsen, Nancy J. *Trauma, Taboo, and Truth-Telling: Listening to Silences in Postdictatorship Argentina.* Critical Human Rights. Madison: University of Wisconsin Press, 2016.

Gavilán Sánchez, Lurgio. *Memorias de un soldado desconocido: Autobiografía y antro-pología de la violencia*. Mexico City: Universidad Iberoamericana; Lima: IEP, 2012.

———. *When Rains Became Floods: A Child Soldier's Story*. Preface by Carlos Iván Degregori. Introduction by Orin Starn. Translated by Margaret Randall. Durham, NC: Duke University Press, 2015.

Giampietri, Luis. *41 Seconds to Freedom: An Insider's Account of the Lima Hostage Crisis, 1996–1997*. New York: Presidio Press, 2007.

———. *Rehén por siempre: Operación Chavín de Huántar*. With Lorena Ausejo. Lima: QG, 2011.

Gill, Lesley. *The School of the Americas: Military Training and Political Violence in the Americas*. Durham, NC: Duke University Press, 2004.

Goldstein, Robert J. "Editor's Preface: Political Censorship of the Visual Arts in Nineteenth-Century France." *Yale French Studies*, no. 122 (2012): 1–13.

Gómez-Barris, Macarena. *Where Memory Dwells: Culture and State Violence in Chile*. Berkeley: University of California Press, 2009.

González Castañeda, Olga. *Unveiling Secrets of War in the Peruvian Andes*. Chicago: University of Chicago Press, 2006.

González Cueva, Eduardo. "The Peruvian Truth and Reconciliation Commission and the Challenge of Impunity." In *Transitional Justice in the Twenty-First Century: Beyond Truth versus Justice*, edited by Naomi Roht-Arriaza and Javier Mariez-currena, 70–93. New York: Cambridge University Press, 2006.

González Salazar, Alfredo. *Caso Leonor La Rosa: Historia de una mentira*. Lima: UAP, 2006.

Granados, Carla. "El desfile de la Semana Patria en el Valle Yanamarca: Una acción pública de reconocimiento y una memoria alternativa a la historia oficial en la Sierra Central Peruana, 1886–2015." MA thesis, Universidad Pablo de Olavide, Seville, Spain, 2016.

Grandin, Greg. "Human Rights and Empire's Embrace: A Latin American Counter-point." In *Human Rights and Revolutions*, edited by Jeffrey Wasserstrom, Greg Grandin, Lynn Hunt, and Marilyn Young, 191–212. Lanham, MD: Rowman & Littlefield, 2007.

———. *The Last Colonial Massacre: Latin America in the Cold War*. Chicago: University of Chicago Press, 2004.

Grinspun, R., and Y. Shamsie. "Canadian Re-Engagement in Latin America: Missing the Mark Again." *NACLA Report on the Americas* 43, no. 3 (2010): 12–17.

Hayner, Priscilla B. *Unspeakable Truths: Transitional Justice and the Challenge of Truth Commissions*. New York: Routledge, 2011.

Heilman, Jaymie P. *Before the Shining Path: Politics in Rural Ayacucho, 1895–1980*. Stanford, CA: Stanford University Press, 2010.

Henríquez, Narda, and Julissa Mantilla Falcón. *Contra viento y marea: Cuestiones de género y poder en la memoria colectiva*. Lima: Comisión de la Verdad y Reconcilia-ción, 2003.

Hermoza Ríos, Nicolás de Bari. *Operación Chavín de Huántar: Rescate en la residencia de la embajada del Japón.* Lima: n.p., 1997.

Hershberg, Eric, and Felipe Agüero. *Memorias militares sobre la represión en el Cono Sur: Visiones en disputa en dictadura y democracia.* Memorias de la represión 10. Madrid: Siglo XXI Editores, 2005.

Huáman Cabrera, Félix. *Candela quema luceros.* 1989. Repr., Lima: Editorial San Marcos, 2006.

Huapaya Amado, César A. "Militares en la décima: Dos casos emblemáticos." *Documenta de historia militar* 4, no. 4 (2013): 173–82.

Huber, Ludwig, and Ponciano del Pino, eds. *Políticas en justicia transicional: Miradas comparativas sobre el legado de la CVR.* Lima: IEP, 2015.

Hurtado Meza, Lourdes. "Ejército cholificado: Reflexiones sobre la apertura del ejército peruano hacia los sectores populares." *Iconos—Revista de ciencias sociales,* no. 26 (2006): 59–72.

———. "Velasco, Nationalist Rhetoric, and Military Culture in Cold War Peru." In *The Peculiar Revolution: Rethinking the Peruvian Experiment under Military Rule,* edited by Carlos Aguirre and Paulo Drinot, 171–96. Austin: University of Texas Press, 2017.

Infante Yupanqui, Carlos. *Poder, tensión y caricatura durante el período final del régimen fujimorista.* Lima: Facultad de Ciencias Sociales de la Universidad Nacional de San Cristobal de Huamanga, 2010.

Jara, Umberto. *Ojo por ojo: "Una historia verídica" del Grupo Colina.* Lima: Grupo Editorial Norma, 2004.

———. *Secretos del Túnel.* Lima: Planeta, 2017.

Jelin, Elizabeth. *State Repression and the Labors of Memory.* Minneapolis: University of Minnesota Press, 2003.

Jiménez, Edilberto. *Chungui: Violencia y trazos de la memoria.* Lima: IEP, COMISEDH, DED, 2009.

Kaneko, Ann, dir. *Against the Grain: An Artist's Survival Guide to Peru.* 65 mins. Blooming Grove, NY: New Day Films, 2008.

Karp, Ivan, Corinne Kratz, Lynn Szwaja, and Tomas Ybarra-Frausto, eds., *Museum Frictions: Public Cultures/Global Transformations.* Durham, NC: Duke University Press, 2006.

Kirk, Robin. *Untold Terror: Violence against Women in Peru's Armed Conflict.* Edited by Dorothy Q. Thomas. New York, Human Rights Watch, 1992.

Kirshenblatt-Gimblett, Barbara. "Museums as Catalyst." In *Museum 2000: Confirmation or Challenge?,* edited by Per-Uno Ågren, 55–69. Stockholm: Riksutsällningar [Swedish Traveling Exhibitions], Svenska Museiföreningen [Swedish Museum Association], 2002.

Koonings, Kees, and Dirk Kruijt, eds. *Political Armies: The Military and Nation Building in the Age of Democracy.* London: Zed Books, 2002.

Kruijt, Dirk. *Revolution by Decree: Peru, 1968–1975.* Amsterdam: Thela, 1994.

Kruijt, Dirk, and María del Pilar Tello. "From Military Reformists to Civilian Dictatorship: Peruvian Military Politics from the 1960s to the Present." In Koonings and Kruijt, *Political Armies*, 35–57.

Lambright, Anne. *Andean Truths: Transitional Justice, Ethnicity, and Cultural Production in Post-Shining Path Peru*. Liverpool Latin American Studies. Liverpool: Liverpool University Press, 2015.

La Serna, Miguel. *The Corner of the Living: Ayacucho on the Eve of the Shining Path Insurgency*. Chapel Hill: University of North Carolina Press, 2012.

Lazzara, Michael J. *Chile in Transition: The Poetics and Politics of Memory*. Gainesville: University Press of Florida, 2006.

———, ed. *Luz Arce and Pinochet's Chile: Testimony in the Aftermath of State Violence*. New York: Palgrave Macmillan, 2011.

Lehrer, Erica, and Cynthia E. Milton. "Witnesses to Witnessing." In Lehrer, Milton, and Patterson, *Curating Difficult Knowledge*, 1–19.

Lehrer, Erica, Cynthia E. Milton, and Monica Eileen Patterson, eds. *Curating Difficult Knowledge: Violent Pasts in Public Places*. London: Palgrave MacMillan, 2011.

Leiby, Michele. "Digging in the Archives: The Promise and Perils of Primary Documents." *Politics & Society* 37, no. 1 (2009): 75–100.

Lerner Febres, Salomón. *La rebelión de la memoria: Selección de discursos 2001–2003*. Lima: IDEHPUCP, CNDDHH, CEP, 2004.

Levitsky, Steven, and Lucan A. Way, "Elections without Democracy: The Rise of Competitive Authoritarianism." *Journal of Democracy* 13, no. 2 (2002): 51–65.

Lladó, Rocío, dir. *Vidas paralelas*. 100 min. Lima: UAP, 2008.

Lucioni, Mario. "La historieta peruana." *Revista latinoamericana de estudios sobre la historietas* 1, no. 4 (2001): 257–64. http://rlesh.mogno.com/04/04_lucioni.html.

Lynch, Nicolás. *Una tragedia sin heroes: La derrota de los partidos y el origen de los independientes, Perú 1980–1992*. Lima: Universidad Nacional Mayor de San Marcos, 1993.

Macdonald, Sharon. *Difficult Heritage: Negotiating the Nazi Past in Nuremberg and Beyond*. New York: Routledge, 2009.

Macher, Sofía. *¿Hemos avanzado? A 10 años de las recomendaciones de la Comisión de la Verdad y Reconciliación*. Lima: IEP, 2014.

Martínez Garay, Hugo. "Héroes y villanos: La deconstrucción del discurso militar en *Desde el Valle de las Esmeraldas* de Carlos Freyre." BA thesis, PUCP, 2014.

———. *Mano poderosa*. Lima: Estruendomudo, 2013.

Masterson, Daniel M. *Militarism and Politics in Latin America: Peru from Sánchez Cerro to Sendero Luminoso*. Contributions in Military Studies. New York: Greenwood Press, 1991.

McAllister, Carlota, and Diane M. Nelson. *War by Other Means: Aftermath in Post-Genocide Guatemala*. Durham, NC: Duke University Press, 2013.

Menchú, Rigoberta. *I, Rigoberta Menchú: An Indian Woman in Guatemala*. Edited by Elisabeth Burgos-Debray. Translated by Ann Wright. London: Verso, 1984.

Méndez, Cecilia. "Las paradojas del autoritarismo: Ejército, campesinado y etnicidad en el Perú, siglos XIX al XX." *Iconos—Revista de ciencias sociales*, no. 26 (2006): 17–34.

Méndez, Cecilia, and Carla Granados. "Las guerras olvidadas del Perú: Formación del estado e imaginario nacional." *Revista de sociología e política* 20, no. 42 (2012): 57–71.

Mendoza Policarpio, Roberto. "El film 'Alerta en la frontera.'" *Documenta de historia militar* 5, no. 5 (2014): 165–66.

Milton, Cynthia E., ed. *Art from a Fractured Past: Memory and Truth-Telling in Post-Shining Path Peru*. Durham, NC: Duke University Press, 2014.

———. "At the Edge of the Peruvian Truth Commission: Alternative Paths to Recounting the Past." *Radical History Review* 98 (2007): 3–33.

———. "Curating Memories of Armed State Actors in Peru's Era of Transitional Justice." *Memory Studies* 20, no. 2 (2014): 1–22.

———. "Defacing Memory: (Un)tying Peru's Memory Knots." *Memory Studies* 4, no. 2 (2011): 1–16.

———. "Parallel Lies? Peru's Cultural Memory Battles Go International." *E-misférica* 7, no. 2 (2010).

———. "The Truth Ten Years On: The CVR in Peru." In *The Struggle for Memory in Latin American Recent History and Political Violence*, edited by Eugenia Allier Montaño and Emilio Crenzel, 111–28. London: Palgrave Macmillan, 2015.

Milton, Cynthia E., and María Eugenia Ulfe. "Promoting Peru: Tourism and Post-Conflict Memory." In Bilbija and Payne, *Accounting for Violence*, 207–33.

Milton, Cynthia E., María Eugenia Ulfe, and Karen Bernedo. "Review: *La Cautiva*." *E-misférica* 12, no. 1 (2015).

Molinari Morales, Tirso. "El Partido Unión Revolucionaria y su proyecto totalitario-fascista: Perú, 1933–1936." *Investigaciónes sociales* 10, no. 16 (2006): 321–46.

Montesinos Torres, Vladimiro. *Operación militar Chavín de Huántar: Con el terrorismo no se negocia*. Lima: Ezer Editores, 2016.

———. *Sin Sendero: Alerta temprana I*. Lima: Ezer Editores, 2009.

———. *Sin Sendero: Alerta temprana II*. Lima: Ezer Editores, 2011.

Morán Reyna, Pablo E. *Complot contra los militares: Falsedades de la C.V.R.* Lima: Editorial "San Agustín," 2006.

Morote, Herbert. *¡Todos contra la verdad!* Lima: Jaime Campodonico, 2014.

Moyn, Samuel. *The Last Utopia: Human Rights in History*. Cambridge, MA: Belknap Press, 2010.

Nance, Kimberly A. *Can Literature Promote Justice? Trauma Narrative and Social Action in Latin American Testimonio*. Nashville: Vanderbilt University Press, 2006.

Noel Moral, Clemente. *Ayacucho, testimonio de un soldado*. Lima: CONCYTEC, 1989.

O'Donnell, Guillermo A. *Modernization and Bureaucratic-Authoritarianism: Studies in South American Politics*. Berkeley: University of California Press, 1973.

Obando, Enrique. "Civil-Military Relations in Peru, 1980–1996: How to Control and Co-opt the Military (and the Consequences of Doing So)." In Stern, *Shining and Other Paths*, 385–410.

Orange, Jennifer, and Jennifer Carter. "'It's Time to Pause and Reflect': Museums and Human Rights." *Curator: The Museum Journal* 55, no. 3 (2012): 259–66.

Ortiz Sotelo, Jorge. *Acción y valor: Historia de la Infantería de Marina del Perú*. Lima: Securitas, 2010.

Pajuelo, Ramón, Maria Eugenia Ulfe, Fernando Calderón, and Jacqueline Fowks. "Reseñas al libro 'Memorias de un soldado desconocido' de Lurgio Gavilán (IEP, 2012)." *Argumentos: Revista de análisis y crítica*, no. 1 (2013): 65–79. http://revista argumentos.iep.org.pe/wp-content/uploads/2014/04/gavilan_marzo2013.pdf.

Patterson, Monica E. "Teaching Tolerance through Objects of Hatred: The Jim Crow Museum of Racist Memorabilia as 'Counter-Museum.'" In Lehrer, Milton, and Patterson, *Curating Difficult Knowledge*, 55–71.

Payne, Leigh A. "Humor That Makes Trouble." In *The Art of Truth-Telling about Authoritarian Rule*, edited by Ksenija Bilbija, Jo Ellen Fair, Cynthia E. Milton, and Leigh A. Payne, 68–73. Madison: University of Wisconsin Press, 2005.

———. *Uncivil Movements: The Armed Right Wing and Democracy in Latin America*. Baltimore: Johns Hopkins University Press, 2000.

———. *Unsettling Accounts: Neither Truth nor Reconciliation in Confessions of State Violence*. Durham, NC: Duke University Press, 2008.

Pérez, Julián. *Criba*. Lima: Ediciones Copé, 2014.

Pita, Alfredo. *El rincón de los muertos*. Lima: Textual Pueblo Mágico SAC, 2014.

Pizarro Romero, Javier. "La construcción de la identidad en los testimonios de los expolicías y exmilitares recogidos por la Comisión de la Verdad y la [*sic*] Reconciliación." In *Dando cuenta: Estudios sobre el testimonio de la violencia política en el Perú (1980–2000)*, edited by Francesca Denegri and Alexandra Hibbett, 310–54. Lima: PUCP, 2016.

———. "Ni héroes ni enemigos: Análisis de testimonies de expolicías y exmilitares peruanos recogidos por la Comisión de la Verdad y la [*sic*] Reconciliación en el contexto del conflicto armado interno." BA thesis, PUCP, 2013.

Rada, José. *Senderos de sangre*. Lima: Mosca Azul Editores, 1995.

Ramal Pesantes, César A. *La paz después de la violencia en el Perú: Seguridad y defensa nacional una política de estado*. Lima: UAP, 2011.

Ramírez Prado, Fidel. *El voto de los militares*. Lima: UAP, 2002.

Reátegui, Félix, Rafael Barrantes and Jesus Peña. *Los sitios de la memoria: Procesos sociales de la conmemoracón en el Perú*. Lima: Instituto de Democracia y Derechos Humanos, PUCP, 2010.

Rendón, Silvio. "La polémica sobre las cifras: Las sobreestimaciones de la CVR," *Ideele Revista*, no. 233 (October 2013). http://revistaideele.com/ideele/content/la-pol% C3%A9mica-sobre-las-cifras-las-sobreestimaciones-de-la-cvr.

Rénique, José Luis. *La batalla por Puno: Conflicto agrario y nación en los andes peruanos 1866–1995*. Lima: IEP, 2004.

Reuque Paillalef, Rosa Isolde. *When a Flower Is Reborn: The Life and Times of a Mapuche Feminist*. Edited by Florencia Mallon. Durham, NC: Duke University Press, 2002.

Richard, Nelly. "Sites of Memory, Emptying Remembrance." In *Telling Ruins in Latin America*, edited by Michael J. Lazzara and Vicky Unruh, 175–82. New York: Palgrave Macmillan, 2009.

Ricoeur, Paul. *Memory, History, Forgetting*. Chicago: University of Chicago Press, 2004.

Robben, Antonius. *Political Violence and Trauma in Argentina*. Philadelphia: University of Pennsylvania Press, 2005.

Rodríguez Beruff, Jorge. *Los militares y el poder: Un ensayo sobre la doctrina militar en el Perú, 1948–1968*. Lima: Mosca Azul Editores, 1983.

Rodríguez Idárraga, Nicolás. "La naturalización de la violencia: Damnificados, víctimas y desarrollo en la segunda mitad del siglo XX colombiano." PhD thesis, Université de Montréal, 2017.

Rodríguez Ulloa, Olga. "Artist Archives: Experimentation in Peruvian Art about the Memory of the Armed Conflict." *E-misférica* 9, no. 1 (2012). http://hemispheric institute.org/hemi/en/e-misferica-91/rodriguezulloa.

Roncagliolo, Santiago. *Abril roja*. Lima: Alfaguara, 2006.

———. *La cuarta espada: La historia de Abimael Guzmán y Sendero Luminoso*. Buenos Aires: Debate, 2007.

———. *La pena máxima*. Lima: Alfaguara, 2014.

Root, Rebecca K. *Transitional Justice in Peru*. New York: Palgrave Macmillan, 2012.

Rouquié, Alain. *The Military and the State in Latin America*. Translated by Paul E. Sigmund. Berkeley: University of California Press, 1987. Originally published as *L'État militaire en Amérique latine* (Paris: Editions du Seuil, 1982).

Sabino, Carlos. *Guatemala: La historia silenciada, 1944–1989*. Guatemala City: Fondo de Cultura Ecónomica, 2009.

Salazar Jiménez, Claudia. *La sangre de la aurora*. Lima: Estación La Cultura, 2013.

Salvi, Valentina. *De vencedores a víctimas: Memorias castrenses sobre el pasado reciente en Argentina*. Buenos Aires: Editorial Biblos, 2012.

———. "The Slogan 'Complete Memory': A Reactive (Re)-signification of the Memory of the Disappeared in Argentina." In *The Memory of State Terrorism in the Southern Cone: Argentina, Chile, and Uruguay*, edited by Francesca Lessa and Vincent Druliolle, 43–61. New York: Palgrave Macmillan, 2011.

Saona, Margarita. *Memory Matters in Transitional Peru*. Houndmills, Basingstoke: Palgrave Macmillan, 2014.

Seligmann, Linda J. *Between Reform and Revolution: Political Struggles in the Peruvian Andes, 1969–1991*. Stanford, CA: Stanford University Press, 1995.

Sikkink, Kathryn. *The Justice Cascade: How Human Rights Prosecutions Are Changing World Politics*. New York: Norton, 2011.

Silva Santisteban, Rocío. *El factor asco: Basurización simbólica y discursos autoritarios en el Perú contemporáneo*. Lima: PUCP, Universidad del Pacífico, IEP, 2008.

Simon, Roger. "Afterword: The Turn to Pedagogy; A Needed Conversation on the Practice of Curating Difficult Knowledge." In Lehrer, Milton, and Patterson, *Curating Difficult Knowledge*, 193–209.

Sodaro, Amy. "Politics of the Past: Remembering the Rwandan Genocide at the Kigali Memorial Centre." In Lehrer, Milton, and Patterson, *Curating Difficult Knowledge*, 72–88.

Sosa Saavedra, Jesús Antonio. *Sueños de justicia: La verdad del llamado Grupo Colina.* Lima: n.p., 2014.

Soto Quispe, Heder, dir. *Caminantes de la memoria.* 74 min. Peru, 2014.

Stan, Livinia, and Nadya Nedelsky, eds. *Encyclopedia on Transitional Justice.* 3 vols. Cambridge: Cambridge University Press, 2012.

Starn, Orin, Carlos Iván Degregori, and Robin Kirk, eds. *The Peru Reader: History, Culture, Politics.* Durham, NC: Duke University Press, 1995.

Stepan, Alfred C. *Rethinking Military Politics: Brazil and the Southern Cone.* Princeton, NJ: Princeton University Press, 1988.

———. *The State and Society: Peru in Comparative Perspective.* Princeton, NJ: Princeton University Press, 1978.

Stern, Steve J. *Reckoning with Pinochet: The Memory Question in Democratic Chile, 1989–2006.* Durham, NC: Duke University Press, 2010.

———. *Remembering Pinochet's Chile: On the Eve of London, 1998.* Latin America Otherwise: Language, Empires, Nations. Durham, NC: Duke University Press, 2004.

———. *The Secret History of Gender: Women, Men, and Power in Late Colonial Mexico.* Chapel Hill: University of North Carolina Press, 1997.

———, ed. *Shining and Other Paths: War and Society in Peru, 1980–1995.* Durham, NC: Duke University Press, 1998.

Stern, Steve J., and Scott Straus, eds. *The Human Rights Paradox: Universality and Its Discontents.* Critical Human Rights. Madison: University of Wisconsin Press, 2014.

Tate, Winifred. *Counting the Dead: The Culture and Politics of Human Rights Activism in Colombia.* Berkeley: University of California Press, 2007.

———. "From Greed to Grievance: The Shifting Political Profile of the Colombian Paramilitaries." *Faculty Scholarship* 61 (2009). http://digitalcommons.colby.edu/facultyscholarship/61.

Taylor, Diana. *The Archive and the Repertoire: Performing Cultural Memory in the Americas.* Durham: NC: Duke University Press, 2003.

———. *Disappearing Acts: Spectacles of Gender and Nationalism in Argentina's "Dirty War."* Durham, NC: Duke University Press, 1997.

Thays, Iván. *Un lugar llamado Oreja de Perro.* Barcelona: Editorial Anagrama, 2008.

Theidon, Kimberly. *Intimate Enemies: Violence and Reconciliation in Peru.* Philadelphia: University of Pennsylvania Press, 2012.

Thorne, Carlos. *En las fauces de las fieras.* Lima: Grupo Editorial Norma, 2004.

Toche Medrano, Eduardo. *Guerra y democracia: Los militares peruanos y la construcción nacional.* Lima: CLACSO; DESCO, 2008.

Todorov, Tzvetan. *Mémoire du mal, tentation du bien: Enquête sur le siècle.* Paris: R. Laffont, 2000.

Tola, Raúl. *Toque de queda*. Lima: Planeta, 2008.

Ubilluz, Juan Carlos, Alexandra Hibbett, and Víctor Vich, eds. *Contra el sueño de los justos: La literatura peruana ante la violencia política*. Lima: IEP, 2009.

Uceda, Ricardo. *Muerte en el Pentagonito: Los cementerios secretos del Ejército Peruano*. Bogotá: Planeta, 2004.

Ulfe, María Eugenia, and Cynthia E. Milton. "¿Y, después de la verdad? El espacio público y las luchas por la memoria en la post CVR, Perú." "After Truth." *E-misférica* 7, no. 2 (2010). http://hemisphericinstitute.org/hemi/en/e-misferica-72/miltonulfe.

Ulfe, María Eugenia, and Vera Lucía Ríos. "Toxic Memories? The DINCOTE Museum in Lima, Peru." *Latin American Perspectives* 43, no. 6 (2016): 27–40.

Valenzuela, Manuel. *El teatro de la guerra: La violencia política de Sendero Luminoso a través de su teatro*. Lima: Areidea, 2009.

Vargas Llosa, Mario. *Death in the Andes*. Translated by Edith Grossman. New York: Farrar, Straus, and Giroux, 1996. Originally published in 1993 as *Lituma en los Andes*.

Vayssière, Pierre. *Les révolutions d'Amérique latine*. Paris: Éditions du Seuil, 1991.

Vergara, Alberto. *Ciudadanos sin república*. Peru: Editorial Planeta, 2013.

———. "Esperando un guion: El Perú y la sombra de Sendero Luminoso." *Letras Libres*, no. 172 (January 2016). http://www.letraslibres.com/revista/convivio/esperando-un-guion?page=full.

Vich, Víctor. *Poéticas del duelo: Ensayos sobre arte, memoria y violencia en el Perú*. Lima: IEP, 2015.

Villanueva, Victor. *Cien años del éjercito peruano: Frustraciones y cambios*. Lima: Mejía Baca, 1972.

———. *Ejército Peruano*. Lima: Librería-Editorial Juan Mejía Baca, 1973.

Walker, Charles. "The General and His Rebel: Juan Velasco Alvarado and the Reinvention of Túpac Amaru II." In *The Peculiar Revolution: Rethinking the Peruvian Experiment under Military Rule*, edited by Carlos Aguirre and Paulo Drinot, 49–72. Austin: University of Texas Press, 2017.

Weissert, Markus. "Entre dos fuegos—Iconografía y narrativa de las 'Casas de Memoria' en Ayacucho." In *Perú: Medios, memoria y violencia*, edited by Klaus Schäffauer et al., 179–90. Lima: Universidad Antonio Ruiz de Montoya, 2014.

Weld, Kirsten. "Writing Political Violence into History." *Latin American Research Review* 48, no. 2 (2013): 175–83.

Wilde, Alex. "Irruptions of Memory: Expressive Politics in Chile's Transition to Democracy." *Journal of Latin American Studies* 31, no. 2 (1999): 473–500.

Williams, Paul Harvey. *Memorial Museums: The Global Rush to Commemorate Atrocities*. New York: Berg, 2007.

Youngers, Coletta. *Violencia política y sociedad en el Perú: Historia de la Coordinadora Nacional de Derechos Humanos*. Lima: IEP, 2003.

Zapata, Antonio. "En honor a la verdad." *Argumentos: Revista de análisis y crítica* 6, no. 2 (2012).

Index

Critical Human Rights

www.ingramcontent.com/pod-product-compliance
Lightning Source LLC
Chambersburg PA
CBHW071015280326
41935CB00011B/1366